D1357005

Windsor and Maidenhead

95800000157133

TIM LANG

Feeding Britain
Our Food Problems and How to Fix Them

A PELICAN BOOK

PELICAN
an imprint of
PENGUIN BOOKS

PELICAN BOOKS

UK | USA | Canada | Ireland | Australia
India | New Zealand | South Africa

Penguin Books is part of the Penguin Random
House group of companies whose addresses can
be found at global.penguinrandomhouse.com

Penguin
Random House
UK

First published 2020
001

Copyright © Tim Lang, 2020

The moral right of the author has been asserted

Book design by Matthew Young
Set in 11/16.13 pt FreightText Pro
Typeset by Jouve (UK), Milton Keynes
Printed and bound in Great Britain by
Clays Ltd, Elcograf S.p.A.

A CIP catalogue record for this book is available
from the British Library

ISBN: 978-0-241-44222-7

MIX
Paper from
responsible sources
FSC® C018179
FSC
www.fsc.org

Penguin Random House is committed to a
sustainable future for our business, our readers
and our planet. This book is made from Forest
Stewardship Council® certified paper.

www.greenpenguin.co.uk

Contents

CHAPTER 5

What We Ought to Do: A 'Great Food Transformation'

List of Figures

List of Tables

Preface

Over forty years ago, I picked up a copy of Le Gros Clark and Titmuss's 1939 *Our Food Problem and Its Relation to Our National Defences* in a junk shop. I have the copy still. It is an early Penguin Special, the series created by the publisher Allen Lane to inform and comment on current affairs. This book gave a sober account of the strategic weakness the UK faced on food. It argued that a country whose state had created a default policy of food imports laid itself open to severe weakness not just in the food itself but in public morale. Reading voraciously about the 1930s debates led me to earlier ones and my interest grew in how complex the politics of food are, and how tricky an issue food security can be and what it means. It also instilled an urgency about food and war which endures. Wars almost always disrupt food systems and often destroy them. Food can be used as a weapon; it can make or break economies. How we manage our food systems is something fundamental to human civilization and culture. We constantly have to update our understanding of what is going on. How societies manage food in war and times of food insecurity necessitates not just public comment but public engagement. In these days when governments bow down to market power, appreciation of what happens when food is disrupted concentrates policymakers' thoughts on how food is a matter of minds and mouths not just dry 'market' economics.

In the mid-1970s, when I read Le Gros Clark and Titmuss, and many others since, I realized this complexity was missing in the UK and rich-world debates. Yet data were emerging about the environment and food, and about psychological traumas over food such as phobias, anorexia, bulimia, body anxieties, etc. My own interest in food policy partly stemmed from doctoral work in this area. Academic understanding of this complexity has grown with the data ever since. And in the 1970s the UK was in the process of joining and then voting on whether to stay in the Common Market (now the European Union). Those politics too have come to dominate domestic politics. Joining, like leaving, the EU restructured everything. It meant changing the post-Second World War system of agricultural support from one format – deficiency payments – to another – production subsidies. To switch from one form to another did not seem earthshattering, if its purpose was to ensure the population was fed. The 1970s, like now, saw an explosion of analyses of global food challenges: poverty, maldistribution, inefficiencies. Mostly, these focused on the developing world. Famines rightly stalked the news. So where does a rich country such as Britain fit into this? I mused. What lay behind the sober analysis painted in that 1939 book? How could the UK have got into that dire situation? How did it dig itself out?

Meeting people who had been involved in trying to sort out the mess inherited in the 1930s and who pushed for post-war reconstruction to prevent it in future taught me the wisdom of earlier generations on UK food security. Many people, both radical and establishment, realized that the UK's imperial model of food supply was weak, and its mix of political arrogance and ignorance risky. Never underestimate the capacity of clever human beings to destabilize food potential in the interests of ideology. One sometimes wonders if those today who paint a rosy UK food future out of the EU are as deluded as those who think business-as-usual is all that is needed. Bigger thinking and planning are needed. While in no way claiming this book has the answers, it is intended to sketch the common good, and to urge that we (and other rich countries) face the realities. We must realize and get our policymakers to realize that we cannot go on eating and feeding as we are, without undermining our own interests.

Food is a matter that goes beyond the modern religion of individual choice. There is such a thing as society and the collective interest. There will always be outliers, variations from the norm, but the common good is sketchable. To use another sector as an example, there might always be petrolheads who want to tarmac over the country in the delusion that this would enable everyone to go faster, but the common good suggests, if anything, we need fewer motorways and more bike lanes. Even if cars are electric, their climate-change-inducing energy source is simply somewhere else. Technical innovation can be valuable but technical fixes often do not resolve social problems. A process of change to enable people to eat and live better, not in hairshirts but within planetary boundaries, surely has to be part of the picture.

The idea for this present book was thus germinating many years ago, as I explored with and learned from many colleagues around the world about the extent of our current food problems. As one who worked in the policy domain, it became clear to me that there was not sufficient political support to address the challenges the food system causes for the environment, and for health, development, culture and the economy. Policy lags miles behind the evidence, yet bland assurances are often given that we live in a world where policy is evidence-based. We do not.

At the end of the last century, an intellectual diaspora existed. Rich-world concerns were said to be totally different to poor-world concerns. This is no longer wholly true. Low-income countries have rocketing diet-related ill-health. Rich and poor worlds' food and farming capacities are being threatened by environmental damage caused, in part, by food systems. There has been a blurring of the policy demarcations. And yet it was apparently unthinkable for a rich country to have a food security problem. Or that is what the UK government says. We get lots of food from many countries, therefore we are food-secure. This is nonsense.

For a while, the financial crisis in 2007–8 shook complacency. It spawned the Great Recession, over which economists and historians now argue whether it lasted one year or six. As austerity was turned into a governmental policy, some of the old certainties about food security for a rich country such as the UK began to erode. An anxiety that the West's food system might not be so secure began to creep up the agenda of the G8, the EU and even momentarily the UK. A rethink about UK food security began, which I describe in this book, only to be swept away after the 2010 election. This was not just a shame – it is what happens when governments change – but a waste of policy formation effort and compounds the UK's current dangerous food insecurity. Climate change, obesity and biodiversity loss clocks were all ticking. Inaction now made crises ahead more likely.

The 2016 Referendum vote to leave the European Union, from where we get around 41% of our food, gradually made even hardened analysts realize that systems built over decades can be rocked in a few months. With colleagues, I spent a year before the Referendum, and the years since, exploring and publicizing the vulnerabilities within the intense, just-in-time efficient, hyperactive food system which has been created in our name and with our tacit acceptance. These briefings were written by academics for and with civil society.* In 2016–19, as in 1936–9, political attention was focused mostly elsewhere, too often making wild assumptions about the ease of doing trade deals with this or that country, which already had trade deals with us via the EU. Food was again becoming a pawn in wider trade thinking. Yet food is a daily activity. The people do not eat widgets.

In this book, I take stock of current UK food security. I do not think we are in a 1939 military position, or hope not, though I note concerns expressed about global tensions, insurgencies, conflicts and risks. I defer to others on those. In homage to the 1939 book and many other writings in that generation, I nevertheless consider the political arguments about the direction and format for UK food. I wrote the book because I consider that the UK, my country, has lost sight of

---

* See Food Research Collaboration: https://foodresearch.org.uk/food-policy-briefings/.

the importance of some of the most fundamental questions which should shape a political economy. These include:

- What version of food security do we want? A neo-colonial one or a sustainable food system? A mixed economy or one entirely traded?
- What does a good food system or a sustainable food system look like?
- What is a good diet and how much control do people really have over what they eat?
- How much are we prepared to pay for decent sustainable means of production?
- What is land for? What is a good relationship between people, land and food?
- How can we resolve massive food-related inequalities, whereby food is too cheap for some but too costly for others?
- Can a food system be fair to producers and workers as well as consumers?
- Are the political institutions in a fit state to steer the food system through known challenges ahead?

These are fundamental questions for any democracy. They should be addressed and, where possible, answered in a national food policy. We currently lack one, although there are elements struggling to get through. This is a call for British food democracy. It's time we stopped telling others how to improve their food systems when we are not doing this for our own.

We have a failure of political leadership. I am not writing this in a fit of petulance. It is simply true. Major challenges are known to be facing the UK food system: climate change and ecosystems stress, public ill-health caused by diet, food poverty caused by social inequality, leading millions to depend on food handouts, and more. But we have no political response getting a grip. Brexit has been seen by many as an opportunity to right wrongs. Disruption-derived opportunity so far actually adds just another layer of risk. Whether the UK is in or out of the EU has never impeded the UK, if it wanted to, from narrowing social inequalities, making sure every schoolchild is well fed, banning food advertising which promotes unhealthy foods, radically reducing food waste, and so on.

Whatever the macropolitics, if we do not analyse what our food problems are, we will squander the chance to set things right. Whether in or out of the EU, these big challenges are often UK-made, certainly UK-manifest, and must be UK-resolved alongside others. This needs to be done in concert with other countries both in the EU and beyond, simply because food crosses borders. Food tastes often precede actual food commodities. Food is an idea not just a biophysical entity. Food operates in a multi-level world from local to global, wherever we source food and however much we produce sustainably here.

Arguments summarized:
the two sides of UK food insecurity

This is a book about the UK's food (in)security. It shows that the UK, the fifth-richest country on the planet in 2016 according to the International Monetary Fund, has a home-grown food security problem. The 2019 Economist

Intelligence Unit's Global Food Security Index assessed the UK at seventeenth out of 113 countries for food security, and its 2018 Food Sustainability Index rates the UK as twenty-fourth out of sixty-seven countries monitored. The UK is awash with food but from modes of production, processing and packaging which are unsustainable ecologically and socially. The book proposes that we need to discuss the UK food system as being insecure on both those two fronts. Meanwhile mainstream politics is in denial or otherwise engaged. The UK has undue food reliance on external sources – about a third of UK food is from the EU it has left. We are not considering our land or what a good food system could be for the mid-twenty-first century. We passively accept that diet is now one of the major causes of premature death and healthcare costs and environmental damage, when we ought to be well underway on a national 'Great Food Transformation'. A post-imperial default policy still rules: that others can feed us.

The UK only grows a little over half its food needs, if measured by value; more in tonnage and quantity terms. Different figures say it imports 39%, 48% or 50% of total supply. Whichever measure is used, it does not feed itself – anything like it. It manages to have consistent deficits in production of *all* food and drink categories measured by HM Revenue & Customs (cereals, meat, fruit, vegetables, milk, eggs, etc.). Only in drinks is there an import/export surplus, due to massive exports of whisky. Paying for food imports puts a burden elsewhere on the economy. The food trade gap in 2017 was £24bn in the red, and this gap has been steadily rising under Labour, Conservative and Coalition governments since the early 1990s.

The UK has a benign but very varied climate. It has some rich soils and extensive upland and grasslands. No critic says the UK should be growing its own bananas or mangoes, but that it imports huge quantities of what it could perfectly well grow here suggests a failure of political economy. Vast amounts of land are used to produce feed for cattle, when almost all scientific advice is to reduce cattle and to shift animal production from red to white meat (but that too has problems).

The UK has a huge food labour force of 3.95 million. Of this, only 11% work on farms, fishing boats and greenhouses. Food is the country's biggest employer but working in food has a low-wage image problem, sometimes undeserved, but not helped by the new gig economy. In 2017, 30% of workers in food manufacturing were EU migrants, 63% of those in red- and white-meat processing plants. UK food manufacturing is the biggest manufacturing sector in the UK, far bigger than the declining car industry. But it feeds the British the highest rate of 'ultra-processed' foods in the EU, contributing to make the UK one of the fattest countries in the EU: 27% of British adults are obese or overweight.

The UK food economy is highly concentrated. There are ten large food retailers. 0.5% of citizens own almost all the land. The top five food manufacturers have a combined £30bn turnover. But 85% of food manufacturers are small and medium-sized enterprises (SMEs), with fifty employees or fewer. Even in food service, giant combines have emerged, particularly in fast food and contract catering, and in home deliveries. Food lorries account for a fifth of all truck traffic on UK roads. Almost all the money made by food companies is accrued off the land and sea. Farming and fishing themselves receive only 8% of the total gross value added of the entire UK food chain. This is a strikingly top-heavy food system.

The people of Britain say they would like to buy British food but do not do so. Partly this is because they do not have the information on what is or is not home-grown – unless it is raw food – and partly because the overriding value is cheapness. Social inequalities and wage squeezes lock this in.

Increasingly the British buy ready-made food, which can be 'food from anywhere'. British food culture is split, half experiencing a renaissance of interest in quality and authenticity, and half trapped by price. This tension goes across the social-class divide. Cheapness consistently comes out as the top consideration for UK consumers.

The UK's food (in)security problem is one which could quickly and easily turn tricky. Official audits are reviewed and found to be complacent. The auditors are either dissembling or not reading their own official reports, many of which express concern. The assumption that money can buy food security no longer quite fits. The UK, as is discussed later, has a long tradition of assuming others will feed us. Leaving the EU with barely a discussion of how it is where most food imports come from is par for the policy course. Politicians talk of new trade deals as though they are flicking a switch, but have little understanding of actual food flows (or of the labyrinthine nature of trade negotiations).

The global food system meanwhile is widely agreed by scientists to be facing a highly dangerous period and combination of challenges. Massive human-made problems are already upon us: climate change, biodiversity loss, water stress, social inequalities, health costs, and labour issues such as skills, availability and wages.

The book proposes that attention needs to be given in the UK to addressing this agenda. We need to revise core food security and national food defences. Some of what needs to happen depends entirely on political outcomes. If the UK switches supply lines, for instance, from Europe to North America or West Africa, or what I term 'outer Europe', the Navy would not be able to mount anything like a requisite support system, should some form of regional or global emergency or even warfare break out. The UK food system is currently torn between being European, globalist, Atlanticist, neo-imperialist and outer-European, when we probably ought to be trying to build a more resilient, bio-regionalist framework to use our land and resources more soundly and use others' less. We ought to eat less but better anyway, and to equalize food patterns to compensate for shocking but known diet-related inequalities. Certainly, the entire UK food system needs to be lighter on the planet. We are getting heavier physically as humans as the nation gets fatter, and also heavier on the land, as the 'footprint' of the food system goes ever deeper.

The book is organized in three parts. Part One reviews the state of food defences and (in)security. Our national food defences (the capacity to protect food lines), food flows, labour force and where the money goes have all quietly put the UK into an unnecessarily weak position. Policy is fragmented, and failing to be effective even against weak criteria. Civil contingency planning is weak. Official audits are complacent and thin. Local-authority powers and funds are also weak after years of cuts. There is no food plan for England, nor are the authorities in a fit state to deliver one. Scottish and Welsh governments have been marginalized despite tentatively entering this policy space. Northern Ireland has been especially weakened by Brexit politics and a collapse of working government from January 2017.

Part Two explores the range and scale of the UK's food problems. It argues that the only long-term route to food security is to make the food system more sustainable. This means more than improving land management, dire though food's impact on the environment already is. Acknowledgement of food's impact on the land crept into UK policy, often due to pressure from the EU (e.g. through water and run-off directives). Integrated food health and environmental thinking was meant to emerge by the creation of Defra in 2000, but has ebbed and flowed. The book urges the need for policymakers to adopt a broad 'multi-criteria' approach to delivering sustainability for food systems. The country needs leadership not just on soil and ecosystems but people, skills, confidence and health. A national Food Policy and Plan to join this up is long overdue but now urgent.

To oversee the transition, UK food institutions need a proper overhaul, outlined in Part Three. Consumed by Euro politics, mainstream UK politics has been either in a state of denial or ignorant and uninterested in the slowly emerging ecological public-health crisis in food. A few state institutions do their best, a select committee here or there, but the UK lacks an overall food plan which provides a framework suitable for the enormous challenges facing the food system in coming years. Those politicians who do see this lack voice in the mainstream parties.

A gap has emerged between the evidence about UK food's systemic distortions and the policies and institutions which nominally could address them and be in charge. A form of policy 'lock-in' is described which restricts new thinking and locks us into inappropriate food supply patterns.

One lock-in is residual imperial thinking which assumes the UK deserves to be fed and retains the power to impose that view, when in fact the armed forces are relatively weak, due to cuts. Another is the belief that, since money buys food (and not necessarily happiness), and we have a rich economy, the UK will always be able to buy food on world markets. This is complacent. It misreads what international assessments argue, that world markets now are subject to inherent volatility and uncertainty. Food we assume to be 'our' food can easily be redirected to other customers with deeper pockets.

Yet another lock-in is a general assumption that food can safely be left to the food industry. This is wrong and out of date, but reinforces policy reluctance to engage with the range and scale of our food problems. Only government has the authority to reframe the food system, but governments have been in some disarray about food, which is why new frameworks and policy leadership are required.

Pressure on government to act in the public interest must be exerted from inside and outside. Many people and organizations now recognize that the current pattern of food capitalism in Britain needs an overhaul and reorientation. A new more devolved regionalism is overdue to rebuild connection and engagement between the people and their food. It can be done, and the criteria by which its direction can be judged are known. We need to decide as a country whether we want to feed ourselves more and better, not at any cost, but sustainably and well.

A secure food system is one in which sustainable diets are the norm and the entire food system is reoriented to be low-impact, resilient and sustainable. This is not the case now but must become so. As a rich country, the UK could and should take a lead in this direction. It is not doing so, and this book is my exploration of how that has come about and what it implies.

PART ONE

Our Food Security Problem

The following three chapters provide an overview of UK food security. I argue that UK food security deserves to be taken more seriously than it has been. Most economists and many food policy analysts will assert that food follows wealth. Demand pulls supply. Historically, this has been so for the UK. It follows that, as a rich if divided society, there is no need to have concerns about UK food security. Indeed, many policymakers dismiss such thoughts, as has been witnessed in Brexit politics. Ignoring reports to the contrary, mainstream policymakers assume food flows are assured. Food security is deemed to be a concern for Africa or poor developing countries, not the UK, they say.

This book suggests this policy confidence is wrong. New stresses and fragilities have been introduced into the UK food system (expanded on in Part Two). The UK is not the only country with access to funds or sources to buy food. World markets have been completely restructured since the days when the Royal Navy could be assumed to protect long colonial seaborne food supply lines. Also experience showed that this confidence was misplaced even then, when the Navy was much more powerful than it is today. UK supply chains have also restructured in the last half-century or so. They have become more European and, above all, been revolutionized by just-in-time supply logistics. Warehousing is thin; the warehouse is actually the motorway.

Part One rehearses the current state of UK food flows, presenting the broad picture. If the UK food system was a bank, it would be bankrupt. There are a yawning trade gap, declining home production, and a system which is akin to skating on thin ice. I reject the official British state assurance that food 'resilience' is high. It is actually stretched, open to disruption and far from resilient. I offer seven arguments for why policymakers should put food security at the heart of planning and policy for food in coming years.

The productionist policy and approach to food which appeared to work so well – more food, cheaper, bigger range – is in fact fragile. In Part Two, these arguments are explored in more detail. A constellation of problems threatens UK food security. There is a lock-in which a tweak here, a nudge there will fail to resolve. A more detailed case is made for restructuring the current model of food supply. In Part Three, an outline is presented of what might be done to resolve our food problems. Part One in the immediately following pages introduces our food security problem. Some of this is peculiar to the UK, but it conveys messages which might not be lost on other affluent societies. One might hope that a benign world would follow from a Smithian free flow of foods, but in fact food is easily taken into a dependent and exploitative relationship unless there is a framework of some kind of equality and mutual recognition. The history of food suggests alas that it is a useful weapon in international diplomacy.

CHAPTER 1
Food and the National Interest: Redefining Progress

The UK has entered an important period of restructuring. Not before time, nor without reason. This book proposes that a hard, cool look at UK food security must be part of that period of reflection and redesign. A review of the policy framework, largely the legacy of the mid-twentieth century, is needed. I want to focus on the present but also look back to explain how we have got to where we are; and look forward to face the known features of future food systems.

We must ask what is different now and what will be different again by the mid-twenty-first century. One could pick other significant periods or processes against which to chart how the UK food system has changed. There was the rise of industrialization and its pull of labour from the land to the towns from the late eighteenth century. Or the agrichemical revolution and its unleashing of efficient production but damage to ecosystems. Or the switch in lifestyles to sedentary work, car use and hypermarkets. I try to include all these, but keep coming back to the 1930s and mid-twentieth century for one main reason. It is when the UK zigzagged into a food security emergency from which it only just ultimately escaped. And in the immediate aftermath it reviewed its food system in cold political light and set on a different course – to produce more itself and to be less reliant on *distant* supplies; first on its own and then as a member of the Common Market/European Union. That is what it has done ever since.

The mid-1930s to mid-1940s were thus an important policy transition period for UK food. Anyone who knows even a little about UK history knows that food was a central challenge in the Second World War. Actually, food problems had been emerging for well over a century – arguably longer – before the 1930s. But that it took a massive crisis to engender significant policy change is a key point to grasp. The evidence of a coming food security crisis was as plain as a pikestaff to cognoscenti in the late 1930s yet was ignored until events struck in 1939–40. I believe we are in a position something akin to that today. Like then we have multiple, well-argued and evidenced calls from different parts of British society for the food system to be reformed. A country which has a boom in food banks is not a happy place. A country with declining food production and with a massive diet-related, NHS-bankrupting food culture is not a good food nation. A country where 60% of farming is propped up by subsidies and producing only 12% of its fruit (which in any event ought to be consumed at twice the level it is) has a mismatch between need and land use. A country in which being overweight and obesity are rampant, and that is locked into car use, not walking or bicycling, to get its food is not a healthy nation. A country with massive greenhouse gas emissions from its food system is not environmentally friendly. And so on. Something is not right with our food body politick.

And yet . . . one could argue – many do – that we in the UK today have, in the words of a former Prime Minister, Harold Macmillan, 'never had it so good'. Full supermarket shelves; historically cheap and plentiful food – surely the food problems we have today do not compare to those of the 1930s. A glance at those black-and-white photos of squalid streets, the pictures of obviously hungry and thin children, and people in ragged clothes: these surely indicate real food poverty and there is nothing like that today. Indeed, today is different, yet the class inequalities are again rampant, the gap in life expectancy just as shocking but shaped by different factors. I shall argue that we need some humility about both past and present. It was not obvious in the 1930s that 'something had to be done'. People had to campaign and shout then, as now. The war heightened the debates, but the dignified Jarrow March by the unemployed in October 1936 had highlighted the issue of hunger.[1] And Sir John Boyd Orr's 1936 *Food, Health and Income* survey of British diets had given a scientific credibility to the critique that hunger lay at the heart of the British Empire.[2] Coverage of his report was front-page news around the world.[3] More followed when doctors and the British Medical Association produced reports on the malevolence of malnutrition.[4,5] Despite these wake-up calls, the food system carried unequally on, shaped by an austerity politics in the central state.

Today, without pushing the parallel too far, the reaction by central government to the 2018 visit, and his initial and final reports, by the United Nations (UN) rapporteur on extreme poverty and human rights, Professor Philip Alston, discussed later, gives some kind of echo of what happened in the late 1930s.[6,7] He described a state of food affairs as bluntly as Sir John Boyd Orr had in 1936. Poor diet and inequalities were normalized. The state and large sections of the population turned a blind eye or blamed families. Too little was changing. The constancy of poverty has also been emphasized by the relatively new Social Metrics Commission, a collaboration between the Legatum Institute, the Joseph Rowntree Foundation and others. Using measurements developed for its first report in 2018, the Social Metrics Commission 2019 report estimated that 14.3 million people (22% of the population) live in poverty in the UK. Within that figure, 34% of children live in poverty,[8] 4.5m of these people live at 50% below the poverty line, i.e. extreme poverty, and three fifths of those in extreme poverty are stuck there. Food 'choice' is inevitably severely constrained under such circumstances.

In the late 1930s, as is known, the food policy temperature changed drastically when Nazi submarines had the capacity to threaten UK food supplies, and new thinking was applied via rationing and a renewed interest in producing more food here in Britain. In 1939, only a third of UK food was homegrown. British agriculture was in a sorry state: unkempt fields, low prices, depression, as observers from the political Right, Centre and Left agreed.[9,10,11] Today, as we'll see, depending on how it's measured, UK food self-sufficiency is at worst about a half and mostly nearer two thirds. The fields are not untidy; indeed, they have been blitzed by chemical farming to the point where wildlife has been ruined. The fields are vast and monocultural, while the supermarket shelves groan under about 30,000 food items. There is product diversity, not biodiversity.

As I mull over the differences between the 1930s/40s and today, what particularly interests me is the social movement which came together to articulate a new 'food national interest'. Those involved came from many parts of society: depressed northern towns and bourgeois London, doctors and social campaigners, the landless and even members of the landed aristocracy, town councillors and MPs. Whatever their starting point, they did not shy from arguing for food system reform. Today, again there is a cacophony of sectoral appeals about food matters, but so far too few systemic appeals. That said, already, as I write, I detect signs that this is changing. The cliff edge of a no-deal Brexit debate at last knocked some heads together, forcing people to see the implications of disruption to the massive flow of trucks carrying food. I argue later that this means we need to ask: what sort of food system do we want for the UK? More of the same or a different direction? If the latter, shaped by what considerations?

Already in the 1930s, and increasingly in the 1940s – when reality was a harsh educator – an emerging food reform movement was arguing that better food should be at the heart of future political reconstruction for a better Britain.[12] Living standards were disgracefully low.[13] Poor standards led to poor diets. Affordable but better food therefore required action greater than the sum of previous political parts. If food rationing helped inject a bit of social justice into the food market but would be unpopular after the war, what should be done to get the UK food system onto a better footing? The mid-twentieth-century food politics were about what would do this. And the new position set on rebuilding home production was based on seeing that there was a direct connection between decay in the countryside and the unmet need in the towns. It shone light on the terrible health distortions that followed from genetic chance: a child born to affluent in-work parents thrived. Others did not. Today, as we'll see, a not dissimilar mix of societal and genetic chance is at work. Life expectancy differences have widened between income groups. This in one of the richest societies on the planet.

That 1930s/40s generation of food thinkers, to which this book offers such respect, laid down a way of thinking which we have inherited for the last seventy years. They churned out data and arguments, shaming British society into aiming for something better.[14] It could be done. Canteens could produce wholesome food at the school, hospital and workplace. Healthier mothers and children would be part of a better society. Those aspirations were and remain honourable, yet this book questions some of the thinking we inherited. It argues that something different is now needed; the old policy recipe is not working. Our food problems are more complex. Before exploring what is different today, I want to restate something I know that the previous generation thought too.

This was a belief that there could be a better food system, that everyone can be fed, that food supply can be made more efficient, and that everyday lives will be massively enhanced by so doing. It is hard to disagree with these sentiments. But there are important differences between then and today. Then, their main goal was to feed people, increasing the quantity and availability of affordable food, whereas today we are awash with food and bombarded with marketing to pick this brand over that. Whereas, then, they sought to make food cheaper, today food is almost too cheap, yet not cheap enough for those eating poorly or on tight budgets. Then the pursuit of a more efficient food supply seemed the clear direction to go, whereas we today know the consequences of some of those efficiencies – the effects of agrichemicals, the legacy of plastics, the loss of biodiversity while bringing more land under cultivation. Today we have to rethink what is meant by efficient production if we accept that food is now one of the major drivers of ecosystem destruction.

What Charles Darwin called 'the web of life' has until recently been swept away by a narrow financial view of efficiency as output and profits. The notion that the food system could be centred on the prevention of ill-health and protection, nay, improvement, of ecosystem resilience while providing decent diets for all (not some) of the population has been deemed wildly utopian. That is our problem today. But we can draw strength from the past. Back then too people saw insurmountable problems. While today few see science as the sole fount of solutions to food problems, it is more commonly accepted that ecological resource efficiency must be at the heart of twenty-first-century food policy and that epidemiology, for instance, offers pretty convincing evidence about diet's impact on population health. So science is a really important source of information and public education about the complexity of food. But it is not alone. Many competing interests vie for policy attention.

Today, even as we talk of good policy being 'evidence-based', we know, as the mid-twentieth-century reformers did, that good policy can only emerge when opportunities arise, and chances are seized. I think we have such a moment now. British society is in the midst of a long-term upheaval about the future, who we are and what kind of society and forms of governance we want. Europe has been the punchball, when it is only one 'level' in a multi-level political framework. There is equal uncertainty about how the UK fits into world affairs, and what kind of more local or regional structures we have.

In the 1930s and 1940s, the urgency of war concentrated minds. With the serious fault-lines fissuring UK society and its political economy exposed even more openly for all to see by Brexit politics, it is no longer wholly inconceivable that modern politics could slide into another European war, when part of the role of post-war food policy in both Britain and Europe was to prevent such calamity. Nor is it inconceivable that trade wars could see economic giants fight for supremacy and for the UK to find itself weaker than it likes to think of itself as being. Mistakes were made in the Second World War but, although tens of thousands of lives were lost and countless ships destroyed in maintaining food supplies in 1940–45, Britain did not lose the war or starve its people. Historians such as Lizzie Collingham and Madhusree Mukerjee have shown how around the world millions of humans died during the conflict from no access to food, whether through collapse of supplies or enemy policy or policy priorities in favour of keeping the UK fed. It is not just others who used and use food as a weapon of war.[15,16] Our own history is not unblemished.

The British grumbled dreadfully about rationing in the Second World War, and the drab state of more equal diets.[17] But a worried state machine was persuaded that British society would only keep supporting the war effort if it was decently fed.[18] And after the war conditions needed to be altered to prevent the gross food injustice that had characterized the 1930s. A remarkable coalition of forces, interests and organizations, a broad and new consensus, won the argument that a different policy framework was needed. Everywhere, they argued, land can be better used, people can be better fed, inequalities can be reduced, children can be fed properly at school. Why not?

Food improvement as progress

I think we need just such a new alliance today and I believe elements of this alliance and consensus are emerging. This book is written to present a case that I think this alliance could promote. At a time when there are powerful appeals for isolation or turning our backs on neighbours, plus a nostalgia for a simpler Britain that did not really exist, it is important to realize that, as ever, we are engaged in a tussle over what we mean by progress. Food offers important lessons and opportunities to chart clearer conceptions of what we want, what food progress should look like. Already bookshops, libraries and media programmes are awash with advice on cooking, diets and lifestyle food choices. These individualize our food problems. They see salvation in private choices. I think bigger questions are at stake. We can raise our eyes to consider what a good food system is, both in the sense of a 'good food' system and a food system which delivers good for the public. I would like to see more attention on arguing about what 'food progress' for a rich country such as Britain would look like. Is it yet more food or better food? Is it more choice or more sustainable choice? Some food voices argue that the world faces starvation unless productivity rises and a new round of intensification is unleashed. Others question that, arguing that immense amounts of waste are now intrinsic to the food system and that there is plenty of food but it is maldistributed. These divergent positions matter for Britain. Resolving them and setting out a clear direction is a priority for British food policy.

Britain does not feed itself. Some say that doesn't matter. I think it does. I do not favour autarky – only food from here – but argue that to allow the current decline is risky. We need closer understanding of what excessive reliance on long food chains and distant supply sources means. We need to realize that simply buying food does not absolve us from responsibility for how that food is produced and sourced. For a country blessed with a relatively benign climate not to maximize its own sustainable food produce is immoral and could come back to haunt us, much as the decision in 1846 to source food supplies from wherever it was cheapest came back to haunt Britain in the Boer War and two World Wars. A powerful strand of both the British political Right and Left subscribes to the view – wrong in the nineteenth century and wrong again in the twenty-first – that all that matters is to fill bellies as cheaply as possible.

This is both stupid and dangerous. UK food supplies are fragile amid plenty. While supermarket shelves are awash with food, this book explores how food insecurity is closer than we might like to think. The logistics revolution which has swept the food system has created seeds for its own downfall, if surprisingly small things go wrong. The data which emerged after the Brexit Referendum, to which colleagues and I contributed,[19] showed that: narrow bottlenecks, oil-dependent trunker routes, just-in-time (JIT) distribution – let alone the massive stresses emerging from climate change.

Later chapters explore these issues and arguments. Suffice it now to state that big things are already going wrong. Much of my immediate motivation for this book was that I judge the slow decline in food self-sufficiency to be risky in itself and to represent a loss of nerve by informed opinion. Britain's reflex is to let others feed it. This is wrong today, was wrong in the past, and is not just hugely risky in security terms, but betrays a malign assumption that we have a right to be fed. We do not. This hangover from food imperialism is a bubble which needs to be burst. Better that we do it now than that events do it later.

The matter of food supply cannot be separated from the wider dynamics of the food system. I argue in subsequent chapters that the politics of British food is not being properly addressed by politicians. They are fearful of intervention when increasing numbers of even the most powerful food companies think a big shake-up is necessary. From science and academia, and from parts of the British state machine, there is resounding agreement. No one is in political charge yet everywhere the case for getting a grip now stares us in the face.

Another intention of this book is to reflect on what we mean by good food at the population rather than individual level. Is it to be a nation of *bon viveurs*, eating *haute cuisine*? (Note we use the French phrases.) Or is it to chart a better everyday food culture, less fixated on the pastiche feast day food we tend to eat daily? Simpler and better, or indulgent and better? It is time we talked about food progress as culture. Arguably, British food culture has never been apparently more democratic – tens of millions of British people can eat like only the rich ate a hundred years ago – yet a food culture is in place which is based on a false belief that individual choice can keep the food flowing at whatever cost to other countries, our health and the planet's. Many of us daily eat quite extraordinary amounts of cocoa, butter and sugar (for example) which would have astonished (and possibly nauseated) a generation back. Is this really just a matter of happiness and choice?

Over the last few decades, the UK has undergone a quiet revolution in what is eaten, how we get it, what food means and its impact. Some of this has been for the better, and some not. The current UK food system has never been so full of food yet its footprint is grossly unsustainable. Eating has become a – often the – major factor in altering the environment, damaging public health and cementing social inequalities.

Readers will have noticed that I have already used the term 'food system'. This clunky term warrants explanation. By food system I mean the complex network of economic and societal relations which organizes how food is grown, processed, retailed, cooked and consumed. Some economists and food analysts prefer the term 'food supply chains'. I use that term too, but only to indicate the actual lines down which foods are sent and merge before food products arrive packaged and sealed on supermarket shelves or our plates.

Food supply chain analysis can lend itself to the corollary that, if any deficiencies are found, the chain simply needs better management. It implies an orderliness and control which are, indeed, sought by food commerce, as the studies show.[20,21,22] Actually, food is underpinned by more than food commerce and its food control tendencies. The state and civil society are completely involved too. I prefer and thus use the term food system, because it allows us to consider the full web of policy actors, in all their messiness, not just a notional orderly sequence. We are definitely beyond thinking of the food system as a simple mechanism, beloved of children's story books about farmers and markets. As a former farmer myself, I know the limits of the image of fluffy lambs and kindly sheepdogs. British farmers themselves have actually been marginalized in today's analysis of what can be done about food problems while being blamed for some of them. The health and environmental critics have been close to running out of sympathy for farming, just when British land use urgently needs a radical shake-up and a case can be made not just for a complete farming make-over but for how land is used and made available in both town and country.[23]

Herein lie deep and difficult politics. As in the 1930s, the British food system is quietly out of control. Neither the state nor markets nor consumers are holding the wheel. Parliamentary politics needs strong, clear champions to push a new food vision through the food system. We have food champions in this food zone and that, but if we scan across existing democratically accountable institutions, there is no unified sense of urgency. No big picture. Although there are many fine statements coming out of, or directed at, the British food system, no one currently is fully engaged in taming and redirecting the machinery of government. Bits, yes, but not fully. This is deeply worrying. As in the 1930s and 1940s, the data are abundantly clear that we need to begin another process of radical change, a process which I and others call the 'Great Food Transformation'. This should start very soon or we will be forced to do it in a crisis later.[24]

People who recognize this sometimes say privately that crisis will force change. This may be the case, but the scale of the crisis sketched across the sciences suggests that it will be dangerously far-reaching. Surely it is better to engage the public in debate before whatever crisis management plan is steamrollered through. Moreover it is wrong simply to wait for a crisis. The data suggest that it has already crept up on us. Climate change is happening; food-related ill-health levels are shocking; the unfairnesses of financial reward in the food system are dreadful. Part of the point of this book is to point out the range and extent of the tensions in and over food. We do not need to wait for trouble. It has been normalized. Open our eyes and it is here now.

The dichotomy of crisis-led versus rationality-led changes matters. I acknowledge that British history is full of examples of where food crises can be presented as causing change. A Whig interpretation of history can be offered that school meals, for instance, were introduced in the 1906 Education (Provision of Meals) Act because the supposedly benign and thoughtful state realized it was in its interests to feed its future soldiers better after the humiliations of the Boer War when healthier, fitter Boers nearly trounced the mighty British imperial forces. Not so. Actually, the number of schools offering meals declined after the 1906 Act because the precious few who had carried out this role as charities withdrew, arguing that responsibility was now up to local authorities, who had been given powers to levy funds on the rates (the then local property tax) to provide meals for needy school-children. Not until the First World War was the Act activated, and then rarely. School meals did not become common until the Second World War, when women were needed in factories and were less available to be home to feed children and their men. Thus improvements in school food took decades, not one Act. Food progress may take decades and come from surprising sources. However, now the warning signals are very loud. Think of Britain's food system as in a war: humans versus security versus health versus the environment versus jobs versus culture. This is how I have structured this account of our food problems.

A note of optimism

The state of UK food is not all bad news. Over the forty-five years I have worked in and on UK food policy – as a farmer, as an academic, in and with civil-society organizations and government bodies, and in a policy think tank – I have seen and joined others in celebrating wonderful improvements, amazing people getting food things done. The sad truth is that it is too patchy. The food scene suffers from projectitis – great projects often started on a wing and a prayer, then winning funding, only to be cut off by short-termism. Perhaps that is inevitable. Overall I agree with many observers of civil society that good things and projects are being countered by the back-pull of wider socio-economic tensions. Despite waste reduction targets, the avalanche of food continues through the food system pipelines. Despite cooking classes and TV shows, the rise of ready-made foods high in salt, sugar and hidden saturated fats continues. Despite growing environmental awareness, the indices on biodiversity generally worsen.

The British food system is so complex, so huge and so fractured that many analysts agree it needs a new framework. Surely Brexit could bring that? some argued. The shackles of the EU's Common Agricultural Policy (CAP) and Common Fisheries Policy (CFP) have stopped progress. Others point out that similar tensions to those we have in the UK are manifest throughout the world and that the CAP and CFP are not alone in suffering from them. Food systems are in a permanent state of change, responding to intra-system pressures such as declining fish stocks, in the case of the CFP, as well as external campaigning. But whether the changes are fast or progressive enough is what matters. The UK cannot bury its head in the sand or fantasize that leaving the EU to buy more food on 'open' world markets or hitch up to the USA or other distant countries will somehow resolve our farm or fishing policy failures.

The scale of analysis must be system-wide. We must take a sober look at how the food system jigsaw fits together. Currently it is characterized by food inequalities within and between countries, huge externalized diet-related ill-health costs, environmental damage from agriculture, runaway giant corporations, a sweetening of diet, and more. All these characteristics feature in British food. The CAP or CFP alone cannot be blamed for this range of policy failure. We need to sort out our responsibilities too.

There are some food matters which can be addressed from within the food sector itself – whether we teach people to cook, whether food labels work, how we farm, whether we are prepared to pay for higher quality – and some issues that cannot. Food poverty and inequalities, for instance, are shaped by forces outside the food sector: jobs, income, social class, taxation, history, genetic chance as to who one's parents are. The general national political orientation – Left, Right, Liberal or Green – goes beyond food matters, yet frames how we do or do not shape national food policy. I try to point to those framing factors outside the food system, where possible, while focusing on what falls within the food system. I am clear that we can do something better with the British food system. There are now many state actors, elected politicians, programmes, departments, projects, NGOs and commercial actors who recognize that it is time we got the British food act together.

Resolving our food problems, Brexit or no Brexit

A caveat. This is not a book about Brexit, although I delayed writing it the moment the Referendum happened, knowing that the policy frameworks would have to come into play and could change significantly. In the name of austerity and rebalancing the books, government ministers had foolishly cut the civil service from 2010 in the Food Standards Agency, the Environment Agency, and in the Department for Environment, Food and Rural Affairs (Defra). Defra, for instance, was cut by 30% in 2010–16. Then it had to rise by 65% in 2016–18 when another raft of ministers (and the Treasury) realized Defra was responsible for at least 25% of EU-derived legislation – 4,000 regulations alone on food – and that Brexit meant they needed to rebuild their in-house expertise.[25] By the end of 2018, staffing was almost back to 2010 levels.[26] Whatever shape Brexit politics takes, the British food system deserves review. Rural Britain, for example, has long been recognized as likely to be affected by changing subsidy levels, Brexit or no Brexit.[27] But the urban food sector matters too, and is where the money is mostly made and mostly goes.

The book, however, is not concerned with Brexit, despite that being both a backdrop and a dynamic. It also had its surreal moments, such as when the government issued advice (coded 'Official Sensitive') to local Resilience Forum chairs on the 'reasonable worst-case scenario (RWCS)' and the shock revealed in the leaked Yellowhammer papers showing the government expected massive disruption to food supply and price rises.[28] Yet it did not tell the public.[29] One wonders what unreasonable worst-case scenarios might look like!

Whatever happens in the short to medium term in UK relations with the EU, it is clear that a food agenda needs to be addressed. Arguably, some of the problems tackled in this book shaped the simmering resentment in the country that found expression in the Brexit vote, understandably so, even though the EU was often not the main driver of such problems. Indeed, often EU programmes gave local politicians opportunities to compensate for decisions made by national politicians, such as applying for regional structural funds to tackle widening inequalities, regional disparities and the decline of old industries. For three years (and counting), Brexit politics consumed energies, but a weakened and Brexit-focused Whitehall and political class had to face realities of severing links with our neighbouring countries, relationships which have been embedded for half a century. Nowhere has this mattered more than for food. But we are where we are. This book is an appeal to politicians, the people and the food sector to engage with what we *ought* to be doing: making the UK food system more food secure and more sustainable.

Defining Britain: what is the nation?

The 2016 Referendum reminded us that Britain was still unclear about Ireland. As Brexit political divisions intensified, there was considerable surprise in many quarters at how important the Irish question became again. Anyone with the slightest understanding of history should not have been surprised. Irish and British political tensions are centuries-old, peppered with invasions, uprisings, struggles, yet proximity, shared language and parallel currencies (until the Euro). The two islands' history is a mix of conflict, tension and peace, at times sullen, sometimes benign. The food relationship between Ireland and Britain matters very much, not least in terms of the status of Northern Ireland. It voted to stay in the EU, yet a sizeable proportion of inhabitants judge remaining part of the UK a higher priority than staying in the EU. Ireland is one of the biggest trading partners of the UK. Britain is the travel route from the Republic to continental Europe.

So for this book, as for many food discussions, where the boundaries are drawn is significant. It can matter whether we refer to the UK – England, Scotland, Wales and Northern Ireland – or to Britain – only England, Scotland and Wales. I decided to assume that political engagement between Britain and Ireland would remain possible and that the slow engagement between Northern Ireland and the Republic would continue, in line with the general majority opinion and the 1998 Good Friday/Belfast Agreement. The text of this book uses both Britain and the UK, not least since the statistics and studies on which I draw vary. But I chose to do this in hope that hard boundaries do not again disfigure the map of these islands. A theme throughout is how food could play a part in a better mix of the local, regional, national and international within the UK, let alone with Europe and other nations.

CHAPTER 2

Why UK Food Security Matters

Britain has a food security problem. It doesn't feed itself. Lessons learned from the total crisis of the Second World War have been forgotten or deliberately undermined or eroded by internationalization and changing food tastes. Some argue that the slow decline of home production does not matter. As a rich society, they say, Britain can buy on open markets and does not need food even from its European neighbours. This chapter sets out seven reasons why we should take food security seriously. It proposes that the only route for food security is to make the food system more sustainable. This is not happening, not least since the British state is not yet interested. This is partly deliberate, a triumph of the New Right's 1970s view that the only good state is a weak state. And partly, it is simply a British idle default position that it expects others to feed it. This is risky, short-sighted and politically illiterate. A prime duty of the state is to ensure its citizens are fed both well and sustainably. We need a national debate about food. Less watching it on TV or Instagram; more talking about what sort of food system we need and want.

In simple quantity terms, we are heavily and increasingly dependent on others feeding us. From a high point in the early 1980s, self-sufficiency has declined once more.[1] We are not yet at the 1930s level where we only produced a third of our food and then had to double production in six years.[2,3] But to be at about 60% home production when there is so much more that could be grown here is, I suggest, immoral and short-sighted. The 60% figure today takes the optimistic view of official statistics. Based on farmgate value of unprocessed food, in 2016 the UK supplied just under half (49%) of the food consumed in the UK.[4] In my view, the UK is in a strange place on food security. More detail about actual food flows is given in the next chapter but this one looks at the arguments.

There is no shortage of food information and attention to food in modern Britain. Entertainment pours out of TV programmes and social media. There are cafés and eating places everywhere. Supermarkets are full of food. British food has been transformed since the 1940s. This is all true, but not the full picture. The food the British take for granted comes from a vast and often hidden food system which urgently needs to be reshaped for reasons explored in subsequent chapters. Amid all the pressing matters within Britain, making us more *food secure* must be a national priority. How the current food system operates, how we eat, has sown the seeds of its own undoing.

Let me state clearly, before we go into more detail, that post-war British food *has* been in some respects a remarkable success: more food, cheaper, bigger range, ubiquity. Yet this success, which we now take for granted, is more fragile than one might think. The dynamics which have transformed British food are now undermining British food security. There is a mismatch between what our current food system delivers and what we ought to be doing to make the UK food secure for the medium and long term. In this respect, British food is not unusual. Some of the main drivers within the British food system are shared by other affluent countries, while Britain has some idiosyncratic features to its food problems, which deserve attention. British science is famed internationally, and our food researchers and advice are in demand everywhere, not least since there are large international aid budgets which include attention to food. That is all well and good, but we do not give enough policy attention to the food fault-lines here at home. I am not arguing a 'pull up the drawbridge' position; simply that we would do well to face our own contradictions while trying to help sort out others'.

Land use everywhere needs to be seen as a prime national consideration, whether one is talking about Malawi or Britain, the Amazon or East Anglia. The UK has a famously benign climate – forget the jokes about British rain, which is essential for growing food, yet we are mismanaging that water, much as we mismanage soil. At the heart of our food problems is that to work on food is seen as, if not low status, then not exactly high status. Food labour tends to be low paid.

Does food security matter?

Usually at this point, thinking divides. One position says this does not matter. The UK is rich. It can always buy its food. Security comes with money. As long as the economy is functioning, the UK will be all right. This is such a British position! We assume someone else will feed us. This is a relic from past times, a post-imperial hangover. There are no colonies to provide food, or only fourteen British Overseas Territories such as the Falklands and Gibraltar.[5] The sole large land mass is the British Antarctic Territory with 660,000 square miles but it is ice, with little capacity for food growing! World food markets have changed since the mid-twentieth century, let alone the nineteenth, but old arguments have a habit of returning in new guises. Colonial power and gunboat diplomacy are history but replaced by modern 'soft' forms of food power such as cultural appeals shaped by huge advertising and brand budgets as well as 'hard' commercial power via contracts, trade deals and market might. There is a long strand of British intellectual critique even of food aid.[6,7,8]

A second line of thinking argues that food security should not be confused with self-sufficiency. A country placed in the north of Europe with short growing seasons cannot possibly feed itself. The growing seasons are against us. We have to import food. Food insecurity is a real concern for Africa or poor developing countries which have clear potential to grow more but not, it is argued, for a rich northern country such as the UK. And yet, while Britain cannot grow bananas, its favourite fruit, for example, it can grow apples and pears beautifully yet does not. And it has systematically destroyed its capacity to do so. This must be reversed and the conditions to do so must be created. This is simply because global pressures require all countries to rethink appropriate land use. UK land use policy is profligate. We ought to be using prime land to produce health-enhancing food, not treating it as expendable. We keep building houses on prime land, or putting motorways across it or (as is explained later when we consider soil) simply degrading our land by treating it as dirt. Land is a precious resource. All humanity depends on that thin layer of matter we call soil (actually a biomass teaming with life),[9,10] yet the food system today actively distorts the human-land nexus. If food security was taken more seriously, we would be making soil and food-growing capacity a top public policy issue. Currently, it is not. But there are signs this might be changing, not before time.

A third argument is that the food critics have lost a sense of proportion. While there might be some issues on the edge of the British food system which need a bit of tidying up, in the order of things British food is a great twentieth-century success story. This shows, above all, in how life expectancy has gone up. It is true. Life expectancy *has* risen. Figure 2.1 gives period life expectancy for males and females in England and Wales from 1850 to 2010. It shows a gently rising curve from the 1870s to 2010, after which it in fact 'slowed down dramatically', as the Government's Actuary Department has stated.[11] Figure 2.2 gives period life expectancy for English men from 2001 to 2017. It shows a decline in life expectancy compared to the dotted line which gives what had been expected if trends continued.

Life expectancy may have gone up but not all those life years are healthy. As the King's Fund explains, an English male could expect to live 79.5 years in 2014–16, a wonderful advance on the mid-nineteenth century. But this average male's healthy life expectancy was only 63.3 years. In other words, he would have spent 16.2 of those years (20%) in 'not good' health.[12] This is not just distressing for the male, friends and family; it is also expensive for society.[13]

The Longevity Science Panel – set up by the insurance company Legal and General and chaired by Dame Karen

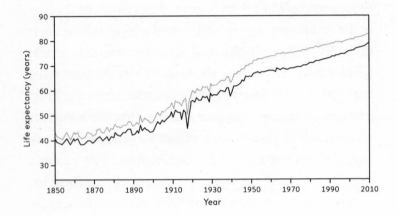

Figure 2.1

Period life expectancy at birth, England and Wales, 1850–2010

——— Females

——— Males

Source: GAD. Mortality insights from GAD. December 2018.[11]

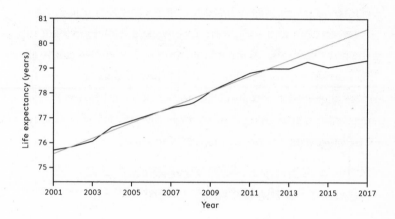

Figure 2.2

Period life expectancy, UK, 2001–17

—— Females

—— Males

Source: GAD. Mortality insights from GAD. December 2018.[11]

Dunnell, former head of the Office of National Statistics – agrees the upward march has halted. The life expectancy gap between the richest and poorest neighbourhoods of England widened between 2001 and 2015.[14] In 2001, a boy born in an affluent neighbourhood could expect to outlive one born in a poor area by 7.2 years. A decade and a half later that gap had risen to 8.4 years. The Panel found that death rates for 60- to 89-year-olds declined for all socio-economic groups between 2001 and 2015, with the biggest advances evident in the most well-off. All the while, other societies as wealthy as Britain show it is possible to do better. And all the specialists suggest that diet and food are a significant factor in this epidemiological change. Another is the politics of austerity. The biggest factor is income, says the Panel.

Is this a 1936 (not 1942) 'Beveridge moment' for the UK food system?

Part of the problem about whether food security matters is that the state has side-stepped the issue. It does not want to engage with it. It was remarkable how, when tensions rose over Brexit, the government denied there might be a problem until it was almost upon it. A transition from complacency to crisis planning occurred in a trice. Meanwhile almost everyone in the food industry here and abroad was astonished at how anyone could consider there might be business-as-usual. Part of the UK's food problem is getting acceptance that the food system might have to change. Government is a major part of the problem. Its default position is to assume business will sort it – what I have called the 'Leave it to Tesco et al.' reflex. Meanwhile, Tesco et al. were telling the Prime

Minister and Cabinet there would be a food security problem and were realizing that, whatever happens with Brexit, there is little hope of sorting out the food system worldwide, if we in rich countries like Britain fail to get our own food act together! And the UK regrettably has failed. A serious review of the UK food system is long overdue. Michael Gove, Secretary of State at Defra, was criticized by a few people (myself included) for focusing on ecosystems (a good thing, and overdue) but without considering food, and for winning space in the parliamentary timetable for an Agriculture Bill which barely mentioned food, and an Environment Bill.[15] Welcome though some features of the proposed legislation were, they did not get a grip on *food* policy as the linkage. To his credit, a longer-term Food Strategy review was slowly set in train in August 2019 by Defra, while Mr Gove was moved to take charge of all Brexit affairs under the Prime Minister, Boris Johnson. In March 2018, Henry Dimbleby, co-founder of Leon, the organic fast-food chain, was brought on to the Defra Board. He had led reform of the English school meals programme when Mr Gove was Secretary of State for Education. The Dimbleby food review is due to report by summer 2020.[16,17] Whatever this has managed to do, it ought to have critically assessed the core policy assumption that others will feed us and that world food trade is a calm pool of supplies from which the UK can draw cheaply and at will.

Sceptics in public policy always say that if a government does not know what to do, it can simply set up a review. But reviews can also be seriously good and effective in changing policy, if well handled and genuinely wanted. There is a precedent for both the sceptical and the positive assessment of

Figure 2.3
Henry Dimbleby
Source: Defra

such a review in the one Sir William Beveridge was asked to chair in 1936. Beveridge was charged to consider administrative plans for food rationing for the augustly named 'Committee for Imperial Defence', in the event of a new war. An economist, he was the senior civil servant in the newly formed Ministry of Food set up in 1916 to address food insecurity then, and he wrote the official history a decade after the Ministry's closure.[18] His 1936 food review is not often acknowledged in modern food policy. It deserves to be, not just for what it proposed but for what happened after it. Having witnessed the fierce arguments over commerce and the national interest in 1916–19 over food supplies and national morale, when the food industry resisted state intervention.

Beveridge knew the importance of food planning as part of national defence.[19,20] He recommended that preparations begin, and a new Food (Defence Plans) Department was set up that same year in the Board of Trade but Beveridge, who expected to guide the preparations himself, was kept off that new Committee, almost certainly because he suggested drastic action such as rationing and food controls. Opposition came not just from industry but from politicians and others in the civil service who thought war and dire conflict unlikely. A softer route was taken and preparations were thin until war actually broke out three years later. The historians agree that the long lull known as the 'phoney war' in 1939–40 was crucial in giving the government and new Ministry of Food (a rapid recreation of its 1916 predecessor) time to get up to speed.[21]

In the second half of the 1930s, other sources of pressure to tackle the sorry state of the British food system emerged.

One was the state of farming itself – in depression and providing only a third of national food. An independent inquiry was published in 1935 by two rich men, Viscount (Waldorf) Astor, the media magnate, and Seebohm Rowntree, scion of the chocolate family, who had spent decades investigating the poor diets of people in his home city of York. Between them, they pursued the dangers of this misuse of land for the next decade, repeating, developing and pushing their findings, in the House of Lords, in the press, anywhere they could;[22,23,24,25] and again after the war.[26] When they started their joint inquiries in the mid-1930s they were concerned about the sorry state of British farming within the web of Empire relations. By the 1940s they were clear as to its security importance.

The other line of policy attack, in which again Seebohm Rowntree featured, focused on food poverty and health. Rowntree's own studies had exposed the lamentable state of working-class diets since 1899. A Quaker, he knew it was partly about pay, but also about lack of infrastructure – poor housing, poor food at work, immiserated food culture, ill-health. He championed works canteens, better welfare, while a remarkable line of British women activists had been championing the need to support women and mothers since before the First World War, and detailing the plight of working-class women lacking kitchens and incomes.[27]

The medical world weighed in too, denouncing the state of diet-related ill-health. Perhaps most important was John Boyd Orr's large 1936 study *Food, Health and Income*. Boyd Orr showed how bad the diet in Britain was. He was a doctor who had been shocked when teaching in Glasgow by the poor

Figure 2.4
Sir William Beveridge
Source: Hans Wild/Time & Life Pictures/Getty Images.

diets of working-class children and had set up the Rowett Research Institute at Aberdeen in 1913 to study animal and human nutrition. Interrupted by the First World War, the Rowett's work took off in the 1920s, championing the connection of farming and public health through food. Boyd Orr, like Beveridge, knew the urgency of improving food supply and quality, especially for people on low incomes, suffering then as now from the effects of poor diet.[28,29,30]

The policy links between the land, food, the towns, health and social policy were beginning to emerge, even if the reality remained dysfunctionally mired. Farming was in recession; hunger and ill-health were widespread; European politics were on the edge. War, when it came, was the opportunity for policy and reality both to be reformed. Beveridge, as is well known, captured the political mood with his 1942 National Insurance report, *Social Insurance and Allied Services*. Not specifically concentrating on food, but laying the shape and rationale for the welfare state via a principle of insurance and the National Health Service, the report's focus was on the state as provider of a minimum standard of existence. Justly celebrated as one of the most influential reports in modern British history, and known as the Beveridge Report rather than by its ponderous title, it was a bestseller.[31]

Having been marginalized over his 1936 pre-war thoughts on food planning for a coming war, Beveridge was not deflected when given the second brief to produce his views on social policy in the war. He expanded his remit and reported what he really believed needed to be said and done. We are in his debt even today for that, but Beveridge deserves to be better known for his earlier food work. He was part of an extraordinary generation of academics and social-policy analysts who viewed food as a national scandal but one which could be addressed and resolved.

Britain today is again at a 1936 'Beveridge moment' on food. There is a stack of evidence that the food system should change, and no shortage of thinking available, yet so far insufficient high-level political leadership prepared to push through that change. There are many reasons – resistance to evidence, fear of the scale of the case for radical change, more pressing immediate political matters, residual belief in the default 'leave it to Tesco et al.' policy, a naïve belief in technical fixes, a lack of advice from a weakened civil service, no champion body for food within Whitehall . . . many reasons. Inactivity, however, is sowing the seeds of a downfall.

In 2007–8, the banking crisis and subsequent Great Recession looked as though they might lead to a food policy rethink among high-income economies. Secure in the belief that their (our) food systems were the epitome of efficiency and success, and that the problems lay in Africa, not America or Europe, G8 leaders were shocked when oil prices doubled and world commodity prices rose, affecting world food prices and thus their own.[32,33,34] The banking crisis and the collapse of Bear Stearns and Lehmann Brothers in the US, on the back of a mortgage bubble, and of Northern Rock and Royal Bank of Scotland in the UK, thus led to a nervousness that the global food system's failings might also apply in the rich West. Oil doubled in price but then crashed. A new era of price volatility in key commodities began.

In the UK, a rapid rethink about food policy was initiated. A Chatham House project, led by a secondee from the

Ministry of Defence, which had started in 2006 to look at UK food risks and food security, had struggled to get interest from across the British state.[35] And then suddenly, as the bank/commodity crisis swelled, interest rose. A Cabinet Office review was initiated, reporting in 2008,* after extensive cross-industry consultation, that a significant change of direction was needed.[36] A Cabinet food sub-committe was instituted. A UK food security review was conducted which mapped new indicators and connected food supply with environmental goals; it was developed via extensive consultation and open drafting.[37,38] This led to an ambitious new national strategy known as *Food 2030* linking health, environment, food industry and national security, together with the need to change diets.[39] Published in January 2010, it was immediately shelved by the Conservative-led Coalition after the May 2010 election.

There then followed nearly a decade in which there was little or no consideration given to food security – or not in any public sphere – until doubts about food security were raised in the event of a hostile or no-deal Brexit.[40,41] This lack of attention was surprising given growing scientific concerns being raised about the fragility of international food systems and the unsustainability of UK and rich-world consumption patterns.[42,43] The concerns colleagues and I raised were initially dismissed, only for a Cabinet member to admit within days that plans were underway for stockpiling, special transport was being booked and contingencies being

---

* I was a member of the advisory group for that Cabinet Office Strategy Unit *Food Matters* review.

activated. Then public and media interest grew but those concerns were really about immediate and 'emergency' planning rather than long-term; shaped by the possible effects of a 'no-deal' Brexit, crashing out into World Trade Organization trade terms, rather than due to any structural analysis from a review of the UK's own potential fragilities.

History teaches that events can rapidly change. It is now widely remarked that across the world a certain volatility and populism have emerged. It is not too far-fetched to imagine that a volatile state in transcontinental, European or world politics could slide intentionally or by mistake into another dreadful war or some other cause of food crisis. Stranger things have happened. Let us hope that rationality will prevail. Even if normality and civility resume, my case is that risks to food security are already with us. The normal is risky, and the UK food system ought to be beginning a measured process of radical change to tackle the fissures within the food system as it is. The rest of this chapter summarizes a number of clear reasons why food security should be taken more seriously, which are expanded and explored in the rest of the book. And then it poses a question about what, how and who can start what the 2019 EAT–*Lancet* Commission called the 'Great Food Transformation'.[44]

Food security

The UK's food system is over-stretched and mismatches food supply, health and ecosystems. One might argue that food security has no place in the environmental or health debates. And one could argue that it does not matter where food comes from as long as it gets to people. I disagree on both counts. Here is why.

REASON 1. THERE IS NO EMPIRE, NOR ARMED FORCES, TO PROTECT LONG SUPPLY LINES

Only a minority of British-born people alive today have adult experience of wondering where their food came from. Rationing ended in 1955. Before that, there were fifteen years of uncertainty. Today, the UK no longer controls agriculture-rich (former) colonies such as Australia, Canada and New Zealand, which shipped food over from the nineteenth century till the tap turned off with war, and then the UK joining the Common Market. Yet today people are complacent about food continuing to flow into UK ports either from Europe or from remoter sources. Present policy options are either to trade (i.e. import) food or to grow our own. The UK 'controls' only fourteen British Overseas Territories, and UK production is on a slow slide down.

When the UK had imperial or colonial food sources, it could protect shipping routes with its imperial military and more importantly its naval power. Today, the British Army, Navy and Air Force are stretched and have been subject to financial cuts, while experiencing rising costs from technological commitments – new weaponry. In crude terms, firepower may be up, but capacity to reach has diminished. In 2019, the Royal Navy had 75 commissioned ships. By comparison, the USA had 490 and Germany 65. In 1939, the Royal Navy had 377, plus 159 being built or on order. These could be spread around the globe and could, as many did, protect food convoys across the Atlantic. Today, if Britain wanted to import food from lands far away, it lacks ships in sufficient numbers to protect the supply lines.

Some think a focus on 'firepower' is too dramatic, and not

needed. 'New' power, they argue, resides with IT industries and the soft technologies of social media, allowing a different and more democratic exercise of power. It's a more complex intertwined world, they say, veering towards Thomas Friedman's argument that no two countries which both consume McDonald's burgers go to war with each other. Such arguments emerged when it was fashionable to think the age of ideology was over; the West had won. Today, that is laughable. And food is still a physical entity which has to be transported. If it comes a long way, opportunities to disrupt grow. IT-based logistics are highly vulnerable. Power resides with whoever controls the growing, distribution and form of that food. If it does not come to the UK from the Netherlands, Spain or France, then it must come from elsewhere, unless the UK grows more and eats less (both are possible strategies).

In the Brexit preparations after the 2016 Referendum, the Secretary of State for Trade set out to initiate new trade deals to replace the EU, assuming these would be food-secure. Trading relations can bind countries together and minimize military tensions, but long supply lines are by their nature open to more risks than shorter ones. A sense of geographical realism helps, too. Some politicians want to push the UK towards the mid-Atlantic. Others even think we are located somewhere in the mid-Pacific; they wanted the UK to join the Trans-Pacific Partnership (TPP). This is risky food politics. The safest food supply lines are proximal not distant.

We cannot assume in the twenty-first century that others will feed us. We could also produce much more food than we do. Indeed, world pressures mean that every country needs to think carefully about *how* to feed its population. It would be a mistake for the UK to relive its imperialist past. There are no colonies.

REASON 2. THE FOOD ECONOMY IS A JUST-IN-TIME ECONOMY, WITHOUT STOCKS

That there are no stocks for many foods was exposed in the run-up to the three times deferred Brexit dates of 29 March, 12 April and 31 October 2019. The modern food system operates on a just-in-time (JIT) basis, with ingredients and products arriving where needed in complex supply chains just before they are needed. It is a management system pioneered in the car industry by Toyota, and first maximally applied in food by Tesco. It's magnificently precise but, as analyses of episodes of failure such as the 2013 horsemeat scandal and 2018 shortage of CO_2 supplies (extensively used in food manufacturing) are wont to comment, 'even a minor disruption can create a ripple effect that magnifies as it widens.'[45] Food contracts are typically set twelve months ahead but delivered just in time. There are only a few days' commercial and public stocks held in the UK's food distribution chain.

The British Retail Consortium (BRC) reminded Theresa May, the then Prime Minister, in July 2018 that about 10,000 containers of food come into the UK from the EU daily, among millions of containers that pass through UK ports annually, supplying about 50,000 tonnes of food to the UK food trade.[46] The BRC made public its letter to Mrs May and Michel Barnier, the EU's chief Brexit negotiator, expressing concern about Brexit. Other senior food industry executives had been expressing concern in private since late 2016.[47] A food system engineered on three-to-five-day just-in-time logistics can break down completely in less than a week, and clog roads for longer. The Prime Minister had been warned in private in 2017 by at least one major food retailer to that effect.*

This should have been no surprise. In the mid-2000s, when the Labour government worried about food security threats from terrorism, a study by the Shrivenham defence management and resilience research group, part of Cranfield University, considered the range of possible disruptions. It showed that, besides the direct impact from terrorism, there could be breaks in IT systems, and loss of some distribution hubs, but it concluded that disruption could be coped with. The food system could bounce back. A disruption to one or even a few of the giant retail distribution hubs could be compensated for by ratcheting up supplies from other hubs.[48]

What the Cranfield report did not address and could not offer reassurance on, however, was the implications of bigger systemic disruptions such as emerged in the Brexit process or might from climate change or infrastructure stress or a breakdown in the Channel Tunnel coinciding with port disruptions. Effects are unknown from bigger threats than the UK experienced in a strike of a few days by 1,000 lorry-drivers in 2000 – after which a minister at the time told me that the food system was five days from crisis.† From a systems perspective, we ought to be planning for whether our highly

---

* Personal communications to the author from top food industry executives in summer 2017 through to summer 2018.
† When I referred to that period at an early meeting of the Chatham House *Food Futures* project in 2007, a number of food industry representatives put me right, saying they judged it as three days not five! Who knows? The Cranfield study was part of the learning from the 2000 internal rather than external threat.

concentrated and attenuated JIT food system can adapt to an above 2-degree rise in temperature, not simply reiterating the belief that we are rich, that we can buy food on 'open markets', and that our modern food system is highly efficient. Its complexity actually opens up risks rather than proves resilience.

REASON 3. THE FOOD TRADE GAP IS ENORMOUS

The term 'food trade gap' refers not to self-sufficiency but to the difference between imports and exports. The UK trade deficit in food, feed and drink increased in 2018 to a new record high of £24.3bn, up from £22.8bn in 2016. The UK exported £22.5bn worth of foods but imported £44.8bn. But the gap had been growing since the turn of the century and the post-Brexit drop in the value of the pound did not help.[49] Most global trade is conducted in $ or €. In June 2016, £1 was worth $1.50; by mid-2019 it was $1.22.

The UK trade is generally in deficit, and relies on financial services to compensate. A seventy-year review of UK trade in goods and services shows that the food trade deficit is nothing new.[50] A 2009 Defra study indicated that the UK was last self-feeding in the mid-eighteenth century![51]

Only in a few years in the 1970s and 1990s was the overall UK trade balance in the black, i.e. exporting food worth more than the cost of imports. Since 1999, the national food trade deficit has yawned. The argument used to be that we need not worry unduly about a growing trade deficit in goods as long as the service economy booms and compensates. The UK, from that perspective, does not need to grow food or to use its land for sustainable food production; it can simply buy much more of its food on world markets; others would benefit from the export markets and income.* This is a modern version of the argument which seduced a powerful section of the British élite in the early to mid-nineteenth century and won favour in the 1846 Repeal of the Corn Laws – those laws which favoured landowners by imposing tariffs (border taxes) on food imports. We will explore this more in later chapters. Meanwhile, some caution is in order today. Firstly, world commodity and food markets cannot be assumed to be stable; the OECD, FAO and others judge that price volatility and uncertainties are the 'new normal'.[52] Secondly, we need to clarify whether the UK actually has rights let alone the sufficiently deep pockets to rely on market purchases. Global economic power distribution has changed. Other countries have equally deep (and some deeper) pockets than Britain as well as mightier military and naval forces able to intervene in long supply routes, should they wish.

REASON 4. PLANETARY ECOSYSTEM PRESSURES ARE UPON US

Food is both a driver of, and affected by, climate change, water stress, population growth and biodiversity loss. Land use pressures on food production have grown. This science is often presented to the British public as though it is 'out there' somewhere, not something that will have a direct impact on us. Or else it leads to wry humour that the UK will be like the Mediterranean. Climate change is no joke. Anticipated and massive pressures on and in Africa – climate, wars, politics, population rise – are already pushing migrants northwards.

---

* A Cabinet Office specialist once told me: 'We don't need farmers, we can buy on open markets.'

The UK itself is not immune from ecosystems stress, and the countries we already rely upon for food will be negatively affected. We ought to be thinking strategically about these matters. We ought to be planning to protect and regenerate land for growing food here, as well as helping others to adapt and prepare – not using them to fill a post-imperial gap.

Already, the UK ought to be applying complex criteria to decide what a good food system will be like. This means more than price or immediate availability or how food looks. We need to redefine efficiency, and reframe food choice. A multi-criteria food world is emerging where environmental, health, social and quality factors need to sit alongside price and not be subsumed by it. This new multi-criteria approach to food systems makes life more complicated but it is more real for all that. This is the approach that policymakers ought to be applying.[53]

The UK could, for example, extend production of tomatoes and strawberries under glasshouse conditions, but we need to think carefully about whether this does in fact make sense. And how to do it: is it actually good to do this under plastic rather than glass? We know that seasonality is returning as an important consideration; energy inputs tend to rise in colder months.[54,55,56] So is it better, if the UK wants fresh fruit such as strawberries and tomatoes in mid-winter, to import them from where they are grown under the sun, not grow them under lights here (or in the Netherlands), and pay the full environmental costs? But, if we now apply water use to our criteria, not just energy, moving production south might simply add to the water stress of countries already experiencing problems. So which matters more – energy (carbon) or water? Eating fresh tomatoes in mid-winter might be nice, but if they are from Murcia or Almería, in southern Spain, the consumer is depleting their water tables.[57] And this complexity becomes even more tricky if we include labour conditions. Buying food that is produced outside the EU – in, for example, Morocco, with whom the EU has a bilateral trade deal – might still leave a lot to be desired.[58]

Optimists hope that the UK might become warmer and wetter with climate change, and that more food-growing opportunities will arise, but this assumes people will want to work on the land, where conditions are hard and pay not so good. For all sorts of historical reasons, British labour is reluctant to work on the land. Europeanization has brought a high dependence on EU migrant labour within the food system. We will explore later whether robots might have a role, but that is some time off. Development is underway and specialists think robots may be usable in ten or fifteen years, but not now. Even if and when they are, the multi-criteria approach to food will remain. Who controls the robots will have power. And what will happen to the displaced labour?

REASON 5. DIET IS A MAJOR CAUSE OF ILL-HEALTH AND A DRAG ON THE ECONOMY

Diet is placing a vast strain on the National Health Service. Poor diet causes slow, not fast deaths. Diet-related non-communicable diseases (NCDs) from excessive consumption of so-called 'cheap' foods are very expensive. Costs fall on society and bring untold emotional cost to families. In theory, consumers understand and agree with the case to eat healthier diets; in practice, we do not. Children are in a more vulnerable position than adults; they under-consume fruit and vegetables, and are becoming more obese. These eating patterns are influenced by commercial interests, and especially by advertising.[59] A 2019 survey by the academic campaign group Action on Sugar found that over half of 500 UK food and drink products, which use cartoon animations on packs to appeal to children, were unnecessarily high in fat, saturated fat, sugar and/or salt (i.e. they contained a red traffic light label). The majority were foods that would not be recommended for regular consumption such as cakes, biscuits, sweets or chocolates. Despite being subjected to years of criticism, the food industry still takes advantage of 'pester power', and use of cartoons exposes holes in supposed restrictions on broadcast and online advertising. The marketing industries are proving to be more nimble (and unethical) than governments, which appear to drag their feet, reluctant to intervene.[60]

Food companies spend an estimated twenty-seven times more on advertising than the UK government spends on promoting healthy eating. Even the government downplays its prevention work. In 2017, it spent £38m on weight loss surgery (such as bariatric operations) in the NHS but only £5.2m on its flagship healthy-eating campaign![61] The NHS, i.e. we as taxpayers, thus pays the cost of an inadequately regulated 'permanently eating' culture. The NHS Chief Executive has acknowledged that the government spent more in 2016 (£16bn) on treating the results of excess eating than the Home Office allocates to the police or fire service.[62]

The sad truth is that poor diet has been normalized in the UK. A 2018 survey found the UK to be eating the most processed diet of any studied in Europe.[63] Good news for the food-manufacturing sector, but less good for health agencies. Analysing data from the UK's National Diet and Nutrition Survey (2008–14) in a parallel study, the same team found that the average energy intake was 1,764 kcal/day, with 30.1% of calories coming from unprocessed or minimally processed foods, 4.2% from culinary ingredients, 8.8% from processed foods, and 56.8% from ultra-processed foods.[64] These 'ultra-processed' food products mean the UK consumes too much carbohydrate, free sugars, total fats, saturated fats and salt, while decreasing intake of protein, fibre and potassium. The people with the 'best' diets consumed about a third of their nutrients via ultra-processed foods, while those with the worst were about 82% reliant on ultra-processed foods. If the UK wants to prevent diet-related non-communicable disease, concluded the researchers, we must reduce the intake of such pre-processed foods low in good nutrients. This sobering study is not alone. Others point to how the growth of consumption of such foods is associated with diet-related and costly ill-health.[65,66]

Britain used to be (in)famous for dreadful food. Now even the French agree that we have some terrific food. We produce more artisanal cheese than they do. But our food culture is massively divided. There is excellent, high-quality food, and there are vast amounts of really doubtful food – cheap, plentiful, energy-dense, salty and fatty, contributing to short-term satiation but longer-term ill-health.

REASON 6. FOOD IS A MAJOR DRIVER OF SOCIAL INEQUALITIES

In her 2018 annual report, the Chief Medical Officer for England stated that, in England, the gap in life expectancy between the most and least deprived deciles (tenths) had increased in 2001–16.[67] The life expectancy gap between the most affluent and most deprived deciles in England had increased from 6.1 years in 2001 to 7.9 years in 2016 for females and from 9.0 years to 9.7 years in males.[68] Since 2011, the rise in female life expectancy has stalled in the third, fourth, and fifth most deprived deciles and had reversed in the two most deprived deciles, declining by 0.24 years in the most deprived and 0.16 years in the second-most deprived by 2016. Death rates from every disease and at every age were higher in deprived areas than in affluent ones in 2016. In everyday terms, this means progress is reversing before our eyes.

The gap between rich and poor now is actually wider than in Victorian times. Rich people can escape many diseases today; then they could not. The good news is that we all live much longer and plentiful food has been part of that advance. The bad news is that we accept that the rich will be able to eat well, be thin, have mental space and life opportunities, and accrue life advantages. We accept that people on low incomes are more obese and die prematurely. This is outrageous, and not civilized. And food is part of the problem. Britain has form on this, as the Chief Medical Officer's 2018 report acknowledged. Back in 1980, when the Black Report on inequalities in health was produced, it was so embarrassing that the newly elected Thatcher government tried to bury it.[69] Nearly two decades later an inquiry set up by the incoming Blair government under Sir Donald Acheson reported a worsening situation in 1998 and charted what needed to be done.[70] Much was done, but a review under Sir Michael Marmot reporting to the Cameron government in 2012 still recorded persistent heath inequalities.[71] These inequalities are stubborn, and not just about direct inputs such as nutrients and quality of diet, but about status, class and identity. Britain's food system is built on and reinforces these fissures and socio-economic class dynamics.

Price is the top factor for UK consumers when choosing food, according to polls and retail behaviour.[72] Governments and the food industry repeatedly commit to cheap food. Today the average British consumer spends about 10% of disposable income on food, but this varies greatly by income. A picture of consistent difference between income and educational groups emerges. One study by two Cambridge researchers, using a sample from the National Diet and Nutrition Survey, found that the highest socio-economic groups consumed up to 128 grams per day (g/d) more fruit and vegetables, 26g/d less red and processed meat, and 2.6% less non-milk extrinsic sugars.[73] Relative to lowest socio-economic groups, highest socio-economic groups were 2.4–4.0 times more likely to eat oily fish. There was a 113.7g/d difference between people working in routine occupations and those in higher managerial and professional occupations. Lowest-earning households consumed 15.7g/d more red and processed meat than the highest-earning households. Those with no qualifications consumed 21.9g/d more red and processed meat than degree-educated participants. Participants in higher managerial and professional occupations consumed 25.5g/d less red and processed meat than those in routine occupations.

The less income people have, the higher the proportion of that income they have to spend on food, and the less the actual amount spent on food is. Poor people spend proportionately more but get a worse diet. In public-health parlance, disposable income is a social determinant of diet-related health inequalities. This might be obvious, but it is not central to UK food policy. The introduction of Universal Credit, the new rationalized welfare system, has not helped. Growth in the use of food banks has been normalized. Public confidence in the welfare state's capacity to provide a safety net is weakening – critics argue that this is the intention, of course – shaped by the moral case that work is good, and the best way to feed oneself and one's family.[74,75]

REASON 7. FOOD SECURITY IS KEY TO DECIDING WHAT FOOD SYSTEM WE WANT

What sort of food system does the UK want? I am arguing that Britain has a false sense of security about food. Partly this is due to rising prosperity, the good times from being a member of the EU: plentiful food, widening cultural choice, ever more conventionally efficient food supply chains, tough regulatory regimes underpinning national interests, a shared commitment to feeding all Europeans. This policy infrastructure and framework received almost no coverage in the 2016 Referendum, other than reference to slights about Brussels bureaucrats making absurd decisions and the flows of money from the UK to Brussels (ignoring flows back from the EU budget to poorer UK regions). Whatever one thinks about the EU, the lack of discussion about the food implications of Europeanization or leaving is remarkable. A country which received over 40% of its food from or via EU membership seemingly chose to (and was led to) ignore that dependency when voting.

Even the most gung-ho Europhiles know that EU policies and structures are by no means perfect, but the lack of discussion about alternatives is remarkable. Gradually since the 2016 Referendum, some issues have emerged over specific matters such as chlorinated chicken and food standards.[76,77] To its credit, the two-year-long Food, Farming and Countryside Commission hosted by the Royal Society of Arts sought to raise questions about the future of farming,[78] but the scale of rethinking required by the UK's entire food system breaking from the EU is immense. The National Food Strategy review led by Henry Dimbleby is welcome and has an uphill task to overcome the legacy of policy myopia. A number of broad options can be charted.

One vision is for a *food importing future*. It rejects concerns about the food trade gap thesis introduced earlier. It accepts an economy in which others feed the UK and the UK produces other goods and/or services sufficient and profitable enough to buy food. The main policy mechanism lies in future trade deals, in which restricted home food production is traded off for access for UK exports to other markets. For some this fits an *Atlanticist* food politics. A key policy instrument is lowering tariffs to attract imports. There is little concern that this would in practice undermine UK producers.[79] A recent Secretary of State for Trade proclaimed the attractions of the UK sourcing food imports from the USA, as part of a wider future UK–US trade deal,[80] but concerns emerged about examples of lower or different US food standards such as for treating bacterial contamination by washing poultry and salads in chlorine.[81] Chlorination became a symbol of what might be at stake.[82]

Another future accepts *some form of loose food integration with Europe*, but is fluid about what Europe means. Rejecting actual EU membership, it sees a looser arrangement such as the European Economic Area (EEA) or European Free Trade Agreement (EFTA), or some bespoke deal to be negotiated by the parties. Theresa May's government's November 2018 Draft Agreement was one such. Any such semi-detached arrangement is liable to meet a crossfire of competing demands, 'red lines' and ideologies. For some, the priority is to stop EU migrants (only to have to accept the pull of non-EU migrants to replace them). For others, the key issue is Northern Ireland and Ireland politics and whether their border is hard, technically managed or non-existent. This future can be taken in diverse directions in all of which food is a sub-theme rather than a priority.

Another future could be described as *anyone but Europe or rejecting the EU in favour of an outer Europe*. This seems hard to take seriously, not least since decades of supply chain networks have been built up within and across Europe, but nonetheless it could be an option. The difficulty is that the EU already has food trade deals with most of outer Europe, such as Morocco for tomatoes and citrus fruit, negotiated by the EU. Michael Gove, later Secretary of State at Defra, at one time supported joining the European Free Trade Agreement, having access to the EU Single Market from outer Europe.[83,84] This envisages positive gains from access to food growing beyond the EU itself, particularly to West Africa, which shares close time zones with the UK (useful for management) and with a warmer climate plus cheap land and labour. One could imagine a food-importing future not from the north of the Mediterranean but from the south and east, favouring countries such as Morocco, Turkey and Israel.

A very different future proposes a *localist or British food first* system. This can take different forms, from a simple flag-waving branding system, such as the Red Tractor symbol, to a more strategic desire to rebuild UK food production. If the latter, better understanding of the costs as well as other impacts would be required. It implies a significant nationalist push for food supplies, and a big effort to increase what could be grown here (and where). Key issues are the labour force (hitherto heavily reliant on EU migrant labour) and the restructuring of currently international supply chains. Limits set by geography and climate would also pose special challenges.

Another vision cuts across almost all of the above positions, the view that the only lasting route to UK food security is to build *a sustainable food system* – low carbon, ecosystems, benign, reliable and affordable. This is not what we have. The UK, proponents argue, can no longer duck the need to address the complex web of challenges raised by food in relation to health, environment, quality, social values, culture, jobs and the wider economy, and of course public trust and good governance. To some, this is what the food system would begin to look like, if designed around ecological public health: a food economy delivering sustainable diets from sustainable food systems.[85] Elements of such thinking were presented to Defra in 2012, only to be pushed away.[86] The Welsh government set ambitions for such a direction with its Well-Being of Future Generations Act 2015.[87] And Scotland's Good Food Nation strategy, too, is in the same terrain.[88] The void has been England.

Against these ambitions, there is another vision for the

future that just sees *food as a matter for the market.* Food is seen as a sub-issue of general economics, with its dynamics best left to market forces. The agri-food sector does not deserve special treatment. If people want to import food from anywhere, it does not matter. Concerns about food standards or quality are over-emphasized, are code for unnecessary impositions on business, and can often be set aside as the expression of sectional rather than general interests.[89] In 2016, for instance, Jacob Rees-Mogg MP mooted to the Treasury Select Committee that standards that were 'good enough for India' could be good enough for the UK.[90]

Each of the above visions has a fundamentally different outcome for the UK food system (returned to in Chapter 5). The institutions and legal frameworks required will vary. To give one example, food standards. As a member of the EU, our standards have been negotiated with other member states, building up a large body of regulations and practice over nearly half a century. As one of the EU's largest economies (and food importers), the UK has had considerable weight in negotiating matters ranging from contaminants to food labelling. Outside the EU, and as a single member state in the World Trade Organization, the UK would negotiate with 164 other member states, and be one voice within the even larger 189-member body Codex Alimentarius Commission, which sets baseline food standards.[91] If the UK negotiated a UK–US food trade deal, we would do so as a relatively small food economy compared to the lobbying power of US-based food giants. The UK Food Standards Agency would have to deal with the might of the US Department of Agriculture. And food would become a pawn of wider strategic concerns.

Reluctant governments

Whether we like it or not, the role of government is now a central issue for UK food security. British scientists from across the disciplines agree that we ought to be changing the UK food system far faster than we are. Climate change looms. But an obesity crisis is already with us and known to be worsening.[92] The Department of Health has been aware for nearly two decades that diet-related non-communicable disease is helping bankrupt the NHS.[93,94] But the flow of calories continues and is unrelenting. Some food product reformulation is happening, but the incentives to eat excessively and inappropriately are not being altered. For about three years after the 2007–8 commodity price spike, as was noted above, there was a period of policy interest in Britain and across the affluent West in the case for reshaping our food systems, but the interest gradually dissipated, eroded by a mix of default policies and business-as-usual. It is not that food's impact on public health or food's reliance on plastics are unknown. It is just that the desire to tackle the scale of what is necessary is absent. We must take stock of why progress is not being made quicker. And that demands that we be clearer about what a food secure Britain needs.

Part of the problem is institutional. Everyone says someone else should be doing something, when the scale of change requires that everyone act in concert. Most analysts agree that, short of authoritarian rule or extreme crisis, it is government which has to facilitate and lead the required process of change. We live, however, in an era of the 'reluctant state' on matters such as food, a policy mindset which predates the post-2007 Great Recession.[95] The British state largely hands over the practical aspects of food to commercial interests despite having some fundamental involvements. These include regulation, subsidies, public accountability and welfare, yet the state has to be dragged into acting. When foot-and-mouth disease broke out in 2001, an exasperated Labour government decided it needed to get a tighter grip on what it suddenly realized was a costly animal economy; zoonoses could jam up the economy. It set up the Curry Commission, reporting in 2002, which recommended greater integration of farming into the market dynamics of the food economy.[96] Environmental considerations were to be given bigger presence, but public health barely featured.[97]

Some critics argue that corporate power in the food system is too strong. Although many companies now recognize big challenges for UK food, their actions tend to be sectoral or at a single-company level; sceptics see this becoming part of commercial branding. To be fair, many food companies – even the most powerful – worry about climate change and are on the back foot about plastic excess. But they are also wary of being accused of anti-competitive behaviour, if they get together to argue a structural case. At the same time, food sectors are highly concentrated, dominated by big players. Even in the hospitality sector, some big firms are dominant – in contract catering, for example, there are two, one British, one French. In fast food, US multinationals are the most important, alongside many thousands of small and medium-sized enterprises (SMEs). In food retail, eight retailers sell about 90% of UK food. One (Tesco) has about 30% of the market, dwarfing the next two (J Sainsbury and Asda) who proposed but were denied merger in 2019 (and blocked from doing so for a decade).[98] In food manufacturing, giant brands dominate almost all sectors.

It would be simple to blame food companies – or lionize the small, while demonizing the large, or vice versa – but we must remember that they have been given space to act as they do by the state, not least by the UK government negotiating at the EU level. Since 1992, there has been an expanding Single Food Market across Europe. It is from here that UK food commerce derives a third of our food. With the exception of farming – for historical reasons dating to the 1930s–40s – the food system is left to get on with driving food security by simply making food accessible and cheaper, so in theory more affordable. Farming's role has been to produce commodities which have increasingly been turned into unnecessarily processed foods. Although the food industry is made up of thousands of SMEs, historically, British governments have tended to champion big players – already well represented in Brussels lobbies – only then to blame Brussels if anything is unpopular at home.

This situation is almost designed to deliver weak leadership at a time when we need to redesign the food system. Ideologically, governments are reluctant to act. For years, they have preferred voluntarism and soft or self-regulation to hard regulation and tough interventionism. In crises, this changes. In the BSE ('mad cow') crisis of the late 1980s and early 1990s, as with foot-and-mouth in 2001, government was shamed into acting. But there was no intervention for the food poor in the Great Recession of 2007–10. It was left to charitable and inadequate provision by food banks.

If there is any 'national interest' over food security, it is often framed in laissez-faire or 'let consumers decide' terms, the default 'Leave it to Tesco et al.' The result of this light-touch governance is everywhere. Stasis triumphs over any evidence which suggests urgent need for action, unless there is a huge scandal such as there was over BSE. We accept outcomes we should not, such as poor diet, obesity, hunger. In a democracy, only government has the requisite mix of legal sanctions, negotiating capacity and democratic legitimacy to reframe conditions. We need government to accept that climate change, not cheap food, is of paramount national interest, and to recognize that food behaviour and health are driven by social and economic factors. Only government can facilitate the rapid process of recalibration at the scale and pace now needed yet we are in thrall to an out-of-date 1970s neo-liberal reflex to leave change to industry. My case here is that industry too is out of its depth.

A shift on this grand scale is precisely what happened from the 1940s, born out of dire wartime crisis. Having ignored Beveridge in 1936 (see p. 35), the British government in 1940 rapidly began to plan mechanisms for ensuring the people were fed equitably. The minister, for example, bought in one fell swoop almost the entire Canadian wheat crop, having realized that unless he did so, the UK could be blockaded by submarines, and that bread – a morale-sensitive food – would be in very short supply. UK production was pitifully low. Today we appear to have forgotten that long trade routes are vulnerable. Fred Marquis, made Lord Woolton to become the new Minister of Food in Chamberlain's government in April 1940, realized the truth very quickly on taking office, and secretly and illegally bought huge stockpiles, an act of rapid and extraordinary political élan.[99,100] I am not suggesting that the UK should start to buy up world crops today; there isn't the warehouse storage, for one thing, and market mechanisms have changed, too. I am highlighting the importance of political will and how we have forgotten that circumstances then forced a reluctant government to recognize that the UK food system needed to be reshaped. The Ministry of Food became a key strategic actor. Food regulations were rewritten to take account of trade and health interests. A conception of the national interest as feeding people, cutting waste, ensuring some civic responsibility was injected into food markets. Existing bread regulations, for example, which had previously specified a *maximum* of 10% Canadian wheat, were altered to specify a *minimum* of 60% Canadian wheat![101] This was not reluctant government. It put health and security top.

Today, although not officially at war – although engaged in many proxy conflicts (think of the Middle East) – the UK is *de facto* facing a wartime scale of food challenge – climate change emergency, runaway health problems, widening food poverty and inequality, distorted marketing, and much more – with weakened, hollowed-out state resources and a complacent default misunderstanding of how food markets work. This combination is hopelessly equipped and possibly so far unable to address the complexity of the multi-criteria food challenge. Whatever one thinks of Brexit preparations or politicians, the change of tone with regard to expenditure in late 2019 did show that funds can be made available, if the political leadership sees fit.[102] Seemingly overnight, as no-deal challenges loomed, the government rapidly expanded its civil service and had to prepare to replace what hitherto it had painted as an inefficient or heavy-handed EU. The role of government and the state is back in public policy, not before time.

It's time again to reform food government

The difference between academic and government life, US politician Dean Rusk once told Denis Healey MP in 1949, was 'the difference between arguing to a conclusion and arguing to a decision – a distinction which many intellectuals in politics are slow to learn'.[103] The complacency about British food security is not helped by the constant churn of ministers. A rule of thumb in Whitehall is that it takes three years before ministers are on top of their job. The first year they learn the terrain; in the second what might be possible, the ropes and scopes; and in the third they can begin to deliver, having thought what to do and how.

There have been sixty-seven top ministers for Agriculture and Fisheries and for Food across 128 years. Scottish and Welsh ministers are much more recent, in the last twenty. The average occupancy of the top political jobs has been about two years. Ministerial 'churn' is normal, even though food security requires continuity. Even if there are no longlasting ministers, at least there ought to be consistency. The ministers have come from across the political spectrum, so there have only been phases of political continuity. Of those ministers or presidents (when the key state body was the Board of Agriculture or Board of Agriculture and Fisheries), forty-two have been Conservatives. One constant has been the heavy emphasis on farming. It might have been right to equate farming with food security in the nineteenth or mid-twentieth century but this is no longer the case in the twenty-first. Farming matters, of course, but what is needed is an overview linking town and country, locating food and farming in their proper systemic places; a policy framework which ensures the emphases are right across the food system, and which enables imbalances to be righted. Since the Second World War, the dominant policy emphasis has been 'productionist', an assumption that public good comes from simply producing more food.[104] This is not adequate. The UK does not feed itself, and food supply distorts British health and society and Britain's environment. An environmental focus belatedly arrived in the 1980s, initially via new EU environmental regulations – to control pollution of rivers, air and food – and egged on by civil society campaigns which successfully embarrassed UK governments as the 'dirty man of Europe'.

The first UK Ministry of Agriculture and Fisheries was created in 1889. A Ministry of Food was created in 1916 in the First World War but closed immediately afterwards in 1919; a second version was started in 1939 and closed in 1955, but this time 'Food' was added – Ministry of Agriculture, Fisheries and Food (MAFF); food coming symbolically last, note. MAFF was itself restructured when environmental and rural matters, previously located in the Ministry of Local Government, were merged in 2001 to create the new Department for the Environment, Food and Rural Affairs (Defra) extant today. Meanwhile Scotland, Wales and Northern Ireland were given varying degrees of autonomy over farming matters, with Defra thus being responsible for England and tending to lead at the EU level. A somewhat messy multi-level system of governance came into existence within the UK. The three 'devolved administrations' of Scotland, Wales and Northern Ireland were smaller in population and economic power than, for example, London, which had few powers over food other than were held by the thirty-three local authorities under its geographical wing. And those powers were mostly rooted in mid- to late-nineteenth-century responsibilities such as to police food quality and safety at the local level.*

The messiness and asymmetry of the UK multi-level food system needs attention. Food may come to consumers locally – in your shop or home – but is actually the result of international, national and regional dynamics. Cities don't feed themselves. If anything requires a city region approach, it is food, yet our towns and cities stand woefully, watching the damage of food systems, yet unable to act. The UK is not alone in experiencing this. It is why, at Expo 2015 in Milan, 100 cities pledged to take food into their policy focus. Some countries – our EU neighbours particularly – already give modern powers to city regions, more than we do. The Milan Urban Food Policy Pact has been signed by more than 140 cities since 2015, suggesting local politicians' desire to take a lead.† They see the problems. In the UK, there is a vibrant

---

* Hence the UK's and Ireland's idiosyncratic system of Environmental Health and Trading Standards Officers and Public Analysts, who traced their roles and powers to the 1848 Public Health Act, the 1865 Food Act and others since. Europeanization from 1973 meant that anomalies of auditing and monitoring to ensure a fair Single Market had to be addressed, which is why meat inspection in abattoirs has been conducted by veterinarians, under the EU Food Safety White Paper 2000.

† I was at (and an opening speaker at) the Milan signing on behalf of the London Food Board under Mayor Boris Johnson.

Sustainable Food Cities movement down to town level. But the UK is not just cities but towns, villages and rural areas too, which is why, almost certainly, we need regional food structures. Rather than bringing some order and coherence to multi-level governance, the UK has a divide-and-rule approach, with Westminster dominant, and arguing about whether to give powers to the regions.[105] London has powers which south-western or northern cities lack. Wales and Scotland are forging elements of food and farming policy, whereas English regions have no powers at all, merely weak Local Enterprise Partnerships (LEPs). The LEPs were created to replace what were becoming more interesting and strategic Regional Development Agencies (RDAs), but they too lacked democratic legitimacy; they were appointed, not elected.

One option, to which I return at the end of the book, would be for the UK – England particularly but also Wales and Scotland – to have new Regional Food Bodies (like France and Italy, which decentralized in the 1980s). These would help develop new multi-level food policies. Is it too much to envisage that each city and town could conduct food audits and citizens' consultations, and plan how their region could improve land use and food systems for their areas? Surely, part of the frustration that was expressed in the 2016 Referendum and 2019 election blamed Europeanization for their troubles, when the centralization of Whitehall deserved more attention. If we want to improve food security, an injection of new regional and more-local food powers is essential. The involvement of local citizens is a key ingredient for building a more resilient food system.[106] Much that needs to be done, as we will explore in later pages, will fail unless it is translated into local terms. There are good arguments, for example, to increase allotments and horticulture around urban areas – part of the original purpose of the UK's 'green belts'. Although few people think cities could feed themselves, more food could be grown in cities, whether on land, on roofs or in hi-tech vertical farms, simply because people want to do it.[107] Urban farming is unlikely to be massive, although it is thousands of years old. Many early big cities practised it.[108] But there is much in favour of a new generation of even hi-tech farming of perishable foods, such as salads and herbs in particular. Sizeable investments are already even being made in automated farms. In 2019, Ocado bought a majority stake in a vertical-farm company based in Scunthorpe, announcing an intention to aim for such green factories near its big warehouse distribution centres, and anticipating growth from a new distribution link to Marks & Spencer.[109]

Such developments excite some analysts and perhaps have their place. Certainly, cities and towns need to be and could be given new food powers as part of a rebuilding of regionalism, a practical way of enhancing people's control over their conditions. It is why consortia of cities such as C40 on climate and 100 Resilient Cities are now interested in food.[110] City-regionalism was a more powerful political force in France and Italy in the late twentieth century. The UK endorsed the creation of strong regional powers in Germany after 1945 but failed to apply that thinking to itself!

The rest of this book explores why I believe this is a time for imagination and debate in food policy. It ends with suggestions as to what might be done. If the evidence for food policy reform won the day in the name of enhancing food security in the dire 1940s and exhausted 1950s, don't today's weight and range of evidence deserve to win leverage now?

The State of UK Food (In)Security

How secure is the UK?

'To expect the unexpected shows a thoroughly modern intellect,' observes the dangerous and disruptive Mrs Cheveley in Oscar Wilde's play *An Ideal Husband*.[1] Wilde's play shows that (un)favourable appearances might not turn out to be true; strange things can happen, the wrong data be misinterpreted; a supposedly ideal husband has feet of clay; and the presumed twit in the tale is the person who actually unlocks the relationship lock-ins. In Wildean terms, my thesis here is that food security, like the marriages in his play, cannot and should not be assumed. Unlike Wilde's play, there are few attempted witticisms in this chapter. No country should downplay its food security. A country which barely provides half its food is putting itself at risk.

Before looking at the data of food security, let us quickly summarize the British food system. This is something that the British statisticians do well, a tradition from the war planning of the 1940s. The first official national nutrition surveys began in 1941 (on-going today), when due attention went to food flows (for military and societal reasons). But the food system has changed drastically since the 1940s.

Even though the UK had been early to industrialize and for its rural labour force to leave the land, then as today farming was a relatively small employer, with 447,000 people in 2018 compared to, say, catering's 1.8 million.

Today's food system is mostly located away from farming or fishing. It is spread liberally almost anywhere except on farmland or the seas, even though they are the primary resource. Entirely new and vast sectors such as food logistics have emerged in a few decades. Logistics means more than trucks; it includes IT systems, satellites which track consignments, and vast distribution hubs to enable just-in-time distribution to service retailers. A useful overview is given in two annual state publications which draw on Her Majesty's Revenue and Customs (HMRC) data, and trade statistics and economic data compiled by the Office for National Statistics (ONS). Figure 3.1 is taken from Defra's annual 'Agriculture in the UK' report for 2018, which gives the conventional economic view of the food system as a supply chain. It tells us for each sector: what gross value added (GVA) it has, how many enterprises there are, how many employees, and on how many sites of economic activity.

The flow of food up and across this system relies on huge imports, worth £46.8bn in 2018. They come in various forms: highly or lightly processed and unprocessed. Food exports, by contrast, were worth only £22.5bn. Here is the huge 2018 Food Trade Gap of £24.3bn, roughly two thirds of what the UK spends on defence. The size of the Food Trade Gap shows how British politicians and the public, cushioned by EU membership, have forgotten the lessons of the world wars, rationing and shortages. In effect, the UK economy broadly buys

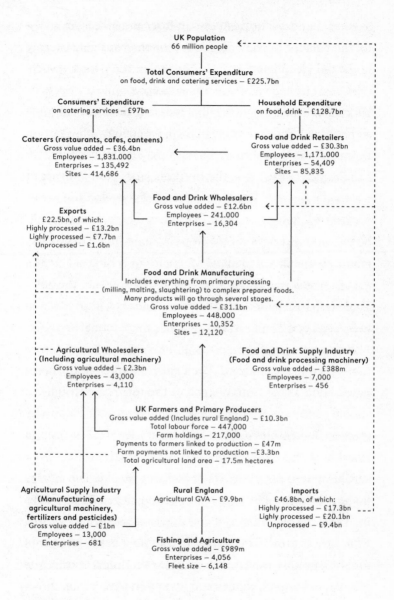

UK Population
66 million people

Total Consumers' Expenditure
on food, drink and catering services — £225.7bn

Consumers' Expenditure
on catering services — £97bn

Household Expenditure
on food, drink — £128.7bn

Caterers (restaurants, cafes, canteens)
Gross value added — £36.4bn
Employees — 1,831.000
Enterprises — 135,492
Sites — 414,686

Food and Drink Retailers
Gross value added — £30.3bn
Employees — 1,171.000
Enterprises — 54,409
Sites — 85,835

Food and Drink Wholesalers
Gross value added — £12.6bn
Employees — 241.000
Enterprises — 16,304

Exports
£22.5bn, of which:
Highly processed — £13.2bn
Lighly processed — £7.7bn
Unprocessed — £1.6bn

Food and Drink Manufacturing
Includes everything from primary processing
(milling, malting, slaughtering) to complex prepared foods.
Many products will go through several stages.
Gross value added — £31.1bn
Employees — 448.000
Enterprises — 10,352
Sites — 12,120

Agricultural Wholesalers
(Including agricultural machinery)
Gross value added — £2.3bn
Employees — 43,000
Enterprises — 4,110

Food and Drink Supply Industry
(Food and drink processing machinery)
Gross value added — £388m
Employees — 7,000
Enterprises — 456

UK Farmers and Primary Producers
Gross value added (Includes rural England) — £10.3bn
Total labour force — 447,000
Farm holdings — 217,000
Payments to farmers linked to production — £47m
Farm payments not linked to production — £3.3bn
Total agricultural land area — 17.5m hectares

Agricultural Supply Industry
(Manufacturing of
agricultural machinery,
fertilizers and pesticides)
Gross value added — £1bn
Employees — 13,000
Enterprises — 681

Rural England
Agricultural GVA — £9.9bn

Imports
£46.8bn, of which:
Highly processed — £17.3bn
Lighly processed — £20.1bn
Unprocessed — £9.4bn

Fishing and Agriculture
Gross value added — £989m
Enterprises — 4,056
Fleet size — 6,148

Figure 3.1
Economic summary of the UK food chain
Source: Defra. Agriculture in the UK 2018.[4]

in goods but pays for them by surpluses in services. In 2016–18, the balance of the entire UK economy was consistently in the red (see Figure 3.2).[2] In November 2018, for instance, the Goods Balance of Trade was –£34.65bn while the Services Balance of Trade was +£26.73bn, meaning there was an overall negative balance of trade in the UK economy of –£7.92bn. Defra and the Department for Business, Enterprise, Industry and Science (BEIS), and their predecessors have long urged UK food industries to export more.[3] But they do little to encourage an increase in what is produced here, which would be the most effective way to stop the drain in the first place. Home production of foods which could easily be grown here – apples, pears, vegetables – languishes. In 2005–18, the Food Trade Gap rose by 41% in real terms.[4] Figure 3.3 illustrates the widening Food Trade Gap, 1993–2018, in real terms.

Table 3.1 gives the imports and exports to both EU and non-EU countries in 2018. The final column gives the combined Food Trade Gap for each of the main foodstuffs. We should note that fruit and vegetables represent by far the greatest food trade deficit, £9.85bn in the red. The gap is sizeable for all food sectors except beverages, which has a surplus due to huge exports of Scottish whisky. The figures do not show the extent of re-exporting either. Britain does not grow the ingredients of cocoa, tea or coffee; it processes what others grow. The 'preps' in the table headings stands for preparations; thus cereals includes the grains themselves plus sweet biscuits, waffles and uncooked plain pasta.

The UK's big failing and trade deficit lie in horticulture, which produces keystone foods for public health – fruit and vegetables. UK consumers say they want more UK-grown

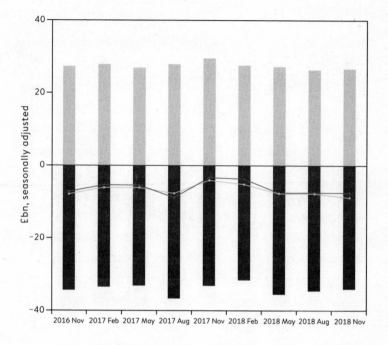

Figure 3.2
UK trade balances in goods and services, Nov. 2016–Nov. 2018, £bn

- ▮ Goods balance
- ▮ Services balance
- —•— Total trade balance
- —•— Total trade balance excluding erratics

Source: ONS. UK trade: November 2018.[2]

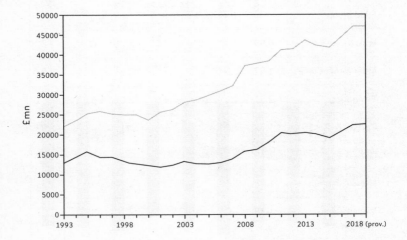

Figure 3.3
The widening Food Trade Gap: value of imports and exports of food, feed and drink, 1993–2018

——— Imports (£m) at 2018 prices
——— Exports (£m) at 2018 prices

Source: Defra. Agriculture in the UK 2018.[4]

Food group	Exports to EU, £bn	Imports from EU, £bn	Exports to non-EU, £bn	Imports from non-EU, £bn	Total exports, £bn	Total imports, £bn	Food trade gap EU + non-EU, £bn
Fruit & veg & preps*	0.99	7.02	0.27	4.09	1.26	11.11	-9.85
Meat & meat preps	1.52	5.59	0.36	1.21	1.88	6.80	-4.92
Beverages	2.87	4.21	4.77	1.62	7.64	5.83	1.81
Cereals & preps	1.52	3.30	0.62	0.80	2.14	4.10	-1.96
Dairy & eggs	1.48	3.34	0.41	0.05	1.89	3.39	-1.50
Fish & fish preps	1.28	1.08	0.52	2.10	1.80	3.18	-1.38
Miscellaneous edible preps	1.38	2.66	0.72	0.61	2.10	3.27	-1.17
Coffee, tea, etc.	1.12	2.56	0.42	1.18	1.54	3.74	-2.20
Animal feed	0.83	1.33	0.36	1.04	1.19	2.37	-1.18
Oils, fats & oil seeds	0.54	1.04	0.08	0.82	0.62	1.86	-1.24
Sugar & preps	0.33	0.81	0.12	0.37	0.45	1.18	-0.73

Table 3.1

UK Food Trade Gap, 2018: imports and exports, by major commodity group, EU and non-EU, £bn

Source: Defra. Agriculture in the UK 2018, Charts 13.1a and b.[5]

* 'preps' stands for prepared foods mainly, of any food group; thus 'Fruit and veg & preps' includes fruit juices, as well as fresh, frozen and prepared fruits, and also nuts.

foods, but they are not receiving them. This market failure needs attention and in Part Two we explore why it is by no means a simple problem.

Each year Defra calculates figures known as the Total Income from Farming (TIFF). Figure 3.4 shows the oscillations in TIFF and subsidy from 1993 to 2017 plus estimates to 2020. In 2016, UK farming made £3.7bn, and 2017's £5.71bn was the highest since 1996. Farming viability has been maintained by direct support in the form of over £3bn in annual subsidy through the EU Common Agricultural Policy (CAP). Remove that support and the viability of a large percentage of farming disappears. Defra estimated in 2017 that two in five farms would be loss-making without the subsidy. The National Audit Office confirmed this again in 2019.[6] It found that, of the 85,000 farmers receiving CAP subsidies in England in 2017, 42% made a loss over the previous two years and were kept afloat by direct payments. 16% of English farm recipients made a loss despite receiving the subsidies. To make matters worse, a 2019 study by Strutt and Parker estimated that 75% of farms would see heavy profit drops (22–68%) from changes to agricultural support planned by the government.[7] The reliance on subsidies and yet the mass fragility of farm viability is surely a total indictment of the farm economic system. Huge profits are being made elsewhere from food, but possibly half of English domestic primary producers are not viable. Figure 3.5 shows the reliance on subsidies, by farm type, in England for 2017, with the line of direct support (i.e. subsidies) oscillating between £3bn and £4bn a year, while the vertical bars give the total income from farming which farmers actually receive. In other words, the subsidy is a large proportion of the

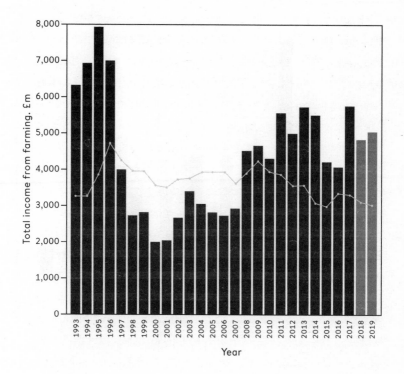

Figure 3.4

Total Income from Farming (TIFF), 1993–2017, plus direct support (subsidy)

▇ TIFF (real terms)

— Direct support

Source: Pelham, J. and King, R., eds. Agricultural outlook 2019. Melton Mowbray: The Andersons Centre, 2018.

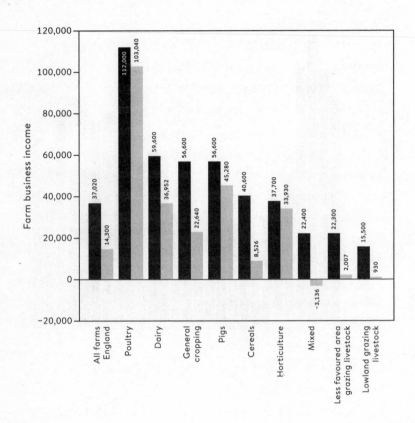

Figure 3.5
Farm income in England 2017, with and without subsidy,
by type of farm business, £

■ Average farm business income
■ Average farm business income
without direct payments

Source: NAO. Report: early review of the new farming programme.[6]

income. Although incomes fluctuate year on year, the general picture is of farming as a financial-dependency culture.

Defra and HM Treasury, meanwhile, have long wished to phase out subsidies, and fought hard in Brussels for CAP reductions.[8] They are seizing their political opportunity in Brexit; the 2019 Agriculture Bill disguised the fact that direct payments are to be phased out while some payments for environmental land management are phased in, but not for food production. National food security was not initially an issue; the assumption is that external sourcing will now accelerate, with a reassertion of the commitment to supposedly cheap food. Cheap food for cheap wages, counter the critics. While analysts agree that British consumers are very price-conscious, less attention is paid to whether cheap food is really cheap, a topic to which I return later.

WHERE WE GET OUR FOOD FROM TODAY

Financial viability lies at the heart of the food security question, particularly for primary producers such as growers and fishing businesses. If the UK does not produce its own food, who will, paid for how?

The high point of self-sufficiency was in the late 1980s. Since then there has been a slow decline. Figure 3.6 gives the figures for foods overall and for foods which can be produced in the UK – 'Indigenous-type food'. Based on farmgate value of unprocessed food, just under 50% of food consumed in the UK was provided by the UK itself (see Table 3.2). Other EU countries provided 30% and 4% each came from Africa, Asia, North America and South America.

The Netherlands is particularly important for the UK.

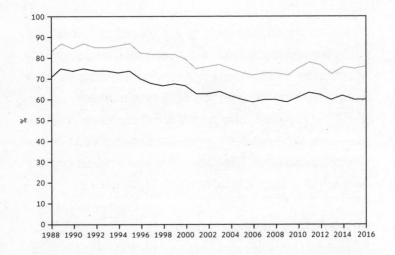

Figure 3.6
UK food production to supply ratio, 1988–2016

―――― Indigenous-type food
—— All food

Source: Defra. Agriculture in the UK 2017.[13]

Source region	% supplied to UK
UK	50
European Union	30
Africa	4
North America	4
South America	4
Asia	4
Rest of Europe	2
Australasia	1

Table 3.2
Where Britain's food came from, 2017
Source: Defra. Agriculture in the UK 2017.[13]

It both provides a lot of food – all those greenhouse-reared tomatoes, cucumbers, peppers and lettuces – but also Rotterdam is the key transit port for many foods coming from outside the EU. Rotterdam acts as go-between and port inspection point. The UK exported food worth £1.185bn through Rotterdam, accounting for 5% of all UK exports to the Netherlands, and imports food worth £4.675bn, accounting for 13.6% of all imports from the Netherlands.[9] When fears of a no-deal Brexit heightened in 2018, most food industry insiders were principally worrying about how to replace Rotterdam as the food gateway at short notice. The policy disconnect between the ideological fever and food realities was exposed in 2018 when the then Brexit Secretary of State, Dominic Raab MP, admitted he 'hadn't quite understood' how reliant UK trade in goods is on the Dover–Calais crossing.[10]

The lack of understanding was surprising because, in the summer of 2018, the issue of supply flows had been raised following a Food Research Collaboration report about food stocks, in the event of a no-deal Brexit. The government first denied there was an issue, then seemingly backtracked when a non-Defra Cabinet minister told the BBC the government itself was undertaking some stockpiling and some planning for shortages and was booking ferries to ensure traffic could be maintained. But even months later it tried to downplay the significance of stocks. In November 2018, a spokesman told the BBC: 'The UK has a strong level of food security built upon a diverse range of sources including strong domestic production and imports from third countries. This will continue to be the case whether we leave the EU with or without a deal.'[11] It is true that the UK sources food from many countries – 168 in

2015 – but there is a concentration of supply from a relatively few. Twenty-four countries provide over 90% of what the UK buys in.[12] Most is from the EU.

STOCKS AND VIRTUAL STOCKS

The basic truth is that food stocks are low intentionally, and reducing over time as part of intra-chain dynamics. The summary in Defra's annual review in July 2018 showed that at least some parts of government know this well.

> The majority of retail supply chains have between one and four weeks of stock, with suppliers tending to hold higher levels of stock than retailers. For fresh produce, stock levels can sometimes be only 24 hours or less. As retail supply chains become more responsive, lead times are reducing and order frequencies are increasing. Retailers are increasingly moving products into their stockless networks, managing products from across their ranges in the same way as the fresh and produce categories. The impact of the current economic climate on consumer spending has helped drive this change as retailers look at ways of funding price cuts; supply chain operating costs and working capital tied up in inventory has provided such an opportunity.[13]

In fact, for many companies, stocks are much lower than four weeks. In the 2001 lorry strike, ministers judged that stocks were about five days. Brexit brought this issue to the fore once more. It had surfaced across the rich world during the 2007–8 commodity price spike, when new volatilities emerged. Volatility, the OECD and FAO recognized, became the new norm.

The quickest way to resolve shortages in times of crisis, as Prof. Alan Matthews wrote in a report on the potential for Brexit to cause disruptions to the EU, is to buy food in. Buying on open markets brings other problems. 'The build-up of intervention stocks can act to depress market sentiment and to delay the recovery in market prices.'[14] Other options to deal with crises include having a fund ready for crises (to be quick off the mark), being flexible about state aid rules and targeting aid. But what if others are doing the same?

The UK puts itself in a tricky position if, as it has been doing, it runs down its own production, hence growing reliance on imports. British food security, in terms of quantity, currently depends on those flows continuing. Reducing stocks at the same time doubles the potential source of risk. Holding stocks of food – the old 'thrifty' approach – is seen as dead capital financially. And cutting that source of financial loading has been part of the rationale for the just-in-time food system. The stocks *de facto* are what is on the motorway, as lorries deliver the next consignment. That is why the UK food industries generally agreed Brexit was problematic and a no-deal Brexit would be potentially disastrous. The freight industry knew this only too well, anticipating hold-ups on roads and at ports.[15]

Importing food means the UK uses other people's land as 'virtual stocks'. The most stark assessment of that is provided in a sequence of studies at Aberdeen University by Henri de Ruiter and colleagues.[16,17,18] This showed that, in real terms, the UK is only 30% self-sufficient in land terms. The enormous quantity of feedstuffs imported and fed to British animals may be recorded as British food because processed here but they have been fed on feed grown elsewhere.

WHAT LAND DOES THE UK HAVE, WHAT IS GROWN AND IMPORTED?

In sector terms, the UK self-sufficiency is 62% in cereals, 75% in red meat, 77% in dairy and only 23% in fruit and vegetables. Any change of trade regime and tariffs (taxes at borders) would alter price signals. The British Retail Consortium (BRC), which represents the retail sector, is obviously exercised about this. Table 3.3 gives the BRC summary of what kinds of foods and how much is imported under different types of trade deal the UK operates as a member state of the EU. It gives four broad types: (a) foods from within the EU single market, where there are no border taxes and free flows; (b) foods brought in under external trade deals negotiated by the EU for all member states; (c) imports under a generalized system of preferences (GSP) under which the EU removes import duties from products coming into the EU market from certain vulnerable developing countries;[19] and (d) imports under the so-called 'most favoured nation' (MFN) status, a baseline for trade.[20]

Why these trade deal types matter is because they have different tariff rates. While the EU Single Market means there are no tariffs and food moves freely, foods from outside the EU will be subject to different types of deal. The BRC calculated that exiting both the Single Market and any negotiated trade arrangement with the EU, and instead being on World Trade Organization (WTO) rates, would add an average of 22% of tariffs to UK food. Tariffs could be as high as 46% for cheese or 21% for tomatoes.[21] Not producing food here means food prices and sourcing become subject to financial matters such as the exchange rate. If the value of sterling falls, there

Trade status type	Category	% of UK food imports in this trade status type	% of total UK food imports
(a) EU Single Market			79
	Beverages	43	
	Fruit and vegetables	21	
	Meat and fish	14	
	Cereal products	7	
	Other	16	
(b) Bi-lateral agreements			9
	Fruit and vegetables	60	
	Beverages	38	
	Other	2	
(c) General System of Preferences (GSP)			1
	Fruit and vegetables	42	
	Fats and oils	35	
	Other	23	
(d) Most favoured nation (MFN)			11
	Meat and fish	30	
	Fruit and vegetables	14	
	Other	19	

Table 3.3
Types of trade deal under which UK food was imported, and percentage of food sectors imported under those deals, 2017
Source: BRC. A fair Brexit for consumers.[22]

is also an immediate impact on costs and thus consumption patterns.

And what about home production? In 2017, the UK had an estimated 17,476,000 acres of land registered as 'utilized agricultural area', 72% of the UK's total land mass. The total croppable area that year was 6,131,000 acres. Of that, only 4,745,000 was actually cropped in 2017. And of that actually cropped land acreage, 4,577,000 was used for arable crops, with just 168,000 down to horticulture.

Arable crop area was dominated by 3,181,000 acres growing cereals; 590,000 for oilseeds (e.g. rape and linseed); 145,000 for potatoes; and 661,000 for other crops such as sugar beet, maize, peas. Grassland for animal production amounted to 10,138,000 as pasture plus 1,144,000 as temporary grassland (in a rotation, for example). Of the rest of the UK's land, only 1,037,000 was categorized as woodland. The UK has one of the lowest rates of tree cover in Europe. And, although trees are important carbon sequesters and useful sources for wood, tree planting is not meeting targets set by the Committee on Climate Change (CCC) and the government. In England the deficit is particularly wide.[23] The CCC estimates that 30,000 ha need to be planted every year to meet the 2050 target. At present total tree cover of the UK is 10% in England, 15% in Wales, 19% in Scotland and 8% in Northern Ireland.

Animal production dominates UK land use. Even prime cereal land is used to produce crops, of which between a quarter and a third are then fed to farm animals. In 2017, the farm census recorded that there were 10,004,000 cattle and calves in the UK; 34,832,000 sheep and lambs; 4,969,000 pigs; and 181,818,000 poultry. Thus over 230 million animals were being kept for 66 million people. Even so, the UK was not self-sufficient in meat; we imported meat worth nearly £5bn in 2017.

Every year the giant HSBC bank publishes a forward look at UK agriculture. In 2018, no doubt influenced by imminent Brexit, the bank made £300m available for farm loans. But its 'Forward planning 2019' report, replete with prices per tonne, profit margins and viability advice for a large range of crops and stock, did not even include vegetable or fruit growing in its list of UK agricultural outputs.[24] Why is horticulture taken so lightly when it is so important for health and for its capacity to feed people so efficiently? The UK historically has been a meat-oriented food culture, for understandable reasons: climate, terrain, tradition. For health reasons alone, this needs to change. The UK did once have a viable and famous horticulture sector, but it has been allowed to decay. Travel the country and you see ruined greenhouses. Talk with local people of a certain age, and they will tell you what land used to grow fruit and vegetables. The Netherlands did not allow its horticulture to decay. It invested, trained, researched, and made it an exciting career route.

In 2017, the UK imported nearly £4bn of fruit and £2bn of vegetables, much from the Netherlands. We still grow fruit and vegetables – about 57%, by value, of the vegetables we consume and about 12% of fruit consumed.[25] In 2014–17, fruit production hovered between 700,000 and 800,000 tonnes, and vegetables just under 2.5 million tonnes (mt). UK vegetable production over the last twenty years has fluctuated between 2.5 mt and 3.0 mt, of the nearly 5 mt consumed. There has been a gentle rise in fruit production but not nearly enough to make a big difference; what there has been is mostly polytunnel soft-fruit production (dependent on EU migrant pickers).[26] But the horticultural food trade gap is large and has widened. This is not just a missed opportunity, it is a drag on health. For two decades, government and health promotion campaigns have urged higher consumption, yet supply is weak and only 1% of subsidies go to horticulture. At the global level, the 2019 EAT–*Lancet* Commission report, which modelled a healthy diet for the world that could be produced without damaging ecosystems, estimated the need to double fruit and vegetable production worldwide.[27] The picture for British fruit production is dire. Only 16% of what was consumed in the UK in 2017 was grown here. This was down in tonnage from a peak in 2012, and down in financial value since 2016.

Production of vegetables under protection (glass or plastic housing) rose over the last decade but declined latterly. This is due to loss of EU migrant labour following the 2016 Referendum. Almost all the horticulture industry knows that the key issue is labour. There is no shortage of lyrical praise for the beauty of apple orchards but someone has to look after them and do the painstaking, skilled work of pruning, training and picking.[28,29] While other EU countries expanded their orchards, UK growers took financial incentives to grub out theirs. There were 3,000 commercial apple growers in the UK in the 1950s but only 800 by the mid-1990s. The Apple Orchards Grubbing Up Regulations, for example, were made a statutory instrument by the UK Parliament in 1991.[30] Farmers were paid to destroy fruit capacity.

Horticulture could and should be increasing in the

UK. Some large enterprises have in fact emerged within horticulture – specialists such as G's. Britain's biggest horticultural firm, it began on three acres in the 1950s but grew to be a major supplier to large supermarkets, and to own land abroad and run a co-op of other growers.[31] Horticultural giants such as G's, Fresh and Barfoots have gone international, becoming gatekeepers which provide retailers with round-year supplies. If they are the success stories, what has happened to other horticultural areas is not so good. An area such as the Lancashire Moss, rich peat lands between Manchester and Liverpool which fed both those conurbations from the nineteenth century, has seen a collapse in horticulture. Glazebrook Moss in Lancashire used to have fifteen farms all producing horticultural crops but now has none. One could argue that farming the Moss was an ecological risk and that rich peatlands ought to be left unturned, storing carbon. Even in 1878, observers noted a seven-foot drop in the depth of the soil once the railway embankment (the world's first commercial railway runs nearby) was made across the peatland, thus drying it out.[32] Be that as it may, as relatively small producers, the farms there thrived from the nineteenth century only to be marginalized and dropped in the early twenty-first century when ever-larger supermarket chains emerged in the 1980s and 1990s. They only wanted big suppliers such as G's or Barfoots who could provide scale. In France, by contrast, farm co-operatives have existed which can provide a co-ordination and pooling system for small growers. The UK's farm sector has resisted such structures, and gone out of business as a result. This is a microcosm of what needs to be sorted out – what mix of business, food security, ecosystems, work and production do we want or are we right to have?

Over the last thirty years, some horticultural experiments have flourished against the odds, reminding us that it is possible to grow fruit and vegetables in the UK. One avenue has been box delivery schemes such as the Devon-based Riverford or Abel and Cole. These pioneered home deliveries well before the big supermarket chains re-entered the home delivery service market. Riverford began when Guy Watson rented a few acres from his father in the 1980s. In 2018, he stood down, handing over 75% of the business to an Employee Owned Trust (John Lewis style). By then it was providing 47,000 veg boxes a week using a network of growers as well as production from its own land.[33] A smaller experiment which has also grown is Hackney Growing Communities in London. This is a local scheme in East London set up in 1996 as a consumer 'club' contracting to growers direct. It sets out to pay growers far more than the rates they get conventionally. Nine small growers are linked up to provide veg for Hackney consumers.[34]

Barcombe nurseries in Sussex also started in the late 1990s.[35] By 2018, it employed ten permanent all-year-round staff, some paid the minimum wage, and some more, but all paid what they report is a fair wage. It has twelve acres, of which two acres are wild, with trees, ponds, nettles and brambles. Of the ten used for growing, about 2–3 acres are glasshouses and polytunnels, allowing it to extend the season and to deliver vegetables every week of the year. In keeping with much of horticulture it has never had funding or grants. All its machinery has been collected from other farms, either upgrading or from farm sales.

We need more such enterprises. Meanwhile, between 2005 and 2015, an estimated 33,500 small/medium holdings went out of existence.

Over recent years, many modelling studies have been conducted which point to the need for increased plant production for direct human consumption. The EAT–*Lancet* Commission's Planetary Diet – outlined in its 2019 report – showed how land use and ecosystem resilience require considerable dietary change. We cannot continue to raise production to eat as the rich world currently does. Most studies have been done at the global level but UK-focused studies such as de Ruiter's at Aberdeen (cited in the previous section) are rare.[36,37] In 2019, Marco Springmann at Oxford University – a key member of the EAT–*Lancet* team[38] – conducted modelling on the UK for the Food, Farming and Countryside Commission to see if more 'progressive' farming systems could help to resolve the mismatch of health, ecosystems and farming.[39] He looked at the effect of switching livestock production to only pasture-fed livestock, for example, and/or organic production. These more progressive systems indeed can reduce greenhouse gas emissions and other environmental impacts. A switch to pasture-fed livestock could retain UK milk output at current levels, for example. But Springmann shows that any production benefits would still have to be accompanied by a change in consumption to more flexitarian and/or vegetarian diets. UK policymakers cannot sidestep the need to alter both production and consumption if UK food security takes its own land use seriously. A drastic reduction of UK meat output plus a massive increase in fruit and vegetable production to meet health requirements is needed. The

evidence points to the UK having to begin large rises in production and consumption of fruit, legumes, nuts and seeds
while lowering beef, lamb, pork, poultry and eggs, plus moderate drops in milk and fish. In other work, Springmann and
colleagues showed that, on average, a plant-based diet had a
three times lower emissions footprint than average diets and
up to four times lower in high-income countries – even in
sub-Saharan Africa that ratio was still two times lower. This
means that, from a food resources perspective, meat eating is
consuming resources at between two and four times what a
more plant-based diet would use. As a rich country, the UK is
in the 'four times more' category.[40]

The yawning gap between health and production is a
major problem which must be addressed in the UK. We must
create 'ladders' into the horticulture industry, and build on
community schemes to help rebuild commercial horticulture
on an extensive scale. This is not happening.

It depends what is meant by food security

The meaning of food security goes wider than the bare facts
of flows of food in and out of a country. Simon Maxwell of the
UK's Overseas Development Institute (ODI) once showed
that scores of different meanings have been ascribed to the
term food security,[41,42] almost to the point of its becoming
meaningless.[43] The term remains in use, however, so some
pragmatic clarification is required. Already, we have seen
how it invokes supply and consumption, and draws on variables such as finance, labour and state support. Indeed, to analyse food security in its full glory requires us to include many
factors, ranging from land use to cultural and taste matters.

At its core, however, is the issue of whether a population is being fed, and how well, by whom and why, or starved. Quite a mix bundled into two words!

Post-1945 history provides many dreadful examples of food insecurity *in extremis*: major famines in Bangladesh in 1974, Ethiopia in 1983–5, Sudan in the 1980s, in 1998 and again in 2017–18. The most recent and brutal has been in South Yemen, brought semi-deliberately into famine in 2015–19 through military devastation by Saudi Arabia, the United Arab Emirates and their allies, the USA and the UK. The disastrous food insecurity of the Yemenis which resulted was widely agreed to be the outcome of regional power play and religious difference.

The FAO applies five grades of assessment of food security (see Figure 3.7). These range from 1, 'generally food secure', to 5, 'famine/humanitarian catastrophe'.

Whether famines are 'natural', such as from drought and disaster, or deliberate, as when they are an act of war, they are the extreme of food insecurity, rarely the outcome of a sudden change, more often the result of a progression from less extreme states. There is much debate about what most affects food security but it includes key matters such as supplies, cost, infrastructure or social support, and whether the at-risk population bows to its fate. A Nobel Prize-winner, Amartya Sen, and his colleague Jean Drèze, called this last point the 'entitlement' factor, showing that there is always food available from somewhere, but people have to be organized into demanding it.[44] The FAO has distilled the vast literature and experience to propose that there are 'four pillars' to food security:

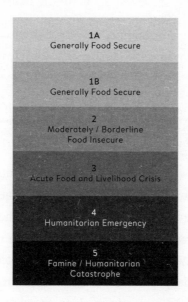

Figure 3.7
The FAO's five grades of food security

Source: FAO. Integrated food security phase classification: the IPC reference table.
Rome: Food and Agriculture Organization, 2011.

- Availability: the availability of sufficient quantities of food of appropriate quality, supplied through domestic production or imports.
- Access: access by individuals to adequate resources (entitlements) for acquiring appropriate foods for a nutritious diet.
- Utilization: utilization of food through adequate diet, clean water, sanitation and healthcare to reach a state of nutritional well-being where all physiological needs are met.
- Stability: to be food secure, a population, household or individual must have access to adequate food at all times.[45]

Conventionally, the UK sees food security troubles as occurring elsewhere, not applying to us. In fact, the UK already has worrying rates of food poverty, with too many people experiencing shortened lives and strains due to lack of food and real financial pressures. No one suggests that the UK as a whole has a food insecurity problem at grades 4 or 5 in the FAO classification. Some individuals and social groups are certainly at 3 or 4. But mostly the country is officially at 1 or 2. In late 2018 the UK government reacted with fury when Prof. Philip Alston, the UN Special Rapporteur on extreme poverty and human rights, published his initial report from a fact-finding tour of the UK,[46] and again when the final report was presented to the UN General Assembly in May 2019.[47] He summarized the rapid rise in homelessness, food bank use, hand-to-mouth existence and enforced poor dietary choice experienced by sizeable numbers of the UK population. It may have been politically embarrassing for a rich country like the UK to have to face unpalatable truths from an outsider, but Prof. Alston's account was supported by anti-poverty groups as real, and it gives an opportunity to clarify what kind of approach to food security we favour and what kind of food system we want to build. It helps if we locate food security within a cluster of terms which offer different but overlapping perspectives. These choices are summarized in Table 3.4 (pp. 106–7) and include the following:

Food nationalism is a perspective which hovers around the surface of UK food policy discussion. It has been historically powerful in various countries such as the Soviet Union under Stalin and Nazi Germany under Hitler (who thought rye bread a factor in why Germany lost the First World War).[48] In the UK, nationalism has not been such a dominant factor since industrialists won the repeal of the Corn Laws and encouraged a 'food from anywhere' price-led food policy. In modern times, there has been some resurgence in food regionalism and localism, more marked than nationalism, which has been left to the preserve of marketers and 'branders'. The Red Tractor scheme – a label run by a not-for-profit company – is one attempt to encourage a UK food pride. This is a brand, set up by the Labour government, to be an overarching 'Union Jack' marketing scheme. It was initially loose in its criteria, but effort has gone into tightening both its criteria and its auditing, although concerns periodically arise about how well it is policed.[49] Consumer polls suggest that the UK public favours buying British but they are less clear about what exactly *is* British.

Food self-sufficiency can be measured as production plus

imports minus exports; it is usually presented in either tonnage or financial-value terms. However calculated, it is and has been a powerful notion in food policy, shaping, for example, the EU's Common Agricultural Policy. It came under sustained attack from neo-liberals from the 1970s, arguing that food trade and macroeconomics were better ways to ensure people are fed. The UK, as we have seen, was forced to think in self-sufficiency terms in both the First and Second World Wars.[50,51,52,53] This led to a rethink after the war and Labour's weighty (125-page) Agriculture Act 1947,[54] which set out to rebuild home production and prevent the country sinking back to the 30% levels of self-sufficiency which had proved so risky in 1939. Land use (estates, farms, smallholdings, allotments) was rethought, and a system of deficiency payments was put in place to ensure that farmers did not produce below the cost of production or become unviable. UK self-sufficiency rose from 50–60% in the post-war period to a heady 80% by the early 1980s (the high point of the EU subsidy regime). It has declined slowly since.

Food defence has not been a term in common usage recently, but was in use in the UK from the mid-1930s.[55] It needs to come back. Defending supply lines became crucial for national survival from 1940 with the Atlantic Convoys.[56,57,58] Food defence becomes militarily important when and if geopolitical uncertainties rise. The term draws policy attention onto whether supplies are vulnerable, how protection can be given, and whether there are resources to enable them to be strengthened. This need not result from actions that directly involve the UK at all; the closure or fragility of a waterway or port can have a devastating impact on food security.

Audits of food defence require weaknesses and risks to be identified. In theory, the UK reviews its food defence annually under the Civil Contingencies Act, but, as is discussed later (pp. 127–36), this is too thinly done.

Food control is the term Beveridge and the First World War food policy administrators used to describe what they had to do to ensure food supplies were maintained.[59,60] The word 'control' drew a line between market thinking and some level of state intervention and reshaping of hitherto normal market dynamics. Control implies actions being taken by powers-that-be to allocate resources, and to make choices about where food goes or does not go. Strategic decisions are made. Lord Woolton, as we have seen, led UK food controls in the Second World War,[61,62] using not just supply measures but also incorporating scientific advice from nutritionists who were tasked with ensuring the population received appropriate levels of nutrients.[63] The resulting system of food rationing was a key policy filter applied in (and intrinsic to the success of) food control.[64]

Food resilience is a relatively modern term in food policy and is borrowed from mechanics but draws on both ecological and sociological systems thinking from the 1970s.[65] Its original seventeenth-century meaning of elasticity and capacity to bounce back from shock is how contemporary ecologists apply it to biodiversity and when webs of interdependent organisms have to change rapidly. A food system is said to be resilient if, when its equilibrium or normal (steady) state is disrupted, it can re-order itself to some new kind of equilibrium. The term has come into common parlance to reflect data on matters such as climate change and concerns about current imbalance and risks in the food system.[66] And this is where social factors become important. Shocks create societal stress affecting multiple actors whose actions can contribute to or thwart resilience.[67] Food resilience requires consumers to act as citizens.

Food risk is a notion widely yet diversely used. It implies a potential source of change or a weakness to 'normal' functioning. The notions of risks and stress (expounded by Hans Selye in the 1950s)[68] have been widely applied in food. The identification of risks to food performance, whether at company or country level, became a key feature of management of complex systems. The Hazards Analysis Critical Control Point (HACCP) approach, widely used in food safety management for example, was created by the US National Aeronautics and Space Administration (NASA) to minimize risks of foodborne disease in astronauts. Diarrhoea in space is no laughing matter. With HACCP, a food chain is subject to rigorous inspection to find where potential weak links are, and then corrective attention is focused on that point. Risk analysis and risk management are widely used in food business and have shaped not just food safety policy but entire management and investment systems.[69,70]

Food capacity is a term used to focus on skills and the capability of countries or food sectors to address problems. It raises issues of human resources as much as environmental or production concerns. One can argue that the entire nineteenth and twentieth centuries have been characterized by applying science and technology and human skills to mine resources and produce fertilizers and minerals that raise the productivity of land. Classical economics viewed food capacity as a function of capital (finance or land) and labour. Systems such as plantation agriculture used slavery (forced unremunerated labour) to maximize output with brutal effects which accrued massive wealth for the owners (and helped make Britain rich).[71,72] Modern approaches to capacity are framed more by socially liberal or neo-liberal economics. Today, food capacity development is mostly discussed in a country such as the UK as a matter of skills, science and technical support rather than colonial land grabbing.[73] But even these are not neutral matters, and raise questions about priorities for investment, land use, food work and the older vocabulary of capacity too.

Food sovereignty is a term coined by the peasant movement La Campesina in the 1990s to express the aspiration that small farmers' interests must take priority within international development.[74,75] Conscious of being squeezed by urban-controlled food interests, the peasant movement argued for more self-determination. Sovereignty implies they, not outsiders, can assert their values and rights. The term became a signifier of radical 'bottom-up' perspectives on food production mostly in relation to developing economies.[76,77,78] It celebrates small, often marginal producers, who in fact produce a significant proportion of food globally (an issue discussed later). The term began to be used in high-income food economies by solidarity movements but has been adopted widely in both rich and poor society deliberations.[79,80] Small-farmer organizations in the UK now use it.[81]

Food justice is a more recent term raising ethical concerns about fairness and equality. Its roots lie in the 1948 UN Declaration of Human Rights, which enshrined freedom from hunger as a human right.[82] It differentiates between the rhetoric and reality of markets, championing that they should operate openly and fairly, and questioning when they are creating unequal outcomes. As with food sovereignty, the term emerged in and about the developing world but spread.[83] Food justice offers a moral stance on how food systems work.[84] A 2009–10 inquiry by the UK Food Ethics Council, for instance, which involved people from industry, civil society and academia, concluded that the British food system discriminated against many sections of society.[85] It argued that these inequalities block progress towards a more sustainable food system. Food workers and consumers are not offered equal opportunities and lack engagement in the process of transition needed. The 2018–19 reports by Prof. Alston, a UN Special Rapporteur, cited above, provide sober verdicts on UK food injustice. Civil-society organizations in the UK increasingly use food justice – not least in relation to climate or environmental justice – as their catchphrase. Food justice thus becomes a multi-criteria term in itself.

Food democracy is a political term to denote the pursuit of open governance and the creation of food systems shaped by the public interest.[86,87] It suggests the importance of understanding and making accountable existing forms of decision-making, and posits that democratization is a key to determining who eats what, when and how. It has been applied as a 'lens' through which to review long-term struggles to improve food security, and to assess national strengths and weaknesses.[88] It asserts the importance of social processes in determining food system outcomes, and broadens the scope of Sen's notion of entitlement.

The distinctions between these ten perspectives matter

for present UK food policy (see Table 3.4). They cut across many arguments about directions for the political economy of food. Our national debate can draw on many policy themes when defining the national interest. Not far below the surface in Parliament and in Whitehall (and commented on in Edinburgh, Cardiff and Belfast) are old imperial perspectives about *trade and empire*, which suggest that the UK does not need to grow so much food (or not unless profitable) and that it is better to import food from wherever it can be sourced most cheaply. Cheap food for cheap urban labour has been a dominant cry since the 1846 repeal of the Corn Laws. A counter-theme was even then championed within UK food politics in the name of *public health*. It was not in the interest of the state to have a population so badly fed as to be unhealthy, inefficient and unfit. What first found expression in the mid-nineteenth century over urban squalor and poverty can again be detected in the debate about obesity. Does it really matter if people get fat and die unnecessarily early? Some blame the poor; others the obese themselves, Boris Johnson once stingingly writing: 'Face it: it's all your own fat fault.'[89]

Here enters another theme – food as a matter of *welfare and morality*. If a rich society does not ensure its people are well fed, can it claim any moral standing? Even if one accepts Milton Friedman's dictum that a company's sole social responsibility is to its shareholders and owners,[90] that food poverty exists in a world of food plenty poses moral and practical questions for corporate capitalism. Charity is a default response, and there's been a rise in food donations, sometimes as a 'fix' for food waste, but wider questions remain

Concept	What it means	Comment
Food nationalism	A country-centred focus stressing national interests, ranging from increasing self-sufficiency to full autarky.	The 'national interest' frames all considerations about food. In extreme, it seeks autarky (feeding within national boundaries) and can mean a desire to maximize home production and consumption, but not at all cost.
Food self-sufficiency	The proportion of food supplies consumed by the population, derived from within that country.	Countries vary in their self-sufficiency and how they measure it. Norway is about 40%. The UK 50–60%. Within the EU, France is almost wholly self-sufficient. This does not mean no trade but that the trade is marginal in meeting the population's nutritional needs.
Food defence	Protecting food sources and supply lines.	This is to cover eventualities and in dire circumstances such as war; although it implies military defence, it also means citizen engagement in protecting food systems.
Food control	Actions by the powerful to exert control over food systems, from production (e.g. farm output) to consumption (e.g. rationing).	Historically this has been top-down action by the State (e.g. in wartime) to manage the food system. The modern argument is that food companies have taken on this role by using contract and specification rather than law and regulations (e.g. 'choice-editing' products before consumers get to see the food).
Food resilience	Capacity to withstand shock and to bounce back after shock or change.	A term much used both by ecologists (drawing on systems/steady-state modelling) and military analysts.
Food risks	Factors which alter the food status quo and whose impacts are measurable.	Used to indicate factors which threaten stability or smooth running. There may be multiple risks and of varying strength with a single or cumulative impact.

Concept	What it means	Comment
Food capacity	Capabilities and skills deemed necessary to produce food to meet needs.	Focus on narrowing the gap between what is and what could be for food systems, drawing on both techno-scientific and social routes to improvement.
Food sovereignty	A term coined by small-farmer organizations to indicate societal control over food supply.	This term is associated with 'bottom up' social movements, particularly peasant/small-farmer movements in developing countries, but now used by others in the developed world.
Food justice	A focus on fairness and rights in the food system.	An ethical perspective on food systems gives priority to equality and human rights. It views the dynamics of food systems as perpetuating inequalities and constraining rather than opening up possibilities for better food and modes of production and distribution.
Food democracy	Political processes to ensure all social needs are met and subject to accountability.	The pursuit of equality in food systems implies pressure from social movements to reform decision-making and to widen social engagement in food policymaking. It also implies a real liberalization of interests.

Table 3.4
Some key concepts in or associated with the food security debate
Source: Author.

(not least food justice). To ensure that houses have kitchens, that people know how to cook, that food is affordable and that incomes are sufficient to enable people to buy adequate decent food – all these have become hallmarks of a civilized food society for good reasons. Their erosion should not lightly be ignored, but has been normalized.

Another theme is *technical efficiency*. A view that technical advance drives societal progress has been a consistent presence in UK food policy since industrialization. In the eighteenth century, it emerged in the form of more refined equipment (ploughs), crop rotation and farm animal breeding (bigger, faster, better), but by the twentieth and twenty-first centuries was more associated with plant breeding, intensification, IT and automation. Whether lo-tech or hi-tech, the goal throughout is to raise productivity. At the same time, arguments about equity and the unfairness of Britain's social divisions bubble away. At times it has taken the form of organized activism – trades unions, campaigns for the vote or school meals, with the role of women one moment recognized, the next demonized (bad parenting) as determining poor diets, as though food quality and control are readily possible when poor. And especially in the second half of the twentieth century, all was subsumed as a new *consumerism* became ascendant with post-war economic expansion. Demand drove production but the moulding of demand also became a battleground over consumer rights and responsibilities. Are consumers responsible for their diets if they barely know their impact let alone what their food contains and the hidden processes that make it? Consumer critics answered 'no', questioning how markets were managed, wanting controls and better protection.

POPULATION

An underlying issue in any consideration of food security, whether globally or nationally, is the existing as well as future pressure on the planet for food from growing populations. The UK population was 65.6 million in 2016. ONS expects this to grow to 72.9 million by 2041, adding 7 million people, all of whom must be fed healthily and sustainably.[91] According to UN projections, the UK population growth of 12% from 2015 to the mid-2040s is low compared to the world average of 25%. India's population is expected to grow 23% in that time but China's only 1%. Niger's population is projected to grow by 150%, while Latvia's will decline by 19% and Lithuania's by 13%. Such changes mean hugely varying regional food demands and almost certainly will encourage changes in cross-border food flows. The UK cannot expect to have first call on regional surpluses – and if we damage European relations that will not help; nor can we make glib assumptions that such surpluses will continue to exist or be priority shipping to the UK. Other countries now have deep pockets and more powerful diplomatic and military influence.

ONS's projections are for an average annual UK population growth rate of 0.5% (see Table 3.5). In 2016–26 the population will rise by 3.6 million, but within the UK growth rates differ. England's population is projected to grow by 5.9% in 2016–26; Northern Ireland's by 4.2%; Scotland's by 3.2%; and Wales's by 3.1%.

Brexit politics might have already altered such projections. People from EU member states resident in the UK are being rejected and have met hostile reactions in some areas. Given the tone of some Brexit campaigning, this is not surprising.

| | | | | | | millions |
	2016	2021	2026	2031	2036	2041
UK	65.6	67.6	69.2	70.6	71.8	72.9
England	55.3	57.0	58.5	59.8	60.9	62.0
Wales	3.1	3.2	3.2	3.2	3.3	3.3
Scotland	5.4	5.5	5.6	5.6	5.7	5.7
Northern Ireland	1.9	1.9	1.9	2.0	2.0	2.0

Table 3.5
Estimated and projected population of the UK and constituent
countries, mid-2016 to mid-2041
Source: ONS. National population projections.[91]

When Prime Minister, Theresa May made halting EU migration one of her 'red lines' in her Brexit thinking, and the government's formal migration advice agreed with this.[92] The share of foreign-born people in total UK employment increased from 7.2% in 1993 to 18.0% in 2017.[93] The public has not been made so aware, however, of mainstream economic thinking that, if not from the EU, the economy will still require more migration to keep essential services going and to provide key expertise as well as less-skilled labour. Already there are strong pressures from food and other employers to reverse blocks on migrant labour.

There are other demographic dynamics besides migration flows. In the 2016–26 period, it is projected that 7.7 million people will be born in the UK; 6.1 million people will die; 5.2 million people will immigrate long term to the UK; and 3.2 million people will emigrate long term from the UK. UK food policy will have to address these flows, not least since these people will all eat and many will be directly involved in the food system as producers, workers, cooks, waiters, fruit pickers.

Demographically, the UK is ageing. Figure 3.8 shows the ageing between 2016 (the filled-in figure) and 2041 (the dotted outside line). The bulging line (breaking away from the filled-in space towards the top) indicates the rise in older people.

Even if the UK were to adopt illiberal or draconian migration rules and literally block all human movement across borders, the reality is that the world population is rising, so our food system will come under greater pressure from outside. Although the twentieth-century food revolution has been an extraordinary success in feeding more people globally, the rise in population maintains the pressure. Whether politicians and

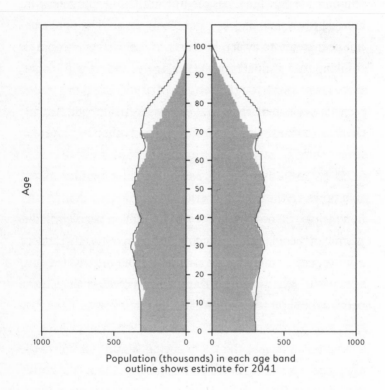

Figure 3.8
Age structure of the UK population, mid-2016–2041
Source: ONS. National population projections.[91]

public like it or not, the UK's food capacity will come under stress which it did not have in the eighteenth, nineteenth or twentieth centuries. Brexit politics ought to be a wake-up call, reminding us that the UK is geographically located in a region, Europe, where population is now fairly stable relative to elsewhere. It grew rapidly in past centuries but no longer. Table 3.6 gives the 2017 estimates of global population and by region to 2100. These are the UN Population Division's medium-variant projections. Note that much Brexit trade talk implied that the UK will do deals with areas of the world which expect massive population growth. Will they, ought they, really decide to feed us? Are we right to want or expect to be fed if we could do more here?

We must be wary of raising the impact of population too crudely in the food security debate. More mouths do not necessarily mean more food is needed, but better distribution, less waste, more sustainable versions of efficiency. Much in the food–population question depends on the status of women, their income and access to fertility support.[95,96] And much also depends on how the food is grown: what methods, what land use, what diets. The more diet is meat- and dairy-focused, the higher the resource use. That is the global assessment, but how that translates to this country compared to others is a matter of capacity, climate, terrain, skills, culture. Incomes and inequalities are also key determinants of who receives what foods. Expectations and rights shape how populations create demands for food. Even in extreme circumstances, people's sense of entitlement shapes how many people succumb to famine.[97,98,99]

Despite these variables, it is clear that the type of diet

Region	2017	2030	2050	2100
World	7,550	8,551	9,772	11,184
Africa	1,256	1,704	2,528	4,468
Asia	4,504	4,947	5,257	4,780
Europe	742	739	716	653
Latin America and Caribbean	646	718	780	712
Northern America	361	395	435	499
Oceania	41	48	57	72

Table 3.6
Population of the world and regions, 2017, 2030, 2050, 2100,
in millions
Source: UN DESA. World Population Prospects.[94]

populations consume varies the impact on land use. The 1940s productionist policy thinking – that simply to produce ever more food will resolve the world's food problems – is now judged to be wrong and too crude, and no longer fits a consumerist, majority-urbanized world.[100] As the EAT–*Lancet* Commission, the inter-academies partnership and others pointed out in 2019, if the extra population were to be fed on a US-style diet high in meat, and if that meat were reared in feed lots fed on grain, the implications for land use change, biodiversity loss, the nitrogen cycle and more are huge.[101,102,103] If the extra population was vegetarian, flexitarian or even vegan, the impacts differ and drop.[104,105] One NGO has estimated that 1.75bn more people could be fed by halving use of cereals as animal feed, an additional 1.4bn by halving food waste, and still 0.4bn more just by reducing over-consumption.[106] Making such calculations – which the government ought to do – highlights the various policy options. The UK cannot escape such choices. How and whence we source our food is subject to political circumstance and framing assumptions. It was always thus. We have simply forgotten some home truths.

PAST ARGUMENTS ABOUT WHETHER THE UK SHOULD ASSUME OTHERS WILL FEED IT

Time and again, when we start to take food security seriously, we re-enter an old and sometimes fraught debate about whether the UK can, should and will feed itself or expect others to. This has been a recurring theme in UK political history. It is a key part of a wider political economic debate about the central features of the UK economy. Are we a manufacturing nation? If so, let others feed us. Are we a service economy? Let us serve them. Or should we consider food security and production as a baseline for any kind of political economy? That emerges only in time of crisis.

The first industrial nation, the UK also became the first – and still a rare – country to *decide* to stop giving priority to its own food. Historically and even today, the most common policy approach around the world is for countries to maintain as high a level of home food production as is possible. Among rich societies, there are others like us with low levels. Japan produces only 38% of food and drink consumed (but its government set a target to raise that to 45% by 2025, so it senses trouble in this low rate).[107] The general argument in Britain is our old, imperialist one: that as a rich country, we can afford to buy food from countries which are not rich and have the cheap labour to help produce cheap food. This cheapness can therefore be passed on to the 'home' population as a bonus. This, so the argument goes, is more efficient and leaves us to concentrate on what we are good at – trade, banking, services. London's role as a global centre of financial services tends to be cited at this point. The general case is a version of David Ricardo's famous theory of comparative advantages, articulated in 1817, in which he argued that Portugal and England should stick to what they were good at, trade those advantaged outputs and thus both benefit.[108] Let England produce wool and Portugal wine, and simply trade to have both in both countries. This economics is increasingly viewed as complacent and inaccurate. Besides the fact that many industries have in reality been nurtured into existence by the state rather than entrepreneurs,[109] modern economics must now also address environmental, health and societal considerations within markets, not just as afterthoughts or only if 'affordable'. The UK is not alone in struggling to face this challenge.

Norway, for example, produces most of its own meat but saw its plant produce (fruit, vegetables, cereals) self-sufficiency decline from 52% to 46% in 2005–13, while exporting farmed salmon, a growth industry, alongside its massive oil trade. Like the UK, Norway buys a lot of food, but unlike the UK has decided it ought to grow more food sustainably itself,* as its 2015 statement makes clear: 'From the viewpoint of emergency preparedness, a society should produce as much as possible of the food its citizens actually need. In war or crisis a reliable food supply is particularly important, and being self-sufficient is a significant factor in food security.'[110] But Norway has a small population, 5.3 million in 2019, and is located further north with harsher growing conditions. It has also built a huge Sovereign Fund from North Sea oil earnings, whereas the UK spent not saved its oil earnings.

UK food production has fluctuated over time, a function of its wider economic position and politics. My concern is whether we might take this more seriously now. In the late eighteenth century, it produced almost all its food, but levels have varied ever since (see Table 3.7). This is not a sign of consistent policy. And we need to understand why.

At the turn of the eighteenth and nineteenth centuries, as

---

* I was made aware of this by being invited to address a review meeting in 2014 hosted by the Defence Research Establishment of the Government of Norway (Forvarets Forskningsinstitutet/FFI), which I was told was the first such gathering for a very long time. Smaller countries do appear to be more sensitive earlier, and it was not a surprise to me that a defence establishment should take this seriously.

Period	Rate of food self-sufficiency
Pre-1750s	Around 100% in temperate produce
1750s–1830s	Around 90–100% except in poor harvests
1870s	Around 60%
1914	Around 40%
1930s	30–40%
1950s	40–50%
1980s	60–70%
2000s	60%
2018	50–60%

Table 3.7
Changing rates of British self-sufficiency
Sources: Defra. Ensuring the UK's Food Security.[111] Defra. Agriculture in the UK 2017.[112]

industrialization spread and wealth grew, the right of large landowners to set the legal and parliamentary conditions for feeding the population was questioned by both the new class of industrialists and the industrial working class itself outside Parliament. Working people, remember, had no voting rights. Writers such as Ricardo and Malthus questioned the intellectual basis of the landowners' protectionist policies.[113,114] After the 1803–15 Napoleonic Wars, with Britain and its allies triumphant, furious political battles broke out about why tariffs were being put on food imports. UK industrialists and the emerging working class generally favoured cheaper food, and the fight over the so-called Corn Laws continued for thirty years, culminating in their repeal by Parliament in 1846. The repeal of the Corn Laws split the Conservative Party for a generation (a lesson both cited and ignored in the recent Brexit debates) and the repeal symbolized the end of the unquestioned power of landed capital and the emergence of two rivals for power within UK politics: finance capital and industrial capital. These gradually tamed landed capital. Food prices became relatively cheaper over the century, particularly when food came in from faraway colonies once technical innovation enabled, for example, meat to be chilled and survive circumnavigating the globe. (The first shipment of frozen meat from New Zealand landed in England in 1882.) By the end of the nineteenth century, British agriculture was in serious decline, whereas British capitalism was anything but in decline. It was expansionist, imperialist and predatory. Tensions over the price of food were not dissipated by sourcing abroad. The worries voiced in the 1840s that cheaper food would simply enable industrialists to keep wages down turned out to be true.[115]

By the early twentieth century, doubts about the wisdom of the cheap-food policy within the British state were being voiced but marginalized. The pummelling of the British Army by better-fed and healthier Boers in South Africa gave rise to eugenicist thinking that the UK troops exemplified the decline of British human breeding stock, a wider concern present in the infamous but influential Inter-Departmental Committee on Physical Deterioration of 1904.[116,117] A less well-known state review was published a year later, the report of the Royal Commission on Supply of Food and Raw Materials in Time of War.[118] This acknowledged for the first time since the repeal of the Corn Laws that there were risks in the decline of home production. Food posed an unnecessary vulnerability. In that report lay the first acknowledgements of the importance of food security as a social good. The case for feeding people decently was voiced in hearings by Commissioners, and noted but still not acted upon.

The dawn of the twentieth century saw both technical change in food – chilled, packaged and mass-processed foods, white bread was normalized by new roller mills – and political demands from the increasingly well-organized and educated working class.[119,120,121,122] State education had begun in 1870. The first twenty Labour MPs were elected in 1905, and the Liberal government sought to nip this political rival in the bud by conceding some social advances. Arguably the first expression of the future welfare state was a private member's bill proposed by a new Labour MP and backed by the Liberal government which allowed local authorities to fund school meals with a levy on the rates (local property tax).[123] In fact, few of them did, but the moral right to do so was now available.

Although there was an improvement in how food was being thought about, generally there was little change in reality despite the Royal Commission's warnings or early welfare measures such as the 1906 Education (Provision of Meals) Act. The First World War, however, shook UK state complacency. Some local-authority school food provision emerged. A Ministry of Food was set up in 1916 to deal with shortages in food markets and to force industrial and agricultural change, only for the default position to be reasserted when peacetime returned. The Ministry of Food was rapidly closed down in 1919 but its lessons were recorded, not least by Beveridge's official history in 1928.[124] As was noted in Chapter 1, his suggestions for war preparation (and more) were ignored in 1936, but seeds of consumer advice had been sown (see Figure 3.9). Food was recognized to be a matter of hearts and minds, not just stomachs and nutrients.

Between the wars, the case to reform food policy grew from many quarters. Nutrition science was still relatively new but recognized as an alterable determinant of public health and national efficiency.[125] There had been considerable UK interest in the findings of US nutritionist Wilbur Atwater, already reshaping US welfare and fuelling a mechanistic approach which saw food as fuel for workers.[126,127,128] By 1929, Sir Frederick Gowland Hopkins had co-won the Nobel Prize for Physiology and Medicine for the discovery of vitamins. The British medical establishment began to express concern that human potential was being destroyed by poor early nutrition. By 1939, a damning report was published by the British Medical Association.[129] In the 1920s, the philanthropist chocolate industrialist Seebohm Rowntree was showing that workers could and

Figure 3.9

1917 poster urging lower consumption of bread from imported wheat, carried by ships which were being threatened by German submarines

Source: Imperial War Museum catalogue number: Art.IWM PST 4470. http://www.iwm. org.uk/collections/item/object/41180.

should be better fed.[130,131] Eleanor Rathbone and thousands of feminists were documenting and articulating the case for better treatment and payment for women.[132] Trades unionists and campaigners were organizing against what today would be called austerity politics.[133] Agricultural scientists were arguing that British farms, which were failing due to collapsed prices and wider recession, could play a central role in meeting dietary needs, if only state economic structures supported them. Sir George Stapleton at Aberystwyth,[134] like Sir John Boyd Orr at Aberdeen, saw food, farming and health as connected. Food availability could be improved. The food system did not have to be as it was. Progress was possible.

In 1938–9, Frederick Le Gros Clark, an army officer blinded on the last day of the Great War who became a significant campaigner for a better food and welfare policy and co-founded the Committee against Malnutrition, and Richard Titmuss, a young researcher who later became the first Professor of Social Policy at the London School of Economics, came together to review UK food security. They did not flinch from criticizing the UK state for allowing food production to be so low and external supplies to be so risky. Had the German Navy attacked UK food supply routes in 1939, the year the two authors' book was published, subsequent national and possibly international events would have been very different.

Le Gros Clark and Titmuss's 1939 book, *Our Food Problem and Its Relation to Our National Defences* – an early Penguin Special book – stands alongside Beveridge's 1928 *Food Control* and the 1905 Royal Commission report as key texts which today's British ministers would do well to familiarize themselves

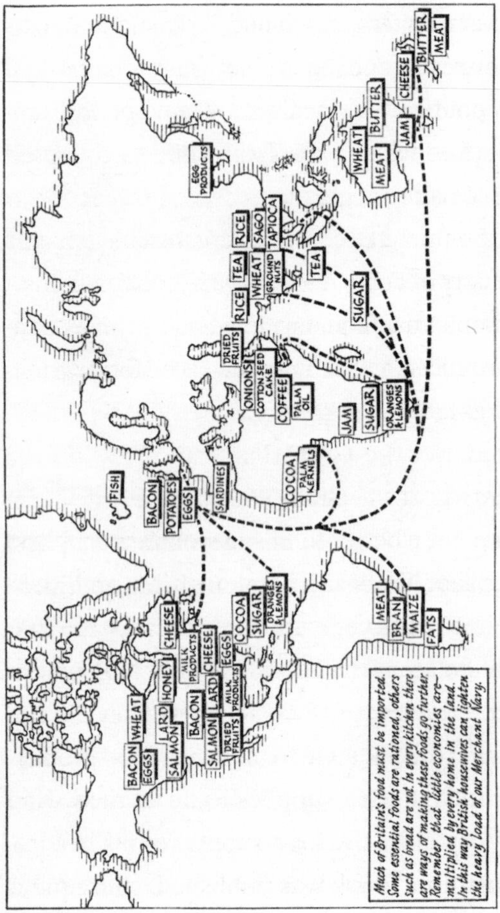
BACON
WHEAT
EGGS
LARD
SALMON
HONEY
CHEESE
MILK PRODUCTS
BACON
SALMON
LARD
CHEESE
DRIED FRUITS
MILK PRODUCTS
EGGS
COCOA
SUGAR
ORANGES & LEMONS
FISH
BACON
POTATOES
EGGS
SARDINES
COCOA
PALM KERNELS
ONIONS
COTTON SEED CAKE
COFFEE
PALM OIL
DRIED FRUITS
RICE
TEA
RICE
WHEAT
SAGO
GROUND NUTS
TAPIOCA
TEA
EGG PRODUCTS
JAM
SUGAR
ORANGES & LEMONS
SUGAR
WHEAT
MEAT
BUTTER
JAM
CHEESE
BUTTER
MEAT
MEAT
BRAN
MAIZE
FATS
Much of Britain's food must be imported. Some essential foods are rationed, others such as bread are not. In every kitchen there are ways of making these foods go further. Remember that little economies are multiplied by every home in the land. In this way British housewives can lighten the heavy load of our Merchant Navy.

THE FIGURES BELOW GIVE SOME IDEA OF THE GREAT DISTANCES WHICH THESE SUPPLIES MUST TRAVEL BEFORE THEY REACH YOUR TABLE

Bacon	2,700 miles	Egg Products	2,700–13,000 miles	Maize	6,200 miles	Sago	11,200 miles
Bran	6,200 miles	Eggs	2,700–2,760 miles	Meat	6,000–13,500 miles	Salmon	2,700 miles
Butter	12,000–13,500 miles	Fats	6,200 miles	Milk Products	2,700–13,500 miles	Sardines	1,000 miles
Cheese	2,700–13,500 miles	Fish	1,000 miles	Onions	5,000 miles	Sugar	4,000–11,200 miles
Cocoa	3,000–4,000 miles	Ground Nuts	11,000 miles	Oranges & Lemons	1,500–6,000 miles	Tapioca	11,200 miles
Coffee	9,000 miles	Honey	2,760 miles	Palm Kernels	3,000 miles	Tea	11,500 miles
Cotton Seed Cake	9,000 miles	Jam	6,000–12,000 miles	Palm Oil	9,000 miles	Wheat	2,700–11,000 miles
Dried Fruits	2,700–12,000 miles	Lard	2,700–2,760 miles	Rice	11,200 miles		

Ministry of Food map showing places from which food had to be brought by sea

Figure 3.10

Where food came from in 1939: Woolton's Ministry of Food map

Source: Ministry of Food, reproduced in Woolton, T. E. *The Memoirs of the Rt Hon. The Earl of Woolton*. London: Cassell, 1959.

with. They were clear and prescient.[135] We need regular such overviews today, conducted by the state, using its convening and evidential powers. Le Gros Clark and Titmuss were right about the risks from extended supply routes. An earlier privately conducted commission led by Viscount Astor and Seebohm Rowntree had concluded the same in 1935 and called for the rebuilding of national supply.[136,137] No one got a grip of the food situation until Lord Woolton was made head of the re-formed Ministry of Food in April 1940. Woolton, a businessman, had a simple map made which displayed the risks and which he reproduced in his memoirs (see Figure 3.10). Britain's food miles problem is not new.

FOOD RIGHTS, FOOD SUPPLY, CIVIL CONTINGENCY, MILITARY/CYBER PROTECTION AND ENERGY

Today, it is a moot point who is responsible for food supplies: consumers or state, families or suppliers, or all. My argument is that, by default, it is surely the state's duty to facilitate this. There continue to be debates and conflicts about where power lies, and over how to unpick ideology from reality, but some policy features are already there. After the devastation of the Second World War, the 1948 Universal Declaration of Human Rights (UDHR) laid out a framework of thinking about various rights to protection and space, including the means of existence such as food.[138] This has been developed ever since.* The 'Right to Food' is now articulated in various channels all traceable back to the UDHR.[139,140,141] In 1966, an International Covenant on Economic, Social and Cultural

---

* The history and development of these arguments is given in Lang, Barling and Caraher, *Food Policy*, pp. 280–83 (see p. 498, n. 88).

Rights (ICESCR) was produced which in 2019 had 196 parties (i.e. states who nominally support it) but only seventy-six countries as signatories (i.e. who have ratified it). The ICESCR lays out duties to ensure the protection of economic, social and cultural rights by specifying the rights to the means of existence such as work, social security, health and education. Article 11(1) of the ICESCR recognizes the right of everyone to an adequate standard of living, including 'adequate food, clothing and housing, and to the continuous improvement of living conditions'. Article 11(2) guarantees the fundamental right of everyone to be free from hunger, and lays down obligations to States Parties (countries which have ratified the Covenant). Article 11(2) is worth quoting in full because it puts obligations on states:[142]

> States Parties to the present Covenant, recognizing the fundamental right of everyone to be free from hunger, shall take, individually and through international co-operation, the measures, including specific programmes, which are needed:
>
> (a) To improve methods of production, conservation and distribution of food by making full use of technical and scientific knowledge, by disseminating knowledge of the principles of nutrition and by developing or reforming agrarian systems in such a way as to achieve the most efficient development and utilization of natural resources;
>
> (b) Taking into account the problems of both food-importing and food-exporting countries, to ensure an equitable distribution of world food supplies in relation to need.

The UK ratified the ICESCR in 1976.[143] As a signatory, the UK might be expected to have a clear Food Plan. In practice, we do not. If it takes a war or emergency to get the UK to act, there are many grounds for assuming we already have food emergencies. Yet, under governments of all persuasions, the UK has been consistently resistant to 'right to food' politics, preferring the more general position of assuring critics that a sound economy allows all citizens to be able to consume and eat adequately. This is patently not the case, as Prof. Philip Alston's report and the reaction to it showed (see above, pp. 98–9). There is an optional protocol allowing individuals to submit complaints to the UN Office of the High Commissioner for Human Rights, and many countries indeed have complaints made against them. Although there have been few from the UK,[144] there have been decades of reports and papers which document what could have been such complaints. UK anti-poverty campaigners have until recently not looked to the UN for protection, seeing that route instead as applying to developing rather than developed countries. This is clearly out of date.

CIVIL CONTINGENCY AND FOOD PLANNING

Under the Civil Contingencies Act 2004 (CCA), the government has a duty to communicate with the public about dangers.[145] There was precious little food communication in Brexit planning as far as the public was concerned other than externally written reports.[146,147,148] Inside Whitehall, however, there was rising concern about the effects on civil society from supply disruption, given UK reliance on EU-sourced food and food trade deals done as a member of the

EU.* The CCA does not specify any special duties with regard to food. It does, however, provide powers for keeping running anything which matters (to the government). Local Authorities – who, as we will see below, carry most Civil Contingency burdens (but without enough resources) – are often unclear about their duties of care.

In law, whether in emergencies or not, Local Authorities appear only to be required to ensure schoolchildren are fed. The Education Act 1996 (S.512) requires Local Authorities to provide meals to pupils at maintained schools whose parents receive benefits, and to do this to the standard required by the School Standards and Framework Act 1998 S.114A (4). Other social welfare legislation appears to be food 'blind'. Neither the Children Act 1989, nor the Care Act 2014, nor the Equality Act 2010, nor the Crime and Disorder Act 1998, nor the CCA 2004 itself places duties on Local Authorities to ensure people are decently fed. On a more positive note, the Health and Social Care Act 2012 does place a general public-health duty on Local Authorities and specifically therefore on Directors of Public Health (DPHs).[149,150] The Health and Social Care Act 2012, steered into law under the Secretary of State, Andrew Lansley, moved the DPHs from working within the Health Authorities and the NHS to being based in town halls under Local Authorities. The DPHs thereby rejoined the locally elected body where environmental health and

---

* Such concerns had surfaced in the British state before, as has been noted earlier, but what matters is that this has been institutionally forgotten. Note, for example, the monumental inquiry recorded in the three volumes of The Report of the Royal Commission on Supply of Food and Raw Material in Time of War, Cd 2643, 2644 and 2645.

trading standards officers have been located ever since they were charged with sorting out the adulteration of UK food under the 1865 Food Act. In theory the co-location of these key functionaries for environment, food and health could be powerful, but they are resource-constrained and politically marginalized by the centralization of the British state.

It is unclear, at time of writing, how real this general public-health duty is with regard to food supply in times of civil unrest or a mass emergency. It is fine to ascribe a 'motherhood and apple pie' duty to ensure everything aids public health but it means little unless there are specific duties, funds, responsibilities and entry points, plus more devolved local and regional powers. What could Directors of Public Health actually do to transform the food system, let alone do it in crises? They can hardly buy the fruit crops of Southern Europe to maintain supplies or dismantle trade barriers. Nor do many set up horticultural enterprises on a mass scale. Actually, when Dr John Middleton was Director of Public Health at Sandwell, West Midlands, he did pioneer exactly that. He set up urban horticultural social enterprises through budgets for special-interest groups. This remarkable pioneering work could and should be built upon.[151,152,153] Arguably, some of the transition towns and urban farming projects which have emerged in recent years do just that.

The lack of central state interest in food – to the point of not even 'dumping' responsibilities onto Local Authorities – seems a surprising policy omission now, just when vulnerabilities in the UK food system are being exposed. Back in the early 2000s, when the CCA was drafted, world politics and EU–UK politics looked different. Fragilities to food and medical supplies began to become clear in the event of a no-deal Brexit; the realities of just-in-time (JIT) logistics systems were explained to ministers, and the possibility of shortages due to lack of warehousing and storage space, in particular, loomed large. Ministerial absence of knowledge was palpable. Whitehall was worried. Political questions emerged: how would shortage be managed? Was it up to consumers to decide whether to have sufficient stores to ride out emergencies? If they did, retailers advised, this might only exacerbate shortages. Consumers today mostly live in houses without larders; they have become used to being able to purchase when they like, whether weekly or daily from ever-replenished stores. There was genuine fear of civil unrest from shortages.[154]

In the run-up to Brexit dates in March and April 2019, a movement known as the 'preppers' – people preparing for food shortages – was publicized in the press. The term 'prepper' was borrowed from the extreme US survivalist movement. The British preppers, however, were presented as benign and often understandably worried mothers whose actions were casting doubt on the modern existence of the British 'keep calm and carry on' ethos.[155] One moment, the need for stockpiling was denied by the government; the next, ships were reportedly being chartered to take food and medicine to ports other than Dover. In one extraordinary episode a company was awarded a Department for Transport £13.8m contract (one of three valued at a total of £107.7m) to carry food to the UK in a crisis but apparently had neither ships nor experience.[156]

In this period, the government gave barely any official advice to the public. In the run-up to the 31 October 2019

Brexit date – defined by Boris Johnson, the new Prime Minister, as the 'do or die' Brexit moment – public information was produced in the form of large advertisements telling people to prepare, paid by a £138m fund.[157,158] A fourteen-page memorandum to the Cabinet (then chaired by the Prime Minister, Theresa May) by Sir Mark Sedwill, the head of the civil service and National Security Adviser, was leaked to the *Daily Mail* and published on 1 April 2019.[159] This indicated that food prices in the UK could rise by up to 10% and there would be disruptions to fresh-produce supplies. The Yellowhammer Cabinet review, leaked in August 2019, spelled out the extent of anticipated disruption, food price rises and shortages.[160]

What could Local Resilience Forums (RFs) do, faced by such uncertain planning? RFs are little-known bodies, co-ordinated by the Cabinet Office, which bring together Category 1 responders under the CCA (2004), such as the NHS, and emergency services. Their published advice in the run-up to the constantly moving Brexit dates (March, April and October 2019, and ultimately January 2020) also made no mention of food or what to do about food shortages other than in the most general terms. This is because no RF had been led to expect disruption on the scale that the government's internal planning assumptions eventually showed the Cabinet in fact did anticipate. The standard booklet for emergencies was titled *Don't panic – prepare* (sic),[161] and gave advice on issues such as what to do in a crisis due to snow, floods and electricity cut-offs.

The Cabinet Office provides Resilience Forums only with the following advice on when to communicate with the public in Civil Contingencies using the 'Ten Step Cycle':[162]

- Step 1: Establish a public warning group.
- Step 2: Use the Community Risk Register as a starting point.
- Step 3: Identify and agree lead responders.
- Step 4: Assess systems and arrangements in place.
- Step 5: Identify target audiences.
- Step 6: Consult the public.
- Step 7: Decide what is sufficient.
- Step 8: Implement a training and exercising regime.
- Step 9: Ensure that all stakeholder communities are informed on a continuous basis.
- Step 10: Measure the effectiveness of your implemented control measures, review, and adjust as appropriate.

A final note is given at the end: 'Don't rush this work. Consider all the possibilities, and talk to all relevant stakeholders.' This has a reassuringly sensible Second World War tone but is pathetically weak and not a contribution to food security policy. It completely ignores public-health implications from disruption to fresh fruit and vegetable supplies and the special interests of the poor.[163] Alas, this situation had more than a whiff of the complacency and lack of preparedness that the country experienced in food planning in 1939. After ignoring Beveridge's sober advice in 1936, rapid action had to be taken in 1940, leading to rationing, food price controls and emergency management.

If public advice up to autumn 2019 has been found wanting and decidedly weak, at least food is considered as part of the Critical National Infrastructure (CNI), alongside transport, health and other matters. The CNI should be important in food security planning. Few have heard of it. It is subject to an annual review co-ordinated by the Civil Contingencies Unit of the Cabinet Office, which publishes summaries of the thirteen key infrastructure sectors; one is food, provided by Defra. The most recent summary (December 2017, updated January 2018) at time of writing warrants scrutiny. This does not take long, as it is barely one page in length:[164]

> The UK Food sector has a highly effective and resilient food supply chain, owing to the size, geographic diversity and competitive nature of the industry. Although there is recognized dependency on other critical services such as fuel, energy, transport and communications, the resilience of the sector has been demonstrated by its response to potentially disruptive challenges in recent years.

The 'Assessment of Continuing Resilience' states:

> Like many industries the Food sector operates just-in-time supply chains which require sophisticated logistics operations and contingency plans to respond rapidly to potential disruption. The industry remains highly resilient owing to the capacity of food supply sectors and the high degree of substitutability of foodstuffs.
>
> This resilience has been demonstrated in the response to events such as the 2015 flooding and disruption to cross-channel transportation, the 2009 H1N1 Pandemic, the 2010 Icelandic volcanic ash clouds, the 2012 potential industrial action by fuel tanker drivers, and severe winter weather experienced over the years 2010–14.

That is not quite all. Under a heading 'Building Resilience', Defra does nod in the direction of climate change inducing extreme weather events such as floods.

> Government and the sector will continue to work together to ensure the resilience of food supply. This will include building on recent research into the resilience of food supply to respond to and recover from maritime transport disruption resulting from a major coastal flooding event, building resilience in supply chains to extreme weather events, and providing good practice guidance on cyber security including by updating PAS 96.

This is misleading and complacent. We could be charitable and take it as typically British understatement, designed not to frighten the horses (the public), or hinting that there are good plans somewhere, held as 'top secret' under the Cabinet Office's classification system (to be released thirty years later, showing there was nothing to worry about).[165] If so, many key people in the food industries are in the dark too. And few believe there is a cunning plan. There is just nothing.

In fact, the prospects of a chaotic food Brexit led to a rapid recruitment of civil servants, but also, elsewhere in the state machinery, an updating of the PAS 96 referenced in the final CNI paragraph just cited. The full title of the PAS 96 document is more sober: 'Guide to protecting and defending food and drink from deliberate attack'.[166] PAS stands for Publicly Available Specification, a system looser than formal British or European Standards, and lacking legal status. The document is clear that 'Compliance with a PAS cannot confer immunity from legal obligations.' PAS 96 was first produced in 2008

in the middle of the financial-commodity crisis which first
alerted the then Labour government not to assume continuity of supply, only for the Coalition to drop such systems work.
PAS 96 has since been updated three times; a sign someone in
Whitehall is aware. It is a fall-back position, not a policy of prevention, however, and a sketch towards crisis management, so
public protection by inference only. It proposes a modification
of the Hazards Analysis Critical Control Point (HACCP) approach developed by the US NASA, discussed earlier (p. 102).
Early in the 1960s space race between the USA and Russia, US
scientists saw the need to ensure completely risk-free food for
the astronauts. But PAS 96 took HACCP one stage further,
proposing an ancillary system to HACCP it named TACCP –
Threat Assessment Critical Control Points.

The committee that drew up PAS 96 suggested six types of
possible disruption, giving case examples of them all (which I
repeat here) but with most cases in the first and second:

- economically motivated adulteration: e.g. adulterating
  olive oil with cheaper oil;
- malicious contamination: e.g. putting needles into a food
  product during processing;
- extortion: e.g. threatening to spike a baby food product
  with glass unless a demand for money is met;
- espionage: e.g. stealing a seed patent;
- counterfeiting: e.g. selling fake gin or wine;
- cybercrime: e.g. hacking Deliveroo accounts.

The examples – much as the Cranfield University 2006 food
resilience study before it[167] – limited the scale of possible
threat to the company level, not to the whole society or even

a societal sub-group. The TACCP method is thus of some-what restricted value for national food security. Its Critical Control Points are designed for use only at product level rather than for entire supply chains or a whole food system. That is what we ought to have.

The PAS 96 document interestingly does use the term 'food defence' right at the start (p. 1), which it defines as 'procedures adopted to assure the security of food and drink and their supply chains from malicious and ideologically motivated attack leading to contamination or supply disruption'. It continues: 'The term food security refers to the confidence with which communities see food being available to them in the future. Except in the limited sense that a successful attack may affect the availability of food, food security is not used and is outside the scope of this PAS.' Just when we might have hoped for a strategic food security overview, it is taken from us. This is not the fault of the British Standards Institute. Could a standards body really be expected to deliver answers to a major strategic-policy review? Unlikely.

The problem exposed is scale; the concern is national. Responses which are more panoramic are needed. Food security is a matter of more than checking tags or labels or tampering. And it is more than having naval ships alongside food-carrying vessels, Second World War style, though it can mean that, too. Where better to start considering food defence than with military capacity, the last line of defence?

UK MILITARY CAPACITY: SHIPS, POLICE, CYBER-GEEKS

In 1939, food came to the UK by ship. There was no Channel Tunnel, no Eurostar, no plane-based freight (or not for the mass population), no Roll on, Roll off (RoRo) fast-turnround ferries, no pallet systems, no containerization. It was a trade based on merchant ships loaded and emptied by stevedores, cranes lifting a bit at a time, considerable manual handling. Ships were slow, and slow to load and unload. This rightly worried the few critics of the late 1930s such as Le Gros Clark, Titmuss and the few members of the 1937–9 preparation committee. The UK's food supply lines were global, long and cumbersome. They were unprotected and vulnerable to submarines and aircraft (depending on fuel range). After narrowly escaping serious attention in 1939–40, a massive system of Navy-guarded Atlantic merchant shipping convoys was initiated to bring in food from the Empire and, after 1941, from the USA under the Lend-Lease funding scheme.[168,169] It suffered immense losses but was a top national-security priority exercising the Cabinet, and was brought home to the public through rationing, which, unlike in the First World War, when it was introduced only halfway through the conflict, was introduced early.[170,171]

It started with one advantage compared to today. The Royal Navy (RN) in September 1939 was the largest navy in the world, with one calculation that it possessed 1,400 vessels, of which the major ships were: 7 aircraft carriers (plus 5 more under construction); 15 battleships and battlecruisers (5 more under construction); 66 cruisers (23 under construction); 184 destroyers (52 under construction); 45 escort and patrol vessels (9 under construction and one on order); and 60 submarines (9 under construction).

In 2016, by contrast, according to the Strategic Defence Security Review, the Royal Navy had just 77 significant ships.[172] It owns more than that – cutters and other small vessels – but not remotely a fleet with the serious scale and numbers of 1939. Military analysts can and do argue that the modern military and navies have unbelievably greater 'firepower' or killing capacity, measured in different ways, but for the function being considered here – protecting merchant food supply ships whether on long or short routes – the UK has an utterly diminished strength. If we choose to shift supplies away from Europe, we have restricted means to protect a globalized food supply system, unless Allies (such as in NATO or a future European Defence Force) choose to make us and that their priority.

In 2017, in the course of analyses of potential threats from Brexit,[173] it emerged that the UK Border Force has just three vessels operational to protect sea borders. Nominally, it had five vessels but one was on patrol in the Mediterranean (dealing with migrants) and one was in dock. Eight new cutters (not large vessels) were on order.[174] On New Year's Eve 2018 (an interesting time to release such data), the Home Secretary announced that as of that date the Border Force had five cutters and six coastal patrol vessels (CPVs).[175] Even if this eleven rises to thirteen, by comparison with other maritime European countries this remains a pathetically small border force to protect ship-borne food traffic, if needed. No wonder Lord West, a former head of the Royal Navy, has said that outside the ports the UK is 'vulnerable'. Table 3.8 lists the UK and six other countries with their relevant naval border forces. Of these, the UK has the second longest coastline at 7,723 miles; this also includes one of the world's busiest sea routes, the Channel. Only Greece has a longer

Country	Name of naval body	Coastline (miles)	Number of vessels
UK *	Border Force	7,723	5
Italy	Guardia di Finanza	4,722	600
Turkey	Coast Guard Command	4,473	107
Spain	Guardia Civil	3,085	147
Greece	Hellenic Coast Guard	8,497	240
Croatia	Croatian Coast Guard	3,625	9
Netherlands	Nederlandse Kustwacht	280	16

* Four of these are 257-tonne cutters; one is a 454-tonne cutter. There are six additional CPVs of a 31-tonne 'rib' type.

Table 3.8
Border protection vessels in the UK and six European countries, 2017
Source: Dunlop, 'UK Border Force fleet size "worryingly low"'.[176]

coastline, 8,497 miles, for the patrolling of which it had 240 vessels. Italy, with 4,722 miles, had 600. Even the Netherlands, with just 280 miles of coastline, had five times more vessels. The tiny size of the UK's coastal force reflects both the lack of threats and UK reliance on the EU Single Market.

The Border Force is also responsible for protecting land-based arrivals into the UK. Security at the Channel Tunnel is a matter for governments and the private operator Getlink under the Treaty of Canterbury 1986 between the French and UK governments. In 2019 Getlink had 300 'security operatives', three times the number in 2014, a rise due to the migrant crisis.[177] The Royal Marines – the Navy's army – meanwhile was cut by 6% in 2011–18, down from 7,020 people in 2011 to 6,580 in 2018, with the Commons Defence Committee anticipating a further 30% of cuts to come.[178]

HM Government does not appear to have a specialized function or body to protect long, non-EU food supply lines, but immediate responsibilities fall to the Border Force created in 2012 to address all movement of people and goods into ports and airports. It sits under the Home Office answering directly to the Home Secretary.[179] Naval capacity meanwhile is in the purview of the Ministry of Defence and has been cut for years but remains substantial in budget terms. In 1980, the RN had 13 destroyers and 53 frigates. In 1990, it had 13 destroyers and 35 frigates. In 2000, 11 destroyers and 21 frigates. In 2010, 6 destroyers and 17 frigates. In 2016, 6 destroyers and 13 frigates. Six of the frigates were reported by the Defence Committee of the House of Commons as having 'power-failing engines'.[180] In its third 'Restoring the Fleet' report, the Defence Committee gamely reasserted the importance of the Navy. 'As an island nation, the importance of the Royal Navy to UK defence must not be underestimated.'[181] While it approved current refitting and restructuring, it expressed deep 'concerns that the number of ships is at a dangerous and an historic low'. As one MP commented, this was 'way below the critical mass required'.

FOOD CYBERSECURITY

Some argue that this naval 'lens' on food supply protection is less relevant today, although UK–Iranian tensions in the Gulf of Hormuz over protecting oil-carrying ships in July 2019 exposed how stretched the Royal Navy was. A British-flagged tanker was easily captured by the Iranians in retaliation for the British impounding an Iranian tanker off Gibraltar. While food shipping traffic is inevitably vulnerable the further the food travels, modern food systems are now even more vulnerable to other forms of disruption such as from software attacks and cyberwarfare. Food logistics are dependent on computers, satellites and information technology (IT), another potential Achilles heel.

The PAS 96 document cited earlier was developed to guide the food industry on how to protect its 'devices, services and networks' from attack. It defined food defence as 'procedures adopted to assure the security of food and drink and their supply chains from malicious and ideologically motivated attack leading to contamination or supply disruption' but expressly does not include a concern about food security.[182] Its focus, as we have seen, is mostly on the scale of threat to individual supply chains – a brand of chocolate or crisps – rather than the whole system, although it notes that actors at the nation state level could disable GPS-based logistics (GPS is owned by the US government and run by the US Air Force; with Brexit, there has been concern that the UK might leave the European alternative Galileo system in preparation).

A more systemic perspective has been adopted by the Joint Committee on the National Security Strategy (JCNSS) of the House of Lords and House of Commons. In a 2018 report, the JCNSS noted that public opinion is barely aware of cyber threats to the national infrastructure – by which it meant the underpinning of everyday life in the UK – and was critical of the government's underinvestment. It urged activity to prevent cyberattacks by hostile states and other interests which it accepted are highly likely – 'not if but when'.[183] JCNSS rightly noted that food is part of that infrastructure. Ironically – given the government's intention to leave the EU – it noted too that advances in cybersecurity had mostly been driven by EU regulation, while the National Cyber Security Centre (see below) took shape.

Perhaps the most important feature of the JCNSS analysis is that it highlighted a gap between insider expertise, which takes cyberthreats seriously, and the general understanding of cyberthreats within business and by the public, which operate in blithe ignorance. This 'hush hush' mentality is probably a mistake. Few doubt the need for experts in this field but, as users, the public is both recipient and potential victim of cyber insecurity. In the Internet of Things and with the ubiquity of web-based activity, consumers might be better alerted than left in the dark. On p. 26 of its sixty-two-page report the JCNSS had a worrying footnote number 134. This observed that the Commission on National Infrastructure leaves food 'out of scope' with regard to cyberthreats. Did this mean not taken too seriously, or that this went beyond an existing remit? The JCNSS recommended that a Cabinet minister responsible for cybersecurity should be appointed. This should include food, in my view.

The National Cyber Security Centre (NCSC) is a relatively new agency of the UK's Global Communications Headquarters (GCHQ) and is now a critical institution for food defence. In the government's words, the NCSC was created in 2016 'to be a bridge between industry and government, providing a unified source of advice, guidance and support on cyber security, including the management of cyber security incidents'.[184] Its purpose was to build capacity and develop itself as the 'single authoritative government voice' not just for cyber security but for cyber infrastructure, seeking to promote 'smart cities', for example, in which cyber defence is a default position. NCSC appears to recognize the centrality of IT to how British society and industry work,[185] but so far its role in food cyber defence remains to be seen; perhaps this is deliberate.

The food industry meanwhile is certainly increasingly aware of how the spread of new technology opens it to new avenues of disruption. Just-in-time systems are impossible without the internet. The food industry may pride itself on being at the technical cutting edge, but its protection measures are judged by many auditors to lag far behind.[186] Entire systems (not just food systems) can be hacked, as was shown by a ransomware attack in May 2017 which incapacitated 200,000 computers worldwide.[187]

For all these warnings, the food industry continues to see web-based technologies such as blockchain as the answer to problems in food authenticity, fraud and traceability. Robots and Artificial Intelligence (AI) are being invested in as routes to labour replacement, increased efficiency and precision control. Blockchain is promoted as enabling only people or firms in a supply chain to have access to what is happening within that supply chain. Blockchain makes possible the sharing of information within a tightly agreed network, to which only its members have the encrypted access.[188] Its rapid deployment is underway 'for food safety and traceability to create product visibility, quality and freshness', but blockchain is not necessarily fraud-proof. An alliance of Walmart and IBM (both US firms) is working on this matter but is reputedly mostly concerned to deliver consistent and properly managed filing in the blockchain. Those who invest in the technical development will, as usual, stand to reap most benefit. Currently this is large food companies, ones which can afford to employ or hire expert staff.

The growth of hacking already suggests that relying on algorithms and other AI tools should not be assumed to prevent attack. Hackers can teach themselves how to hack and defraud systems. Smaller food companies arguably offer less weighty targets for hackattacks, but as one specialist informed me, 'their links into large company supply chains through Blockchain, distributed ledgers and Internet of Things, as well as the Inventory and Order IT links already in place may make smaller companies conduits into the larger ones for organized criminals.' If a company puts its data on a cloud system, the contents of its computers might be less vulnerable to devastation when or if the firm's offices burned down, but they become more vulnerable to cyberattack. This could take various forms including: disruption of delivery; alteration of food recipes and commercially confidential formulations; interceptions; threats – and ransom demands – for example, of tampering.

One study showed that, for all these risks, firms in the food and hospitality sector invested only about £900 per year in cyber security, whereas finance and insurance companies invested an average of £17,900 – still a low sum.[189] This low level is despite a PWC study reported in the same source showing that any firm which has fallen foul of cyberattack suffers an average annual cost of £857,000. The low level of investment is perplexing given the vulnerabilities at stake, but it reflects the confidence and security of trading systems and European frameworks until recently. In 2019, however, a report from Europol and the European Union Intellectual Property Office (EUIPO) showed that organized crime gangs have moved into food commodities (and many others), and found counterfeit products such as baby formula powder, stock cubes, cheese, coffee, olive oil and pasta on sale, including in major European supermarkets. EUIPO's 'Intellectual property crime threat assessment 2019' estimated that counterfeit trade in goods could amount to 6.8% of all EU imports, with food and drink 'highly popular items for counterfeiters'.[190] If this rate applied in a food-independent UK, it could cause serious loss of public trust. Even now, new risks to food security and defence are emerging.

SPENDING ON SECURITY

The UK government's 2016–21 budget for cyber security was £1.9bn, or about £400m a year. In a 2019 review of how the budget was being managed, the National Audit Office (NAO) was critical of how this budget was allocated in the first place, arguing that the Cabinet Office, which leads the work, first decided on the budget rather than clarifying the tasks the NCSC should undertake and then giving it the appropriate funding .[191] Time will tell. But if food systems are disrupted, the costs could be immense. And the cyber-security budget will almost certainly look tiny in retrospect.

It is hard to estimate quite what current spending is on conventional forms of food defence – such as the doughty convoy protections of the UK in the Second World War. Historians agree that spending on the armed forces, unsurprisingly, rockets in times of war. And public expenditure as a whole rose in the twentieth century, from 12% of national GDP in 1900 to about 40% today. Within that, in 1900 defence spending was 3.69% of GDP, rising to 9% in 1939 and to a massive 40% by the end of five years of war, then dropping afterwards to the current budget of about 3% of GDP. The budget was raised in the new millennium, reflecting combat after the 9/11 al-Qaeda attacks in the USA and elsewhere.

Today the Ministry of Defence (MOD) has the fifth-largest budget of the British state. *UK Defence in Numbers* provides a breakdown of the 2016–26 expenditure: submarines – £44bn; combat air – £18bn; ships – £19bn; air support – £16.6bn; helicopters – £10.6bn; land equipment – £19.1bn; weapons – £13.5bn; intelligence, surveillance, target acquisition and reconnaissance – £4.6bn. These are huge sums, but planes, ships and other equipment and forces are not cheap. The 2018 MOD budget was £35.3bn. The point here is that from a food defence perspective, we need to ask whether this is the best use of huge sums. With just a handful of 20-metre 'rib' CPVs, which are mostly focused on illegal drugs and migrants, one wonders whether the UK's food defence is receiving the attention and budget it is due.

Reviewing equipment budgets in reports published in 2018 and 2019, the House of Commons Public Accounts Committee (CPAC) noted drily that there appeared to be an expected overspend of between £7bn and £14.8bn, and concluded: 'we remain sceptical that the Department is close to reconciling what it says it needs with the funding it has available.'[192] The PAC 2018 report identified a £2.9bn gap between expected costs and received budgets for 'four nuclear deterrents, six attack submarines, an estimated 30,000 people and the infrastructure to support them'.[193] It noted that there were 201 active contracts, worth £48.9bn, given to cover 'the designing, building and maintenance of submarines, nuclear propulsion systems and warheads'. Nuclear submarines are not likely to have a role in protecting food supply chains (or one hopes not), but if the MOD's expenditure is so focused on these massive capital outlays, there is likely to be little budget left for investing in more routine ships or cybersecurity needed for food defence. T45 destroyers cost at least £1bn each, and engine and intercooler failures exposed within a few years of use have required an additional £0.28bn refit for the six in service in 2019–21.[194] T26 frigates cost about £0.25bn each. If the UK is to reorient its food supply lines overseas and away from neighbouring EU states, more such vessels might be required, and so presumably fewer nuclear submarines – unless there is a vast increase in MOD budgets on a quasi-war footing. One could buy many coastal patrol vessels for that, and do a lot of cybersecurity, too.

If the UK remains in food-trading relations to and from the EU, we might still require more land-based personnel and equipment to be able to defend the millions of tonnes coming through Dover. Let us hope not. In the first annual National Security Strategy and Strategic Defence and Security Review 2015 (published in 2016 by the Cabinet Office rather than the MOD), the only mention of food was in relation to Southern Africa and the effects of El Niño.[195] This is comforting, as it suggests there are people in the Cabinet Office alive to the effects of climate change on food supply somewhere. Meanwhile, in 2019 most food imported to the UK came via the EU, with the majority of that coming through the South of England, much in trucks through the Channel Tunnel and through ports. If so much comes on ships, surely the RN capacity to protect shipping lines remains important. Quite how important can be seen from the section immediately following which provides information about the scale of the food flows.

PORTS, ROADS AND RAIL: ALL ENERGY-DEPENDENT, ALL LINKED

All the means for moving food have undergone extensive rationalization and change in the twentieth century. All freight mostly moves by land. 76% of freight (not just food) was moved by road in 2015–16, 9% by rail and 15% by ship.[196] Food is the most trucked freight, 326 million tonnes (mt) in 2016, accounting for 17% of all freight by weight. The second was ore and minerals at 316 mt (also 17%), with waste matter third at 263 mt (14%). Road traffic is immense. Goods moved 147 billion tonnes kilometres (tkm) in 2017, travelling 18.6 billion kilometres that year.[197] Traffic is now long-distance, with GB trucks doing trips averaging 105 kilometres. No wonder roads feel full. Trucking fluctuates with economic activity; it was down in the Great Recession. In 2017, 287 mt of food products were trucked by GB-registered heavy goods vehicles (HGVs), 21% of traffic that year. Most goods moved are urban to urban. Food is also the top category for 'intermodal' freight, moving from, say, ship or plane to truck or vice versa. In 2017, 9.1 mt were intermodal.

Airfreight is tiny, accounting for only 1% of all UK freight tonnage moved, but it accounts for 40% by value of all non-EU airfreight according to the National Infrastructure Commission (NIC).[198] It has grown massively since the Second World War, of course, partly with a growth in dedicated freight flights but mostly on the back of passenger air travel. There was a drop from a peak in 2007 to 2016. Heathrow airport's freight handling is far the biggest of the UK airports, but four others are also important: East Midlands, Stansted, Gatwick and Manchester. Airfreighted food is then trucked by road, sometimes simply to another airport, if it is international goods from outside the EU.[199] Most UK airfreight comes in the belly of passenger planes; Paris, Frankfurt and Amsterdam airports by contrast carry far more dedicated freighter goods, being better located for EU road distribution. Airfreighted food is overwhelmingly perishable – such as mangoes from the Indian sub-continent or asparagus from Peru – and requires specialist containers and handling. Public data on airfreighted food is scarce, but it accounts for about a sixth of airfreight imports by value.[200] Salmon has become one of the most valuable and fast-growing exports, worth £0.6bn in 2017, the vast majority going to the USA and China. Even though from Scotland, 90% of it goes through Heathrow. London is thus, by far, the major location for any strategic food security risks, if there are any. Most airfreighted food imports are from Brazil, Kenya and South Africa.

In a report considering the future of freight, the NIC saw three linked issues looming. The UK freight system, it stated, is 'one of the best in the world, but there is a major problem. The negative impacts of freight – carbon emissions, poor air quality and congestion – need immediate focus and coordinated action. We should not accept that the challenge of cleaning up freight is something for another time.'[201]

In 1939, the UK could use UK coal to power its own merchant fleet. This fleet has long gone and, like many countries, we pay others to ship our daily needs. The rise in airfreighted food is considerable but starts from a very small base. Unlike many other countries, and apart from the Channel Tunnel's road freight, we are almost entirely dependent on ships to import food, cross-channel and beyond. Today, it is not coal but oil that provides the energy for this transport. Research is in fact being conducted into making ships more energy-efficient, including an interesting hi-tech use of wind power.[202] A driver for such innovation has been pollution. Sea shipping is dirty. In 2018, the 174 member states of the International Maritime Organization (IMO) committed themselves to halve world shipping's carbon emissions by 2050,[203] and the search for low-sulphur fuels and liquid natural gas is underway. The US Navy is even reported to be experimenting with using seawater for hydrogen. The search for 'cleaner' fuels is also under way for planes, lorries and cars. Solar-driven planes already

Figure 3.11
Freight through UK airports, 2018, tonnes
Source: Civil Airports Authority, 2019.

London Area Airports

Gatwick	112,600
Heathrow	1,685,137
London City	7
Luton	26,193
Stansted	226, 128
Total London Area Airports	2,050,065

Other UK Airports

Aberdeen	5,706
Barra	13
Belfast City (George Best)	227
Belfast International	27,672
Benbecula	24
Birmingham	33,709
Bristol	7
Cardiff Wales	1,459
Doncaster Sheffield	7,107
Durham Tees Valley	1
East Midlands International	334,536
Edinburgh	20,316
Glasgow	15,466
Humberside	121
Islay	283
Isles of Scilly (St Mary's)	74
Kirkwall	38
Lands End (St Just)	65
Leeds Bradford	3
Liverpool (John Lennon)	159
Manchester	114,131
Newcastle	5,524
Newquay	3
Norwich	220

exist but have little immediate chance of being available for heavy freight such as food. Oil and alternatives are thus likely to be the key energy infrastructure for food transportation. HM Government recognizes that, despite other possibilities ahead, the UK runs on oil. 38.8 mt of oil were imported into the UK in 2017, compared to just 8.4 mt of coal (down from 50 mt in 2005, which itself had risen after the UK coalfields were closed).[204]

PORTS ARE KEY

This is why the ports matter so much for food defence. There are 112 ports in the UK (see Figure 3.12). Fifty-one of these are designated as ports which can handle significant freight, but within that group there is very uneven throughput. A few points of entry are disproportionately busy. There are clusters of immense significance such as Goole, Immingham, Grimsby and Hull on the Humber, or the vital Thames and Kent cluster (from Tilbury round to Dover), or Southampton. It would be nigh impossible suddenly to switch port use between these, with their different parameters and specialisms, let alone others in the fifty-one major ports and certainly not the sixty-one smaller ones.

Major Waterways (downstream of the point indicated)

1 River Thames
2 River Medway
3 River Severn
4 River Mersey
5 Manchester Ship Canal
6 River Clyde
7 River Forth
8 River Humber
9 River Ouse
10 Aire and Calder Navigation
11 River Trent
12 River Orwell

Figure 3.12
Ports in the UK
Source: DfT. Port freight statistics 2017.[204]

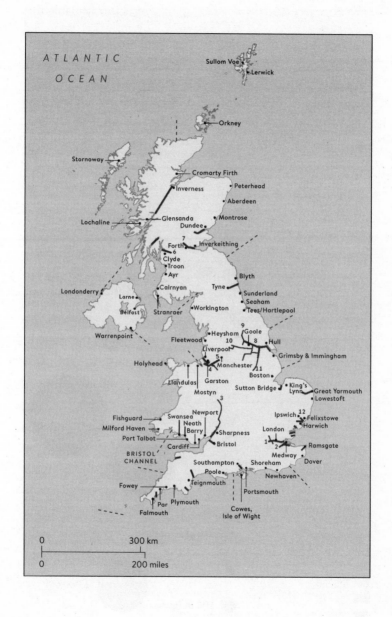

ATLANTIC

OCEAN

Sullom Voe

Lerwick

Orkney

Stornoway

Cromarty Firth

Inverness

Peterhead

Aberdeen

Lochaline

Glensanda

Montrose

Dundee

7

Forth

Inverkeithing

6

Clyde

Troon

Ayr

Blyth

Cairnyan

Tyne

Sunderland

Londonderry

Seaham

Larne

Workington

Tees/Hartlepool

Belfast

Stranraer

Warrenpoint

9

Goole

Fleetwood

Heysham

Hull

10

8

Liverpool

Grimsby & Immingham

5

Holyhead

Manchester

11

4

Boston

Garston

Llandulas

Sutton Bridge

King's

Mostyn

Lynn

Great Yarmouth

Lowestoft

3

Newport

Ipswich

12

Felixstowe

Fishguard

Swansea

Harwich

Milford Haven

Neath

London

Port Talbot

Barry

Sharpness

1

2

Ramsgate

Cardiff

Bristol

Medway

Dover

BRISTOL

CHANNEL

Southampton

Shoreham

Poole

Newhaven

Fowey

Teignmouth

Portsmouth

Par

Plymouth

Cowes,

Falmouth

Isle of Wight

0   300 km

0   200 miles

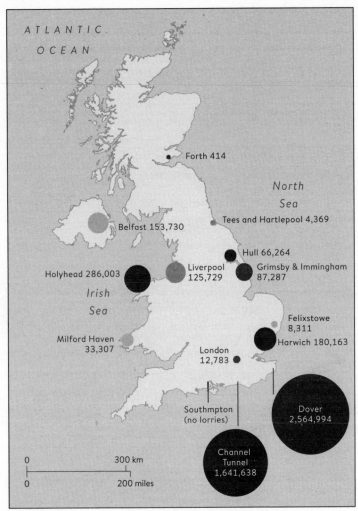

ATLANTIC OCEAN

North Sea

Forth 414

Belfast 153,730

Tees and Hartlepool 4,369

Hull 66,264

Holyhead 286,003

Liverpool 125,729

Grimsby & Immingham 87,287

Irish Sea

Milford Haven 33,307

Felixstowe 8,311

Harwich 180,163

London 12,783

Southmpton (no lorries)

Dover 2,564,994

0   300 km
0   200 miles

Channel Tunnel 1,641,638

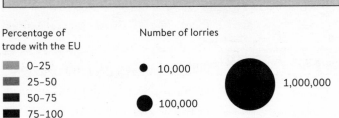

Percentage of trade with the EU

- 0–25
- 25–50
- 50–75
- 75–100

Number of lorries

- 10,000
- 100,000
- 1,000,000

In 2015, 2.56 million trucks came through Dover and 1.64 million through the Channel Tunnel (see Figure 3.13). These two dwarf the next-biggest truck flows: 286,003 through Holyhead from Ireland, 180,163 through Harwich, and 125,729 through Liverpool.[205] Other ports are tiny both in numbers and capacity. Food is part of that total.

ROAD MOVEMENTS: FOOD TO THE PEOPLE/ PEOPLE TO THE FOOD

The Transport Resilience Review (TRR) also expressed concern about 'natural' disaster shocks (if that is what climate change is) and their possible impacts on the vast network of roads. There are 183,300 miles of English roads alone (ranging from 'A' roads to narrow country lanes), which are managed by 152 local-highway authorities, plus the 4,300 miles of Strategic Road Network managed by the Highways Agency. This has complex governance. Although a semblance of resilience thinking is visible in the Department for Transport (DfT), its default policy has for years been just to help increase road traffic flows rather than to prevent unnecessary traffic, which would be the sustainable route. In fact there have been more motorways built over prime agricultural land. And the more space is given to roads, and the more vehicles there are, the more bottlenecks are cited as requiring yet more roads. Economic growth is equated to ever-expanding vehicle movement. The EU Single Market helped drive this expansion from 1992 by delivering a continental 'trunker' system. Cross-border and internal traffic has risen. One fifth of all UK lorry traffic is food. Figure 3.14 gives

Figure 3.13
Flows of lorries and trade source

Source: After Owen, Shepheard and Stojanovic, Implementing Brexit, p. 12.[205]

Year	Agricultural goods, mt	Food goods, mt
2004	117	245
2005	112	236
2006	103	267
2007	107	266
2008	102	261
2009	100	259
2010	106	285
2011	103	279
2012	110	290
2013	98	277
2014	104	235
2015	97	258
2016	94	272
2017	97	287

Figure 3.14
Agricultural and food goods moved by UK-registered heavy goods
vehicles, 2004–17, mt
Source: DfT. DfT statistics: Road freight statistics.[206]

the tonnage of food-related UK-registered HGV movements, measured by the Department for Transport.[206]

Besides this freighting, our roads are full of people going about their daily business – taking children to school, going to work, going out for entertainment or on holiday, and going to buy food.

One of the trends of the second half of the twentieth century was for both people and food to travel further. The term 'food miles' was coined in 1992,[207] and immediately developed at length,[208] to highlight the cultural implications and hidden choices being made by food brokers in the move to all-year-round supply of single commodities. The inherited culinary acceptance that foods come in seasons has been made obsolete. In rich societies like the UK, peaches or strawberries can be supplied for most months in the year from within the EU or via EU trade deals. There has never been any serious policy discussion of the desirability or otherwise of this huge change. It is assumed to be progress. This transition in taste and availability has favoured large-scale horticultural agencies over the small-scale. 'British' enterprises in fact have international webs. A new financial and managerial layer has also been inserted between grower and consumer, altering power and nurturing a-seasonality. Food miles have been much debated, criticized for being a poor proxy for carbon,[209] for discriminating against developing nations' food exports,[210,211] for over-emphasizing one feature of mass logistics above others,[212] and more. But the public understood what lay behind it. How can it make sense to buy an apple from Washington State, in the USA, halfway round the world (and also in the northern hemisphere), when we could buy one from Kent or Herefordshire? Why buy a lettuce grown under lights in the Netherlands or in polytunnels in water-scarce southern Spain, when we could get it from Lincolnshire or Lancashire using similar technology (whatever its footprint)? 'Food miles' thus remained in use, not least since the food industry realized it highlighted the industry's vast trucking ('trunker') use and the related problem of returning empty lorries; it set out to cut food miles for cost and environmental efficiency.

What has changed in recent decades has been not just how the food gets to us, but how we consumers go to the food and where that sits. In the 1950s, people – almost always women – shopped on foot or by bus. Shops were local, and specialized: grocers, bakers, butchers, fishmongers. By the 1980s, supermarketization was in full swing, leading to a decline of the local and specialist shop. Hypermarkets offering 20,000–30,000 food options were built out of town, requiring car access and leading to a concentration in food markets and decline of independent shops (and not just food ones). By the 2010s, a counter-trend was underway – a rise of online shopping accompanied by home delivery, a growth of restricted-range food shops, a rise of café society and niche delicatessens. How we travel to shop has changed. Figure 3.15 (p. 162) shows car shopping trips every two days, and Figure 3.16 (p. 163) shows what trips are for.

In the last decade or so, having concentrated market share under the multiples, a new generation of smaller supermarket has emerged, first via the German-owned so-called discounters Aldi and Lidl and then with the big retailers setting up their own equivalents. The shopping picture has shifted

Classification	Total units	Total units, %
Non-food stores, e.g. fashion, books, shoes	163,000	28.0
Supermarkets and convenience food shops, e.g. Nisa, Asda	74,484	12.8
Service shops, e.g. nail salons, dry cleaners, hardware	162,325	27.9
Leisure food, e.g. entertainment outlets, mid-range eateries, hotels	146,078	25.1
Miscellaneous (everything else!)	35,715	6.1

Table 3.9
Comparison of food to non-food shops, UK, 25 July 2019
Source: Local Data Company.

again. Table 3.9 gives a snapshot of British shops as at 25 July 2019, collated by the Local Data Company, a specialist analyst. Food shops are a minority of shops in Britain. Supermarkets are very much a physical minority, even though their market share is immense.

Table 3.10 gives a more detailed breakdown of what these stores are and of how many outlets there are and what proportion of the total British market is held by which type of store. There are many stores competing for our favours.

After years when shopping by car became the norm, today there is a return of more frequent and 'local' shopping. Individually, people are making fewer car trips each year and covering less distance. Fewer younger people in big cities are even taking driving tests. The cost of motoring is the main determinant. For food, the key issue is that the number of shopping journeys, in any mode, appears to be in decline. Yet the roads are full, for the simple reason that there are more cars. At the end of September 2018, there were 38.4 million vehicles licensed for use on the roads in Great Britain. 31.6 million of these were cars, about one for every two humans alive in Britain.[213] Vehicle numbers have grown every year since 1945. In 1997–2007, an average 670,000 more vehicles were on the road every year (i.e. new cars less scrapped ones). That growth rate has slowed slightly to an average of 640,000 since 2012. About 2.5 million new cars are registered each year. They are very little used; they move (their purpose) on average for just 4% of the time.[214] With a decline in bus services, this is not surprising but is not healthy. A rise in walking and bicycling would be better for health but requires town planning and a complete rethink about energy, health

Category	Total units	% of total GB units	Independents	Multiples	Independents, %	Multiples, %
Bakers	6,213	1.1	2,474	3,739	39.8	60.2
Bars, pubs and clubs	28,925	5.0	16,843	12,082	58.2	41.8
Butchers and fishmongers	3,602	0.6	3,467	135	96.3	3.7
Cafés and fast food	64,061	11.0	48,671	15,390	76.0	24.0
Confectionery, tobacco, newsagents	11,897	2.1	8,523	3,374	71.6	28.4
Entertainment	14,670	2.5	4,784	9,886	32.6	67.4
Groceries, supermarkets and food shops	43,465	7.5	14,930	28,535	34.3	65.7
Off licences	2,736	0.5	1,915	821	70.0	30.0
Petrol stations	6,571	1.1	93	6,478	1.4	98.6
Restaurants	27,983	4.8	22,118	5,865	79.0	21.0

Table 3.10
Breakdown of all food-related shops, UK, as at 25 July 2019
Source: Local Data Company.

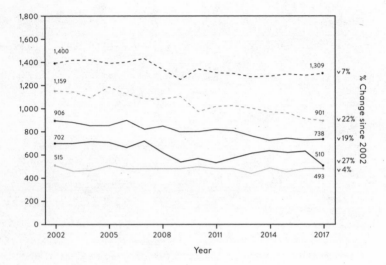

Figure 3.15

Average miles travelled per person, per year, England, 2002–17

——— Shopping

- - - - Commuting

——— Personal business

- - - - Visit friends at home

——— Business

Source: DfT. National travel statistics England 2017.[215]

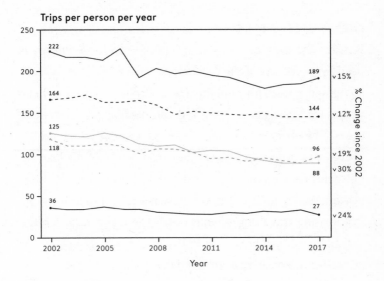

Trips per person per year

Figures shown on chart: 222, 164, 125, 118, 36 (left side, 2002); 189, 144, 96, 88, 27 (right side, 2017)

% Change since 2002: ∨15%, ∨12%, ∨19%, ∨30%, ∨24%

X-axis (Year): 2002, 2005, 2008, 2011, 2014, 2017

Figure 3.16
Purpose of car-based trips, per person per year,
England, 2002–17

—— Shopping
----- Commuting
—— Personal business
----- Visit friends at home
—— Business

Source: DfT. National travel statistics England 2017.[215]

and environment to be delivered. Meanwhile, cycling rose in 2002–17 by 54% to an average of sixty miles a year – hardly Dutch rates – but with young people cycling far more, which is better for their health, street life and air quality.[215]

ENERGY USE FOR FOOD

Besides the moving of food and people to food, energy is used by all sectors of the food supply chain, not least by consumers in homes for cooking. Here, a policy battle has been waged for years about sourcing: oil, nuclear, gas or renewables. The electricity which drives equipment which grows, moves and processes food comes from a mix of nuclear, renewables (wind and solar), coal, gas and (in Scotland) water power. Mostly food is trucked, flown and shipped using oil. But anyone travelling up and down the UK can notice the arrival of renewables: windmills, solar panels and crops grown for biomass have sprouted everywhere, encouraged by subsidies but also now for their efficiency and cost cutting. For food and farming policy, the key issue is land use and amenity. If land is used to grow biomass to feed into a power station such as the giant Drax station in Yorkshire, critics argue it cannot be used to grow food direct for humans. Solar panels have spread across farmland, incentivized by subsidies or forward contracts from electricity companies wanting to increase their renewables use.

In fact, the food–energy mix might be less intrinsically conflicting than it can seem. In Oregon, researchers found that photovoltaic (PV) panels across fields actually increased grass crop growth because they protected the plants from wind and weather. The biomass (the weight of the biological/plant matter) of several key grazing grasses increased by 90% in areas partially or fully covered by solar panels.[216] In Germany, where the government committed in 2011, after the Fukushima disaster, to ending nuclear power by 2022, a technical innovation bonanza followed. The University of Hohenheim, for example, has experimented with lifting the PV panels onto much higher gantries which allow 'normal' farm equipment and cropping to occur underneath, permitting dual food and energy output.[217] New studies are underway. Some show that a variety of crops can be grown on the farms, with only small reductions in yield. Others suggest an increase in growth and biodiversity because the panels protect plants. Others criticize the aesthetics; the technology is ugly but the incentive is that farmers or landowners make money (often more money) from energy production as well as from food. Ideally, surely, solar panels should mushroom on the UK's roofs, not its fields.

In the UK, government policy has retained a mixed-economy approach, but by early 2019 the high cost of nuclear investment meant Japanese, Chinese and French funder-contractors halted work on two of the three planned new nuclear plants. It remains to be seen if the UK government will fund nuclear whatever the cost. Critics find the government's approach to renewables too thin. The UK's Export Finance (UKEF) system, for instance, overwhelmingly favours fossil fuels. In a pointed and unusual criticism of UK energy policy, the UN Secretary-General, Ban Ki-moon, called on the UK to stop funding fossil fuel use in developing countries.[218] In 2010–14, the UK allocated 99.4% of its funding for developing countries to fossil-fuel-related work, leaving a pitiful amount for renewables. This is poor leadership, he wrote. He was right. In 2010–16, UKEF spent £4.8bn funding fossil fuel use for developing countries, while, in roughly the same period (2010–17), the UK government gave £4.9bn to the International Climate Fund! One was adding to climate change while the other was trying to mitigate it! This is policy incoherence but perhaps not surprising when, at home, the UK government cut financial support for renewables. This dented but did not obliterate the growth of renewables; they are simply becoming more cost-efficient.

A problematic source of renewable energy of significance for UK land use is biomass, which uses fast-growing plants as fuel for generation. In 2018, the Committee on Climate Change (CCC), the statutory body monitoring performance on achieving targets set by the 2005 Climate Change Act, reviewed biomass.[219] The CCC was broadly favourable, noting that biomass can be well or poorly managed, but seeing a positive role in the UK energy mix. The priority was to ensure that biomass is sustainably harvested, while not deflecting a growth in forestry, so essential to store carbon. It recommended a new system created to collect food and biodegradable waste. This would need to be done by local authorities, which are both underfunded and have been badly served by government over recycling paper, tin and plastic waste. There is no unified national system for such household waste, let alone any plans to create a new channel to collect food waste for electricity generation.

Energy analysts used to be enamoured of biofuel and saw a big role for it in transport. Since then, worries about land use have increased; growing crops to convert into gas is parallel to growing grain crops to feed to animals. The conversion losses are inefficient; the subsidies have been distorting.[220,221,222,223] Yet by 2017 the UK was providing 25% of what was used in transport, France 19%, Spain 9%, the USA 6%, and France and Germany 5% each.[224] The Department for Transport reports a long-term drop in use of both petrol and diesel for transport due to improved vehicle efficiency. The use of subsidies to drive use for biomass has been contentious. £1bn is spent subsidizing use of biomass – trees – for burning in power stations. Drax power station, for example, received an estimated £1bn subsidy across 2016–18, a huge sum; according to the European Commission, in 2016 the UK spent over £10bn subsidizing fossil fuel use compared to £7bn on renewables.[225] Nuclear would not exist without handsome state support, but so high are its costs that even governments can be reluctant to put up the vast sums to build nuclear plants.

Whichever political party is in power, the trend to renewables in the UK is probably unstoppable simply because the technologies have become cheaper. The government's Energy Transitions Commission, whose 'mission' is to 'de-carbonize hard-to-abate sectors' – air, ships, road – believes the UK could achieve zero greenhouse gas (GHG) emissions from energy.[226] But one additional 'mission' goal perhaps ought to be added to the Energy Transitions Commission's aims: to reduce transport in the first place. That would require working with intra-national bodies and economic actors to de-carbonize the food system, not just its transport. A land use review is required to assess the competing demands of energy use and generation, food production, and CO_2e and H_2O sequestration, alongside other uses, including fibre, timber and amenity, let alone beauty and identity. Certainly, more policy attention is needed on the connection between energy security and food security.[227]

THE RISE OF CONTAINERS, LOLO AND RORO

Docks have shed their labour and replaced it with containers and lift-on, lift-off (LoLo) systems of giant gantries at increasingly automated docks. Truck transport has been altered by the rise of ever larger wagons driving up and down motorways. The big change, arguably, is how all the modes are managed by the logistics IT revolution with its computers and satellites. This infrastructure of the modern food system is strategically crucial.

Fourteen million tonnes of agricultural products are handled by UK ports annually. This accounts for only 15% of the total dry bulk which is handled by UK ports. In 2016, 8.5 mt came into the UK, and 5.5 mt went out.[228] Over the ten years 2006–16, agricultural dry-bulk imports rose by 7%. Even London, which historically was a huge food terminal but then declined, has seen a growth in recent years. The port at Sheerness, for example, now has the capacity to handle 12,000 tonnes at any time, and saw an 8% growth in exports in 2015–18.

Alongside the information technology revolution involving computers in logistics, modes of transport have also changed, from loose to containerized, coming in the standard 20-foot equivalent unit containers known as TEUs. Containerized food imports have become immense. Of the total of 4,771,536 tonnes of food and drink imported into the UK in 2014, 1,503,513 (31.5%) came from eight countries providing ten commodity groups (see Table 3.11).[229]

Rank	Region	Exporting country	Commodity	Tonnes
1.	Sub-Saharan Africa	South Africa	Fruit and nuts	315,289
2.	Asia Pacific	Australia	Wine	252,132
3.	Asia Pacific	Thailand	Meat and fish	144,189
4.	North America	USA	Beer, wine and spirits	139,075
5.	South America	Chile	Fruit and nuts	125,101
6.	South America	Brazil	Fruit and nuts	118,242
7.	Sub-Saharan Africa	South Africa	Wine	111,463
8.	South America	Chile	Wine and beverages	106,000
9.	Mediterranean	Turkey	Citrus and grapes	100,011
10.	North America	Canada	Vegetables	92,011
	Total			1,503,513

Table 3.11

Top ten 'containerized' UK imports of food (2014)

Source: Morgan. Sustainable supply chains.[229]

Containers have revolutionized handling and restructured who does the work. Dockers and their union power have been broken, and lorry drivers now do the bulk of movement. Motorways are the internal arteries and constantly moving 'storage'. At the edges, the logistics revolution is represented by the rise of the roll-on, roll-off ferry (RoRo). Figure 3.17 gives the top five ports, by tonnage, where RoRo movement occurs. Traffic between the UK and EU accounted for 76.7% of all Ro-Ro movement (not just food) in 2016. Within that general flow, one company dominates. Getlink, formerly Eurotunnel, handles over 20 million passengers, 1.6 million trucks and 2.6 million cars. It accounts for 25% of trade in goods between the UK and continental Europe, 1.7 billion tkm of freight and 1 gigawatt of electricity (about the amount of power to run 700,000 homes).[230] This work enabled it to pay €600m in dividends to shareholders in 2008–18.

UK ports through which food imports come are officially categorized in three ways.[231] They can be a Designated Point of Entry (DPE), a Designated Point of Import (DPI) and/or a First Point of Introduction (FPI). DPEs need to receive Common Entry Documents (CEDs) at least one working day before the physical arrival of the consignment. DPIs are those ports approved under an existing set of regulations. And FPIs are places where at least two working days of notice must be given before the arrival of a food consignment.

WHO IS ABLE TO SHIFT WHAT?

Some ports and airports are designed and registered so as to be able to take some kinds of food freight and not others. In the mid-2010s, for instance, Belfast could be used for all

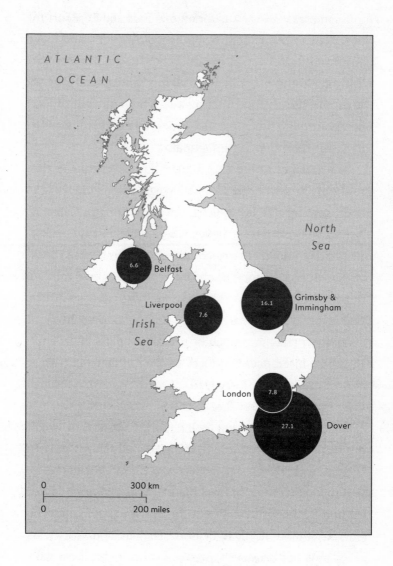

Figure 3.17
Top five ports for UK RoRo movement, mt
Source: DfT. Port freight statistics (2016 revised).[228]

foods, whereas Bristol was for animal feed and Teesport for both. Doncaster Sheffield 'Robin Hood' Airport could move chilled and ambient stable products not frozen, whereas Gatwick and Heathrow could move all food and animal feed. By the turn of the century, Heathrow had become a major food entry point, with other regional airport owners committed to increasing their freight throughput.[232]

As a member of the EU, the UK had border inspection posts only at ports and airports which dealt with non-EU goods, such as Heathrow, Felixstowe and London Gateway. There have been none at Dover, where 10,000 lorry consignments a day – not all food – come through (sometimes peaking at 16,000).[233] A total of 470 mt of freight passed through UK ports in 2017, with 110 mt more coming in than going out. Food is a relatively small but still significant percentage of this freight, 18.25 mt, much of it fresh or perishable: fruit, vegetables, meat, dairy products. In the run-up to Christmas 2017, for instance, 130 lorry-loads of citrus fruit came through Dover from Spain every day.[234] This is a huge operation.

Much of the UK's recent food imports from non-EU countries has come via Rotterdam. If the UK fully leaves the EU, the time currently taken to inspect non-EU foods could be applied to foods coming in from the EU. Port authorities agree that non-EU imports can be got through the port in under an hour, but if more needs to be done, such as laboratory tests for example, or because paperwork is not right, it can take days. There are three levels of inspection: documentary (e.g. authenticity of certificates), identity (e.g. correct labelling, packaging or the physical seals) and physical (e.g. opening up the product to check by sight, smell and test).[235] That is why the freight industry joined with the ports to express worries about leaving the EU without frictionless borders.[236]

Under EU regulations, 20% of consignments of meat and fish had to be tested, and 50% of poultry meat, honey and dairy products, but only 1–10% of products inedible to humans such as hay. As a sign of concern, the UK government's advice was for importers to test 100% of Brazil nuts from Brazil, 100% of pistachios from Iran, 10% of peanuts from China, 20% of peanuts from Egypt, and 5–10% of figs, hazelnuts and pistachios from Turkey. Imports from Canada and New Zealand were deemed less in need of inspection other than as per trade agreements, since those countries were judged to have high safety standards.[237]

PORT OWNERSHIP

In 2000, the Labour government set out its vision for ports as part of its commitment to 'modernize' infrastructure. The 'Modern Ports' strategy report outlined the importance of ports to the UK economy and wanted this to grow, operate to higher standards and deliver competitiveness – a familiar mixed-policy aspiration.[238] A *National Policy Statement for Ports* produced by the Conservative-led Coalition in 2012 continued the policy but usefully recognized how ports have environmental and land impacts. Taking over marshland, for instance, destroys biodiversity.[239] A central purpose, however, was to enable planning procedures for new or enlarged ports. The *Policy Statement* anticipated static liquid and bulk freight but growing RoRo and containerized.

The big issue for huge infrastructure like this is how to get the investment. As with other sectors – schools, hospitals, transport – the means have been privatization, pursuit of efficiency, and a more arm's-length approach to state strategic oversight. British ports have experienced decades of deregulation and privatization. A sector pilloried by economists in the 1970s and 1980s as rife with fraud, corruption and inefficiencies – often blamed on dockers' and stevedores' trades unions which had grown to counter the casualized basis of dock labour – then underwent massive change; automation shed labour. Some ports have gone into decline, others emerged and grew; some are entirely new.

Today, ports fall into one of three ownership categories: private, municipal or trust. Most trust ports are small, but a few are large, notably Aberdeen, Belfast, Dover, Milford Haven and the Port of London. In legal terms, trust ports are independent statutory corporations, operating commercially but answerable to their stakeholders. The Port of London Authority and Belfast Harbour Commissioners are independent statutory corporations managed by a board of trustees, for example. Municipal ports are local authority-owned, such as Portsmouth and the oil terminals in Orkney and Shetland. They too operate on a fully commercial and competitive basis but the returns accrue to the local authority. There is a lobby group for the big port actors, the Major Ports Group, formed in 1993 (see Table 3.12). It shares offices with the British Ports Association and Port Skills and Safety.

Britain actually has hundreds of ports, not surprising for an island nation. The vast majority are small harbours with mostly leisure or other private boats. The significant ones are the 120 or so cargo-handling ports; and there are over 400 non-cargo-handling ports and harbours.[240] Food imports

Group	UK ports operated	Ownership
Associated British Ports	Ayr, Barrow-in-Furness, Barry, Cardiff, Fleetwood, Garston, Goole, Grimsby, Hull, Immingham, Ipswich, King's Lynn, Lowestoft, Newport, Plymouth, Port Talbot, Silloth, Southampton, Swansea, Teignmouth, Troon	Private holdings
Belfast Harbour Commissioners	Belfast	Public-owned; directors appointed by N. Ireland government and include members of Belfast City Council
Bristol Port Company	Bristol	150-year lease sold in 1991 by City Council to private company
DP World	London Gateway	Dubai-owned after purchase from P&O
Forth Ports	Burntisland, Dundee, Grangemouth, Leith, Methil, Rosyth, Tilbury	Part-sold in 2018 by one investment fund into 100% ownership by a Canadian pension fund
Hutchison Ports	Felixstowe, Harwich International Port, London Thamesport	Registered in the Virgin Islands but headquartered in Hong Kong
PD Ports	Hartlepool, Tees	Bought by a Japanese company in 2000 and sold to a Canadian one in 2009
Peel Ports	Glasgow, Heysham, Liverpool, Manchester Ship Canal, Medway Ports	Privately owned by Peel Group (also owner of Liverpool airport)
Port of London Authority	Port of London	Self-funding public trust set up in 1908, amended by Port of London Act 1968

Table 3.12

Major ports groups

Sources: Company data and websites.

and exports go through the huge ports, now often container-ized. Twenty ports account for 88% of total UK imports and exports, including food.

The privatization of ports has been extensive. And a creeping 'financialization' of national assets has been underway with barely a murmur. As one critical summary put it: 'UK ports are now more or less all in foreign ownership having been privatized', citing ownerships by banks, family trusts, funds registered offshore or in tax havens or by foreign sovereign wealth funds.[241] Does it matter if they are foreign-owned? When all goes smoothly, some might argue perhaps not. But earnings go offshore rather than being retained or recycled for national investment. In 2011, for example, Forth Ports, the last British port group listed on the London Stock Exchange, was sold for £0.75bn to a financial consortium facilitated by Deutsche Bank. Seven years later, in October 2018, it was bought out fully for an undisclosed price by a Canadian pension fund which already had a major holding.[242] In 2015, the US bank Goldman Sachs and others sold a 30% stake in the giant Associated British Ports (ABP) for £1.6bn to Hermes (owned by the BT pension fund) and the Canadian Pension Plan Investment Fund. Goldman Sachs had delisted ABP from the stock exchange nine years earlier in 2006, valuing the whole group at £2.6bn. In nine years, group value had grown to £4.8bn.

Dubai, trading as DP World (whose chairman is Sultan Ahmed Bin Sulayem), now owns Southampton and London Gateway ports, for example, and has set out to be able to handle the largest container ships in the world, each carrying 21,000 TEU containers.[243] London Gateway was entirely new, receiving its first ship in 2013, a 58,000-tonne container ship carrying South African wine and fruit.[244] DP World bought the Gateway site from P&O ports in 2006 and spent £0.6bn on the new port. DP World 2017 revenues were US$4.71bn. A rivalry has ensued between Felixstowe and London Gateway as to which can process containers faster and cheaper.

The emergence of these relatively new private groups means the power of publicly owned docks has gone. Ports' value lies in both their land assets and their trade role. Other countries would not allow this sell-off to have happened. Infrastructure ought to be seen as a public good. Today, the UK state has few points of leverage and the conduit for food flows lacks publicly accountable strategic oversight.

Potential for disruption

At present, the majority of food imports are from the EU and through south-east Kent. Brexit preparations (after a delay in getting started) quickly exposed potential for disruption: clog-ups and motorway jams from concentrated just-in-time logistics.[245] The UK food system is complex both internally and externally. It lacks the decentralization needed by resilient food systems.[246] Various studies have been conducted into potential disruption of food supplies and the ports, in particular. The structural fragilities reviewed and suggested here include: the just-in-time system, motorway logjams, limited warehousing, potential to be affected by sudden changes in consumer expectations (stockpiling), breakdowns in external sources, failures in privatized infrastructure, lack of central government understanding, and wider ecosystems pressures such as looming climate change.

There is, in the legal and insurance fields, the notion of an 'act of god', meaning a natural occurrence beyond human control, something insurers would not insure for, something so beyond control that they would not accept blame or pay compensation or prevention. Today, science is collectively generating a new list of what we might term 'acts of humans' which are beginning to reshape food capacities. These impacts already face the UK. In December 2013, for example, a combination of very bad weather, high tides and sea surge inundated the port of Immingham, Humberside, which is a major port in tonnage terms but also, as the government states itself, 'a crucial conduit for petro-chemicals and fuel'.[247] Water levels rose 50 cm above the port's flood defences and 75% of the port area was submerged. Serious IT and power supply failures resulted.

The 2013/14 weather was presented as 'extreme', when it probably heralds a new normality. It led to the worst coastal flooding since 1953. The storm surge at Dover was estimated to be a one-in-1,000-year event. Until the next one. In view of such events, a Transport Resilience Review (TRR) was conducted for England.[248] The TRR's scope was not very wide. It did not consider whether disruption risks might rise with growing reliance on imports for strategically important freight such as food. It did, however, identify threats across all modes of transport from climate change.[249]

The TRR recommendations ranged from suggesting that every transport sector conduct its own weather resilience review (i.e. more local reviews). It recommended that the owners of Railtrack cut down trees near railway lines and offset this destruction by enhancing biodiversity elsewhere.

Its argument was that delays are caused by trees falling onto lines in bad weather! The scale of action implied would be considerable; National Railways (the state-owned tracks) has 18,200 km of rail embankments and cuttings, some of which are already vulnerable to flooding even before sea rises, let alone having trees. In May 2019, Emma Howard Boyd, chair of the Environment Agency, accepted that 'we cannot win a war against water' by building higher flood defences and that local communities will have to be prepared to be more resilient. This affects not just coastal populations. Two thirds of properties in England are served by infrastructure in areas at risk of flooding.[250]

A more prosaic list of potential causes of disruption was given by a different independent report into ports (see Table 3.13). These included climate change, of course, but also mechanical breakdowns, labour problems, power failures and terrorism. Simply, it argued that, as infrastructure, ports are vulnerable. And if there is concentration through some more than others, the risks are greater. The investment which private owners have made into particular 'channels', 'corridors' or 'clusters'[251] may exert their control but means the state has little oversight or indeed understanding. In addition, shipping routes can, of course, be disrupted by hostile naval or military action.

Where does this leave protection of the UK food supply? No amount of small-scale managerialist interventions such as TACCP or HACCP, as suggested by the PAS 96 report, or Border Force assessment can avoid the conclusion that UK food supply chains are already potentially vulnerable. To lengthen them further, switching a massive amount from

Cause	Duration	Impact level	Intervention level
1. Mechanical failures (bulk discharge equipment, cranes, RoRo ramps, etc.)	Short	Port	Port
2. Peak-time arrival traffic congestion or temporary control system (technical) failures	Short	Port	Port
3. Bad or extreme weather (high winds, snow, etc.)	Short/ Medium	Regional	Port / Regional Government
4. Power failures (leading to control system and equipment downtime)	Short	Regional	Port / Regional Utilities
5. Industrial action (port workers, government agency employees, road haulage drivers, rail workers, etc.)	Short?	Port / National	Port/Transport Industry / Regional And National Government
6. Lock gate failure	Short/ Medium	Port	Port
7. Vessel breakdown, grounding, collision, sinking (at berths or in access channels), including ongoing environmental impact of fuel spillage	Short / Medium / Long	Port/Range Of Ports (With Single Access Channel)	Shipping Lines / Ports / Marine Authorities / Repair And Salvage
8. Road and rail transport problems (fuel prices, accidents causing blockages, shortage of drivers, etc.)	Medium	Port / Regional / National	Transport Industry/ Government

Cause	Duration	Impact level	Intervention level
9. Fire and / or disruption in the Channel Tunnel	Medium	Tunnel	Tunnel
10. Terrorist activity (bombs, hijacking)	Medium?	Regional	Government
11. Earthquake, tsunami, flooding, volcano eruptions at foreign ports	Long	National	International
12. Tidal surge (will impact Continental ports as well)	Long	International	Government
13. Climate change / rising sea levels (longer-term likelihood and planning?)	Long	International	Government

Table 3.13
Possible causes and impacts of port disruption
Source: Morgan. Sustainable supply chains.[229]

Europe to North or South America, for instance, might over-extend already stretched naval forces. The UK must decide on what sort of food system we want and whether and how we are prepared to defend our food sources, and consider whether we have sufficient flexibility to be resilient under duress or emergency. If politicians wish to switch trade deals to sources further away, almost inevitably increasing investment in food defence will need to be considered. Surely this is of sufficient magnitude to warrant the appointment of a Royal Commission to review:

- the adequacy of current food defence;
- whether port infrastructure under foreign control has sufficient strategic oversight;
- how to improve and fund resilience;
- where options for the national interest lie.

There is little in the public domain so far on this score, yet some actors in the system are aware of a number of the issues, particularly climate change. The scope of a Royal Commission type of inquiry needs to be wide. In May 2019, the Committee on Climate Change (CCC), a statutory body, recommended that the UK should tighten its carbon emissions target from the current 80% by 2050 to net-zero greenhouse gases by 2050, with Scotland aiming for net-zero by 2045, reflecting Scotland's greater relative capacity to remove emissions than the UK's as a whole (sequestering carbon in land), and Wales achieving a 95% reduction by 2050. The CCC calculated that this is achievable with known technologies but needs to be 'clear, stable and well-designed [. . .] without delay'. Adding that 'Current policy is insufficient for even the existing targets.'[252]

If these are wide-reaching aspirations, an inquiry of the status of a Royal Commission is surely also required to address the immediate problems of personnel, co-ordination and capacity for food defence. Eurotunnel, for example, doubled its security budget in 2017 due to pressures from desperate migrants,* as well as terrorism threats.[253] Even before the Brexit discourse, the possibility of localized disruption to food flows – to this or that port or this or that regional retailer hub[254] – began to emerge. But the state still failed to conduct a systemic analysis.[255] This is a serious failure in national food policy, which may look reckless in the future. Unfortunately, we appear to be repeating the default failing: it takes a crisis to get a rethink, and then the crisis narrows the possibilities.

Part Two now considers what the evidence suggests we really ought to do if we want to address the combination of immediate and longer-term structural pressures known to be emerging. These include wider ecosystems pressure, labour and societal tensions, economic dynamics and food's role in health. Along with many academics and analysts, I know that the tensions in the UK food system are extensive. Food security is more than just tonnage and flows. It requires a rethink about how food is grown, what is eaten and who gets most, best and affordably, too. The long-term route to food security will be making our food system more sustainable, not just environmentally but socially and economically too.

---

* An exploitative trade in people exists with boats chartered by or paid for by would-be migrants, some of whom are picked up in the Channel.

PART TWO

Tackling Food Problems is the Key to Security

The UK food system is a major force in how humans manage ecosystems, public health, social relations, consumption and the economy. Historically, much that has been done has improved life quality for our species but now the damage and distortions are severe – so severe that we should not and must not continue to run the food system as we are. UK food is a bundle of paradoxes. It is a major employer and has been seen as a post-1945 success story, yet contributes to premature death and disease. UK food and diet used to be an international joke, but now its supply chains are respected worldwide for being super-efficient, delivering more food to the previously badly fed British, and taking a declining proportion of household expenditure, thus liberating spending to fuel consumption elsewhere – clothes, houses, cars, holidays. In towns, cities and villages across the UK, food has been transformed, yet everywhere big brands dominate sales, and huge chains control outlets and high streets. While British cuisine and restaurants have ramped up their standards and respect, too much of the mass food on offer is sweet, fatty, salty and ultra-processed.

This mix of success and problems does not fit industry's and government's narrative that it's all one big success story.

Severe problems are upon us and many are deepening. Some challenges are acknowledged while others are not. Collectively the paradoxes are weakly addressed. Charting future policy requires us to accept both faces of the food system; co-existence of success and policy failures is a sign that paradigm change might be upon us. I think it is. It would be absurd to bask in the glories of having more plentiful food if its consequences are lasting damage and change in the environment on which it depends. We cannot simply keep the success and resolve the failures in a benign 'trade-off'. The harsh reality is that current food practices – how we resource, grow, process and consume food – are undermining present let alone future generations' capacity to feed themselves decently, healthily and in a way which not only protects but positively enhances the natural world on which we all depend. A cycle of demand for apparently cheap food is warping the interplay between UK food culture and the food economy. Mutually reinforcing pressures stop the right thing from happening. The smooth running of the food system is fraying.

Part Two provides an overview of what I see as the UK's 'food problems', and gives the evidence for why I think they matter, and how they interconnect. It proposes that these problems are beyond a state of normal wear and tear, and cannot be dumped back onto consumers to resolve; the framework needs major overhaul and reorientation. Parts of the food system have such deep fissures that they even show some portents of implosion – the runaway rise of food poverty, for example, drags people on low incomes into poor diets which then add burdens to an over-burdened NHS. Biodiversity, too, is in serious trouble – here, not just in suitably distant foreign parts which allow us to ignore it or leave it to our TV screens. And our food supply systems are so finely tuned that it takes little to disrupt them, should anyone wish to. In this part of the book, I provide an outline of what I see these food problems as being. Others – a Royal Commission such as I recommended at the end of Part One – might conceivably draw up a different list. But I doubt it. What I summarize now is well evidenced but too rarely drawn together.

If ignored, these food problems will continue to narrow future chances of the UK being a good-food society. By this, I do not mean eating posh food every day; far from it. I mean decency every day. All people being healthily and sustainably fed without dumping problems elsewhere. Many of the food problems in the following pages are by no means only the UK's lot. Other countries exhibit some of them too. But if we want to become a more food-secure society, we must make our food system fit for purpose. We cannot shed responsibility onto 'the other' – be that blaming foreigners, or Europe, or consumers, or Parliament. We must see Britain's food problems as our share of global collective problems. That said, the UK does have some which are peculiarly British: the naïvety of assuming food somehow arrives in shops, the romantic ignorance about primary food production (despite efforts by the media or farm organizations to educate the public), the class nature of food, the legacy of Empire, the contradictory demand for cheapness, as though that is the most important value to impose on food, despite its meaning we pay more later, too.

Whereas Part One suggested that UK food supply chains are more fragile and insecure than most British consumers might think, Part Two summarizes the breadth and weight of pressures on the food system now emerging from environmental damage, ill-health, social inequalities, distorted consumption, undervalued food work, and underrecognized complexity of land use. The argument I propose here is that the UK's food security problem suffers a double burden: chronically weak supply and alarming levels of ecosystems and societal damage, and fraying or absent capacity. The political task, therefore, is to unpick the mutually reinforcing dynamics which stop us from putting the UK food system – from production to consumption – onto the right footing for the rest of the twenty-first century. While calamitous climate change looms, failure to address it is a symptom of other food problems and, notably, a failure of governance. The UK currently lacks the mechanisms with which to get a grip on our food problems.

The following pages summarize the kind of evidence which specialists have been presenting for years. Barely a month or week goes by without a huge report or new scientific overview being published on health or economic or environmental threats associated with food. Often these are couched in global terms which can leave the UK feeling untouched, blithely thinking that these are problems in Africa or the Middle East and don't affect us. This 'anywhere but not here' default thinking is out of date. The UK food system is a major player in the web of food systems relations which drive this combination of factors and outcomes. Our food companies source raw commodities, not least from former colonies. The UK takes 40% of world cocoa for chocolate, for example. It may not be pleasant, but we must recognize that the UK food system contributes to environmental damage, is feeding people so amply that we are a fat and unhealthy nation, is draining health budgets to a point of crisis, is distorting culture by permitting marketing messages which insult health requirements, and is further dividing an already divided society and enforcing regional disparities. Our food economy is our largest employer, with 3.9 million workers, but is squeezing too many of them. Price signals reinforce unhealthy dietary patterns, burdening the NHS, wrecking our lives. As supply chains have lengthened, the market share of big British as well as foreign food firms has enlarged. A pretty ruthless internal struggle is being waged here, not just internationally, over market share, wages and jobs. We cannot say that this has nothing to do with us.

While some problems do receive ample hearing, others do not. There may now be regular reports about threats to the global ecosystem but there are few on the power accrual through 'big data', or the vice-like grip that Britain's social inequalities have over life expectancy. I have tried in the following pages, therefore, to give a measured overview of where I think our structural problems lie.

The problem of food governance

This nexus of food problems must be faced, not bit by bit, tweaking a little bit here and a little bit there, applying a fashionable 'nudge' or 'trade-off' here or there, but taken as a whole and changed extensively, constructively but decisively in the next two decades. If we do not do this, the UK will fail to meet goals our government has signed up to for 2030–50 – zero emissions on climate change,[1] and the UN Sustainable Development Goals, most of which require food change.[2] Whether we act slowly and gradually or, as some scientists now argue, speedily and more radically to address accelerating climate change or economic disruption, we have to recognize that our food problems are linked, in a pattern, in a combination of lock-ins. To see food's water impact as nothing to do with consumption patterns, for example, would be to miss the point. The draining of East Anglian aquifers to irrigate crops which are then wasted is nigh criminal. Yet we do this. To do so while destroying biodiversity is to turn spring silent – no insects or bees, no pollinators, no birds. To judge UK food as good if it is simply cheap while watching mounting type-2 diabetes drug costs or other NHS costs is to restrict our potential to put things right. To see the answer to rising food poverty as providing more food banks is to miss the point. Sticking plasters do not resolve the cause of wounds.

The food problems discussed below are not just problems in themselves. They cannot be understood unless we recognize how they connect. And we are unlikely to resolve them unless we get a grip on food governance generally. The cross-cutting nature of the food problems summarized in the following pages is what we actually have to address if we want to provide lasting food security. We need to recognize the systemic nature of the food challenge, by which I mean the entire web of resources, ideas, biological and physical entities, decisions and finance which permeate food as it travels from primary production to end consumer.

Conflicting appeals made by single-issue lobbies, each arguing that its problem is a top priority, actually contribute to a politics in which UK food problems can be cherry-picked, marginalized and sometimes incorporated but watered down. We will not make UK food secure for the twenty-first

century unless we address how these food problems inter-
act and lock into each other. The difficulties outlined in Part
Two are what I suggest the UK as a society must address simultaneously. As ever, there is good news here. The UK is not a
totalitarian state. Problems do get voiced – some more than
others. But *how* do we manage them, and *how* do we distil
them? For the last three decades, UK public policy has instilled a quasi-market bidding system for addressing problems. Equally pressing ones are championed by equally good
projects and entire funding streams to compete against each
other. HM Treasury or research councils act as gatekeepers,
reducing everything to value-for-money and downplaying the
actual values embedded in choices. Some food problems are
ignored, others tackled too little, too lightly and with excessive reliance on market mechanisms which seemingly cannot
realign production, consumption and impacts. The net effect
is that the big picture is lost, an irony in this supposed era
of big data when transparency rules. Indeed, as is explored
later, big data illustrates the problem; it is a vehicle for power
concentration not just information access or democracy.

The crisis of food governance in the UK is that problems
are normalized rather than prevented. Policy processes are
not helped by lack of political leadership where it should be
integrated, in the Cabinet and Cabinet Office, to meet overall national goals. A Cabinet Office sub-committee on food
was created in 2008, as this failing was realized, only to be
abolished in 2010. Over the decades when the food problems
outlined below began to emerge, from the 1980s on, they were
dealt with partially. Governments quietly vacated the overall policy driving seat, and left it to negotiations at the EU

continental level, and also to business when, powerful though it is in parts, business cannot sort out this systemic mess. (The EU also only has partial powers.) UK engagement kicked in mostly in times of crisis – BSE, food poisoning – or when forced by EU pressure, as over the environment. Three parallel tracks of food governance now compete for policy space: state, commercial and even some shaped by civil society organizations acting as corporates or setting standards for business. The result is lack of overall direction, messy or absent co-ordination, and an arm's-length political culture. That this is often rationalized as being to the advantage of consumers compounds the difficulties. When things go wrong, a blame game is set in train. The system is fine, we have the wrong consumers. Then when we consider how consumers operate, it is little wonder patterns of consumption are as they are. Price signals, the ubiquity of value-added over-processed foods, town planning favouring car use (which adds to climate change and obesity) rather than bikes and walking (which 'burn' food as fuel), the immediate food environment, advertising and cultural signals, plus human desire can easily combine to unravel good intentions. The possibility of a rapid move to a rational sustainable food system is thwarted by unnecessary lock-ins.

No food analysts think the twenty-first-century food challenge is simple. Instead of coherence and consistency, the world of food policy suffers from cacophony: multiple voices all saying, 'Me, me, ours, ours', from diverse strands of food governance, let alone the public. No wonder the common good is dissipated. Ambition is weakened. Ministers prefer to 'leave it to Tesco et al.' In the last decade, that default position turned into 'Business Leadership Councils', in the case of agri-food technology, and a 'Sector Council', for the entire food and drink industries. No wonder few public targets are set and the lowest form of policy intervention – labels – is often the most we get. The old Roman maxim *caveat emptor* ('buyer beware') no longer provides appropriate advice because it assumes consumers possess full information. It also subtly puts the onus on the consumer, implying that the food system is fine, if only consumers would do the right thing.

Against this sober analysis, I repeat, we must not lose sight of improvements too. British awareness of and interest in food has blossomed in the last half-century. Things are not all bad. British tastes have altered. British food is not all brown any more. Some colour and pleasure through food has come into British culinary culture. There has been a rise of food-related environmental and health consciousness. The previously conservative and faddy British now dip into food tastes from around the world. All this is widely celebrated. There is much to build on. Yet the policy lock-in to low-level or slow action remains when the data suggest that a 'Great Food Transformation' (to use the EAT–*Lancet* Commission's phrase) is sorely needed.[3]

Part Two thus explores why making the UK food system more sustainable is not just a good, indeed the only, way ahead, but it is also the answer to some – not all – of the food (in)security problems and risks raised in Part One. And in Part Three I sketch what needs to be done.

Our Food Problems: Recognizing the Lock-in

The term 'locked-in syndrome' is used in the medical literature to describe an extreme but paradoxical state of consciousness in which the patient is awake and conscious but
has lost his or her power of speech and bodily controls, remaining comatose and as though in a vegetative state when
not being so.[1] First diagnosed in 1966 and refined in the
1980s, the locked-in state is extraordinary and still challenges physicians.[2,3]

Policy analysts use the term 'lock-in' to describe how social
forces and decisions can reinforce a lack of change or com-
pound failure. So here, the term 'lock-in' is used in that looser
metaphorical way. The earth and the UK have never been in
the situation they now are, where how the food system operates is a significant threat to the ecosystem's future and
humanity's within that. Many people, policymakers, consumers, companies and civil-society organizations, recognize
this. Calls are made, partial actions are taken, but the food
system continues to exert damage. Despite good intentions,
and some useful steps, the broad picture is still sobering. A
carbon reduction or fat shift here is counteracted by growth
elsewhere; a low-fat product adds a niche in the market, while

calories pour out overall. The pursuit of health is too easily commoditized as merely this or that product or range.

There are understandable reasons for the policy lock-ins. The food system is Britain's largest employer and these jobs depend on what harms society and the environment. It makes huge amounts of money and represents huge investment. It is subject to squeeze on multiple fronts yet wastes immense amounts of food. It is a dynamic system, constantly changing, but the drivers of change are in conflict. We should eat less but better, yet the food system pours out ever more food, and not everyone over-eats anyway. Food poverty and under- or malconsumption have been normalized again, differently to the 1930s, but shockingly nonetheless.

A web of fundamental conflicts and contradictions such as these is hard to untangle, let alone redirect. It is why some analysts privately think only crisis will allow the conditions for suitable scale of change. The problem is that the crisis would itself be of terrible consequence. My judgement is that signs of cracks are apparent already. We know enough to begin a radical but reasoned policy realignment.

Part Two summarizes twelve food problems where the lock-in must change (and Part Three gives pointers as to how and by whom), if we are to make the UK food system sustainable and thereby more secure. Some argue that Brexit is the opportunity for progress; others that it is a deviation. Whatever ultimate form Brexit takes, Britain's food problems are clear and need to be addressed. We might think of the UK as an island (or many islands) but we are affected by events – climate, resource use, behaviour – beyond us. What we do affects others and they us. The pages which follow inevitably move between the global, continental, national and local levels. I begin with the thorny issue of money, before going on to food's impact on the environment, and then farm size, the labour process, consumption, health, culture, inequalities, power in the food economy, the role of science and education, and who controls data. But, first, let me give a short clarification of what is meant by this now ubiquitous word 'sustainability'.

What is meant by 'sustainability'?

Sustainability is one of those words, like 'community' or 'family', which can mean very different things.[4] It tends to be used in three way: first, as a synonym for the environment; secondly, to denote continuity and survival (as in business or organizational sustainability); and, thirdly, the broad alignment of people and planet. The most common use of sustainability in relation to food is the first: sustainable food is a code for the environment. Thus, we find in the scientific literature a distinction being made between a healthy diet and a sustainable diet.[5,6] In the 1980s, the word 'sustainable' was used with a broader meaning. Sustainable development was defined by the 1987 Brundtland Report as about addressing the overlap of societal, economic and environmental issues.[7] Those three headings are fine but very general. If we are to address food policy lock-ins, we need a more nuanced understanding without drowning in complexity.[8] The complexity needs to be ordered, which is why policy analysts now use more detailed 'multi-criteria' approaches. The Brundtland trio and the business 'triple bottom line' which translated it both need to be amended.[9] Changing the food system affects

ECONOMY
Food security and resilience;
Affordability (price);
Efficiency; True competition
and fair returns;
Jobs and decent
working conditions;
Fully internalized costs.

HEALTH
Safety; Nutrition;
Equal access;
Availability;
Social status/
affordability;
Information and
education.

SOCIAL VALUES
Pleasure;
Identity;
Animal welfare;
Equality
and justice; Trust;
Choice; Skills
(citizenship).

SUSTAINABLE FOOD

GOVERNANCE
Science and
technology evidence
base; Transparency;
Democratic accountability;
Ethical values (fairness);
International aid and
development.

ENVIRONMENT
Climate change;
Energy use;
Water; Land use;
Soil; Biodiversity;
Waste reduction.

QUALITY
Taste;
Seasonality;
Cosmetic appeal;
Fresh
(where possible);
Authenticity.

Figure 4.1

A multi-criteria approach to food system sustainability

Source: After Mason and Lang, *Sustainable Diets*[10]; and Sustainable Development
Commission. Looking forward, looking back: sustainability and UK food policy
2000–2011. London: Sustainable Development Commission, 2011.

culture, governance, politics and people's understanding of quality, not just the intersection of economy, society and environment. I have argued elsewhere that one way to capture the complexity of sustainability for food is to group policy concerns under six broad headings: food quality, socio-cultural values, health, environment, economy and governance (see Figure 4.1).[10] This multi-criteria understanding of food sustainability lies behind how I describe the twelve food problems in the following pages.

Food problem 1: The money flows send the wrong signals

Time and again, when discussing the rights and wrongs of the UK food system (and Europe's and the world's too), the fundamental unfairness of food's financial flows emerges. We cannot expect better land or sea management if primary producers continue to be squeezed and lack funds to help them do the right thing. Almost all the money made out of food flows immediately away from the land and sea, its sources (see pp. 72–81). This is not just a problem of long supply chains in which everyone takes their cut, but a fundamental problem of power and maldistribution.

A straightforward, and stark, example is a cup of coffee. If a customer pays £2.50 in a café, according to a *Financial Times* estimate, 10p (4%) is for the coffee itself. Of that, just 1p (0.4%) goes to the grower far away. 18p (7.2%) goes on the cup, stirrers and napkins. The good news is that the café staff receive 63p (25.2%) but even so remain in a low-paid sector, while the largest share is accrued by the café's property owner, as 88p (35.2%) goes on the rent.[11] Figure 4.2 gives the breakdown.

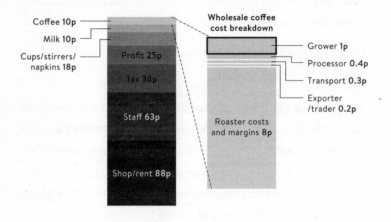

Figure 4.2
Where the money goes from a £2.50 cup of coffee
Source: Bruce-Lockhart and Terazono, 'From bean to cup'.[11]

Another simple example is bananas, which are Britain's favourite fruit. These are almost always today the plantation monocropped Cavendish variety *Musa cavendishii* – so called because it was first grown not in the tropics but at the Duke of Devonshire's Chatsworth House in 1830. This variety now accounts for 99% of all traded bananas but is only one of a thousand varieties available worldwide. This monocropping puts banana production at risk of disease. It also narrows their nutritional value.[12,13] Banana Link, the excellent small NGO which monitors this trade from Norwich, calculates that of the price a British consumer pays for a conventional banana from Costa Rica the workers receive 11%, growers (landowner farmers) 22%, exporters 14% and shippers 21%, the EU tariff takes 10%, and the UK importer/ripener and retailer receive the final 22%. If this was a Fairtrade banana from Colombia, however, the returns would be tweaked by the workers receiving a welcome 7% more, and the retailers about 2% less.[14]

In 2015, the National Farmers Union ran a campaign alleging that UK dairy farmers were being pushed to sell milk below cost. The Agriculture & Horticulture Development Board (AHDB), a statutory body, estimated that farmers were being paid 23.66p for a litre of milk when the full cost of production was 30p, yet retailers were cutting the selling price of a two-pint milk carton from 85 to 75p, blaming price competition. Prices paid to dairy farmers fluctuate, but mostly across 2013–19 AHDB figures show they have been well below 30p per litre. This situation is ruinous, and drives dairy farmers out of business. One could argue that this is the market working, albeit ruthlessly, to the consumers' advantage. But how far can this go? When one supermarket chain in 2015 introduced a 'For Farmers' own-brand range of milk guaranteeing that an extra 23p per four-litre plastic carton would go to the dairy farmer, by default it appeared to accept this criticism. Although that range has continued, it emerged that the extra payment mostly went to the farm co-operative rather than direct to the primary farmer.[15]

Price wars and fights over where the money goes are hard enough to track for single products like milk or bananas or coffee, but very much harder for processed products containing many ingredients and compiled from many suppliers. Supply chains can be long. A study by the Centre for Food Policy found even for a simple processed product such as bread, commercial actors in the chain contributing to the production of bread did not really know what others were supplying them with.[16] And just look at the list of ingredients on many packaged processed foods. Although in tiny writing (barely legible to some), the list goes on for line after line, often with ingredients one has never heard of. Product recipes are commercially confidential as brands fight it out.

One thing analysts agree on, however, is that the gate-keeping power of supermarkets in this flood of products is immense.[17] Actual cashflows within food supply chains are hard to ascertain as there are tens of thousands of food products making up the UK food market. And the majority of these are processed, not fresh and simple like our milk or banana examples; coffee is actually surprisingly highly processed. The truth is only the retailers have a good understanding of where the money goes in a high-value-added ready meal made up of multiple ingredients, and even they might not. If we want a fair food system rewarding people to produce sustainable food from the land and making better, more sustainable use of resources to feed the UK well, we need the money flow to be more transparent.

Food is big business. In 2018, UK consumers spent £225.7bn buying it. £97bn of this is spent with caterers, while retailing takes £128.7bn. Of the food systems' £125bn gross value added (GVA) within that quarter of a billion, catering has the highest GVA, with an estimated £36.4bn GVA, while retailing's GVA is £30.3bn and food processing's is £31.1bn. Farming and primary production's GVA is a third of this, at £10.3bn, but even that is princely compared to fishing at just under £1bn. (We are advised to eat more fish but it turns out we don't want to pay for it.) The harsh reality is that primary production, for all its necessity, is at the wrong end of the value chain.

No wonder, as was shown in Part One, that the viability of UK farming is dependent on subsidies, which currently contribute about one third of its income. New Zealand's farm subsidy by contrast is about 1%, after it axed almost all farm support in 1984.[18] As an EU member, UK farm subsidies have been set by membership of the Common Agricultural Policy (CAP) and are to be phased down in 2026, under plans prepared for after Brexit. Many NGOs back a shift of subsidy from supporting food production to being for ecosystems management, in line with the thinking of Michael Gove, when Secretary of State for Environment, Food and Rural Affairs.[19] The impact of a drop in subsidies would be immense, with 75% of English farmers seeing cuts in profitability of 22–67% by 2027, according to a 2019 Strutt and

Parker study.[20] What on earth is going on if primary production is so reliant on subsidy to keep afloat, let alone that profitability is so tight that viability of the majority is threatened by loss of taxpayer support? The price system is unjust. Either prices need to rise, and more of the money to be returned to those currently squeezed, or the length of the value chain needs to be shortened or short-circuited to cut sectors out. Consumers could also of course just do more cooking from raw ingredients, thus cutting costs by donating free labour.

At stake is the UK's 'cheap food' culture, discussed in Part One. A long-term reorientation is long overdue, but unlikely to be delivered, if current thinking remains. The emphasis is on the advantage of and right to low-priced food, from wherever it is drawn. The wider UK economy, meanwhile, has been distorted by property values which either exclude millions of people from owning housing or drives them to pay high rents. Expensive housing squeezes disposable income and thus maintains the desire for cheap food. At the same time, food prices ought to rise to give fair rates of return to producers while delivering good-quality diets to prevent ill-health. None of this is happening, as the Food, Farming and Countryside Commission's two-year inquiry showed.[21,22] There is a disconnect between what farmers do, their financial returns and food's public-health role. Diet-related ill-health adds enormous externalized costs onto what, to the consumer, is 'cheap' food. And the NHS is tacitly forced to accept the normality of poor diet which now globally kills more citizens than smoking.[23,24] The public sector carries the can for distortions in the private sector which are themselves shaped by inappropriate public support. One couldn't make it up!

Different calculations of the externalized costs of food all point to huge sums. One study estimated that the total societal cost of obesity – just one of food's externalized costs – was £47bn in the UK in 2011, a figure second only to smoking.[25] That includes lost productivity. The NHS itself accepts that the cost of obesity to the NHS in 2014–15 was £6.5bn, with a further one to society of £27bn. The UK-wide direct costs of overweight and obesity to the NHS are projected to reach £9.7 billion by 2050, with wider ones to society estimated to reach £49.9bn per year.[26] A 2012 study by the London School of Economics concluded that the total cost of diabetes (types 1 and 2) was £13.75bn.[27] Then there are the terrible 'human costs', loss of loved ones, family dislocation, etc. While type 1 is hard to resolve, with susceptibility inherited, type 2 is preventable. And if we turn to effects on the environment, similar vast externalized costs to the UK food economy are calculated, whether from water pollution, soil loss, CO_2 emissions or biodiversity loss.[28] As with health, why are such costs being normalized?

While farming as a whole is being squeezed – with a majority kept afloat by subsidies – some farmers are doing well enough, due to size, or simply through ownership of valuable capital assets. They can be asset-rich but with comparatively low rates of return on capital employed. A later section looks at the issues of farm size and ownership, but, meanwhile, the problem raised here is the failure to get fair returns from the vast sums spent by consumers back down food chains to primary producers. The 'fair trade' movement began in the 1970s to do just this for commodities such as tea, coffee, sugar or bananas.[29,30] It had some success but on a tiny scale compared to what is now needed. Routinely, extraction flows the other way. There is no full disclosure of where the consumer's money goes. Imagine a supermarket display which told you where the money went. In fact, consumers have little idea. Competition policy barely scratches the surface of the problem. The Groceries Code Adjudicator scheme was set up in 2013 by the Coalition government to inject some fairness into intra-chain relations, and focused as its title indicates on the power of retailers.[31] It offers primary producers an independent office to ensure, if not total fairness, at least protection from being squashed by naked power.

How can we judge when a price is fair or true? There is a difference. Fairness is a social judgement. True cost is about whether the price fully reflects the costs which have actually been incurred in creating a product or getting it to the consumer. This is of great interest to environmental and health economists, who conduct many such studies. Most show that prices do not actually cover real costs. But then what? One argument is for taxation to help prices become more realistic; another is for consumers voluntarily to pay more, or for a benign authority (perhaps government) to 'nudge' processors to improve and reform their pricing. The taxation of soft drinks and sugar to alter consumer behaviour, for example, is intended to do this and can work. Faced with a sugar tax – even if they have lobbied hard to prevent it – soft-drink manufacturers do seem to lower the amount of sugar used, or to drop below a threshold at which the tax kicks in. In the battles which rage over such fiscal measures, consumer awareness tends to rise. Some studies suggest significant drops in intake,[32] but it is unclear whether this changes 'sweet tooth' norms in the long term, if added sugars are simply replaced by artificial sweeteners, thus keeping the product tasting sweet.

Intervention can be anathema to mainstream economists. Somehow food economics must be unlocked from the present combination of effects, which include unfair money flows and high externalized costs. Price signals need to align more fully with health and the environment. Good food produced by decently remunerated primary producers should be our goal and is essential to rebuilding UK food security. Price setting should certainly not be left out of the policymakers' armoury.

Food problem 2: Food damages the environment on which it depends

In 1992, 1,800 scientists signed a joint paper warning the world that it needed to address environmental trends which were going in the wrong direction.[33] The biosphere – all the ecosystems on which human and planetary life depends – was under stress. They urged a reduction in greenhouse gas emissions, the phasing out of fossil fuels, a reduction of deforestation and a reversal of biodiversity loss. Twenty-five years later, another generation of scientists reviewed the data on ecosystems across half a century (1960–2016) and published a 'second warning', signed by over 1,570 scientists.[34]

The good news was that ozone depleters which had been rising have been brought under control, but water availability, marine catch, dead zones, forests, species counts, CO_2 emissions, temperature, and human and animal population growth were all going in the wrong direction towards more, not less, stress. The authors implored policymakers to cut greenhouse gas (GHG) emissions, phase out fossil fuel use, reduce and reverse deforestation, reverse the trend of collapsing biodiversity, halt the decline in fish stocks and reverse 'dead zones' in the sea. Those all require changes to transform the food system. The problem is that we have become used to these sober global analyses.

A high-profile example is the sea that surrounds the UK. The fishing industry has a particular emotive appeal in British politics. Over long periods, our seas have been polluted and marine environments have been heavily damaged. Fish stocks dropped and quotas on catches had to be imposed to protect them. The number of fishing boats allowed to fish was reduced. This has not stopped tensions between fisherfolk, governments and policymakers, one moment over the folly of throwing away fish disallowed in quotas, the next moment about the structure of the EU Common Fisheries Policy (CFP). What underlies all this is a failure to realign the relationship between ecology, finance, work and food.

What shapes this state of affairs? The biggest impact on fish stocks, arguably, remains over-fishing and the destruction of stocks. This has not been helped by the sheer scale of fishing technology – the huge equipment, the massive trawlers and decline of small-scale line fishing. An investigation by Greenpeace in 2018 found that over two thirds of the UK's fishing quota is controlled by just twenty-five businesses and that four fifths of the English fishing quota is held by foreign owners or domestic Rich List families.[35] The five largest quota-holders control more than a third of all UK fishing quotas. One trawler, the *Voyager*, based in Northern Ireland, accounts for more than half of Northern Ireland's fishing. Small fishing boats working near UK shores are 77% of the total fishing fleet but have 'less than 4% of the quota'. Business concentration, in other words, is part of the policy lock-in. UK governments have done too little to rebalance this misalignment of power, policy, food supply and work, and have been happy to blame Brussels.

LAND USE AND AVAILABILITY: ALL CHANGE

'Land – not technology – is the real capital of civilization. Ultimately, everything comes out of it, and everything goes back into it,' wrote Victor Bonham-Carter in his gloomy 1971 look at the English countryside.[36] Today, we can agree that land is much more than a source of capital. Although economists keep trying to capture just what it is by labelling almost everything 'capital' – natural capital, social capital, human capital, finance capital, etc. – it is worth remembering just how important land is. It is a country's carbon and water sink; landscape provides meaning and culture; it is highly political, not least over ownership and access; and it is also the source of most food. Today it is under harsh human-made pressures, and a battleground of competing interests.

To feed growing populations, we now know that humanity must not continue to bare soil or chop down woods or drain deep aquifers, justifying this by the need for more food. To expand agricultural land use globally is counter-productive.[37,38] This applies to the UK, too. As we saw in Part One, the UK too easily slips into using other countries' land to feed itself. Yet everywhere the scientific advice is to eat within ecosystem and planetary boundaries. That means reducing rather than expanding our food footprint. This means we must take our land use more seriously. Let us consider how UK land is currently used.

The UK has 18.835 million hectares (mha) of total agricultural land.[39] Within that, 17.468 mha are actually used for agriculture, 72% of the total UK land mass. And within that 4.745 mha are cropped: 3.181 mha to cereals, 0.590 mha to oilseeds, 0.145 mha to potatoes, 0.661 mha to other crops, and 0.168 mha to horticulture. Woodland accounts for 1.037 mha. But grassland dwarfs all those uses, covering 10.138 mha, over half of our landmass. It is why the UK looks green from the air (except in droughts), and it is historically why there is so much animal production in the UK, about which there is now such a significant debate. We are using a lot of our arable land for grain to feed animals.

UK land use has changed ceaselessly over centuries, shaped by ownership, demands for food, population changes, threats of invasion and wars, and, in recent centuries, food production techniques. Woods and forests have been felled and converted into pasture or arable; today the UK is only 13% wooded, low by European standards. The medieval system of open and strip fields has been changed into enclosed fields; and even larger fields saw hedges and copses bulldozed to enable large machinery to operate in the second half of the twentieth century. Since Roman times, 90% of the wetlands in Britain have been lost but most have been lost since the Industrial Revolution.[40]

In the last millennium, animal husbandry changed from pastoralism (roaming animals) and hunting to rotation farming within farm boundaries (after the enclosures) and latterly intensive indoor or feedlot systems.[41] Vast metal sheds pepper the landscape in which farmers store animals and their food. And different crops, plants, varieties, processes and animals have all helped constantly alter the UK landscape, as a result. Huge investment has been poured into the land, draining and rationalizing fields, and replacing human labour with machines and chemicals.

Over the last 250 years, agricultural revolutions have accelerated UK land use change faster and more extensively than ever before. Earlier times also had their moments of massive change, of course. The Black Death wiped out whole villages; wars led to forests being chopped down to build ships; the Protestant revolution led to the sell-off or annexation of the huge landholdings by monasteries. But the changes since the late-eighteenth-century industrial revolution dwarf these, not least in the effect of population growth on how much land is used to feed people. The biologist Lynn Margulis and her son, Dorion Sagan, memorably once estimated that a Palaeolithic diet was derived from using about 1,000 hectares per person (hunter-gathering), which Neolithic use of tools later cut down to around 10 ha, and medieval times refined to about 0.67 ha, while modern intensive rice production could mostly feed each person on about 0.064 ha.[42] UK land cannot grow rice and our cropping potential is subject to shorter seasons and a northern climate, but the point about productivity progress is clear. More people can be, and have been, fed from less land over time, and with economic and technical advance. So today, if the UK does not try or want to increase home production, the only other route is simply to colonize land elsewhere, either directly or via trade. This is what the UK once did – getting its Empire to feed it.[43] Without an Empire and trade-dependent, as we saw in Part One, the UK again needs to review its land use, and now faces a choice again: grow more, taking up more land away from non-food functions, or import more to maintain current dietary trends with all their consequences, or alter diet to reduce land use to within environmental limits while rationalizing crop and animal production. In simple terms, this is the food versus non-food land use question.

Using the European Environmental Agency's detailed land-mapping Corine system, Prof. Alistair Rae of Sheffield University identified thirty-four different current uses of UK land. In descending scale, they start with pasture (28.7%), non-irrigated arable land (27%), peat bogs (9.4%), moors and heathland (7.5%), down to airports (0.2%), saltmarsh (0.19%), and further down to a long list of tiny usage such as permanently irrigated lands and vineyards (both 0.0001%).[44]

The Committee on Climate Change has presented a simpler set of seven broad uses (see Figure 4.3).[45] Grassland (for animals) is the largest (31%), then cropland (26%), rough grazing also for animals (17%), forestry (13%), urban and developed land (8%), freshwater (1%) and other natural uses (4%). We should remember that urban and developed land is often on what was prime good-quality land, because it is where towns and villages could feed themselves and prosper. Many towns have spread out over their surrounding fields, often (but not always) fertile because towns were often sited for proximity to food production. Food transportation on a mass-bulk scale is a relatively recent phenomenon. It used to be restricted to, most notably, the spice trade, which is centuries old, but

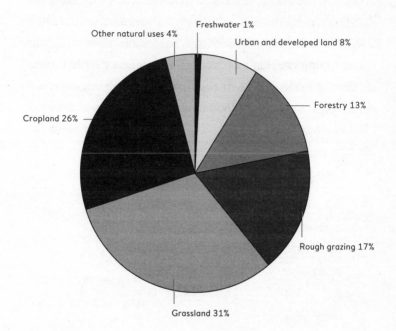

Figure 4.3

Current use of all land in the UK

Source: CCC. Land use: Reducing emissions and preparing for climate change. London: Committee on Climate Change, 2018.

spices are relatively light, could be stored in enormous quantities in a ship, and were expensive.

CARBON AND GHGS FROM THE FOOD SYSTEM

The CCC's statutory interest in land use lies in seeking greenhouse gas reductions. It calculates that agricultural land emits 11% of all UK GHGs, 53 mt of CO_2 equivalents ($MtCO_2e$). The CCC recognizes that a key to future significant reductions is to adopt healthier diets, thus siding clearly with one approach to the food versus non-food land use question posed above. This would prevent GHGs in the first place. An estimated 35–80 $MtCO_2e$ could be saved as follows:

- 4–11 $MtCO_2e$ by restoring peatlands;
- 8–18 $MtCO_2e$ by increased woodland and hedgerow planting;
- about 9 $MtCO_2e$ by better soil and livestock management;
- 2 $MtCO_2e$ by planting bio-energy crops;
- 20–50 $MtCO_2e$ by reducing food waste.

The British public, industry and politicians should be under no illusions about the urgency of the need to address the food and climate change connection. Rich coastal and river plain food-growing areas will be under threat – floods are already more likely, the Environment Agency has warned.[46] Every year, the news tells us of 'unprecedented' floods, but slowly it is being realized we need to rewood uplands, slow down rivers, move horticulture higher up, and rethink food land use with climate in mind. Progress is slow.

While the food system remains stubbornly resistant to

change, UK energy consumption has been changing remarkably. As we saw in Part One, the UK food system relies on energy such as oil to fuel the lorries which truck food across the country. As a primary source of energy, coal is in decline but still present as imported rather than UK coal. While home energy use has risen slowly, that for transport has risen rapidly. Consumers as well as businesses are heavy energy users and thus emitters whether travelling to work, shop or go on holiday. In 2017, the UK transport sector accounted for 34% of all carbon dioxide emissions.[48]

The 2017 UK Climate Change Risk Assessment said we can expect significant risks from climate change to public health, flooding, water supply, biodiversity, soil, and right across the gamut of domestic and international infrastructure for food production and trade.[49] It anticipates new diseases affecting both plants and humans. Yet the government puts an official gloss on the state of UK emissions, saying they have declined in 1990–2016.[50] This is largely due to shifts away from high-emission-energy generation and by not including 'embedded' energy, which is when the energy used to make something before it comes to the UK – a car, plastic toys, clothes, food – has been used in another country not the UK. Objects have hidden energy embedded in them, but even though they are consumed and purchased in the UK, they count as other countries' GHGs. Some caution is needed when reading that UK agriculture's GHGs have declined in 1990–2016 by 16%; more food imports means emissions in our name occur elsewhere. A recent global study estimated that food accounts for 26% of all world GHGs.[51] Agriculture is no longer the whole picture. Of food's 26%, animal products account for 58% and other

How much impact does food have?
Proportion of total greenhouse gas emissions from food

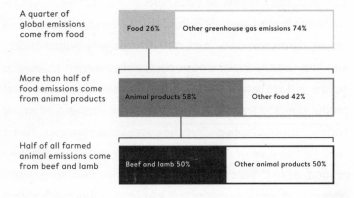

A quarter of
global emissions
come from food

More than half of
food emissions come
from animal products

Half of all farmed
animal emissions come
from beef and lamb

Food 26%   Other greenhouse gas emissions 74%

Animal products 58%   Other food 42%

Beef and lamb 50%   Other animal products 50%

Figure 4.4

Food's greenhouse gas emissions

Source: Poore and Nemecek, 'Reducing food's environmental impacts'.[51]

food products for 42%. Of the 58% impact of animal products, beef and lamb account for 50%. A UK study estimated that UK food production as a whole accounted for 20% of all UK GHGs.[52] Whether global or national, studies consistently suggest that GHGs would come down considerably simply by eating a healthier diet, such as the UK government's Eatwell Plate. Dutch scientists, for example, found that if the UK and other high-income Europeans simply ate the nationally designated healthy diet, their GHGs would fall by a startling 17%.[53]

The Food Climate Research Network (FCRN) summarizes the overall picture as food accounting for 20–30% of GHGs, with agriculture contributing the largest share of this, and within that livestock having the biggest impact. It also rightly notes that 'protected horticulture' (energy-guzzling greenhouses) can have high GHGs, as can some forms of transport, packaging, preparation and storage.

NITROGEN AND PHOSPHORUS

Nitrogen is an essential ingredient of life and makes plants grow. The nitrogen cycle is one of the fundamental planetary processes.* The world has pumped out ever more

---

* A good summary of the nitrogen cycle is given in the House of Commons Environmental Audit Committee's 2018 'Reducing Nitrate Pollution' report: 'The nitrogen cycle is the biochemical cycle by which nitrogen is converted into its multiple forms as it circulates among the atmospheric, terrestrial and marine ecosystems. There are two main forms of nitrogen – organic and inorganic. Organic nitrogen is found in proteins and is continually recycled by plants and animals, including tens to hundreds of thousands of compounds that make up dissolved organic nitrogen and dissolved particulate nitrogen. Inorganic nitrogen occurs as nitrogen (N_2) nitrate (NO_3-), nitrite (NO_2-), ammonia (NH_3+) and ammonium (NH_4+).'

nitrogen since the Haber–Bosch process was invented in the early twentieth century. This made possible the fixing of nitrogen for use as farm fertilizer,[54] and has been key in the remarkable rise in food production ever since. For its development, Fritz Haber received the Nobel Prize for Chemistry in 1918 and Carl Bosch the same in 1931. This 'artificial' nitrogen, however, has become a pollutant as used by modern food and farming systems, causing waterways to malfunction and contributing significantly to global warming. Nitrogen in fuels and the air combine to produce nitrogen oxides, NO and NO_2 (jointly known as NOx).

A 2016 global study showed how agricultural practices, livestock production and nitrogen fertilizer use have a direct impact on near-surface air quality, the air we breathe. This is particularly troubling if such farming occurs near densely populated areas.[55] Aerosols formed from gases released by fertilizer application and animal husbandry have been found to have a bigger effect than all other 'human-made' pollution.

A 2018 report from the joint UK governments' Air Quality Expert Group (AQEG) summarized how fertilizer use, farm machinery and livestock waste emit a range of pollutant gases, particularly nitrogen compounds (NO_2, NO, NH_3, N_2O) to the atmosphere.[56] It was already known that cattle emit 55% of ammonia (NH_3).[57] The AQEG accepted that fertilizer impacts have been under-acknowledged in the past as a contributor to nitrogen oxides, despite contributing an estimated 80% of N_2O emissions, and that is before GHGs from the production processes are included. The nitrogen cycle is one of the planet's fundamental mechanisms, and now known to be massively exceeding planetary boundaries.[58,59]

The global use of 150 mt per year is overwhelming the atmosphere's capacity to stay in balance. A stabilizing level of use would be only 62 mt a year.[60] Worldwide agricultural use has been estimated as about 100 mt per year, with only 17% ending up in food.[61]

This is disruption on a vast scale, so vast that it appears to be defying policymakers' capacity to address it. The House of Commons Environmental Audit Committee (EAC), for example, has described over-use of nitrate fertilizers as a nitrate 'time-bomb'. Back in 2006 Lord (Nicholas) Stern's report on climate change for the UK Treasury noted that nitrogen fertilizers were the largest source of GHGs from agriculture (38%),[62] yet use has not been heavily constrained, other than for appeals to use them more effectively. These appear not to be effective, as UK farming accounts for the highest number of infringements of EU regulations designed to stop excess nitrogen either seeping into groundwater or running off into rivers and the sea.[63] Leaving the EU does not escape the problem. To make matters worse, UK agriculture operates on an imbalance not just for nitrogen but also phosphorus, another planetary cycle key to plant growth. It is not alone in this.[64]

The UK is thus in an almost ludicrous situation where farming has been over-using two inputs – as it was encouraged to do – resulting in environmental distortion which water companies then have to pay to try to take out or compensate for by blending in water from different sources. Professor Johnes of Bristol University told the EAC in 2018 that the cost of fertilizer use in UK lowland farming is of the order of £10,000–£20,000 per km^2.[65] This is thoughtless economics as well as ecosystems damage. It shows how what happens in one sector of the environment or society does not necessarily stay there. It spills over into other sectors. A technocratic response is to see this as resolvable by so-called precision agriculture: more careful application of chemical sprays. It is technically smarter, to be sure, but still missing the ecological point. Intensive food production disrupts the very ecosystems dynamics on which we depend.

WATER

The further west one travels in Britain, the wetter the weather, hence the broad rule for food production that the east grows crops and the west grows animals. This historical division is likely to be disrupted by water stress. Floods and droughts are becoming more common. The old east–west assumption needs to be rethought. Water has not been taken seriously enough by the British. We joke that it rains a lot in the UK. In fact, we import huge amounts of other countries' water in the form of food, while our own water systems are in part also becoming stressed. Globally, water stress is recognized to be worsening. In 2018, the UN's World Water Development Report estimated 5 billion people could suffer water shortages by 2050 due to climate change, increased demand and polluted supplies.[66]

The UK National Infrastructure Commission (NIC) has been sufficiently concerned about water to include it in its Resilience Study (due to report by 2020).[67] The immediate cause for NIC's water concerns is that the 'country' (does it mean water bill-paying public?) looks set to have to pay £40bn a year for emergency water supplies unless something is done to prevent supply problems. NIC's focus is on stemming the considerable leakage of water from pipes and drains. That this problem has been raised for decades is certainly true, but it also misses a trick by focusing on pipes, not food.

In the nineteenth century, water infrastructure was engineered mostly by private companies at a municipal level, but these were reorganized into public utilities on public-health grounds. A century later, in 1989, these public Water Boards were privatized in England and Wales. The argument (as with privatization of the railways) was that this would unleash investment and efficiency savings, and put financial incentives in the driving seat. In fact, the newly private companies were immediately made to invest massively in improving their water quality controls. There had been years of rising concern about agrichemical residues and wastewater pollution. A new infrastructure of inspectorates, agencies and audits was created, too. It all looked promising.

More than two decades since privatization, waste of water continues on a massive scale.[68] Pipes still leak. The House of Commons' Environment, Food and Rural Affairs (EFRA) Committee reports that 3 billion litres of water are lost through leakage every day. An average of 9.3 m^3 seeps out of pipes every kilometre the water travels per day.[69] Analysts agree that cutting water waste and redesigning supplies – possibly transferring water between water companies – is needed but this says little about consumption. The EFRA Committee took the water companies' view that compulsory metering of households would help companies monitor leakages. Others disagree, and point to the 'financialization' of water – money being made from this basic need and natural resource by trade deals, debt swaps being sold to foreign investors. Welsh Water is the sole UK company not to be part of this capitalization market. It was technically privatized but, due to long-term political sensitivities about England asset-stripping Welsh water, a different corporate structure was allowed in Wales, with Welsh Water being a private company but a 'single-purpose' one without shareholders. The Welsh are right to retain room for the public interest through ownership. About three quarters of English water companies are now foreign-owned, the profits flowing elsewhere.

In its first report on the state of water resources in England, the Environment Agency warned in 2018 of significant water supply problems by 2050, particularly for south-east England. 9,500 billion litres of freshwater were taken from underground water in 2016, enough to cover the whole of Greater London in nearly six metres (20ft) of water. Yet 3 billion litres a day are still lost through leaking pipes – equivalent to the amount of water used by more than 20 million people in an average day. Nearly a third of groundwater resources – the natural wells deep underground – were deemed to be in a poor state.[70] In 2016, the Environment Agency judged that 86% of river water bodies had not reached good ecological status. The main reasons for this were agriculture and rural land management, the water industry, and urban and transport pressures.[71]

The good news is that pollutant loads to rivers from water industry discharges have declined in recent years, with reductions of up to 70% since 1995; this is actually the result of strong EU legislation and UK governments having been embarrassed into action. But still the Environment Agency notes that water quality issues were the cause of 38% of all fish test failures, and 61% of invertebrate test failures in rivers in 2015. The level of 'serious water pollution incidents' from water companies has remained broadly the same, about sixty incidents each year, more than one a week. For assessed river water bodies in England, 55% were at less than good status for phosphorus in 2016, and nearly half of groundwater bodies will not reach good chemical status by 2021. For groundwaters protected for drinking water, nitrate levels were responsible for 65% of failures to achieve good chemical status. This is hardly a ringing endorsement. No wonder the World Wildlife Fund (WWF), the conservation NGO, has estimated that a third of UK farmers are not complying with water protection laws.[72] Part of the problem is that enforcement has dropped (cuts in agencies), whereas a mere £10m would bring inspection and enforcement up to scratch, a tiny sum.

If water supply is not in a good place, what about the use of water in primary food production? Travelling around East Anglia, one sees vast pumping systems, jetting water over crops. This ecologically inefficient water use is extremely costly. Technocrats rightly argue that smaller droplets near each plant would be more effective but would be costly to re-engineer (all those plastic pipes). The elephant in the policy room is the UK importation of 'embedded water', or what Prof. Tony Allan of SOAS and King's College London called 'virtual' water.[73,74] This embedded water is the water which has gone into food products, such as when growing fruit and vegetables. If this is from countries which are much more water-deficient than the UK, it is a kind of water 'imperialism' and likely to become more politically sensitive over time.

Tim Hess and Chloe Sutcliffe at Cranfield University in

the Research Councils' Global Food Security programme applied a standard water scarcity index approach to the UK, based on estimates of water use in and to the UK. They concluded that 13.5 billion kilos of fresh fruit and vegetables are supplied to the UK each year, equivalent to 211 kg/capita/year. When the UK imports 90% of its fruit and 50% of vegetables (excluding potatoes), it is actually importing products which used 560 million cubic metres of freshwater per year in these products, 74% of which is withdrawn overseas from countries that themselves have water vulnerabilities.[75] Such exposure has increased over time by 36% in 1996–2015 as the British switched the kind of fruits they ate to ones which cannot be grown here such as avocados, citrus fruits and mangoes, and switched where they came from, mostly Spain. Taking just one example, avocado consumption, Hess and Sutcliffe calculated that the water consumption associated with the UK's avocado intake from just five countries was 25 million cubic metres – 'equivalent to 10,000 Olympic-sized swimming pools'.[76] This hidden trade in embedded water underlines the prescience of Prof. Tony Allan in arguing years ago that this virtual water trade is inadequately acknowledged or compensated for.[77,78] Thus the UK might like to think of itself as awash with water, while actually accelerating stress elsewhere. Figure 4.5 shows how UK food imports draw hidden water from countries which experience water stress for more than a few months in the year. They include India (water-stressed for nine months), South Africa (ten months), Mexico (5.8 months), and Turkey (3.5 months).[79]

We are not alone in having these water responsibilities through food. The European Commission's Joint Research

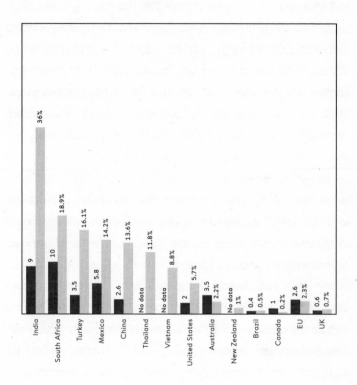

Figure 4.5

Water stress in non-EU countries exporting food to the UK

■ Number of months of water scarcity per year

░ Water use in agriculture as % of total renewable water

Source: Elliott and Tipper. Protecting standards in UK food and farming.[79]
Reproduced by permission of Green Alliance.

Centre conducted a comprehensive study of the water foot-prints of the diets of three rich Western European countries, the UK, France and Germany, taking account of regional and local variations. The researchers analysed 43,786 differ-ent geographical entities. They found that the average British diet used 2,757 litres per person a day. The German average was 2,929 litres a day and the French 3,861 litres a day. The French being highest was due to wine consumption; grape production has a high embedded-water use. But these three European countries used only a third of what the average US person consumes, more than 9,000 litres a day.[80]

There were important sub-national differences. Rural areas have higher diet-related water footprints than cities. Diets in French wine-growing regions, for example, averaged around 5,000 litres per person a day. And because London eats on average less red meat, its dietary water footprint was lower than Yorkshire's or Lincolnshire's. The researchers analysed 43,786 different geographical entities and found a consistent trend was for the water footprint to decrease, the closer to a healthy diet the regions consumed, although eating less meat generally reduced the water footprint by 35%. Larger reductions were found for a healthy pescatarian (fish not animal) diet (an estimated 33–55% reduction) and healthy vegetarian diet (a 35–55% reduction). That healthy pescatarian and vegetarian diets were roughly similar in water footprints perhaps shows the effect of irrigation.* But the general picture was clear – healthier diets use less water.

---

* Even sea-caught fish are then washed, gutted and processed. Aquacultured fish can have higher water use if freshwater-reared.

As they concluded: 'shifting to a healthy diet is not only good for human health, but also substantially reduces consumption of water resources, consistently for all geographical entities throughout the three countries.'[81]

Almost certainly, in the future, the UK will have to audit food choices for its water use. Trying to weigh up what water stress is, and how to measure and pay for it, is complicated.[82] But consumers quickly grasp the concept and varieties of embedded water in food. The calculations by the UNESCO–IHE Institute for Water Education in the Netherlands are already an invaluable database, but the UK ought to begin such calculations of our consumption. Curry, for example, is one of the UK's favourite meals, and rice sales in 2017 were worth £0.4bn. The UK grows no rice yet consumption has risen from just over 20 g per person in 1970 to nearly 100 g in 2018. There are eleven rice mills in the UK, polishing, sorting and bagging rice imported from India, Pakistan, Thailand, Cambodia, USA, Italy and Spain.[83] EU-produced rice (mostly risotto-type) comes from Italy, Spain and Greece. Water use in rice growing varies across these countries and by type, but average production of a kilogram of milled rice (white/polished rice) involves evaporation of about 1,444 litres of water (680 green and 764 blue – see p. 232), pollutes 131 litres of freshwater, loses 1,098 litres of water in the field as a result of percolation and unused soil moisture and uses 575 litres of irrigation plus 523 litres of augmented water in the field. So the total 'water footprint' of 1 kg of milled rice is a staggering 2,672 litres![84] This is before cooking.

UNESCO–IHE has also shown the form in which the EU imports water as rice and from where (Figure 4.6). Most 'blue'

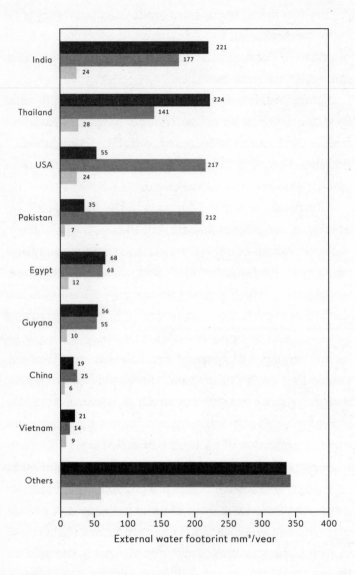

External water footprint mm³/year

■ Green-water footprint
■ Blue-water footprint
■ Grey-water footprint

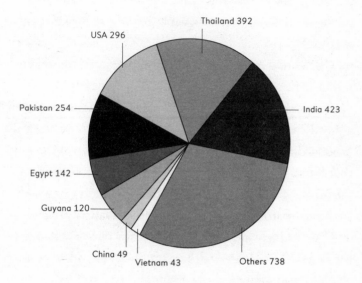

Figure 4.6

The external water footprint of rice consumption in the EU27 in 2000–2004

Source: Chapagain and Hoekstra. The green, blue and grey water footprint of rice.[84]

water is from the USA and Pakistan, but most 'green' water is from India and Thailand. Green water is the rainwater which falls onto crop fields and is absorbed by the plant. Blue water is water from rivers, lakes and groundwater abstracted to enable crops to grow and is either evaporated (e.g. in irrigation) or taken into the plant. Grey water is water used to dilute any pollutants caused while growing the plant to original levels.

Calculating embedded water casts an interesting and different light on many dietary choices. For example, a study of the water footprint of soy milk and a soy burger and their equivalent animal products found that one litre of soy milk produced in Belgium had a water footprint of 297 litres, and that for a 150 g soy burger produced in the Netherlands was 158 litres. 62% of the soy milk's total water footprint was due to the water in the actual soybean rather than its processing, and 74% of the water footprint for a soy burger was due to the soybean. Compared to these products, the global average water footprint for a 150 g beefburger was 2,350 litres and the water footprint of one litre of cow's milk was 1,050 litres.[85] The water footprint of organic beef and milk was lower, the researchers found. This kind of meticulous work will begin to guide consumption and land use.

Finally, on water, the policy failures implied above are compounded by the distortion of how Britain now drinks water. In a relatively short period, the UK took to drinking bottled water. This is a completely unnecessary use of plastics, but a huge market. In 2017–18, UK bottled-water sales were £243.5m for still water (duplicating tap water!), £134.3m for flavoured still water (often simply a subtle sweetening),

£107.7m for flavoured sparkling, and £73m for plain sparkling. Three quarters of British households buy bottled water, according to Kantar Worldpanel, but there have been signs of 'shoppers moving away from plastic' after Sir David Attenborough's 2017 BBC *Blue Planet 2* exposé of plastic pollution in the seas.[86] If it became fashionable to drink bottled water, it can become fashionable to change again. The argument that tap water is more environmentally sustainable may be clear, yet UK bottled water sales rose each year in 2013–18.[87] This ought to reverse.

SOIL

It has been said that soil is the basis of civilization and the most complex system on earth.[88] If so, Britain has been undermining its civilization. For years, soil scientists have been showing UK soils are under stress from farming practice and changing land use. A recent review found the situation problematic,[89] citing that one third of all UK soils are thought to be degraded, with just over a third of all UK arable land judged to be at risk of erosion; the total estimated organic carbon loss from the soil in England and Wales each year is 5.3 mt, or on average 0.6% of the existing soil carbon content; peat is still being removed for horticultural use faster than it can replace naturally, despite peat being known to be an important carbon sink; and farm land is still being built on, tripling from 5,200 ha a year in the 2000s to 15,800 ha in 2013–17, undermining food-growing capacity. This is all worrying.

A more welcome thought, however, is that UK soils remain a remarkable resource, albeit being weakened. They store around 10 billion tonnes of carbon or the equivalent of seventy years of annual UK greenhouse gas emissions. This must not be degraded further. Indeed, the damage must be reversed by regenerating soil and by proper recycling of nutrients on ecological public-health principles.

Phosphorus has been raised earlier. It is a key input into UK farming to raise productivity, and British soils have had a surplus, although that has been declining.[90] Its use as a fertilizer is much criticized by environmentalists.[91] It is also wasted by the UK's water-based sewerage system. Nineteenth-century engineers canalized streams and rivers as conduits to remove human effluent from houses and to wash it out of sight, mostly to sea. The environment was the dump; the nutrients once consumed and excreted were lost. Historically in many cultures 'night soil' used to be collected as a valuable resource, but such recycling was made obsolete by the water closet. Using human excreta may seem retrograde but global harvesting of human urine and faeces could replace almost a quarter of current phosphorus use in agriculture.[92] The challenge is how to do this safely on a mass scale. This is the kind of problem which should be posed to and by the National Infrastructure Commission if only it took food security more seriously. It should also be on the agenda of the National Security Strategy since mined phosphates come from parts of the world with tense politics, such as the Western Sahara, occupied by Morocco since 1975 and subject to a guerrilla war.[93]

Meanwhile, the Committee on Climate Change reported in 2015 that the UK has lost 84% of its fertile topsoil since 1850, with the erosion continuing at a rate of 1–3 cm a year. In 'financialized' terms, soil degradation costs for England and Wales have been estimated by a team at Cranfield University as between £0.9bn and £1.4bn per year, mainly linked to loss of organic content of soils (47% of total cost), compaction (39%) and erosion (12%).[94,95]

The Commons Environmental Audit Committee reports that approximately 300,000 ha of UK soil are thought to be contaminated with toxic elements – such as cadmium, arsenic and lead – as a result of the UK's industrial past. Defra short-sightedly withdrew capital grant funding for local authorities to clean up this contamination.[96] The Parliamentary Office for Science and Technology (POST) has estimated that the cost of damaged soil could be broken down as nearly £600m on greenhouse gas emissions, around £240m on agricultural and productivity losses, £233m on flooding, and well over £100m on water quality; these are annual costs.[97]

The Sustainable Soils Alliance, a coalition of farm organizations, cites English farmers as losing a valuable 235,000 tonnes of nitrogen and 8,391 tonnes of phosphorus every year by pollution which could otherwise be retained within agricultural systems.[98] When Sheffield University scientists looked at soil health on English allotments in comparison to soil on farmland, they found soil in much better condition in the small-scale allotments than on farmland, estimating that at the current rate of loss, the farmland would only be likely to yield for another century or so.[99] Soils on the allotments had 32% higher soil organic carbon (SOC) concentrations and 36% higher carbon to nitrogen (C:N) ratios than pastures and arable fields, and 25% higher total nitrogen (TN) and 10% lower bulk density (BD) than the arable soils studied. This research suggested for the first time that the care which small-scale growers traditionally lavish on their soils in the form of returned compost and manures 'can occur without the penalty of soil degradation seen in conventional agriculture'.

Defra's own studies have pointed to a coming soil crisis and in 2011 it reported that soil degradation costs were rising. The Soil Strategy for England estimated then that the total cost of soil degradation was £206–£315m per year, probably an underestimate.[100] Seven years later, in the 'Health and Harmony' consultation paper which led to the proposed new Agriculture Act (for post-Brexit Britain), Defra accepted that soils needed proper attention as part of a renewed focus on ecosystems.[101] This was welcome, but that document then ignored food, when the policy schism between food and soil is the problem.

The Intergovernmental Science-Policy Platform on Biodiversity and Ecosystem Services (IPBES) is an independent intergovernmental scientific consortium established by governments in 2012 (with 129 members by 2018), rather like the IPCC. In 2018, it produced a major review suggesting that land degradation now threatened the food security of 3.2 billion people, nearly half humanity.[102] It prophesized that land degradation and climate change are likely to force tens of millions of people to migrate by 2050, and that crop yields will decline by an average of 10% globally, and up to 50% in certain regions. The capacity of rangelands to support livestock, for instance, is expected to continue to diminish in the future, due to both land degradation and loss of rangeland area. Biodiversity loss is projected to reach 38–46% by 2050. In its 'middle-of-the-road' scenario, IPBES estimated that biodiversity reduction will be equivalent to a complete loss of the original biodiversity of an area about 1.5 times the size of the USA. With that mid-range scenario, one can imagine the worst-case scenario.

This again emphasizes why the UK must get on the right food policy track itself.

PESTICIDES AND BIODIVERSITY

In 2019, a study of soil samples across the EU found that 82% of agricultural soils producing the main crops in Europe had traces of at least one pesticide. 25% of the samples had one residue but 58% had mixtures of two or more residues, in a total of 166 different pesticide combinations.[103] Agrichemical use has been central to the shift in how UK land is used and the decline of UK biodiversity. The agrichemical industry counters that UK pesticide use has dropped and farming has responded to growing evidence about intended and unintended consequences of heavy pesticide use. This is not the whole picture.

The Pesticides Action Network UK (PAN–UK) is the NGO which monitors agrichemical use and impact. It points to four aspects of change.[104] Firstly, the *toxicity of pesticides* has increased, allowing a drop in quantity. Some neonicotinoid insecticides, for example, are up to 10,000 times more toxic than DDT; DDT was phased out and 'neonics' phased in. Secondly, the *area of land sprayed* with pesticides has risen (see Table 4.1). Thirdly, the *number of times crops are treated* with pesticides has gone up. And, fourthly, the *variety of pesticides* being used on particular crops has increased. No wonder a large international science task force concluded that pesticide use has been excessive and damaging.[105]

The EU has fewer permitted pesticides than does the USA, which has nearly three times more 'active substances' that can be legally used than does the EU (about 1,430 vs 486).[106,107] This is a reflection of different regulatory regimes and thinking. The

	Area treated ha 1990	Area treated ha 2000	Area treated ha 2016	% increase in area treated from 1990 to 2016
All pesticides	44,981,520	59,063,553	73,172,193	+63%
Fungicides	21,471,678	27,298,559	36,369,847	+69%
Herbicides	14,438,110	20,287,443	23,099,598	+60%
Insecticides	5,926,245	5,084,694	5,126,906	−13%

Table 4.1
Increases in area treated (shown by type of pesticide)
Source: PAN-UK. Hidden rise of UK pesticide use.[104]

EU applies a 'do no harm' approach, whereas the US tends to be more permissive, then reviews studies on effects.

As lands were cleared for cultivation over the centuries, and rapidly in the last century across the globe, few thought about biodiversity loss or its long-term impact on climate change.[108] To be against industry was retrograde, the preserve of rural romantics or 'dog and stick' farming. The future was said to lie in the agricultural intensification we now know has polluted soil, seas and air. Run-offs of fertilizers and hormones (and other pharmaceuticals) end up in the sea, affecting fish, which we then eat,[109] and which are also in decline. What to do about biodiversity and food is one of the most pressing food problems. Warnings about declining biological diversity were voiced by specialists decades ago and did lead the UN to adopt the Convention on Biological Diversity (CBD) in 1992.[110] This has been followed up by regular Conferences of the Parties (COPs) at which new agreements and targets are set, based on the latest evidence. In 2010, at a meeting at Aichi, Japan, new Biodiversity Targets were agreed.[111]

For the UK, the Joint Nature Conservation Committee (JNCC), covering all four countries of the UK, provides detailed and regularly updated overviews of the state of UK biodiversity.[112] These reports are the UK's contribution to meeting the Aichi Biodiversity Targets. The first in 2013 showed progress on getting organized.[113] The picture in July 2018 was mixed.[114] Improvements had been made on some aspects, such as animal management, but not on others, such as invasive species in freshwater and rivers. The sixth report, in 2019, acknowledged that the UK had missed fifteen of nineteen targets.[115] These are mostly 'process' targets such as reducing distorting subsidies, controlling invasive species and increasing conservation management of marine eco-systems rather than specific goals for particular species.

The picture given by the civil-society experts is a sober one. The UK is 'one of the most nature-depleted nations on earth' according to the global rankings reported in the *State of Nature* report, produced by fifty UK nature conservation bodies, co-ordinated by the Royal Society for the Protection of Birds (RSPB).[116] The UK was ranked 189th on the Biodiversity Intactness Index. 15% of the 8,000 species on the international 'red list' are threatened with extinction in the UK. Although some species are increasing and others are declining, a great extinction seems to be underway here not just abroad, and intensive farming is a main driver. Farmers have been encouraged to intensify, unleashing the armoury of chemical controls – pesticides and fungicides – while increasing output by using artificial fertilizers. The result has been water and land pollution (which then has to be paid for in the 'clean-up') in return for higher yields. No wonder bird species are affected, whether seasonal transients or all-year-round UK inhabitants. Drawing on forty years of data and the monitoring conducted by Britain's remarkable and knowledgeable specialists, the 2016 report concluded: 'The intensification of agriculture has had the biggest impact on wildlife, and this has been overwhelmingly negative. Over the period of our study (c. 40 years), farming has changed dramatically, with new technologies boosting yields often at the expense of nature.'[117]

The *State of Nature* report did not explore those dynamics but showed some of the consequences. The index of change in the abundance and occupancy of farmland species has declined by 20% over the long term, and by 8% over the short term. Farmland birds have gone down in numbers by 54% since 1970, and butterflies by 41% since 1976. Bats have increased by 23% since 1999. 137 out of 1,118 farmland species (12%) are threatened with extinction from Great Britain.

Defra accepts that England's farmland and woodland bird populations have dropped by 70% in 1970–2016, and by 9% between 2010 and 2015.[118] For seabirds and wetland birds, the figures are more static. Figure 4.7 gives the half-century trends. According to the British Trust for Ornithology, the status of farmland and woodland birds is poor due to habitat destruction and pesticide use destroying the insects and 'pests' which birds live off. The status of pollinating insects is terrible. We are not yet at the point where humans will have to be employed to pollinate fruit and flowers, as is happening in some polluted parts of the world, but this possibility should not be dismissed, though who would do it is uncertain. Why not leave it to insects in the first place?

With such data, no wonder conservation NGOs such as the RSPB and the Wildfowl and Wetlands Trust (WWT) say we should treat land differently, and, from within farming, groups such as LEAF (launched in 1991) and the Nature Friendly Farming Network (launched in 2018 at the Oxford Real Farming Conference, set up to counter the establishment Oxford Farming Conference) have emerged.[119] Even the Common Agricultural Policy began serious funding from the 1990s through increasingly valuable grant schemes. But the total realignment of food production, ecosystems and human health is not happening fast enough.

In 2014, only 8% of UK land was designated as Sites of

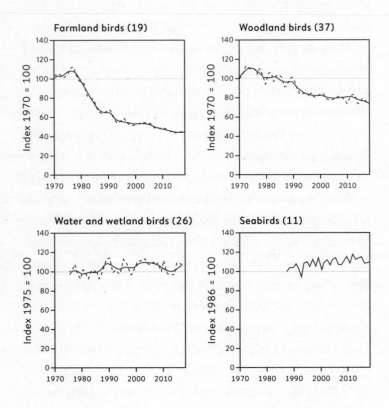

Figure 4.7
Population of wild birds in England by habitat, 1970–2017
Source: Defra. Wild bird populations 1970–2017.[118]

Special Scientific Interest. This has risen. In 2018, 28 million hectares were given protected status for biodiversty.[120] The rise of nature-oriented sites has been mostly marine, either estuaries or offshore. These are covered by the so-called Blue-Belt scheme, applying protection to marine areas around the UK and its Overseas Territories.[121] In 2019, the UK had 355 marine protected areas. This is a step in the right direction, not least for protecting fish stocks. A similar approach to land use is sorely needed, since 75% of UK land is farmed in one way or other. The designation of only some land as of special value for biodiversity tacitly ushers in acceptance that the rest of the land has little role in biodiversity.

The future of food security requires nature to be protected by food production as well, not despite it. Food production should integrate biodiversity into how it is managed, not assume token edges on the field will suffice. Arguments for wilding and rewilding are powerful,[122,123] but they tend to ignore food production, and could frame UK food security as a new (perhaps hidden) form of imperialism – 'We keep the view, and look after nature, while you feed us.'

With regard to biodiversity, there is a strong argument for eating it. A broad variety of species is positively associated with health.[124,125] It makes sense to build dietary adequacy by maximizing biodiversity in the field, not just at its edge or in 'wild' parks. The UK or Canada have low indigenous plant biodiversity compared to, say, Brazil; their diversity has expanded due to trade and plant hunters over the last five centuries. In effect, the UK relies about 90% on crops originating from other parts of the world.[126] Membership of 'nature' bodies such as the RSPB, the British Trust for

Ornithology, WWT and the National Trust are huge but the public finds the food–biodiversity connection hard to translate. A long-term study of attitudes in the EU found only just over 30% of people in 2017 said they were aware of what biodiversity is. Just under 30% had heard of it, but did not know what it is. Nearly 40% had never heard of it. The study found knowledge in 2017 had declined since 2013.[127] The UK public is more aware of climate change than biodiversity, Defra's long-term attitude tracker suggests. In 2011, only 18% of the UK public felt they knew a lot or a fair amount about biodiversity, and another 30% reported they knew a little.[128] Eurobarometer, however, found evidence of quietly growing public awareness in 2007–13, but it is seen as 'out there' rather than in what goes into mouths.[129] On one issue in recent years, the connection is coming to the fore: plastics.

PLASTICS

It is difficult for consumers not to realize the food–plastics connection because it is hard to avoid buying food without plastic wrapping. The UK packaging industry is huge, worth £11bn a year, more than farm output. Everything, not just food, is wrapped in plastic. UK supermarkets have been estimated to account for 1 mt of plastic use annually.[130] An estimated 8 mt of plastic go into the sea every year. In the UK only a third is recycled.[131] A 'moral panic' may have ensued after the BBC's *Blue Planet 2* sequence illustrating just a tiny part of the widespread dreadful impact of plastics on sealife, but some of this public concern is turned into PR froth. Cutting out plastic straws is a tiny contribution to halting the avalanche of plastic used by the food system; a gesture, yes, but of slight impact unless it leads into systemic change. To eradicate plastic would require a revolution in supply chains. Substituting wrapping made from plants (e.g. potato starch) still reflects a particular land use. More important is probably the exposé that the UK has played a charade with consumers for years over recycling, encouraging us to recycle but then mostly simply shipping the result to the Far East; out of sight, out of mind.

The lock-in became apparent when, in 2017, China stopped accepting plastic waste. The UK could no longer send the 2.7 mt of plastic waste it had sent in 2012–17 to China and Hong Kong, supposedly two thirds of its total plastic waste.[132] Instead of backing up in the UK, the waste was diverted elsewhere. In 2018, 15,000 tonnes went to Turkey, 4,000 tonnes to Indonesia, 3,500 tonnes to Hong Kong, and so on. The UK government's overall policy response has been to eliminate 'avoidable plastic' (whatever that is) by 2042. Critics rightly say this is ridiculously far ahead. Iceland, the UK frozen-food supermarket chain, committed in 2018 to phase out plastic use in its own-label products within five years. Fifty UK food and drink businesses, responsible for an estimated 80% of plastic use in UK food, have now committed with the waste consultancy WRAP to 'slash' use by 2025.[133] Meanwhile, some defenders of plastics argue that no one is overtly making the case for how good plastics are and have been for the food industry and that their elimination will simply generate more spoiled food and waste.

In 2018, the Great Pacific Garbage Patch in the middle of the Pacific was estimated to be between 45,000 and 129,000 tonnes of ocean plastic floating inside an area of 1.6 million square kilometres, a figure 4–16 times higher than previously reported.[134] This new plastic floating continent accumulates via five circular sea currents around the globe. Technological optimists hope to develop technologies to corral this loose plastic into scoops which then could remove the plastic, perhaps by 2040, but, meanwhile, large plastic would continue to break down into microplastics. Again, we must ask: why keep putting it into the sea – and air and land – in the first place? The sad answer is that the entire food system, as the whole consumer economy, depends on plastic.

The scale of the problem is immense, a symbol of the Anthropocene. If we humans die off, the plastic residues of our culture will remain everywhere, and food has been one of its central drivers. A global review published in late 2017 estimated:[135]

- 8.3 mt of plastics have been used since the 1950s.
- Of this 6.3 mt has become waste, migrated into the environment.
- Of this 6.3 mt, roughly 9% had been recycled and 12% incinerated, and 79% was accumulated in landfills or just out there in the natural environment.
- If current production and waste management trends continue, roughly 12,000 mt of plastic waste will be in landfills or in the natural environment by 2050.

According to the UN Environment Programme, the world's oceans now contain an estimated 51 trillion microplastic particles, broken down tiny bits from the various forms of plastic waste, and 80% of the litter in the seas is estimated to be plastic. The brilliance of the discovery of plastic as a clean and easy-to-use material has turned out to be short-lived.

99% of seabirds eat plastic one way or another. Plastic adversely affects at least 800 species of birds, marine mammals and turtles.[136]

Microplastics are now found in many fish. A 2018 study by scientists at Hull and Brunel Universities found them in mussels round UK shores, more in 'wild' mussels from Edinburgh, Filey, Hastings, Brighton, Plymouth, Cardiff and Wallasey than in farmed mussels.[137] In the words of one author, Prof. Jeanette Rotchell: 'It is becoming increasingly evident that global contamination of the marine environment by microplastic is impacting wildlife and its entry into the food chain is providing a pathway for the waste that we dispose of to be returned to us through our diet.'[138] The biggest impact on fish stocks, arguably, remains over-fishing and the destruction of stocks by the sheer scale of fishing technology, with its massive equipment and giant trawlers, accelerating the decline of small-scale fishing.

A 2018 report by the Environmental Investigation Agency for Greenpeace UK says that the grocery retail sector is the largest user of plastic packaging, accounting for over half of the 1.5 mt of consumer plastic packaging used in retail every year. Notional recycling, encouraged by the EU-designed logo, is low. The top ten UK supermarkets use more than 810,000 tonnes of single-use plastic on the market every year but had recycling rates for consumer plastic packaging of only 30–34%.[139] Over 1.1 billion single-use bags and 1.2 billion produce bags for fruit and vegetables are used. Only four of the ten offered reusables, but all began to act after the BBC's *Blue Planet 2* TV series. The 5p charge for plastic shopping bags was gradually introduced across the UK – led by a 5p charge per bag introduced in Wales in 2011 (but nine years after Bangladesh banned them). This reduced use by 80% by 2019. Welcome though this is, the UK was shamed into it by China.

The obvious answer to plastics is to phase them out. The problem is that plastics are cheap, easy to use and light. Longer-lasting or recyclable materials such as glass, tin, aluminium, paper or cardboard are energy-intensive, and require whole new industries to be scaled up if they are to replace plastic. The ideal principles for waste management are to reduce, replace, reuse and recycle. Faced by the combination of campaigns, public concern and fear of blame, parts of the food industry have been embarrassed into action. Globally twenty-five transnational corporations created the Alliance to End Plastic Waste; its strapline is 'We're all in this together.'[140]

One possibility is to return to the past: people bring containers to the store. If you want to buy a coffee 'on the go', think ahead and take your own reusable cup with you everywhere. This implies a cultural reversal; it also raises issues of hygiene. Who is responsible if there is contamination? But experimentation has begun. In 2018, a pop-up plastic-free shop called the 'Refill Larder' opened as a temporary two-year pop-up shop in Clapham, London.[141] It reprised 1970s anti-packaging movements.[142,143] In the Netherlands, a plastic-free aisle was trialled by the Amsterdam branch of the seventy-four-store chain Ekoplaza. It offered products in either 'old' packaging of glass and paper/cardboard or 'new' compostable biodegradable plastics. Cellulose trays can now be biodegradable. Its biodegradable cellulose film costs four times more than ordinary film and, if scaled up, requires massive new infrastructure to deal with the degrading and composting. In 2019, Waitrose trialled some weeks of allowing customers to fill their own containers from larger containers in-store.[144]

Such developments fit into the practical direction of the circular economy, championed by the EU.[145,146] It has been much influenced by the Ellen MacArthur Foundation, which in 2016 proposed that recycling and reusing plastics could itself herald a new plastics economy.[147] To date, there appears to be more investment into reuse and recycling than in phasing out, judging by big-food-company pronouncements.[148] It is good that at last the issue is on the agenda, but whether it is being fundamentally rethought is less certain. However, that is true of many of the issues sketched in this section. The food system's environmental lock-in is deep and hard.

Food problem 3: Farm size and labour lock us into intensification

The UK food system is highly stretched, in that a large number of consumers (66 million) are fed by a relatively small percentage of that total, the nearly 4 million food workers. We will consider the lock-in over food work in more detail later but here let us focus on farm size.

By Australian or North American standards, the average UK farm size is small. By EU standards it is large. Visually, the UK landscape is tens of thousands of often small fields. In fact, field size has grown compared to much of the world, where small plots are the norm. It was long ago recognized that small-scale growers can produce relatively more from a given land space than do larger farmers.[149] The latter may make more money due to their scale of production, but their output can be less in quantity and diversity per acre. A recent large, international study found that small and medium-sized farms (less than 50 ha) produce 51–77% of nearly all commodities and nutrients for which data could be assessed.[150] And the UN Food and Agriculture Organization (FAO) is often cited as judging that small, rather than medium or large, farmers produce three quarters of the world's food. Recent assessments suggest that this is no longer so. Taking the accepted definition of a small producer as one who has 2 ha or less, a Canadian team (highly supportive of small farmers) used new mapping and other data sources from fifty-five countries – so not the whole world – and concluded that farms under 2 ha globally produce 28–31% of total crop production and 30–34% of food supply on 24% of gross agricultural area.[151] A key finding was that small farms use a higher proportion of their land to grow food for direct human consumption than do large ones. While small farms use an interest in feeding their owners directly, bigger farms are inevitably drawn into the agri-industrial complex, producing commodities for processors to add value to. Whether small farms produce the bulk or merely a third of food, it is a lot. In the UK, meanwhile, it is the small farm enterprises which declined throughout the twentieth century. That is why the UK has the largest average holding size of Europe.

UK land ownership has gone from wealth being the ownership of 20 acres (8 ha) in the thirteenth century, to 200 acres (80 ha) not being enough for the average farmer today to make a living.* As we saw in Part One, the process accelerated in the

---

* The issue of ownership and subsidies which keep 'smaller' farmers afloat is addressed later.

Holding size	England		Wales		Scotland		N. Ireland	
	No. of holdings	Size, ha	No. of holdings	Size, ha	No. of holdings	Size, ha	No. of holdings	Size, ha
Under 20 ha	42,000	303,000	19,000	112,000	32,000	159,000	10,000	107,000
20–50 ha	21,000	692,000	6,000	206,000	6,000	188,000	9,000	273,000
50–100 ha	18,000	1,283,000	5,000	347,000	5,000	343,000	4,000	289,000
100+ ha	25,000	6,898,000	5,000	1,022,000	9,000	5,064,000	2,000	350,000
Total	106,000	9,176,000	35,000	1,687,000	51,000	5,754,000	25,000	1,020,000
Av area, ha		87		48		113		41
Av area of holdings of more than 20 ha		139		99		292		62

Table 4.2

Number and size (ha) of holdings in England, Wales, Scotland and N. Ireland, 2017

Source: Defra. Agriculture in the UK 2017.[39]

nineteenth century when the UK opted to import more cheap food from its colonies. The shock of the First World War led to a short-lived policy to rebuild farming, but the land area under cultivation in Britain fell from 12 million acres (49,000 km²) in 1918 to 9 million acres (36,000 km²) in 1926. Farm prices continued to decline and then fell by 34% in the three years after 1929. After another bout of emergency rebuilding of home food production in the Second World War, farm support was put onto a longer-term footing, but the number of actual farms continued to drop.[152] The total number of holdings in England and Wales declined from 296,000 in 1950 to 168,000 by 1980 (a trend well underway before CAP membership). While the number of holdings of 2–20 ha fell from 158,000 to 62,000 in 1980, the number of farms of over 100 ha grew from 18,000 to 24,000. Table 4.2 gives an overview of current size and proportions for England, Wales, Scotland and Northern Ireland. In all countries of the UK, holdings of over 100 ha account for the majority of holdings. Larger farms now dominate, and in England and Scotland the average size is far larger than in Wales or Northern Ireland.

CROPS: PLANTS AND ANIMALS

As we saw earlier (see p. 215), UK land is mostly pasture or used for animals. Of the crops, wheat for bread (and some animal feed) and barley mostly for alcohol dominate. Table 4.3 shows land use, in ha, for the main arable crops. Most, not all, are for direct human use. By comparison, the area down for horticulture is very small (see Table 4.4), a mere 168,000 ha out of the UK's 18.8 mha. If the UK were to eat

Arable crops	Hectares
Wheat	1,792,000
Barley	1,177,000
Oats	161,000
Rye, mixed corn and triticale	52,000
Oilseed rape	562,000
Linseed	26,000
Potatoes	145,000
Sugar beet (not for stockfeeding)	111,000
Peas (for harvesting dry) and field beans	233,000
Maize	197,000
Total	4,456,000

Table 4.3

Arable crops in the UK 2017, ha

Source: Defra. Agriculture in the UK 2017.[39]

Crops	Hectares
Vegetables grown outdoors	117,000
Orchard fruit	24,000
Soft fruit and wine grapes	11,000
Outdoor plants and flowers	13,000
Glasshouse crops	3,000
Total horticultural crops	**168,000**

Table 4.4
Total UK area of horticultural crops 2017, ha
Source: Defra. Agriculture in the UK 2017.[39]

a healthier diet, more plants, this proportion would need to change while staying in line with sustainability criteria.

PEOPLE ON THE LAND

Agriculture is dangerous work. The Health and Safety Executive records farm, forestry and fishing as having the highest rate of fatalities of any industry in the UK in 2018–19, eighteen times the rate of other main industries.[153] In that one year, of the 39 fatalities, nearly half the agricultural workers killed were over 60; 2 young children were also killed; 14 were killed by overturning or moving vehicles, 9 were killed by cattle and 7 falling from heights.

The number of people working on UK land is low by European standards, in part the legacy of the UK not feeding itself except under duress. The farm labour force at 474,000 people is less than an eighth of the entire food chain workforce of nearly 4 million. Table 4.5 shows that less than a half of the land workforce is full-time – 115,000 full-time farmers and 73,000 full-time employees. In 2013 the government abolished the Seasonal Agricultural Worker Scheme (SAWS) despite much opposition. Its argument was that it was not needed since we are members of the EU. Hence the asterisks (*) in the 2017 column for that element of the labour force compared to the one for 2015. Under duress and because of alarm about Brexit cutting off friendly EU labour sources, the government introduced a 'temporary' new SAWS for just 2,500 people in 2019. If this continues, it will seal the end of what little UK horticulture there is.

UK agriculture now faces a conventional productivity problem: whether or how to continue to eradicate labour

			2015	2017
Farmers, business partners, directors and spouses			294,000	294,000
	Full-time		142,000	141,000
	Part-time		152,000	153,000
Regular employees, salaried managers and casual workers			183,000	180,00
	Regular employees		115,000	*
		Full-time	73,000	*
		Part-time	43,000	*
	Seasonal, casual or gang labour		67,000	*
Total labour force including farmers and spouses			477,000	474,000

Table 4.5
Agricultural labour force on commercial holdings, 2017
Source: Defra. Agriculture in the UK 2017.[39]

on the land. It could squeeze it by pitching UK production against distant lands via trade deals flooding markets with cheaper imports, or by increasing output through technology, such as robots (see pp. 402–7). The latter implies more regimentation of cropping and land use, making plants and land management fit the machinery rather than the other way round. But, centrally, the wider issue is of financial returns to farming itself. As we saw earlier, UK farming achieved a mere £8.4bn GVA in 2017 out of the £220bn spent by UK consumers on food and drink, of which the food market was £111bn (6% of national GVA). Everyone except the fishing industry, it seems, makes more money than the farm sector as a whole. This inequality of returns is not in the public interest but is the logic of our current system.

Food problem 4: The production–consumption mismatch

We are not listening to the feedback we are receiving from the environmental and health outcomes of how we produce and consume food. Worse, there is a lock-in to this mismatch.

One of the basic arguments underpinning market economics is that efficiencies follow if informed consumers make choices in the marketplace. This does not fit what we see in food. For decades there has been a stream of information appealing to consumers to eat differently – from NGOs, from scientists and from parts of government. But are UK consumers fully aware of the scale of the problems? I am not sure. This is not wilful resistance but due to complex drivers. They may say, for example, that they are troubled by social, environmental or ethical concerns, but their purchases are actually based on other considerations – what is on sale, offers, prefer-ences. The Food Standards Agency (FSA) conducts a biannual food tracker survey of UK consumer attitudes.[154] According to this, the 2018 top food safety concerns for British consum-ers were: food hygiene when eating out (36%); food poison-ing (30%); chemicals from the environment, such as lead, in food (29%); and food additives (26%). And the top wider food issues of concern were: the amount of sugar in food (52%); food waste (48%); food prices (46%); and animal welfare (43%). (Not plastics, note.)

Like all consumers everywhere, UK consumers' attitudes are many-layered. If they are asked about attitudes to local foods,[155] or to healthy eating,[156] or to animal welfare,[157] or to food waste,[158] or to food miles,[159] or how much they are prepared to pay for public goods, different priorities emerge from when they are asked about everyday purchasing practic-es. This is not surprising. We all have an attitude–behaviour gap. Companies which monitor food sales such as Kantar Worldpanel, which tracks what around 30,000 shoppers actu-ally buy, show we buy on price, familiarity and convenience – what is in the shops we go to. That is not to say our values and attitudes are unimportant or that we are simply all hypo-crites. It is just that our realities are framed by circumstances. I might want food systems to be like X but if they are actually Y, what do I do? Starve the children? No, they/we all continue to buy as we can, juggling practicalities – time, cost, availabil-ity, preference, household tastes, income, etc. Willingness-to-pay studies may be useful to map consumer aspirations but do not necessarily indicate what actually happens.

Food is not the only issue in which an attitude–behaviour

gap exists, to be sure, and equally it would be inaccurate to say that efforts by campaigners to alter and improve consumer behaviour have been wasted. Supermarket shelves carry many products which reflect pressure from campaigners for consumer choice to include environmental and other considerations in what is on offer and how it has been grown or processed – Fairtrade, organic, free-range eggs, for example. Long-term campaigns to alter behaviour can have a drip, drip, drip effect, all the while hoping for a breakthrough moment when an outside event hopefully opens the policy gates, as happened for plastics with the BBC's *Blue Planet 2* TV series, or for obesity from the late 2000s.

There is a problem at the heart of choice culture. Consumer attitudes might be primed to eat in line with what the evidence says we should – for health, the environment, justice – while our circumstances do not yet frame or push us to do so. We are surrounded by and experience competing drivers. Meanwhile the evidence about how different foods have varying environmental effects continues to emerge. Figure 4.8 summarizes the EAT–*Lancet* Commission's calculations of the environmental effects per serving of a range of everyday foods. This shows that whether we look – moving from left to right across the table – at GHGs, land use, energy use, acidification (sulphur dioxide) or eutrophication (excess of minerals leading to run-off into water or soil), the big impacts are from meat, dairy and eggs. There is a range of impacts, of course. How the ruminant meat is produced – to take the top row – can affect how much of an impact it has, but the averages (represented by the bold bullet shape at the centre of the range) are high relative to plant production.

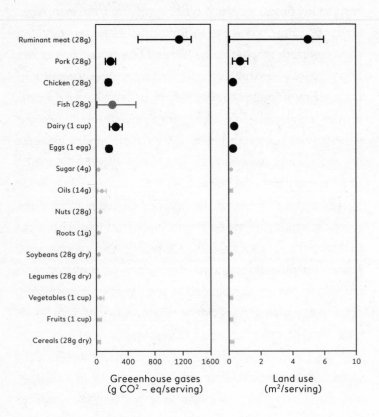

Food group:
- Plant-based foods
- Fish
- Dairy and eggs
- Meat

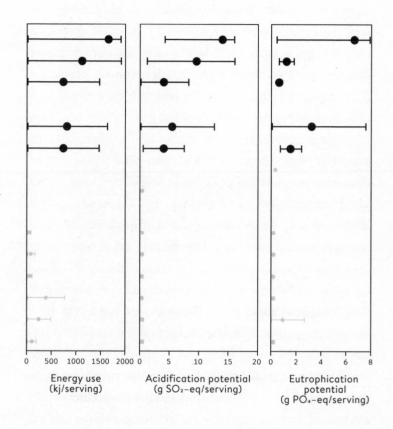

Figure 4.8

Environmental effects per serving of food produced

Source: Willett, Rockström, Loken, et al. Food in the Anthropocene.[5]

A large UK–Swiss study by Joseph Poore and Thomas Nemecek pooled information on the different geographies, practices and environmental impacts of forty major foods, using data from almost 40,000 farms and 1,600 processors, packaging types and retailers.[160] The study was essentially redefining what might be meant by the word 'efficient', distinguishing between high- and low-impact producers. High-impact beef producers, for instance, created 105 kg of CO_2e and used 370 m^2 of land per 100 g of protein, which was 12–50 times greater than low-impact beef producers. Meanwhile low-impact beans, peas and other plant-based proteins can create just 0.3 kg of CO_2e (including all processing, packaging and transport), and use just 1 m^2 of land per 100 g of protein. Simply, foods vary not just in intrinsic effects – meat generally causes more GHGs than plants – but in how they are produced. Figure 4.9 gives the variation within and between food outputs for nine animal and six vegetable products from their sample of about 9,000 farms around the world. Huge variations in GHGs, acidification, eutrophication and land use can be observed by the width and location of the bars representing impacts on the graph. Poore and Nemecek concluded that 'impacts of the lowest-impact animal products typically exceed those of vegetable substitutes, providing new evidence for the importance of dietary change.' In other words, although good agricultural practice can lower impacts, even 'best in class' is not going to reduce the necessity for consumers to eat differently and for land use to change, too.

Figure 4.9

The range of GHGs, acidification, eutrophication and land use for different foods

Source: Poore and Nemecek, 'Reducing food's environmental impacts'.[51]

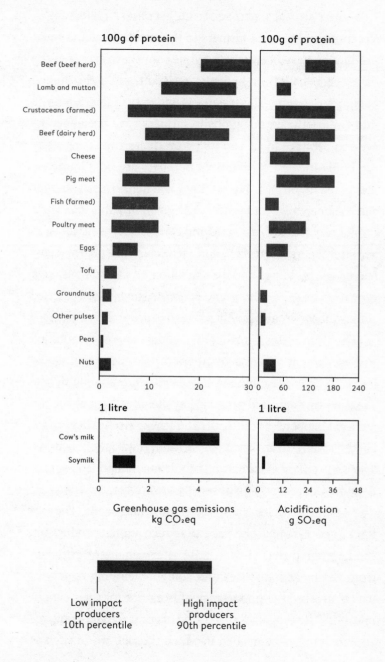

100g of protein

100g of protein

Beef (beef herd)
Lamb and mutton
Crustaceans (farmed)
Beef (dairy herd)
Cheese
Pig meat
Fish (farmed)
Poultry meat
Eggs
Tofu
Groundnuts
Other pulses
Peas
Nuts

0   10   20   30

0 60 120 180 240

1 litre

1 litre

Cow's milk
Soymilk

0   2   4   6

0   12   24   36   48

Greenhouse gas emissions
kg CO₂eq

Acidification
g SO₂eq

Low impact
producers
10th percentile

High impact
producers
90th percentile

TOO MANY ANIMALS, TOO ECOLOGICALLY INEFFICIENT?

Reactions of livestock farmers to the criticisms about meat production have been mixed. While some have accepted the data, others have been in denial, resistant, angry, threatened or simply unhappy. This is entirely understandable. Since the mid-twentieth century, globally, farmers have been encouraged to produce meat and its by-products and to intensify methods. In the UK, livestock numbers are now immense compared to the past. The UK flock and herd sizes in 2017 for cattle, sheep, pigs and poultry are given in Table 4.6. Their output requires not just grass and cereals but resources such as water, energy, fertilizer, agrichemicals, and pharmaceutical drugs, buildings and human labour. As farm sizes have grown, so huge new metal and concrete sheds have sprouted across the landscape, and lagoons to capture their effluent.

The Committee on Climate Change has recommended to government that the numbers of UK cattle and sheep halve.[161] This may happen if subsidy cuts sought by the Treasury for years and promised by the 2019 Agriculture Bill are what happens, as the Strutt and Parker studies have modelled.[162] Many meat-producing farms may go out of business. The EAT–*Lancet* Commission report recommended big production reductions globally too: 65% less meat, but +75% veg, +50% fruit, +75% legumes, +150% nuts and seeds. The UN FAO in 2006 agreed the need to reduce animal production, then softened that view in 2013 after vehement criticism from the meat industries and some developing countries which stressed the importance of livestock for their economies.[163,164] It recognizes that a kind of contract-and-converge approach might be needed in which the rich world such as

Livestock category	Stage	Numbers (in June)
Cattle		10,004,000
	Cows in dairy herd	1,891,000
	Cows in beef herd	1,589,000
Sheep		34,832,000
	Female breeding flock	16,669,000
	Lambs under 1 year old	17,340,000
Pigs		4,969,000
	Sows in pig and other sows for breeding	361,000
	Gilts in pig	55,000
Poultry		181,818,000
	Table fowl	117,619,000
	Laying flock incl. pullets	39,510,000
	Breeding flock	13,429,000
	Turkeys, ducks, geese and all other poultry	11,260,000

Table 4.6
UK livestock numbers, 2017
Source: Defra. Agriculture in the UK 2017.[41]

the UK reins back output while developing countries raise it a bit for assumed economic and possible nutritional reasons. For the UK and Europe, however, the emphasis must be on reduction. The Rural Investment Support for Europe (RISE) Foundation, for instance, calculated in 2018 that while Eastern European countries might not have to cut hard numbers by much, Western EU member states should.[165]

Any talk of animal reduction understandably meets opposition. This is not just a case of big business but small too. Some state that climate and terrain mean only animals are possible sources of sustenance; this can indeed be true. And farmers already committed to sustainability have argued, not least in the UK, that cattle are essential for long-term soil fertility; others that fertility maintenance and biodiversity restoration require a variety of species not any one.[166] Some point out that farm animals are useful within rotations; others say technical efficiencies can be made to reduce emissions; and still others that it's all about politics. Of course, this does become highly charged. The economic stakes are high but the science is clear, too. The issue of UK animal production and land use will not go away. Animals are slow converters of plants. (We humans are too, but we do not normally eat ourselves; cannibalism is a nigh-universal taboo.) One of the claims for human progress in twentieth-century food has been the remarkable increase in output from land and animals. Gerbens-Leenes and colleagues have estimated that, while humans obtain more calories per kilo in meat than from vegetables, fruit or potatoes, land use is almost the reverse. 8,178 m^2 of land is needed to feed a person for a year from beef, 2,592 m^2 of land for pork, 1,369 m^2 for fruit, 1,314 m^2 for vegetables and 274 m^2 for potatoes.[167]

Future UK food policy will have to start reusing measures such as Feed Conversion Ratios (FCR) if we are to take food security more seriously. FCR is a measure for how much nutrient value can be 'harvested' from a given amount of feed fed to the animal. A rule-of-thumb estimate for FCRs today can be given of 6.0–10.0 for beef, 2.7–5.0 for pigs, 1.7–2.0 for chicken and 1.0–2.4 for farmed fish and shrimp.[168] Animal conversion rates vary, not least by breed and how the animals are reared. Their digestion rates vary, as do fermentation rates and maintenance requirements. Cows have double stomachs and chew the cud; sheep, poultry and pigs do not. Of the four, cattle are the slowest growing. A comprehensive review for Defra concluded that there were considerable efficiencies possible, some made and more underway.[169] In 1976, for instance, it took an average of sixty-three days to rear and feed a broiler chicken to 2 kg weight, but by 1999 it was possible to do this in thirty-six days. In the 1930s a Dutch Landrace pig might need 3.5 kg of feed to gain 1 kg in weight, whereas it could put on that 1 kg from only 2.8 kg in the 1990s, a significant gain in 'efficiency'. But feeding even in this way is still a nutrient loss. The animal is not kept on thin air. Efficiency and productivity, beloved of economists and management consultants, are not simple concepts, nor the only measure.

Emily Cassidy and colleagues in the USA looked at nutrient efficiency – how many calories and how much protein are produced – and found that 100 g of grain fed to animals would yield 40 new calories of milk, or 22 of eggs, or 12 of chicken, or 10 of pork, or 3 of beef. Every 100 g of grain fed would yield 43 g of protein in milk, 35 in eggs, 40 in chicken, 10 in pork, or 5 in beef.[170] They argued that, in the future, we need to measure land use by how many people are actually fed per acre, not just financial output. A 2018 global study by Mike Berners-Lee and colleagues at Lancaster University showed that farmers grow 5,935 kcal per person per day (kcal/d) of crops directly edible by humans; plus a further 3,812 kcal/d of vegetable matter eaten by other animals but not directly digestible by humans.[171] This total of 9,747 kcal/d is four times the average intake which the WHO and FAO estimate is needed to feed humans adequately. Animals, of course, can eat plant matter that we humans cannot, such as grass and wild herbage. They make the inedible (e.g. grass) edible (e.g. dairy and meat). In fact, about half that total – 4,260 kcal/d – is directly edible by humans but 1,738 kcal/d (41%) is fed to farmed animals, which also eat the equivalent of 3,812 kcal/d from the other plant sources – what humans cannot eat.

This study was a powerful reminder at the world scale of how a *danse macabre* between farming and consumers has in effect turned farm animals sometimes into our competitors. We have become so meat- and dairy-oriented that cattle, in particular, are now living off what we too can consume. Land which could feed us is growing food for them which they convert inefficiently and then partially feed us. One study provided a nuanced analysis. It showed that livestock consume 6 billion tonnes of feed (dry matter) annually – including one third of global cereal production – of which 86% is made of materials that are currently not eaten by humans.[172] Soybean may have a negative profile for its association with deforestation of the Amazonian rainforest, but soybean cakes account for only 4% of the global livestock feed intake. Actually, the production of 1 kg of boneless meat for humans requires an average of only 2.8 kg of human-edible feed in ruminant systems and 3.2 kg in monogastric systems. The study concluded that, given livestock uses 2.5 bn ha of land globally, its feed efficiency could be improved with no expansion of land use. This is a bit disingenuous. A 3:1 conversion loss is still huge!

Another factor is animal housing – is it better to free-range or control animal conversion by keeping them indoors, not walking much and 'burning' off the food? In simple energy-in/energy-out terms, it is of course more 'efficient' to keep poultry indoors. They cannot and will not expend as much energy as when outdoors. Broiler systems (which opponents term 'factory farms') are more efficient in that strict sense than beef or lamb production.[173] But, whether measured in calorie conversion efficiency or protein conversion efficiency, beef is among the least efficient ways of using cereals.[174,175] Cows are slow converters, which is why bodies such as the World Resources Institute are now rightly working with the UK food service sector to shift consumption patterns away from meat to lower-impact staples, fruit and vegetables for direct human use through their Cool Food project and the Foodprint pledge.[176]

A big policy battle ought to be over UK imports of animals fed on grain, and the imports of grain such as soy to feed to animals here, and our feed exports. The USA is in some respects the global leader of this version of intensive agriculture. Growing maize (corn) in particular is central to the practice of feeding cattle in vast feedlots, euphemistically called 'concentrated animal-feeding operations' (CAFOs). A CAFO is defined by the US Department of Agriculture as an operation with more than 1,000 cattle kept for at least forty-five days. While the size of farms 'finishing' beef has grown, the UK at present has nothing like the huge US CAFOs, but skirmishes as to whether such feedlot systems could begin here have already started over planning applications for 'super-dairies' of 3,000–4,000 cows in Lincolnshire and giant pig factories in areas like Derbyshire. This is as much a battle for hearts and minds – the image of British farming – as over economics, but at the same time it is a tightening of the lock-in.

In the traditional-farming camp are those who argue that cattle can and should deliver food from land which otherwise would be unproductive: the uplands, moors, marshes, scrub. Others counter that such land would be better wilded or forested. The Pasture-Fed Livestock Association (set up in 2009) champions cattle and sheep reared only on grass, arguing that this retains the animals' fertilizer functions while reducing their footprint.[177] (This echoes Mao Zedong's statement in the Cultural Revolution that the pig is both a meat producer and a 'walking fertilizer factory'.) The problem is that rearing cattle in that way means they take longer to 'fatten' so they are alive emitting methane longer. Another argument is that cattle and sheep are essential for good mixed farming and rotational use of land; animals can help build soil structure and diversify any farm's output. They prevent monoculture.[178] The use of pigs and poultry is somewhat different. They are not primarily grass eaters but can be reared outdoors. Consumer pressure has indeed taken many producers to 'free-range' both animals. And both historically were used to recycle waste, but that was largely banned in the UK after disease outbreaks. Be that as it may, what kind of animal production and how much of each type is now a matter the UK cannot fudge, as long as we follow the overwhelming evidence that animal production broadly needs to be reduced and that the inefficient use of grain as feed must be phased right down.

When designing a new UK animal policy, we will require new and better indicators of efficiency and land use. A 2018 study by Tim Searchinger and World Resource Institute colleagues proposed that a new carbon efficiency index would be useful. This would be a measure of whether and how land stores carbon while producing food without extending land use.[179] Applying this to Northern Europe, they estimated that carbon emissions of average European diets were 9 tonnes of CO_2 a year, *twenty* times higher than previous figures such as by David Tilman and Mike Clark.[180] If this index was applied to the UK, it would mean that UK consumers are each emitting far more GHGs than officially estimated. Simon Evans writing in *Carbon Brief* calculated the UK average as 5.4 tonnes per person per year but acknowledged this impact has been dropping since the 1970s, as the UK phased out coal-fired power stations and offshored its manufacturing abroad.[181] But applying the Searchinger carbon efficiency index would mean recognizing the far higher effects of dietary change to more meat. Other academics have proposed that instead of looking at the (in)efficiency of animals, it would be better to assess how much nutritional output the land produced – a simple indicator of nutrient output per acre.[182,183] This would allow land to rewild.

In her bestselling book about the rewilding of her husband's estate, Isabella Tree argues that wild-reared meat has a different nutrient profile to – and emits less CO_2e than – intensively reared animals. The renaissance of biodiversity on the 1,400 ha Knepp Estate in Sussex is now celebrated.[184] Putting English Longhorn cattle, Tamworth pigs and Dartmoor ponies to roam freely, and reversing a lot of the farming revolution's infrastructure – drains, fences, demarcation – has created a magnificent biological environment. Under its former management regime of intensive dairy and wheat production, the estate was not profitable. Now it is, with eco-tourism helping, as does the conversion of farm buildings into light-industrial use. While Knepp now produces 75 tonnes of 'wild range' (free-range and pasture-fed) meat a year,[185] someone's land needs to produce the horticultural products necessary for health. The problem would be familiar to many landowners and farmers: what is the best use of this land, this terrain, these conditions? But at what scale – 50% or 30% of the UK? This is surely not just a matter for landowners' individual choice but a national concern requiring both science and debate. If every landowner did a Knepp, this would be dire for British food security. Nor does Knepp claim it wouldn't be. I agree with Ms Tree that a food cultural shift would have to happen if more (re)wilding went on – a 'return to less meat and traditional methods of rearing animals'. This is the 'less but better quality' route that I think actually summarizes the way forward for UK animal rearing. This must be accompanied by a massive effort to increase fruit and vegetables.

In sum, there have been numerous studies over the last two decades exploring the impact of diet on environment and health. On land use, they may have employed various methods or proposed a variety of indicators or investigated different regions of the globe, but it is impossible to escape the broad conclusion that somehow there should be a reduction in consumption and production of high-emitting meat and meat products. The 2019 IPCC *Climate Change and Land* report confirmed this strongly.[186] The UK cannot duck this; we must change too, as the Committee on Climate Change (CCC) has advised. Consumer choice, whether we like it or not, is in the frame. Other than the CCC, other food-related official advisers are keeping their heads down, or speak when they have left office. It is time there was a coherent position, not least to help producers and the public.

There is still a strange faith that somehow the pursuit of a productionist notion of efficiency will resolve the problems. Technology can help but not alone; and it will not resolve cultural food problems, or heal all land misuse or rationalize all animal production. We need to put farmed animals back into a better ecological niche. The Agriculture and Horticulture Development Board claims that the best-performing (top 10%) UK farmers can get animals reared and off to slaughter far faster than the worst-performing 10%. This is true. But what does this imply? Licensing only the top 10%? Taxing the inefficient? Hmm. Historically, growing crops to be able to feed animals over winter made sense if it then enabled the animal to be used to convert plant growth that humans couldn't eat in the summer. Hay was gathered in summer to feed cattle over winter. Today, highly productive land is being used to feed excessive numbers of animals. Both production and consumption are locked into undesirable outcomes. This is true not just for animal production but also for horticulture.

TOO MUCH MEAT AND HFSS FOODS, NOT ENOUGH FRUIT AND VEGETABLES

The UK is awash with some foods and is not producing enough of others. We are short of foods which we could grow and consume more of here but are held back for some reason. How can we unlock this? Land use ought to be re-oriented around public health but in reality the UK diet is distorted by under-consumption of fruit and vegetables and over-consumption of processed foods, many including meat. Atleast two thirds of the UK countryside services livestock production. Only 165,000 ha of the UK's 6,084,000 ha of croppable farmland is for horticulture. This should surely increase for the sake of health.

Take Scotland. Accoding to a 2016 study, only 20% of Scottish adults had consumed the recommended five portions of fruit and vegetables on the previous day, a *decrease* from 23% reported in the previous study in 2009. The number of Scottish adults meeting the five-a-day guidelines was the joint worst rate recorded. And the proportion of adults eating *no* fruit or vegetables on the previous day – 12% – was the highest, i.e. worst, recorded since 2003. Consumption in Scotland as elsewhere in the UK is age-related: 16- to 24-year-olds consumed just 2.5 portions a day, and 55- to 74-year-olds consumed an average of 3.3 portions.[187]

No one expects our favourite bananas to be grown here, but apples, pears, nuts and soft fruit can be. Horticulture statistics show production of vegetables as barely fluctuating in 2007–17, the period of massive encouragement to the public to eat more. UK production delivers about 55% of what is consumed (and that still fails to meet health advice), while

UK fruit rose slightly from 12% of national consumption to about 15% in the same period. Fruit consumption too is lamentable. In tonnage terms there was a rise of fruit production in 2014–17, much of it popular strawberries, but this dropped back, mainly due to Brexit-related labour concerns since.[188]

Interest in the nutrient value of seeds and nuts has grown in recent years. The UK used to produce a lot but nut production has fallen dramatically, also in part due to labour issues – someone has to pick the nuts. The potential to increase production exists, however, both within the old Kent Cobnut Triangle and elsewhere.[189] Even in Wales, hazels and walnuts can be grown.[190] In 1913, cobnuts were grown on 7,000 acres of Kent – the historic nut-growing heartland – but this declined to just 250 acres by the 1990s with barely a comment from government or dietary health advocates.* Importation of brazils, cashews, almonds and macadamia nuts, as well as peanuts (actually a legume), which cannot be grown here, meanwhile rose. Thus, when evidence of the nutritional advantages of nut and seed consumption for health emerged in the 2000s,[191] this UK food capacity was already weakened.

The mismatch between production and health is on a grand scale. In 1997–2017, according to the Agriculture and Horticulture Development Board statistics, annual pig production fell from 1,100,000 tonnes to around 900,000 tonnes. In the same period beef and veal rose from around 700,000 to 900,000 tonnes while lamb and mutton stayed

---

* A government health adviser once told me that he didn't care where nutrients came from as long as the public ate a healthy diet. In fact, it does matter where they come from if the environmental footprint is high or there is sweated labour or if they come from countries which feed their own populations inadequately while exporting nutrients to the affluent.

more level at around 300,000 tonnes.[192] To put this into a different form, in just one *month* (February 2019, not a special period such as Christmas) this kind of production level meant that 62,217 heifers, 81,931 steers, 11,851 young bulls, 1,266 adult bulls, 52,132 cows, 7,639 light calves, 1,302 heavy calves, 125,018 ewes and rams, 972,314 other sheep and lambs, 867,549 pigs and 21,652 sows and boars went to slaughter in the UK.[193] That is a lot of meat to come onto the market.

The argument often given is that the UK's terrain and climate lead us to produce meat on this scale. In fact, land use has been skewed to do this, using prime land to grow grains which are fed to animals rather than that land being used for horticulture or field crops. Animal production has come under criticism most in recent years over animal welfare and ethical concerns about handling. Pressure from NGOs has led to welfare standards slowly but steadily improving; for instance, the practice of tethering sows when farrowing has been banned, poultry debeaking stopped, and more free-range pig production encouraged. Connecting how farm animals are reared delivers a broadly positive effect on the animals' health.[194] If animals range over land, they grow more slowly than if kept and 'fattened' indoors, and that there is some evidence that their meat nutrient composition alters – clearer for some such as free-range beef than for others. A summary of data was produced by Compassion in World Farming in 2012.[195]

Meat or dairy products from higher-welfare animals cost more. The argument then is that if a consumer wants such products, then eat less but better quality.[196,197] Cattle fed only on pasture offer a definite improvement, but take longer to come to market, being less intensively reared. At the global level, if the number of cattle continue to grow, while the UK reduced production, any planetary advantages would be eroded. But it is hard not to conclude that the UK needs fewer cattle, and it would be better to return farmed animals to their ecological niche, and thus simultaneously reduce their impact on land use, climate and health.[198] Less but better meat is probably the right policy direction.

The third and most recent meta-analysis from the World Cancer Research Fund (WCRF) in 2018 extended the advice given in its 2007 report. While more note is taken of the value of physical exercise in 'burning' the fat intake, the warning by WCRF in 1997 that rising meat consumption has some cancer connections has strengthened.[199,200,201] WCRF now recommends: limits on consumption of (a) red and processed meat, (b) sugared sweetened drinks, (c) processed foods high in fats, starches and sugars, and (d) alcohol consumption; and, on the positive side, eating a diet rich in wholegrains, vegetables, fruit and beans. Red-meat consumption increases the risk of cancer of the colorectum, nasopharynx, lungs and pancreas, and processed-meat consumption that of cancer of the colorectum, nasopharynx, oesophagus, lungs, stomach and pancreas.[202]

In 2015, an expert group from the WHO-affiliated International Agency for Research on Cancer (IARC) produced a statement on meat and cancer.[203] Reviewing 800 papers on red and processed meat, it concluded from the best evidence it could assemble that red and processed meat should be classified as 'probably carcinogenic to humans' (on its classification as in Group 2A).[204] This is not as dangerous as tobacco but foolish to ignore.

Important synergies also emerge between health and

environmental impacts of meat consumption. One such study by Pete Scarborough and colleagues at Oxford compared diets which were: high in meat; lacto-vegetarian (containing animal-based dairy products but not meat); and vegan (eschewing all animal-based products). They looked at the diets of 2,041 vegans, 15,751 vegetarians, 8,123 fish-eaters and 29,589 meat-eaters. The high-meat diet averaged 7.2 kg of carbon dioxide emissions a day, whereas the vegetarians averaged 3.8 kg and vegans only 2.9 kg.[205] These effects suggest a progressive health and environmental improvement would follow an increasing cultural shift from high meat → medium meat → low meat → fish-eaters → vegetarians → vegans. But food choice is rarely made on the basis of health and environmental scientific data! Veganism has grown in profile in the UK in recent years, particularly among younger people, but remains a tiny proportion of the UK diet. But it has become much more common and acceptable for there to be vegan options. A 2018 Harris Interactive poll of UK consumers found 25% said they were looking to cut down on meat, with 35% of 18- to 34-year-olds saying they were.[206]

Meat consumption is a battle for minds not just nutrients and health. Meat consumption is deeply rooted in culture and aspirations; its consumption increases with wealth. Despite and also because of the strong evidence that the world, let alone the UK, needs to cut back on animal production, particularly cattle, strong lobbies and vested interests have become more resistant and vociferous. The US meat lobby, for example, neutralized the official scientific advice that the statutory US Dietary Guidelines for Americans should take note of environmental as well as nutritional science.[207],[208] Around the world, various attempts to create sustainable dietary advice have met sometimes furious and sometimes below-the-radar but effective opposition; in the UK, such moves have been resisted and marginalized too.[209]

Once more, some advocates see technology as the solution, the creation of lab-based meat. The right-wing Adam Smith Institute backs this.[210] Some environmental analysts agree; it is 'land-sparing' and would generate new possibilities for feeding people in ways they like but with lower impacts. It would be, however, another transfer of power and profit away from the agriculture sector. At present, the production of artificial meat is tiny and peripheral, although noisy in media terms. The more pressing need is to reduce the rising impact of existing meat production. For the UK this means planning a sensitive reduction and alternative livelihoods for producers. This might be forced anyway, if investment in 'industrial' forms of non-meat meat (either cloned from real meat or as meat substitutes from plants) advances. Large, heavily capitalized manufacturers have moved into this sector in the USA; a third of all money in US food and beverage innovation funding in 2018, according to one report, went on dairy and meat 'alternatives'.[211] In Europe, Coca-Cola owns Innocent Drinks, which has introduced dairy-free milks. In 2017, Danone, the huge French dairy company, bought the Belgian soya-milk company Alpro. Tyson Foods, the large US meat group, took a stake in Beyond Meat. Unilever owns soya-ice-cream maker Swedish Glacé.[212] Even before consumer trends have taken deep root, corporate diversification can gobble them up.

The 2019 report by the EAT–*Lancet* Commission on Food in the Anthropocene revisited another and older perspective on meat. Favouring a drastic reduction, it proposed that more pigs and poultry should be reared on waste, the so-called 'livestock from leftovers' case. The EAT–*Lancet* Commission calculated that meat produced in this way could amount to about 11–35 grams per person per day.[213] Feedback, the UK-born but now international food waste campaign, suggests an area the size of Yorkshire is currently used to grow soya (much in the Americas) to feed UK pigs. This is food 'offshoring' with consumers in the dark and no declaration on the label. Feedback argues the UK should carefully revisit the possibility of feeding 'swill' to pigs. This practice was banned following the devastating 2001 foot-and-mouth disease outbreak. Better hygiene and technology, it argues, should improve and prevent such outbreaks.[214] Studies and pilot plants should perhaps be conducted to see if risks could be contained if it was used on a small localized basis only.

The examples considered above show that the production–consumption mismatch is extensive and serious, and should not be fudged or ignored. The dietary challenge for the UK is how to rebalance not just diets for health but the environment at the same time. This immediately raises another British food problem.

Food problem 5: Diet-related ill-health has been normalized

In the period 1961–2011, the UK had nutrition sufficiency for energy, macronutrients and key micronutrients, with the exception of total carbohydrates and fibre, according to a study by Jennie Macdiarmid and colleagues at Aberdeen University.[215] In other words, there was a roughly adequate nutrient supply in total (from wherever sourced) to feed the population healthily. Despite this, somehow the UK has created a health disaster out of what ought to be health success. We are not alone in this self-inflicted health damage but we are among the worst. The bizarre thing is that the cost is accepted. There is a steady stream of criticism from academics and health economists, and some acknowledgement in parts of government, but the food system and its externalization of healthcare costs continues, when it ought to be radically changed. There is an evidence–policy–reality gap.

By 2015, nearly two thirds of adults (63%) in England were classed as being overweight (a body mass index of over 25) or obese (a BMI of over 30).* In 2017, obesity alone created £27bn of costs to wider society and these costs are on track to rise to £49.9bn per year by 2050, of which £9.7bn would be direct costs to the NHS.[216] Figure 4.10 compares the number of overweight and obese people in the UK against other EU countries. The bar indicates the percentage of overweight people in each country, and the line across the bar gives the level of obesity within that.

Diet has long been known to be a major driver of non-communicable diseases (NCDs) such as cardiovascular disease, type-2 diabetes, hypertension, coronary heart disease and certain cancers. Since work on these large-scale trends began in the 1970s, the evidence has become stronger and

---

* A body mass index (BMI) of less than 18.5 is defined as underweight; 18.5–24.9 is deemed healthy; 25–29.9 is overweight; 30–39.9 is obese; above 40 is morbidly obese.

clearer.[217] Communicable diseases are still immensely damaging worldwide, and feature most heavily in poorer countries which lack medical services, but in the rich world the NCDs dominate healthcare concerns. The UK is the fourth-fattest population of the EU.[218] In 1998, there were 1.8 million Britons with diabetes. By 2018, there were 3.6 million, 90% of whom have type-2 diabetes, for which obesity is the leading cause in the majority of preventable cases.[219] It is a slow, debilitating and costly disease.

The 2018 results from the National Diet and Nutrition Survey (NDNS) paint a poor picture. It shows that the average saturated-fat intake for UK adults (19- to 64-year-olds) is 12.5% of daily calorie intake, above the 11% recommended maximum; adults consume on average 4.2 portions of fruit and vegetables per day, 65- to 74-year-olds consuming 4.3 portions and teenagers just 2.7 portions per day; only 31% of adults, 32% of 65- to 74-year-olds and 8% of teenagers meet the five-a-day recommendation for fruit and vegetables; and average fibre intake in adults is 19 g per day, well below the recommended 30 g per day, and a sign of consuming over-processed foods.[220]

From a concern about nutrient deficiency in the past, the UK has shifted in a century to having problems of over- and mal-consumption. Nutrition guidelines are not met. According to Public Health England (PHE), of people aged 65–74 only 31% of men and 32% of women eat five portions of fruit and vegetables a day, itself far

▪ Overweight

I Obese

Figure 4.10
Prevalence of overweight and obese women in the EU, twenty-eight member plus three non-member states, 2014, %
Source: Eurostat 2017.[218]

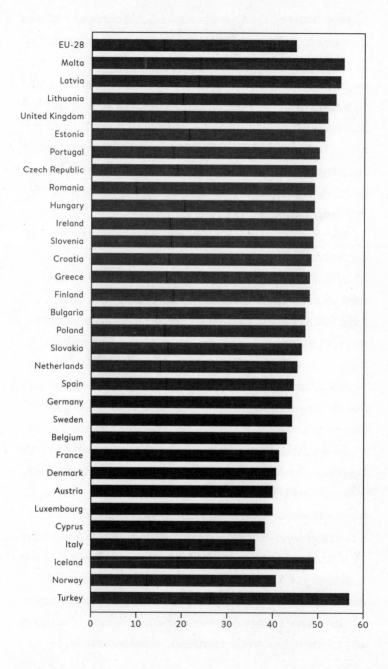

too low a target. Of over-75-year-olds, this drops to 18% of men and 20% of women.[221] At the same time, it is known that if UK diets did meet health guidelines such as PHE's Eatwell guide, their environmental impact would also lessen. A study by a team from the London School of Hygiene and Tropical Medicine shows that if the UK ate a diet as per WHO guidance, there would be a 17% GHGe reduction compared to the present; this would save almost 7 million years of life lost prematurely in the UK over the next thirty years and increase average life expectancy by over eight months.[222,223]

The proportion of UK adults who are obese or overweight is now 26.9%.[224] The UK is the fifth most obese or overweight of all thirty-five OECD countries. Number one is the USA, with 38.2%. This is sad but not surprising. Our daily lives have almost been designed to make us fat. Distances between work, home, school or shops 'make' us use cars rather than bicycles or walking. The food supply over-produces, and advertises sugary, fatty foods (see pp. 308–9). The projections are for the number of people in the UK who are obese or overweight to increase to 25% by 2030 (see Figure 4.11).[225]

When children go to school, they walk through a mostly health-unregulated set of messages – eat this sugary, fatty food, drink this sweet drink. Academics have become increasingly interested in how the built as well as the cultural environment favours health-damaging consumption and affects children's eating culture. The CEDAR research group at the University of Cambridge developed a Food Environment Assessment Tool (FEAT). This shows that 400 schools across England have twenty or more fast-food takeaways within a 400-metre radius, while a further 1,400 have between ten and

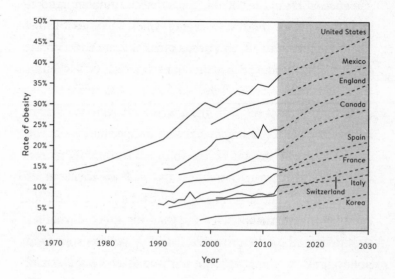

Figure 4.11

Trends in people being obese or overweight, nine countries, 1970–2030

Source: OECD Obesity update 2017.[230]

nineteen outlets within the same distance. London has the worst problem of any region of the UK. There, the number of fast-food outlets has grown in 2014–17.[226] There were an average 2.3 outlets within 400 metres of schools in 2014 but this had risen to 2.6 outlets by 2017.[227] The FEAT method tracks the number of fast-food outlets, cafés, restaurants and convenience stores in the UK, and finds that the number of take-away food outlets tends to be highest where incomes are low. There are fewest in affluent urban areas such as York, Windsor or Maidenhead, and most in poor areas such as Blackburn, Darwen, Hackney or Bradford (see also pp. 300–301).

In theory, most retail chains are committed to encouraging healthy diets. A study of sixty-nine supermarkets in the east of England, varying across fourteen formats, explored what foods were actually on offer on or near the checkout, as a test of this.[228] The supermarkets were found to vary considerably in their actual policies and that this affected whether they delivered on the promises. Two had no checkout food policy at all, six did have 'clear and consistent' policies and six 'vague or inconsistent' ones. The retailers with clear policies were more likely to deliver the promise.

REINFORCING UNDESIRABLE TRENDS

The UK's rate of morbid obesity – a body mass index (BMI) of over 40 – is expected to double in 2015–35 from 1.9 million in England, Scotland and Wales in 2015 to 4.1 million by 2035.[229] This is the first time it has been possible to extrapolate trends of morbid obesity because today *there are so many British people who fit into that category*. Figures for obesity in English children aged 3–17 years rose from 1995, then dropped a little only to rise again (see Figure 4.12).[230] These are rapid changes which the food industries initially said were not their fault but due to lack of exercise. In truth, it is a function both of food supply and lack of exercise. But obesity rates have put all food industries a bit more onto the defensive.

Fewer than one in ten children in the UK meet even the moderate five-a-day target for fruit and vegetable consumption.[231] Other countries think that target is too weak in the first place. In the UK, more than one third of the vegetables that children eat are processed, with 17% of the veg in their diets coming from pizza and baked beans.[232] Children in England consume in six months more sugar – the equivalent of 4,800 cubes of sugar – than they should consume in a year if PHE guidelines were followed.[233] On average, 4- to 10-year-olds were consuming thirteen cubes of sugar a day compared to the maximum of five to six. PHE data show the top ten items in which children consume this sugar are:

- Sugary soft drinks (including squashes, juice drinks, energy drinks, cola and other fizzy drinks) – 10%
- Buns, cakes, pastries and fruit pies – 10%
- Sugars, including table sugar, preserves and sweet spreads – 9%
- Biscuits – 9%
- Breakfast cereals – 8%
- Chocolate confectionery – 7%
- Sugar confectionery – 7%
- Yoghurt, fromage frais and other dairy desserts – 6%
- Ice cream – 5%
- Puddings – 4%

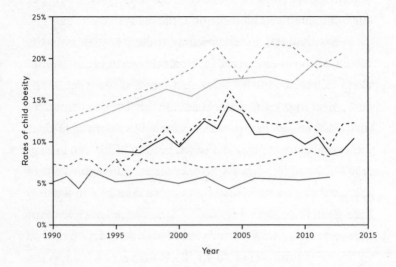

Figure 4.12
Obesity in boys and girls aged 3–17 years, England,
France and the USA, 1990–2015

- - - - Boys, England
——— Girls, England

- - - - Boys, France
——— Girls, France

- - - - Boys, United States
——— Girls, United States

Source: OECD. Obesity update 2017.[230]

As official nutrition adviser to government, PHE's strategy is to encourage parents to 'make simple changes', to 'swap sugary drinks for plain water, lower fat plain milks, sugar-free or no added sugar drinks', and to 'cut back on sugary snacks' by e.g. 'swapping' cakes, biscuits, chocolate and sweets for fruit, plain rice cakes, toast, fruit teacakes, malted loaf or bagels with lower-fat spread. In practice, signals far stronger than advice shape behaviour and gradually PHE has had to recommend a more thorough and coherent battery of change agents. The 2015 PHE review of the evidence on sugar found that price and price promotions (such as price cuts, 'buy one get one free' offers), not surprisingly, affect food purchases.[234] A 2018 study saw that an immediate 17.3% reduction in unhealthy food purchases occurred if health guidelines not to promote 'unhealthy' foods at supermarket checkouts were properly applied. Reductions in purchases were maintained. Over a year later, there was still a 15.5% reduction from before the policy was applied.[235] Cancer Research UK, in a contribution of research to the government's 2019 childhood obesity review of price promotions, used Kantar Worldpanel data to conclude that a third of food purchases are price promotions.[236] The 25% who bought most in line with price promotions were 28% more likely to be obese than 'low promotional shoppers', perhaps helping understand how obesity becomes normalized within households. Almost half of all chocolate, crisps, popcorn and savoury snacks were bought on promotion, and shoppers more likely to purchase in line with promotions bought 30% less fruit and nearly 25% fewer vegetables than others.

A year after the threat of sugar tax, PHE's own data showed that supply went down by a mere 2% – something, but not yet the big transformation needed. The problem is that a continuous flow of sugar pours into the food supply. Meanwhile, farm policy arguments are mainly about whether that flow comes from UK or European sugar beet, former colonies' sugar cane, US maize-derived corn syrup or artificial sources such as aspartame. In 2017–18, 2.4 mt of beet and cane sugar were sold in the UK, 87% of which was ingested via manufactured food and drinks, including net imports.[237] Sugar is a cheap commodity which processors can put quite legally into foods, arguing that consumers like it as it makes foods 'palatable' (i.e. reinforces existing behaviour rather than change), while these four vast industries vie with each other over how, not whether, to sweeten the diet. Each seeks to provide the cheapest offer. The diet is maintained as sweet, even by artificials.

The UK's diet is afflicted not just by excess sugar. Liking sweet foods is a habit which can be reduced, as can salt, but is best done by gradual reduction rather than going 'cold turkey'. As has been noted before, the UK has the most 'ultra-processed' diet (i.e. from foods high in fat, salt and sugar) of nineteen EU member states on which there were good data.[238] The study's own summary is worth citing here in full:

> Across the nineteen countries, median average household availability amounted to 33.9% of total purchased dietary energy for unprocessed or minimally processed foods, 20.3% for processed culinary ingredients, 19.6% for processed foods and 26.4% for ultra-processed foods. The average household availability of ultra-processed foods ranged from 10.2% in Portugal and 13.4% in Italy to 46.2 % in Germany and 50.4 % in the UK. *A significant*

positive association was found between national household availability of ultra-processed foods and national prevalence of obesity among adults. After adjustment for national income, prevalence of physical inactivity, prevalence of smoking, measured or self-reported prevalence of obesity, and time lag between estimates on household food availability and obesity, *each percentage point increase in the household availability of ultra-processed foods resulted in an increase of 0.25 percentage points in obesity prevalence.*

What explains this sorry state of UK affairs? One factor is that the UK provides few counter-drivers to the normalization of ultra-processed foods and their effects. Other countries are more successful in building exercise into daily life (e.g. the Netherlands or Denmark with mass-bicycling cultures, roads engineered to make biking more safe) or may have a culture which more recently has roots in the Mediterranean diet (e.g. Portugal and Greece), but few have the relentless combination of drivers that the UK suffers from. As we were the first industrial nation, our food culture was long ago 'deracinated'. We were known for a culinary culture of brown food, but that began to be changed with Europeanization, immigration and increased incomes from the 1970s. But the ubiquity of cheap ultra-processed foods, combined with the 'good value' ascribed to cheapness, locks us into consumption and lifestyles almost designed to deliver obesity and diet-related ill-health.

Inequalities contribute to this, too. Obesity rates are correlated with levels of inequality within societies.[239] The UK is a highly unequal society, with the top 10% of people by wealth owning as much as the bottom 50%. And the top 20% of UK earners proportionately earned twelve times more in wages and benefits than the poorest 20%.[240] In 2019, the Resolution Foundation reported that for the first time in four decades Britain had seen a drop in the number of people receiving low wages. Twenty years after Labour introduced the Minimum Wage and three after the Conservatives introduced a new National Living Wage for people twenty-five years old or above, the percentage of employees paid less than two thirds of median hourly pay had fallen from 20.7% in 2015 to 17.1% in 2018.[241] This showed that policy can be effective, but cuts in the welfare system and particularly the arrival of Universal Credit and accompanying implementation problems undermine the effect of wage baselines.

A study which compared UK health performance to other countries concluded that while some trends were improving, the UK was generally lagging behind other high-income nations. The UK performs worse than other countries for child life expectancy, low weight, breastfeeding, obesity, parents or family in work, infant and childhood mortality, and neural-tube defects.[242] Except for whether the infant's family members are in employment, diet is involved in all those indicators. This is a sad judgement on our society and reflects how we and the government accept the unacceptable. In the early 2000s, children's diet-related health had a high profile and gained considerable government attention due to campaigns on school food such as that by Jamie Oliver, to the extent that the government created the School Food Trust as a non-departmental public body, part of the government machinery. This became the Children's Food Trust, but was pushed away from Whitehall by the Coalition government in 2011, gradually whittled down and closed in 2016. Funding had thus moved from being part of core Department of Education and Science budgets to being dependent on bidding for charitable funds. Other NGOs have moved into this policy space, but it is a sad state of affairs that charities now carry the flag for child health.[243,244,245] What could and should be normal governmental action has been offshored to NGOs with effectiveness only as good as their lobbying power.

The challenge is how to unlock the lock-in to poor diets. When the Chief Scientist's Foresight team analysed what to do about obesity in 2006–8, it produced a much cited report acknowledging the complexity. This was captured by what was known to some as the 'spaghetti' chart because it showed the simple mismatch between people's energy intake and energy expenditure as being subject to many contradictory forces.[246] Trying to untangle the seemingly tightly woven bundle of factors shaping obesity looked at first sight to be impossible. In fact, one can find clusters of factors which matter: the immediate environment, price, family patterns and background, income, psychological pressures from culture (media, etc.), and so on. Cities have taken up the baton, since their planning can help and often they have public-health responsibilities. Amsterdam has begun to stem runaway childhood obesity.[247] More recently, the Leeds HENRY study has shown that upward trends in early-age child obesity can be reversed by putting large efforts into pre-school child support. The reduction in Leeds was primarily among the most deprived of the city's inhabitants, but also changed the behaviour of the affluent.[248] Forces created by people can be altered by people, but this requires effort and resources.

READY-MEALS: AN EXAMPLE
OF THE CHALLENGE

If ever there was a clear and much acknowledged lock-in in food policy, the problem of obesity is it. The real problem is what to do about it. Short of food rationing or oil shortages forcing people to take exercise – neither being great policy options – is there anything that can be done about it? One strand of analysis suggests that consumers cannot be expected to be so knowledgeable that they can improve both their health and their diets' environmental impact by leaving them to 'do the right thing' simply by exerting choices. It argues that it's more effective to persuade manufacturers and retailers to 'choice-edit'. Campaigners argue that getting those who process or sell foods to lower carbon or apply tough criteria when setting contracts is quicker than trying to achieve culture change. The theory might be neat but reality does not work out quite like that, as one can see from a 2018 survey of 1,350 ready meals by Eating Better, a coalition of fifty UK NGOs promoting in sustainable diets. Eating Better was interested in UK supermarket performance.[249]

The British spend about £5bn a year on this segment of the market, which nine out of ten UK consumers use at some time. The Eating Better survey found that availability of vegetarian meals was 'limited' and what there was sold at premium prices. Meat was the main ingredient in 77% of the own-brand and branded ready meals from the ten retailers surveyed (Asda, Aldi, Co-op, Iceland, Lidl, Marks & Spencer, Morrisons, Sainsbury, Tesco and Waitrose). 3% were vegan; here Tesco was the top performer, with eighteen vegan meals, while Waitrose offered the highest percentage of vegetarian or plant-based meals of the range each retailer provided. 184 meals (14% of total number) were vegetarian, meat substitutes or plant-based, containing, for example, pulses or tofu (3%), meat substitutes (1%) or mainly vegetables (2%).

Eating Better was critical of the apparent reluctance of the retailers to disclose on labels how the meat in these meals had been reared. There was inconsistency between admirable commitments to animal welfare and the information provided on their own products. 'Country of origin' labelling was not given by nearly a third (not least because any ready meal could have contents from different countries), and only the Co-op and Waitrose used British meat in all their own-brand meals. 80% of the premium ranges used UK meat, compared to 52% in regular ranges and only 32% in value ranges. A significant amount of chicken (35% of meals where provenance was indicated) and all of the chicken in value-range meals was sourced either from Thailand or, less frequently, from Brazil.

As to the nutrition, the retailers' product designers seemed to assume vegetarian food must mostly include cheese: 90% of the vegetarian ready meals were cheese-based and typically higher in calories – on average 497 calories per serving – compared with tofu or pulses-based dishes (390 calories) or vegetable-based ones (418 calories). Even meat-based ready meals were on average lower (483 calories). The highest-calorie vegetarian meals were a macaroni cheese at 760 calories and an 'Italian Macaroni Cheese with Cauliflower and Squash' yielding 696 calories. Cheese has 8–10 times the GHG impact of milk, higher per kilo than pork.

The picture from this section is of consumers being

symbolically and actually surrounded by messages and food offers which normalize poor diets. If we won't face up to this for ourselves, I often wonder might the British do so for our pets? We are said to love our pet animals. According to the eighty-one companies who are members of the UK Pet Food Manufacturers' Association (PFMA), in 2018 the UK petfood market was worth £2.6bn.[250] As with human food, the trend is for 'specialist, niche [. . .] and health benefits' and, like some of their owners, UK pets suffer from over-eating. While a 2010 study estimated 59% of UK dogs were overweight, a 2017 study by veterinarians at Liverpool University and Crown Pet Foods of dogs brought by owners to seven family pet shows up and down England in 2016–17 found 65% overweight and 9% obese.[251] Even fat dogs are now normalized.

Food problem 6: Food culture and choice: the battle for the mind

What exactly do the British want from food? The UK default (governmental) food policy may be that food must be cheap, but what is meant by cheap, and does the public actually see matters so starkly? The argument has been built for years by academics that health and environmental costs attributable to diet are not included in the bill consumers pay at the checkout.[252,253] We pay in other ways – disruptions to work and domestic life, NHS bills, strains on future generations – hence arguments for interventions such as the sugar tax or meat taxes.[254,255] If food was sold at its full cost, 'cheap' food would become more expensive. Would the public buy this? Unlike two centuries ago, UK food is today historically cheap; even a century ago, it took half or more of most household incomes.[256]

Surveys suggest the cost of food consistently comes top or high up on the UK public's list of priorities for their food, together with convenience and choice. But other issues vie for their attention: health, environment, taste. After David Attenborough's *Blue Planet 2* TV series, plastic use on food, for example, rocketed up public awareness, with one survey by YouGov (of 2,041 people) in late 2018 suggesting the public expected such issues would shape their food choices, if not now, by 2030 (see list below).[257] Such surveys could be viewed cynically – a secular version of St Augustine's 'Lord make me pure but not yet' – but they indicate cognitive scanning too, and a preparedness if conditions changed.

Factors the UK public say will become more important in their decisions on what food to buy in 2030

- Reducing packaging and using more recyclable materials – 62%
- The price of food – 57%
- Food waste (i.e. the amount of food that gets thrown away) – 48%
- Tackling obesity – 41%
- Where food comes from (e.g. where it is grown, fished, reared etc.) – 36%
- A greater focus on fresh food – 36%
- Supporting local farmers/producers – 34%
- That the food is ethically sourced/has an ethical supply chain – 32%

- Scarcity of certain foods – 32%
- The convenience – 31%
- Greater interest in food as an intrinsic part of health and wellbeing – 30%
- The amount of energy used in food production – 24%
- Shopping for meals not just ingredients – 15%
- People not eating meat – 14%
- People no longer having a family meal together – 14%

Source: YouGov survey for ThoughtWorks, 8–9 August 2018[258]

How good intentions are or are not translated into dietary choice is an issue over which the food industries, academics and civil society tussle all the time. There is agreement that there is a thought–action gap but less on what to do next. Cambridge University FEAT data (referred to earlier) usefully bring the discussion down to earth. Whatever the messages to eat healthily are, low-income consumer choices are affected by the food offer where they live. Despite health messages, fast-food outlets are disproportionately clustered in low-income towns and areas. In 2017, the now deindustrialized former textile town of Blackburn was assessed to be the takeaway food outlet capital of England. Per capita it has the highest presence of all Britain's 56,000 fast-food outlets. Table 4.7 gives the top five and bottom five local authorities for Wales, Scotland and England.

Compared to before the Second World War, when most British households were spending a high proportion of their incomes on food, post-1945 consumer culture has experienced a steady drop in the relative cost of food and a vast expansion of product choice. The UK's food problem now is that spending less money on food may have enabled more people to eat sufficiently compared to the past, but food is now so relatively cheap that over- and malconsumption are normalized, and locked in by the messages, the locality and the content of food products. UK consumers are given full rein to indulge our every food whim. If I want to eat foods high in fat, sugar and salt (HFSS), firstly, who are you to tell me not to and, secondly, why shouldn't I? The culture reinforces that my private space can override the public space in which you and everyone pay for my healthcare. Our 'lifespace', our mental map, is built on choice, and now choice locks us in. It is easier to say yes than no.

Choice is often characterized as a decision-tree, an array of on–off switches, much as computer architecture works. In fact, choice is shaped by context, not just the thought processes or volition of the chooser.[259] Food choice is on a spectrum which ranges from the unbridled choice associated with the seriously rich through to choice in what the Canadian-American sociologist Irving Goffman called 'total institutions' such as prisons, where it is heavily constrained or denied. Figure 4.13 represents this spectrum. In the middle sits restrained or simple choice. Most ecological public-health analyses today point to a de-emphasis of choice, while the dominant culture points in the other direction. How can we normalize 'no' to unhealthy, high-impact diets, while supporting 'yes' to softer, simpler diets?

A study of how UK consumers use food labelling, for example, found that the 'red' warning in nutrition labels was

Rank	WALES Local authority name	Takeaways, %
1	Torfaen	33.1
2	Caerphilly	33.1
3	Blaenau Gwent	31.9
4	Newport	31.6
5	Rhondda Cynon Taf	30.9
...	...	...
18	Monmouthshire	21.0
19	Gwynedd	19.4
20	Pembrokeshire	18.9
21	Ceredigion	16.5
22	Powys	16.0

Rank	SCOTLAND Local authority name	Takeaways, %
1	North Lanarkshire	34.5
2	East Renfrewshire	32.8
3	West Dunbartonshire	32.1
4	Renfrewshire	31.9
5	East Ayrshire	31.9
...	...	...
28	Highland	19.0
29	Argyll & Bute	15.9

30	Shetland Islands	12.7
31	Eilean Siar	11.9
32	Orkney Islands	11.3

Rank	ENGLAND Local authority name	Takeaways, %
1	Blackburn with Darwen	39.0
2	Hyndburn	38.2
3	South Ribble	38.2
4	Harlow	37.5
5	Rossendale	36.8
...	...	...
322	Rother	14.6
323	West Devon	14.3
324	Kensington and Chelsea	13.9
325	Cotswolds	12.1
326	Isles of Scilly	6.5

Table 4.7

Takeaway presence: local authorities in Wales, Scotland and England with the five highest and lowest presences of takeaway outlets, %

Source: Food Environment Assessment Tool (FEAT) 2018, UKCRC Centre for Diet and Activity Research (CEDAR), University of Cambridge, http://www.feat-tool.org.uk. Leaflet | Map data copyright © OpenStreetMap | © Crown Copyright and Database Right 2018. OS (100059028) | Copyright and database right © 2017 CEDAR/MRC Epidemiology Unit. All rights reserved.

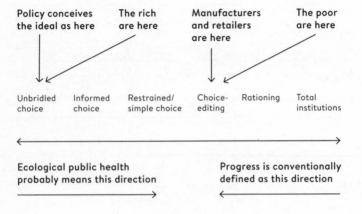

Figure 4.13

The spectrum of choice

Source: Lang, Barling and Caraher (2009).[259]

more powerful in shaping their choices than the positive attributes of 'green' labels.[260] As parents know with children, careful framing can work. While food industries often argue against unnecessary standards and regulations as a burden on business, they in fact 'choice-edit' themselves. Decisions they make – pricing, offers, packaging, marketing, ingredients – all shape choice before the consumer even sees food on the supermarket shelf and selects between products.[261] They also, of course, set the recipes for food products through their contracts.

In Japan, a culture whose diet-related health has come under strain from a rise in 'Western' HFSS food products, the continuing success of its school meals system depends on restriction of choice. The *kyushoku* system was introduced in the 1950s partly to address post-war dietary privations. Like the UK school food standards introduced by the Conservative 'Rab' Butler in the wartime 1944 Education Act, Japanese nutrition standards were used to stipulate menus for all children up to junior high school. Their system remains, whereas a later Conservative Secretary of State under Thatcher abolished standards in the 1980 Education Act. They were an impediment to the privatization of school catering (and this heralded the same for all public catering).[262] An uphill thirty-year successful fight-back then ensued to reinstate some kind of nutrition benchmark for children, which Jamie Oliver and others partly managed.

The role of standards is important – they provide not just 'advice' to consumers but can shape service delivery. They matter, but so does choice, which is accorded perhaps too much uncritical support within consumer affairs. In public health, choice is more usually seen as potentially (but not necessarily) problematic. Public-health advocates know that unfettered choice can be used to justify loosening standards and undermine herd immunity (in the case of vaccination) and make the unhealthy acceptable. The 2019 *Lancet* Syndemics Commission, for example, strongly argued for health to be more central to the framing of choice.[263] The immediate environment in which consumers choose their food contains many hidden as well as overt signals, carefully built into the physical, economic, socio-cultural and political context; lighting, sound (music), colour, smell, position and height on shelves, age appeal, packaging – these can all be moulded to entice. How these forces combine was simplified graphically by the international INFORMAS project (see Fig 4.14).[264] The eating environment is not just physical but mass psychological. Culture is malleable not fixed.

While the value of choice is often defended as a political principle, it is actually context-dependent. A rich person has more choice than a poor person. Someone choosing food in a British supermarket in 2019 enters the store already carrying vast numbers of messages. Young people today cannot imagine a world without ubiquitous marketing pressures targeting them. Although in theory there are restrictions on food advertising targeting young people, studies show they are subject to many advertisements on TV for HFSS foods. The Obesity Health Alliance, a coalition of forty health groups, commissioned a University of Liverpool research group to review the situation. It found the majority (59%) of food and drink adverts shown during family viewing time should be banned from children's TV. The worst case it saw was

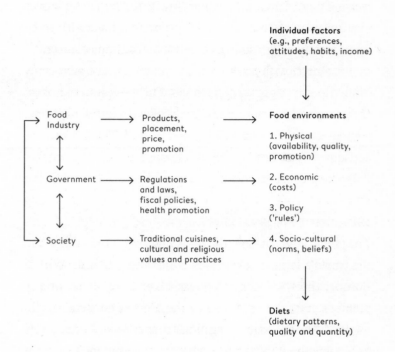

Figure 4.14
The INFORMAS model
Source: Swinburn, Sachs, Vandevijvere, et al. 2013.[264]

children bombarded with nine HFSS adverts in just a thirty-minute period. Any pretence at 'balance' was absent. Advertisements for fruit and vegetables constituted only a little over 1% of the food and drink adverts shown during family viewing time! Those for fast food and takeaways were shown over twice as often as any other type of food and drink adverts, mainly due to sponsorship of popular family shows.[265]

Presented with such data, simplistic choice advocates often flip into blaming consumers. The food system is fine; choice is good; signals are easy to decode; if only 'literate' consumers used their brains, all would be well. This blames the consumer for not acting rationally or appropriately. I call this the 'wrong consumer' theory.

INSIDIOUS MARKETING AND THE ROLE OF INFORMATION

The global advertising industry is huge and powerful. WPP, the world's largest advertising company, is British. Within Europe, the UK has the highest advertising spend of any member state, but the US has the highest adspend in the world.[266] The UK advertising industry spends on food and soft drinks ads about thirty times what the government spends on promoting healthy diets, according to a study by the Obesity Health Alliance which compared government spending with reports of adspend by the top 100 food companies in the food trade journal *The Grocer*.[267]

This 'walk-over' is relentless and gets children when young. A 2019 survey by Action on Sugar and Action on Salt, based at Queen Mary University of London's Wolfson Institute, looked at 526 food and drink products which use child-friendly cartoon animations on their packaging to appeal to children, and found 52% were unnecessarily high in fat, saturated fat, sugar and/or salt (i.e. they contained a 'red' traffic light label).[268] One in five used licensed figures easily recognized by young children such as Peppa Pig (UK-invented, sold to US Hasbro in 2019), Disney characters or Paw Patrol. While there are restrictions in place for broadcast and online advertising, some food and drink products, which would not pass eligibility criteria for such advertising, are still able to promote their products through the presence of well-known cartoon characters simply by putting them on the packaging.

The marketing drive starts young and sets children on a lifetime of this kind of messaging. In 2016, the UK food industry spent £0.927bn on advertising and was the third-highest sector after Entertainment and Leisure, which was top, and Finance. No wonder a panel study by the Food Foundation concluded that there are not enough controls on total marketing (e.g. placement in stores).[269] For a decade, the Children's Food Campaign and its campaign offspring AdEnough have been pointing out the gross inequalities in spending power. Adspend by individual companies may be fluid year to year but the totality is unrelenting.

In 2017, Coca Cola spent £16.4m on advertising in the UK, up from a mere £9.6m in 2016. Of the top 100 adspenders in the sector which industry knows as 'fast-moving consumer goods' (fmcg), forty food and drink companies spent £222m in the year. Table 4.8 gives those food and drink companies and the change on the previous year. Owners switch emphasis between their own brands. PepsiCo, for instance, owns four brands: Pepsi Max (17th highest), Walkers Crisps (31st), Quaker (3rd), and Doritos (90th). Spending on marketing

Rank in top 100 fmcg (2017)	Brand/owner	Product	Spend 2017, £m	Change 2016–17
1	Coca-Cola (Coca-Cola)	Soft drink	16.4	+71.4%
13	Cadbury Dairy Milk	Chocolate	9.4	−24.1%
14	Quorn	Protein food	9.1	+10.5%
17	Pepsi Max (PepsiCo)	Soft drink	8.1	+8.1%
20	Aptamil (Danone)	Baby milk formula	6.6	+10.2%
21	McCain	Chips	6.5	−33.9%
29	Lurpak (Arla)	Butter	6.1	−6.4%
31	Walkers Crisps (PepsiCo)	Crisps	6.0	+95.4%
33	Quaker Oats (PepsiCo)	Porridge	5.9	+42.3%
35	Birds Eye Chicken	Frozen chicken	5.9	+274.1
36	Wrigley's Extra (Mars)	Chewing gum	5.8	+6.5%
40	Diet Coke (Coca-Cola)	Soft drink	5.6	+32.2%
42	Birds Eye Fish	Frozen fish	5.6	+25.8%
43	Ben & Jerry's (Unilever)	Ice cream	5.5	+123.1%
44	Kellogg's Crunchy Nut	Breakfast cereal	5.5	+252.8%
48	Actimel (Danone)	Flavoured yoghurt	5.3	−19.6%

Rank in top 100 fmcg (2017)	Brand/owner	Product	Spend 2017, £m	Change 2016–17
49	Kellogg's Corn Flakes	Breakfast cereal	5.2	n/a
52	Warburtons	Bread	5.1	n/a
54	Coca-Cola Zero Sugar (Coca-Cola)	Soft drink	5.0	−54.2
55	Müller Corner	Yoghurt	4.9	−34.4
57	Hellman's (Unilever)	Mayonnaise	4.9	−9.4
58	M&M's (Mars)	Confectionery	4.8	−18.8
60	Maltesers (Mars)	Confectionery	4.8	−49.0
65	Galaxy (Mars)	Confectionery	4.6	−56.3
67	Carte D'Or (Unilever)	Ice cream	4.6	+444.3
68	Activia (Danone)	Yoghurt	4.5	−35.3
69	Lucozade	Soft drink	4.5	+230.5
72	Yorkshire Tea	Tea	4.5	+4.9
74	Haribo	Confectionery	4.4	0.0
75	Weetabix	Breakfast cereal	4.4	+77.0
76	Yakult	Fermented milk	4.3	+42.9
81	Lindt Excellence	Chocolate	4.1	−4.1
83	Red Bull	Soft (energy) drink	4.1	−9.6
88	Arla Skyr	Yoghurt	4.0	−24.5

Rank in top 100 fmcg (2017)	Brand/owner	Product	Spend 2017, £m	Change 2016–17
89	Innocent Smoothies	Fruit juice	4.0	+40.3
90	Doritos (PepsiCo)	Crisps	3.9	–18.2
91	Arla Food and Milk	Dairy	3.0	+2,083.1
93	Kellogg's Special K	Breakfast cereal	3.8	–15.2
94	Toffifee	Confectionery	3.8	+1.2
95	Dolmio Bolognese (Mars)	Spaghetti sauce	3.8	+3.9
97	Skittle (Mars)	Confectionery	3.7	+149.9
	Total		£222m	

Table 4.8
Food and drink company rank and adspend in fifty top UK fmcg*, 2017

Source: Tatum. The dark side of digital.[271]

* fmcg = fast-moving consumer goods. Here only companies marketing food-related fmcg are listed.

depends on whether the company has the cash, a new line, or a new threat/competitor. In 2017, Birds Eye Chicken's adspend increased by 274.1% on the previous year, while Actimel's declined by 19.6%. Dairy company Arla's spend rose by a massive 2,083.1% on the previous year and Unilever's Carte D'Or ice cream by a mere 444.3%!

With spending such as this, it is little wonder that WHO Europe in 2018 roundly criticized how marketing undermines health, particularly by targeting children.[270] Marketing is ubiquitous via papers, hoardings, TV, radio, e-media. Product placement permeates drama, games and schools. This imbalance compared to public interest information is staggering and has not gone unnoticed. In 2019, following advice from the London Food Board, Sadiq Khan, Mayor of London, banned HFSS food advertising on London Transport, a rare push-back in the name of health. To its credit the Department of Health and Social Care began a consultation about whether the restriction on TV ads before 9 p.m. was having any effect, given young people's use of e-media. We await its findings but a total rethink is in order. Most public research concludes that, with honourable exceptions, current policies and regulations are unable to stem or shape the avalanche.

A significant change in the advertising and marketing landscape has been digitalization. Overall spending on 'traditional' print advertising fell in the UK by 9% in 2016–17. Even industry observers express 'serious concerns about . . . the wild west nature of some of the practices in the online space'.[271] UK online advertising is dominated by two US corporations which account for 61% of all fmcg such as food. And new forms of marketing have emerged, like the use of so-called 'influencers'. These are people who build up sometimes vast online supporter lists on Instagram, TikTok, Snapchat, their own YouTube channels, and other such outlets, which they turn into income by selling their favours to promote products. So far, this escapes particular regulation.

Some influencers are not even human. Agencies have realized that creating a digital person can have the same effect. Lifelike CGI – computer-generated images – influencers become brands themselves and gain hundreds of thousands of followers.[272] Whether these influencers are live or digital, brand managers want their products associated with them, and will pay. By 2018, there were 740 new agencies worldwide specializing in placing marketing through these new digital media. Their skill in matching brands to suitable influencers is now yet another sector adding to the value extraction from food. The 2019 annual spend on this influencer marketing rose to well over €6bn worldwide, up from €5bn in 2018. According to the new sector's own trade group, 11% of such marketing is 'fraudulent' (its word), building notional online followers to boost supposed appeal, or with influencers simply supporting each other's tastes.[273] While these new marketing forms have emerged to shape consumption, there is also an interesting counter-trend in a return to 'traditional' print advertising; some big food advertisers have pulled out of online, worried about brand damage, particularly in relation to parental concerns. In 2016–17, the 100 biggest fmcg adspenders actually increased their spending on traditional media by 20%, but this has not yet altered the general trend away from print media.

Whatever the ebbs and flows of arguments about power

and responsibility, that advertising does shape food culture was settled in the early 2000s when the Food Standards Agency funded a systematic review of its impact. This review and a subsequent one, both led by Prof. Gerard Hastings of Stirling University, concluded that food advertising works.[274],[275] It affects choice. In the fifteen years since, although there have been some policy attempts at control, the reality is that the stable door is only partly being closed on horses which have anyway already bolted. This is not helped by how the advertising industry pulled off a brilliant coup decades ago when offering to regulate itself. Moves led then by UK and Nordic health bodies to toughen up regulations constraining the industry at the EU level were defeated by the argument that advertising is the free movement of ideas. In the UK, the Code of Advertising Practice today is an industry-run body, sanctioned by government, a champion and beneficiary of self-regulation.[276] Thus the unmanageability of modern digital media – not just advertisements but the Twittersphere – has now taken root in already fertile under- and de- and self-regulated policy soil.

Far from the culture battle over food being controlled by a nanny state, the reality is that today we have nanny corporations dominating food messages. And these corporate nannies alas are not always benign, appearing to have little interest in preparing a balanced diet for their young charges. The 'wrong consumer' is apparently again at fault. And even when and if the state tries to rein in food messages, it finds itself up against the sheer buying power of big corporations. Coca-Cola, for example, spends about $4bn a year on ads worldwide. This is twice the total budget of the UN World

Health Organization and twelve times the WHO's health promotion budget stream.[277]

A long-running example of the inequality between health and corporate influence is the distortion of baby foods and breastfeeding practices. The UK has patchy rates of breast-feeding, low for a high-income country. UNICEF runs the UK Baby Friendly accreditation scheme in hospitals. All mater-nity units in Scottish hospitals are accredited as supporting breastfeeding, and as a result Scotland's rate of breastfeeding is rising, and Wales claims a hospital rate of 92%. Figures for England in 2015/16 showed that while almost three quarters of mothers started breastfeeding (73.1%), this fell to 43.2% at 6–8 weeks. In Scotland, 49.3% of women were reported to be breastfeeding soon after birth, but only 38.9% at the 6–8 week review.[278] Mayor Khan's London Food Strategy noted these disparities and set a target to raise London's breastfeeding rates in 2018–23.[279] Despite hard data on the value of breast-feeding, the commercial subversion continues. For comp-anies manufacturing infant formula, the mother's breast is simply a competitor to be neutralized. Besides solid health arguments in favour of breastfeeding, it also starts infants off on a low-carbon footing.[280] If the evidence was followed, there ought to be no contest; the market and marketing are currently framed to undermine what ought to be normal. We need to unpick this culture-health-messaging lock-in. The public's behaviour might indeed often be 'wrong'; how-ever, that is not because we have the wrong consumers, but because the signals are wrong and policymakers are failing to shape the conditions for good human and environmen-tal health.

Food problem 7: Food waste is systemic

According to the Waste and Resources Action Programme (WRAP), the UK wastes over 10 mt of food after the farmgate or an average of 156 kg per person per year. Household food waste is 7.3 mt, estimated by WRAP as worth £15bn and emitting 22 mt of CO_2e. Industry wastes 1.7 mt (worth £1.4bn), the hospitality sector wastes 0.9 mt, and retailers 0.25 mt.[281] In 2017, the House of Commons Environment, Food and Rural Affairs Committee reported that 60% of this waste is avoidable, and the total worth of food waste is £13bn a year.[282] By 2018, using the new international Food Loss and Waste Accounting and Reporting Standard (FLWS), WRAP estimated wasted food as worth even more, £20bn.[283] However calculated, these are huge sums. Figure 4.15 provides an overview. About two thirds of UK food waste is directly by consumers and a third by supply chains. But we should not be complacent about relatively low industry waste figures. That it over-produces food makes waste inevitable. That pricing entices over-purchasing adds to it. That retail power pushes waste back down the chain – rejecting wonky vegetables, for instance, which are perfectly nutritious and sound – means no one is exempt from responsibility. We should not then be surprised that only half of all potatoes bought here, according to WRAP, get to be consumed.

Waste is rather like plastic in public discourse. Everyone now seems to be against it, yet it continues apace. UK consumers are locked in on both and cannot easily do the right thing unless the signals are right, systems are redesigned and behaviour changes. Consumers need help, not

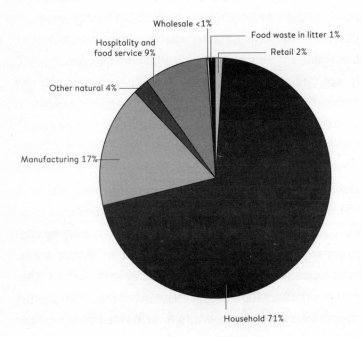

Figure 4.15
UK food waste 2017, by sector, %
Source: WRAP. Estimates of food surplus and waste arising in the UK.[281]

an undercurrent of blaming them in the first place.[284,285] Initially the government targeted consumers with 'shock' tactics, but latterly realized that waste was a systemic rather than an individualized failure; rightly it then started a more 'shared responsibility' approach.[286] Then, following EU leadership, the UK adopted the language of the circular economy, which sees food waste as an economic opportunity. The problem is that a 'tyranny of structurelessness' can emerge where, if everyone is involved, and there is no firm government leadership, the framework slips into a voluntarist approach, or, worse, there is a fixation on only some parts of the problem (plastic straws rather than all plastic packaging).

International waste studies show that consumers in low-income economies waste little food because it is so valuable, whereas those in high-income societies such as the UK waste up to a third of all food because it is so cheap, the culture is so lax and systems of recycling and reuse are either under-funded or disparate. For example, there are at least thirty-nine different sets of rules alone for what plastic can be recycled in the UK. According to WRAP data analysed by the BBC, only 1% of expanded foam packaging can be recycled, 11% of films and food bags, 22% of black plastic, 74% of margarine tubs, and 99% of milk bottles, water bottles and detergent bottles.[287] Design locks us into waste.

Local authorities have too few resources to restructure this, unless forced or funded to do so, yet they carry much responsibility for dealing with waste. Much of what nominally is their responsibility has also been contracted out and privatized. Recycling schemes do not fill the promise on the logos. Much ends in landfill or is sent abroad, or was until China closed its doors to receiving any more.[288] WRAP summarized the facts in early 2017 as the UK still wasting 15 mt of food annually, which cost over £17bn, with 20 mt of associated GHG emissions. Of this wasted food, 9 mt was accepted by WRAP and the industry to be 'avoidable', food that could have been fed to humans or animals.[289] From the mid-2000s, we can detect some strands of action emerging.

One was to turn food waste into bio-energy through anaerobic digester systems.[290] This has been slow to take off, despite initial government pump-priming. By 2017, 20,000 tonnes of perfectly edible food went to produce biogas, a tiny proportion of total waste. This is widely seen as having growth potential, particularly if located at farm level, where farm waste and other waste can be mixed. Biogas – a mixture of methane and CO_2 – can be produced for fuel use (see Figure 4.16). It is debatable how much this reduces greenhouse gas emissions, but the consensus is that broadly it is positive.[291] Germany and Italy are significantly the biggest users and developers of this technology in Europe. One policy danger is that, once expensive plants are built, crops rather than waste are then grown to feed into the machinery. The tail wags the dog.

In the early 2000s, mindful of the huge scale of the food waste problem, the Labour government created WRAP. At first government-funded, it had to switch to become more commercial as a consultancy, and it became a charity in 2014.[292] In its early days, WRAP conducted well-funded, heavily messaged public advertising to generate awareness but that public outreach has dwindled. Since 2005, it has co-ordinated a series of voluntary Courtauld Agreements – so

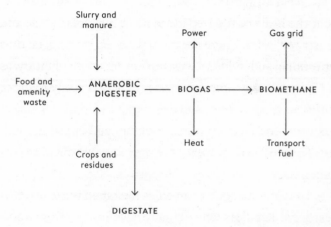

Figure 4.16
A schematic representation of bio-energy production
Source: NNFFC consultants and Oxford Energy Institute, 2017.[291]

called because the first of the series was launched by ministers at the Courtauld Gallery in London. These continue to
be brokered by WRAP with industry today. The latest Courtauld runs till 2025.[293] WRAP now champions the notion of
circular economies, also promoted by the Ellen MacArthur
Foundation,[294,295] and can point to some successes and good
practices in resources efficiency and closed-loop material
flows. What is missing is not WRAP's fault. Food waste is
not at the heart of the Departments of Business, Trade and
Industry or Defra. There are too few legally set targets; thus
institutional and industry engagement remains voluntary, as
are Courtauld Agreements. Waste reduction really requires
a different food system, and delivering this requires action
from everyone – government, industry and consumer culture. This will not happen unless driven by tough, legally
binding targets, incentives and controls.

To be fair, some food companies took food waste seriously early on. Retailers who actually have low profit margins
but from huge turnover saw food waste as a chance to ratchet
up efficiency and reduce costs. They did this partly by pushing responsibility back up supply chains. The low waste figures reported by WRAP for UK retailing cited above disguise
the power retailers have through contracts and specifica-
tions. The head of FareShare, a charity which takes industry-
surplus food and provides it to needy groups, has said: 'we
work with 450 food manufacturers and most big supermarkets and they all initially protest that they have no waste.
Four years ago, Tesco gave us no food, now they give us five
million meals a year and are our largest supplier.'[296]

Retailers have also stepped into the governance vacuum.

Tesco, for example, took on chairing the global industry Champions Group on food waste to meet targets set under the UN Sustainable Development Goal (SDG) 12.3. This aims to halve per capita global food waste at the retail and consumer levels by 2030.[297] The food service sector now also hosts a judicious mix of cajoling and knowledge sharing through trade bodies such as the Sustainable Restaurants Association,[298] and consultancies such as Winnow, which helps chefs cut waste in the kitchen, rationalizing ordering and portion control.[299] These do a good job and have built up experience of what can work or not, but know that unless all workforces, all businesses, all consumers are pushed in the same direction, waste reduction might remain an uphill task.

Since WRAP's information campaign stopped, NGO activism took on trying to reshape consumer behaviour. In the 2000s, 'dumpster-diving', 'freeganism' and 'foraging' thrown-away food had become momentarily chic. Pioneers such as Tristram Stuart shifted this individualized civil reaction into more public engagement,[300] through the Feedback campaign and events such as Feeding the Five Thousand, in which thousands of consumers were fed good wholesome meals from 'waste' at rallies around the UK, starting in Trafalgar Square, London. Community-level experimentation has also bridged civil society and the small-business sector. Restaurants such as Silo, a zero-waste restaurant in Brighton, used waste food for its menu, and Bristol's Poco Tapas adopted a principle of using the entire item of food, with its reduced waste composted. Civil-society schemes also emerged determined to change industry, such as FareShare, which takes misshapes and other about-to-be-wasted food from manufacturing, and makes these available to charities feeding the needy. There have been many such initiatives and enterprises, all doing good work, but still the tide of waste flows out of the food system.

In Britain, we call the receptacles used for food waste 'dustbins'. This is because when coal was the prime source of domestic heating, households needed somewhere to put the residual dust. Local authorities took on the role of collecting household waste. Today, they still have that role, although often privatized to specialist international conglomerates such as Biffa and Suez. British local-authority practices have been significantly altered by EU legislation on landfill, and the landfill tax, as well as stipulations for metal recycling and biological waste. Water companies – the privatized relics of public water boards – have also been legally bound to stop polluting waterways and seas. Yet, in 2017, according to government statistics, the amount of food waste sent for composting (including anaerobic digestion) was 386,000 tonnes, only 2% of total waste collected.[301] What is needed is a fundamental review of how to re-engineer the entire food waste system. It's an elephant in the food system room.

Globally, food waste is estimated at a food worth of almost US$1tn, and adds uncosted effects onto natural resources, livelihoods and human health. The FAO calculates that if food waste was a country, it would be the third-largest CO_2-emitting country in the world, after China and the USA.[302] In 2011, the global carbon footprint of food waste was 4.4 gigatonnes CO_2e per year; that's equivalent to 87% of all global road transport. If the target for the UN's Sustainable

Development Goal 12 to reduce food waste by 50% by 2030 was met, 1.4 gigatonnes CO_2e/year, equivalent to the greenhouse gas emissions of Japan, would be cut. EU food waste, according to the INHERIT project, is 88 mt of food at different levels of the food chain: 53% is at the household level, 19% in the processing sector, 12% in food service and 5% in the wholesale–retail sector.[303] The EU created a Platform on Food Losses and Food Waste to bring together member states and food chain stakeholders to create strategies for food waste reduction.[304] It has also set out to simplify date labelling on food products – a source of confusion to consumers – by extending the list of food products *not* required to have a 'best before' label and clarifying what is meant by this term.[305] Tesco, for one, dropped such labels, while the Co-op decided to donate any foods approaching this date to charity. We shall see what effect such responses have.

It is clearly time that the British dropped any claim that our agri-food system is super-efficient. As the Ellen MacArthur Foundation has noted, it is not just the food which is wasted. The misapplication of fertilizers – applied at the wrong time, run off without affecting intended plant growth – counts for perhaps 70% of fertilizer use. McKinsey & Co. and the Ellen MacArthur Foundation calculated that 'collecting waste from humans, food, food production and agriculture could replace current chemical fertilizer use by 2.7 times'. Within that, the UK could create an income stream of US$1.5bn annually at the municipal level by processing mixed food waste discarded by households and in the hospitality sector.[306,307]

After decades of promoting growth economics, the World Bank now recognizes that growth also creates gross inefficiency; it accepts that this is a 'potential time bomb' and that a circular-economy approach is needed.[308] The problem is that it is hard to redirect speedily enough a system honed in other directions. It is almost as though the system is designed to waste.

But who is to lead this transition? The food waste problem has complex policy lock-ins; we should not be surprised at the slowness of change. A new moralism (the 'wrong consumers' again) about food waste does not help. Food is so cheap, it is sometimes not valued. Indeed, consumers in affluent societies do waste more food than consumers in poor societies. There, food is wasted due to lack of storage, logistics and connection to markets. Economists argue there are no incentives to include waste as costs. Commodification devalues food. Raw food is cheap and the riches from food lie elsewhere. Mass factory-based production inevitably delivers scale of output but also creates food misshapes, equipment breakdowns, recipe failures, human mistakes. It seems hard to avoid the conclusion that mass waste is unavoidable in vast, complex food systems; it's a matter of scale. Mass-production systems have a tendency to over-produce food. There is too much, not too little food.

The waste problem suffers lack of overall leadership. Good people and organizations do their best but there is no central drive. NGOs are unable to fill the vacuum left by government stepping away. Figure 4.17 gives a standard but simple five-tier approach to food waste. Feedback promotes a variant of the five-tier hierarchy. Its top priority is to reduce; then to feed people in need; then to use waste food for livestock; then to compost or use it for bio-energy;

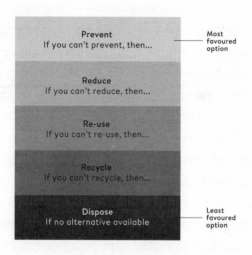

Figure 4.17
An example of a five-tier approach to food waste

and only finally to dispose of it. In the UK, feeding waste to livestock has been banned since the 2001 foot-and-mouth outbreak. It used to be central to pig and poultry production before grain use and factory-farming systems. We need new, more decentralized waste systems which have barriers to cross-infection.[309],[310]

Feedback's argument is that only by admitting the problem can it begin to be addressed. For years, the issue has suffered from 'projectitis', a limited initiative here or there. In 2016, *The Grocer*, the UK retail industry magazine, weighed in with an anti-waste campaign. Whereas in 2014/15 a mere 7,961 tonnes went to the charity FareShare, two years later this has doubled to 13,552 tonnes, and donations to other charities had more than trebled from 1,923 tonnes in 2014/15 to 6,723 tonnes in 2016/17. This may be admirable but it is tiny – affecting roughly 15,000 tonnes out of 1.9 million tonnes.

Britain's food waste problem is policy failure on an institutionally grand scale. An ad hoc web of partial interventions exposes the lack of a clear, firm policy direction. It is time waste reduction became one of the key drivers of the UK food system. This needs legally binding targets and duties. A new Food Act must set these, allocate institutional responsibilities, and see this as essential for food security.

Food problem 8: Social inequalities keep food poverty going

Social inequalities are a running sore of UK politics and society. They lock unacceptable numbers of fellow citizens into poor diets and life chances. The UK is the ninth-most income-unequal society of the thirty-six member states of the

OECD.[311] It would be wrong to blame the food system entirely for this but food both illustrates and contributes to the problem. Food wages are relatively low and top food CEO salaries and corporate profits are bountiful. One of the most obvious manifestations of UK food poverty is the rise in the number of food banks and their use. Food banks are a modern version of medieval welfare when, in theory, most people could turn to an abbey or monastery for sustenance if in need. That social 'contract' was broken by the Reformation, modified by Elizabethan Poor Laws, and tested over who should pay for welfare (and how much) after the so-called 1795 Speenhamland system of payments kicked in when the price of bread got too high. Speenhamland put financial responsibility on the local wealthy, and it was gradually dismantled both by their reluctance to shoulder the burden and by the emergence of a new ethic of individual responsibility within industrial capitalism during the late eighteenth century and early nineteenth, a pattern which the social historian E. P. Thompson described as a new 'moral economy'.[312,313]

The UK has a long history of unmet food need, and there are a number of lasting themes and tensions from the past still infusing UK politics. They include: how to locate individual versus collective responsibility for diet; the role of family values (often a code for mothers) in relation to children's food; whether food prices and affordability should be factored into welfare systems; whether unmet food need is a moral or political failure; and who sets standards of food adequacy and how. These are immense issues, much debated and real but divisive nonetheless. They need to be put firmly on the food security policy table, not least because new responses to unmet food need have crept in, carrying 'moral economic' baggage.

Food banks are one such approach. In their modern form, they began in the USA and rapidly spread to other Western countries applying neo-liberal social policies, such as Canada and Australia,[314,315,316] but only took off in the UK after the fall of the Labour government in 2010, as austerity politics created the opportunity.[317,318,319] Voluntary action replaced declining levels of state responsibility and budgets, but, as has been found in previous times,[320,321,322] charity can be good at highlighting need, can meet some of it, but is unable to provide lasting or adequate safety nets.

The rise in food poverty is the result of macro-policy choices beyond the control of any individual who has fallen on hard times.[323,324] The new Universal Credit scheme, for instance, was introduced to rationalize and cut welfare but has quickly been criticized for adding to food poverty by delays in initial payments. The number of emergency three-day food parcels given by the Trussell Trust, a large church-founded organization which runs a national scheme of food banks, grew from 913,138 in 2013–14 to 1,583,668 in 2018–19. In five years, there was a 73% rise, 19% in the last year alone.[325] Half a million food parcels went to children. Figure 4.18 shows the regional disparity of use. They are literally everywhere. The Trussell Trust is large and well organized but not the only umbrella for direct food aid in the UK. Over 800 other schemes and consortia also exist.[326] In 2018, there were an estimated 2,000 food banks (1,200 overseen by the Trussell Trust) in the UK. These delivered food to 1.6 million people.[327] All the major retailers now liaise in one way or another with food banks, and with other charitable food welfare schemes such as homeless charities, school breakfast clubs and women's refuges.

If the UK goes the US route, retailers and other businesses making such donations will start claiming tax benefits, which merely adds financial insult to nutritional injury. While the motives of people working in such schemes are often honourable, most are aware that food banks do not resolve systemic failure but in fact normalize it.[328] This is why there are divisions as to whether food banks should be accepted as permanent features of social policy or opposed and replaced by financial measures.[329,330,331] Supporters now argue that this is a rational means of disposing of food surplus,[332] which some food companies back, obviously. Others – myself included – see them as well-intentioned fingers in a dyke which is springing ever more leaks.

Is there food poverty because food is too expensive? Unaffordable due to lack of income perhaps. But is it a matter of price? Since the Second World War, the proportion of domestic expenditure on food has dropped from around a third to about 9%, or 12% if eating out is included. In real terms food expenditure has risen, however, jumping from 2007 as commodity prices rose worldwide in the financial crisis. Figure 4.19 shows average UK food prices at constant 2015 values from 1998 to 2018.[333] As the subsequent Figure 4.20 shows, distinguishing between food and alcohol, spending gradually rose in 2000–2012 but declined thereafter, an effect of austerity politics. Households on the lowest 20% of incomes in the UK spend proportionately far more on food than others; the richest also spend far less, of course. Figure 4.21 compares the poorest to the average.

Figure 4.18

Number of three-day emergency supplies given by Trussell Trust in 2018–19, by region

Source: Trussell Trust, End of year stats 2018–19.[325]

The issue of how to decide on what is an adequate diet remains important – is it 'minimum', 'adequate', 'sustainable' and healthy'? And once defined and set, should it be costed into any welfare estimates? Governments are reluctant to admit such processes, but the living-wage campaigns in the 2000s rekindled the matter once more.[334,335] The Living Wage Foundation, an offshoot of Citizens UK, which campaigned for an official rate, reported that 37% of people paid below the rate say they skip meals regularly for financial reasons.[336]

The government offers the Eatwell Plate as the official guide for dietary health. In 2018 the Food Foundation compared the cost of following the Eatwell Plate, using household expenditure data from the 2015/16 Living Costs and Food Survey and data on disposable income in the 2015/16 Family Resources Survey.[337] It found that 26.9% of households would need to spend more than a quarter of their disposable income after housing costs to meet the Eatwell Guide. For households with children in the bottom 20% of earners and on less than £15,860 annual income, 42% of after-housing disposable income would have to be spent if the Eatwell advice was met. In other words, a complete shift in national priorities and consumption patterns would be needed if health genuinely was at the core of how all UK citizens lived. The cost of housing, and other prices, would need to come down dramatically to release purchasing power sufficient to meet health needs. Meanwhile the Dickensian problem of having children in poverty is once more with us.

This should be no surprise to government. The Coalition had received the review by Lambie-Mumford and colleagues

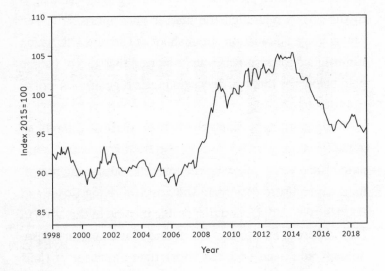

Figure 4.19
UK trends in food and non-alcoholic beverage prices in real
terms, January 1998–December 2018, in constant 2015 prices
Source: Defra. Food statistics pocketbook 2018.[333]

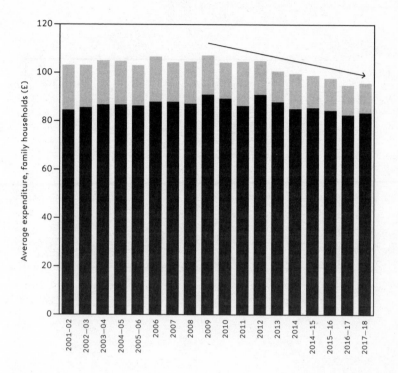

Figure 4.20
Family spending on food and non-alcoholic drink, and on alcoholic drink and tobacco, 2001–18, in real terms at 2017–18 £ value

■ Food and non-alcoholic drink
▢ Alcoholic drink and tobacco

Source: ONS/IGD.

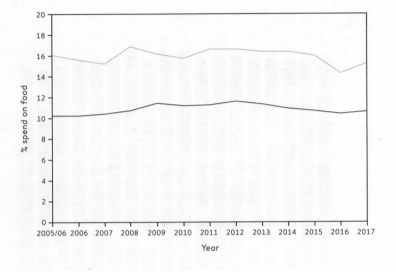

Figure 4.21
Percentage of income spent on food by UK households and
the lowest 20% by income, 2005–17

——— Lowest 20% by equivalized income
——— All UK households

Source: Defra. Food statistics pocketbook 2018.[333]

for Defra in 2014, and in 2017 the minority Conservative government received the Food Standards Agency's 'Food and You Survey' inquiry into food security.[338] This ascertained whether households run out of food due to lack of money, or experience worry this might happen, rating findings on a score of 0–10, with 0 or 1 meaning they had no food security problems and 10 meaning these were severe. The survey covered England, Wales and Northern Ireland but not Scotland in 2016. Of those surveyed 80% reported they had not worried about food running out in the last twelve months, and 88% said that their household had never experienced not being able to afford to eat *balanced meals* in the last twelve months (see Table 4.9). This relatively rosy view was tempered by other findings, particularly in relation to working status and income. 28% of people in households in the lowest income quartile lived in food-insecure households, compared with only 6% in the highest quartile. And 12% of respondents with an 'other' working status (which included part-time or casual or gig-type work) lived in food-insecure households compared with 9% of those in work and only 2% of those who had retired; one benefit of retirement is that flows of income and outgoings tend to be more predictable.

The country and governments alike have had ample evidence for years that something is going structurally wrong on food poverty, a reflection of wider poverty and inequalities. UK social policies have gone dramatically wrong. A Unicef comparative study in 2017 found the UK either the worst or among the worst for children experiencing food insecurity in the European countries investigated (see Figure 4.22[339]). This used FAO data from its 'Voices from the Hungry' study.

Status (0–10)	Wales	England	N Ireland
0 High food security	74	80	78
1–2 Marginal food security	17	12	12
3–5 Low food security	6	5	5
6–10 Very low food security	3	3	5
Bases (unweighted)	492	2,105	521

Table 4.9
Food security status, England, Wales and N. Ireland
Source: FSA. Food and You Survey, Wave 4 (conducted 2016).[338]

The 2018 Poverty report by the Joseph Rowntree Foundation (JRF) estimated 4 million UK workers live in poverty, a rise of over half a million over five years, while 'in-work poverty has been rising even faster than employment, driven almost entirely by increasing poverty among working parents'.[340] This is the underbelly of the UK's 'success' of full employment. The squeeze from welfare cuts has pushed people into work but too many at sub-standard pay. As was summarized earlier (see Chapter 1, p. 8), the Social Metrics Commission in which JRF is a partner, estimated in 2019 that 22% of the UK population (14.3 million people) live in poverty, with 4.5 million of these existing in 'extreme poverty', 50% below the official poverty line.[341]

A study by the British Association for Parenteral and Enteral Nutrition (BAPEN) of 34,699 people admitted to British hospitals across four years, 2007–11, for example, showed that a remarkable 29% of adults when admitted displayed some signs of malnutrition.[342] BAPEN found that rates varied by season (highest rate in the winter at 34%, lowest in spring at 25%). The study – conducted for NHS England and the Welsh and Scottish governments – noted that admissions data were skewed by this being an older than average group.

When Prof. Philip Alston, the UN Rapporteur on extreme poverty and human rights, visited the UK in late 2018 (see Chapter 1),[343] he was met by a range of submissions, as well as days of visits around the UK. His official final report to the UN General Assembly in April 2019 was damning and worth citing here in full:[344]

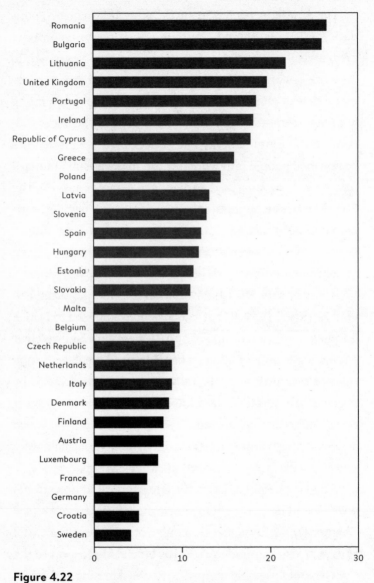

Figure 4.22

Percentage of children under fifteen living in a moderately or severely insecure household (this page) and in severely food-insecure households (opposite)

Source: Pereira, Handa and Holmqvist. Prevalence and correlates of insecurity.[339]

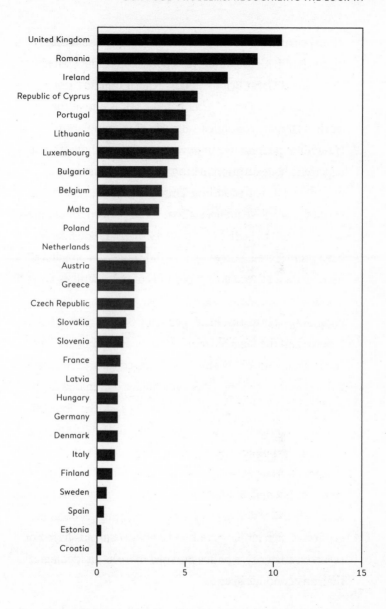

The Special Rapporteur on extreme poverty and human rights, Philip Alston, undertook a mission to the United Kingdom of Great Britain and Northern Ireland from 5 to 16 November 2018. Although the UK is one of the world's largest economies, one fifth of its population (14 million people) live in poverty, and 1.5 million of them experienced destitution in 2017. Policies of austerity introduced in 2010 continue largely unabated, despite the tragic social consequences. Close to 40 per cent of children are predicted to be living in poverty by 2021. Food banks have proliferated; homelessness and rough sleeping have increased greatly; tens of thousands of poor families must live in accommodation far from their schools, jobs and community networks; life expectancy is falling for certain groups; and the legal aid system has been decimated. The social safety net has been badly damaged by drastic cuts to local authorities' budgets, which have eliminated many social services, reduced policing services, closed libraries in record numbers, shrunk community and youth centres and sold off public spaces and buildings. The bottom line is that much of the glue that has held British society together since the Second World War has been deliberately removed and replaced with a harsh and uncaring ethos. A booming economy, high employment and a budget surplus have not reversed austerity, a policy pursued more as an ideological than an economic agenda.

The earlier study by academics for Defra in 2014 had already given clear evidence of parents (usually mothers) having to choose – if that is the right word – not to feed themselves in order to feed their children.[345] Sustain, the NGO alliance, has summarized UK food poverty: (1) a worsening in food poverty wherever the new system of Universal Credit was introduced, with debt rising and a squeeze on domestic expenditure following; (2) a reduction of local-authority budgets available to mitigate food poverty; (3) a rise in diet-related problems due to trading down in quality, sharpening obesity rates.[346] When Prof. Alston's final report was published in 2019 by the UN,[347] the Adam Smith Institute dismissed it, commenting that people 'shouldn't believe a word of what Philip Alston said'.[348] The UK government reaction was simply to state that the UK was a happy society.[349] Indeed, the UK came fifteenth out of 156 countries measured for happiness by the UN Sustainable Development Solutions Network's seventh report in 2019.[350] Alas, that does not mean it is not unequal.

So fragile are some families' circumstances that their children are fed not too badly in term-times when and if the school meal provides a core of nutrition, only for this just-about-adequate status to dip into inadequacy in the holidays, when there are no school lunches or breakfasts. Families on low incomes are eligible for free school meals but their children enter 'holiday hunger' when they are not there. A 2018 study by Newcastle academics suggested that this meant the parents had to find an extra £10.24 per child per week to duplicate (i.e. replace) the free school meal. The study found that while holiday clubs are broadly located in low-income areas, they carry other forms of discrimination, particularly a low representation from ethnic minorities, and rely on charity.[351]

StepChange, the UK debt charity, estimates that 8.8 million people in the UK used debt to pay for everyday essentials in 2017. Of these, 1.1 million used 'high-cost credit'. Of people who resorted to high-cost credit for essentials 49% cited need for food as the principal cause.[352]

The reasons people gave for being locked into punitive high-cost credit to buy food and groceries were clear.* Asked by the researcher: 'Please describe the reasons why you had to go into your overdraft?', answers such as these were given:

- 'Food was needed asap.'
- 'High rent, cost of food for my wife and son, sometimes no food for me.'
- 'I would go into my overdraft 4 days before getting paid and would need it often for diesel or food shopping.'
- 'My ex-husband stopped paying child maintenance, my wages did not cover all the living expenses, so needed overdraft to pay direct debits and food.'

Other comments on food from StepChange clients include:

- 'This meant I was always short at the end of the month and sometimes had to choose between buying food and paying the bills.'
- 'The Universal Credit cap has meant that once I pay my rent and DD's [direct debits] I have virtually nothing left to spend on essentials like food.'
- 'Had to go without food shopping sometimes or resort to credit cards to buy food for family or petrol to get kids to school because of bank charges.'

---

* My thanks to Laura Rodrigues and StepChange for providing this unpublished data.

- 'I get paid weekly on Mondays sometimes I run out of food and make do with bread more so when I have direct debts coming out it's very hard at times and feel like running away.'
- 'When you have no money in your account, no way to pay your rent, and no food – and you see advertisements for pay day loans pretty much everywhere, it's hard not to make a desperate choice.'

The level of UK food poverty indicated here is not surprising but unacceptable nonetheless. For four decades, the literature has pointed to the re-emergence of a 'modern' form of food poverty within 'food choice' culture.[353,354,355,356,357,358,359,360] We must remember that this is not because the UK is a poor country. It is an unequal country. The 2018 ONS Wealth and Assets Survey indicates that the wealth held by the top 10% of households was around five times greater than the wealth of the bottom half of all households combined.[361] Median household total net wealth was £262,400 in 2014–16, up from £223,100 in the previous period (an increase of 18%), but, when debt is included, the median net financial wealth of the bottom 50% was £400 and their median net property wealth worth £0! The UK as a whole is fabulously wealthy – much due to inflated property prices. Aggregate total net wealth of all households in Great Britain was £12.7trn (trillion) in the period 2014–16, up 17% from 2012–14, when it was £10.9trn. Within this property wealth – driving it in parts – was a debt of £1.22trn, which had grown 8% since 2012–14. £1.11trn was mortgage debt and £107.3bn was financial debt.

The Oxfam annual Wealth Inequalities Report for 2019

suggests how UK inequalities nestle within a picture of staggering global concentration of wealth.[362] The wealth of more than 2,200 billionaires across the globe increased by $900bn in 2018 ($2.5bn a day). The wealth of the very richest in the world increased by 12% while the wealth of the poorest 50% of humanity declined by 11%. In 2016, the wealthiest sixty-one billionaires owned as much wealth as the poorest 50% of the global population. In 2017 it was forty-three people, and in 2018 just twenty-six. Oxfam estimates that, within Britain, the poorest 10% of citizens pay proportionately a higher effective tax rate than the richest 10% (49% compared with 34%) once taxes on consumption such as VAT are taken into account. The Institute for Fiscal Studies calculated in 2019 that the share of national income received by the top 1% of the population rose from 6% in 1981 to 14% by 2015.[363] This is almost certainly an underestimate since really rich people have assets which are in trusts or offshore, or have incomes in other countries, which makes income hard to attribute.

The existence of relative as well as absolute food poverty is one of the oldest and most fraught issues in British food policy.* A new geography of work has emerged with economic restructuring and the decline of UK manufacturing, and changed consumption patterns have accompanied shifting aspirations and demands on household purses. Inequalities are easily accepted and rationalized as reflecting effort, but seen at the population level they become harder to accept. One response, since the late nineteenth century, has been for the state to chart certain pathways to mobility – education,

---

* See the discussion in Lang, Barling and Caraher, *Food Policy*, pp. 253–87.

resource allocation. A modern example was the Social Mobility Commission (SMC), created under the presumably not ironically named Life Chances Act 2010 and first reporting in 2012. Its own organizational lifespan coincided with worsening inequalities within Britain, a decline not lost on the SMC chair, Alan Milburn, a former Labour MP and minister. Together with other commissioners he resigned at the end of 2017, so bad had the situation become.*

The SMC's fifth report in 2017 stated that a 'stark social mobility postcode lottery exists in Britain today where the chances of someone from a disadvantaged background succeeding in life is bound to where they live'.[364] It found a 'self-reinforcing spiral of ever-growing division' and called on the government to inject more funds into those underfunded regions and towns. It calculated that the North of England was underfunded by £6bn compared to London – not that there are not stark inequalities of provision and wealth within London, too. Indeed, the SMC debunked the simplistic North–South divide analysis. Almost all regions have internal divergences.

INEQUALITY, INCOME, LIVING COSTS AND LIFE EXPECTANCY

That British food expenditure has dropped as a proportion of incomes can be painted as a great post-Second World War success story, and, in some respects, it is. It has freed disposable income to be spent on other features of consumerism and enabled new mass markets to emerge. This sits ill

---

* Alan Milburn was replaced by Dame Martina Milburn, no relation, former head of the Prince's Trust.

with data on terrible inequalities. Greater London is the second-richest city in Europe with a notional 'GDP' equivalent to $714.975bn, 22% of the UK's national GDP, and that wealth is from work now mostly in the service sector. Yet four in ten Londoners cannot afford a decent standard of living, according to the Trust for London.[365] Applying a calculation of a minimum income standard (MIS), the Centre for Research in Social Policy at Loughborough University found the MIS would have to be 56% higher for a single working-age adult in Inner London than for the rest of the UK, and 39% higher in Outer London than the rest of the UK. This was heavily due to the cost of renting. For a dual-earning family of two adults and two children it was 18% more in Inner London and 21% more in Outer London. 27% of pensioners living in London did not meet the MIS, compared to 15% in the rest of the UK.

This is not special pleading for London but to highlight that important regional, age and income differentials are manifest everywhere and shape food poverty. As a flexible item in household budgets, food is highly sensitive to such determinants. So it is not surprising that health is affected or that the Food Standards Agency has found that one in four people skip meals to save costs.[366] Or that the Food Foundation calculated there were 8.4 million food-insecure people in the UK, applying UN definitions.[367] Or that in a 2018 survey of 2,032 UK adults, the End Hunger coalition (campaigning to create a proper measure for food poverty in the UK) found one in three people reporting they skip meals due to lack of money.[368]

Disparities between UK regions are extensive and an entirely justified source of political resentment. The UK2070

Commission, for example, has already confirmed that inequalities radiate out from the South-East, where unemployment is relatively low to the far North and West, where it is higher.[369] But the Commission's point is that the UK lacks regional bodies who can do much about it. Indeed, local authorities have become supplicants to the central state rather than providing a more local form of governance near to the people.[370] UK political transfer of power to its regions has been tentative. It is a highly centralized state. After the Second World War, the UK helped create strong regional bodies in Germany but would not do so at home. And attempts at decentralization and devolution have been patchy and divisive. Ironically, given hostility to the EU from some regions, it was actually the European Investment Bank and the EU's Committee of the Regions that provided a mix of political and financial support aiming to narrow UK regional disparities. As the UK2070 Commission showed (see Figure 4.23), the 'South' of the UK (defined as London, the South-East, South-West and East of England, and the East Midlands) has steadily drawn away from the 'North' of the UK (defined as the West Midlands, Wales, the North-West and North-East of England, Yorkshire–Humberside, Scotland and Northern Ireland), with London steaming upwards as itself a region. Figure 4.23 shows the cumulative percentage point differential growth in gross value added in these three 'blocs' of the UK.[371]

Macro-economic drivers, captured by such political realities, shape what happens in food. Food spending follows wealth and determines health. The international, not just UK, academic evidence is clear that people living on tight budgets are pressured into consuming high-calorie

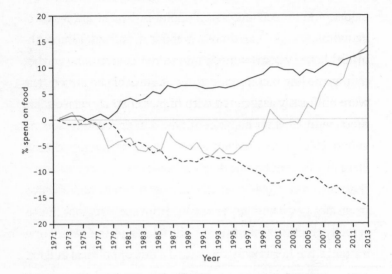

Figure 4.23
Cumulative percentage point differential growth in gross
value added, South UK, North UK and London, 1971–2013

——— London
——— South (inc. London) UK
- - - - - North UK

'South' defined as: London, South-East, South-West,
East of England and East MidlandsYorkshire-Humberside

'North' defined as: West Midlands, Wales, North West,
Yorkshire-Humberside, North-East. Scotland and
Northern Ireland

Source: UK 2020 Commission. Fairer and Stronger.[371]

cheap food. A 2015 meta-analysis of international studies by Darmon and Drewnowski showed that foods of lower nutritional value and lower-quality diets generally cost less per calorie and tended to be selected by groups of lower socio-economic status.[372] Low-cost, nutrient-dense foods might be available but were not always palatable or culturally acceptable to the low-income consumer. Acceptable healthier diets were uniformly associated with higher costs. Lower-quality diets, with a higher content of added sugars and fats, were generally less expensive on a per-calorie basis. Food budgets were insufficient to ensure optimum diets.

Perhaps because it is such a persistently unequal society, the UK has an honourable counter-tradition of social research about food inequalities and poverty. When John (later Sir and then Lord) Boyd Orr conducted his studies of food, low income and health in the 1930s,[373] the findings became front-page news around the Empire, embarrassing the mother country and adding doubts as to whether it really did occupy the high moral ground.[374] Today, food poverty in the UK takes different forms – obesity more than stunting – but the poverty connection has not been resolved; nor is it front-page news. As a result, according to the Institute of Health Equity (IHE) at University College London (UCL), led by Professor Sir Michael Marmot, the long-term rise in life expectancy has stalled, and gaps between rich and poor social groups and geographical areas are wide and sometimes widening.[375] Unemployment has gone down, which is a good thing, but the number of people not achieving the MIS for a decent quality of living has gone up. Using two indicators by which to measure income – the Minimum Income Standard and whether the income reaches 75% of the MIS – UCL's IHE has shown that both measures grew between 2008/9 and 2014/15 (see Figure 4.24).

Inequalities within and between local authorities are also deeply rooted. Booth showed it for London in the late nineteenth century,[376] Engels for Manchester in the mid-nineteenth[377] and Seebohm Rowntree in York from 1901 to 1941.[378,379] Yet today life expectancy for men varies from seventy-four years in Blackpool to eighty-three years of age in Kensington and Chelsea, a nine-year gap. Among women, it varies from seventy-nine in Manchester to eighty-six in Kensington and Chelsea, a seven-year gap.[380] Within local authorities, there are also considerable inequalities due to deprivation levels. For men, in the London Borough of Barking and Dagenham, the gap between most and least deprived was slightly less than three years, while in Blackpool, Stockton-on-Tees, and Kensington and Chelsea the figures were in the region of 14–15 *years*. These gaps are *within* spatially tiny areas! A worrying lock-in to disparity means that deprived people spend more years in a state of ill-health; they become ill or unhealthy and spend over-long periods in that state before dying. In the London Borough of Tower Hamlets, for example, females are likely to spend thirty years in ill-health and males twenty-four years.

The Marmot UCL team estimates that 40–50% of variation in health outcomes is caused by unequal distribution of social and environmental factors. Here is where diet plays a significant role, featuring in all six of the changes the earlier 2010 Marmot Review recommended government should tackle to reduce UK health inequalities:[381,382]

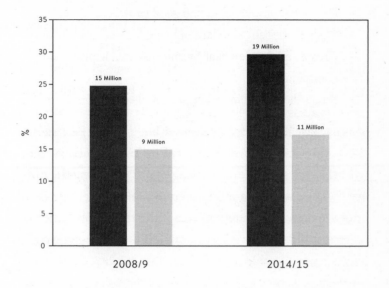

Figure 4.24
Percentage of all individuals in households below Minimum
Income Standard, UK, 2008/09 and 2014/15
■ % Below MIS
▨ % Below 75% MIS
Source: IHE. Marmot indicators briefing 18 July 2017.[380]

- Give every child the best start in life.
- Enable all children, young people and adults to maximize their capabilities and have control over their lives.
- Create fair employment and good work for all.
- Ensure a healthy standard of living for all.
- Create and develop healthy and sustainable places and communities.
- Strengthen the role and impact of ill-health prevention.

This package has not been delivered, but it should be. In 2018, the Royal Society of Arts consulted its 28,000 Fellows as to what they felt were the over-riding challenges facing UK society.[383] They wanted a modern equivalent of the 1942 Beveridge Report, something which captures the national interest by resetting the table. RSA Fellows felt that large-scale challenges loom – problems in facing sustainability, democracy, ownership, income and work. They are right. Food sits across all of them, and inequalities frame the lock-in.

Food problem 9: Food power, competition and control

The UK food economy is highly concentrated. Power has accrued slowly but inexorably – despite 'disruptors' – to a relatively small number of enterprises within each major sector.[384] At the end of the second decade of the twenty-first century, nine large food retailers dominate food shopping; 0.5% of citizens own almost all the land; the top five food manufacturers have a combined turnover of £30bn; and 85% of manufacturers are small companies with fifty employees or fewer.[385] Even in the food service sector, large companies have emerged. This is particularly so in the fast-food and contract-catering sectors. In home deliveries, Uber, Deliveroo and Just Eat dominate. This sector is relatively new. Instead of individual restaurants having their own couriers, these new giant companies have emerged fusing food and transport, thus extending the logistics sector. Although much is made of the ruthless competition within sectors, the remarkable concentration of power between sectors is being weakly addressed by public policy. When Adam Smith described this country as 'a nation governed by shop-keepers' (a phrase repeated by Napoleon),[386] he could not have envisaged what now exists – a nation whose diet is funnelled through a handful of companies in almost all sectors.

A century ago, it was the manufacturing sector which was emerging as the food powerbroker. Processors were beginning to brand foods, and sell to the fast-growing urban market. Today the retailers – and to a lesser extent the fast-growing food service sector – have food manufacturing under their control. Of 6,800 food-manufacturing businesses in the UK, 96.4% are small and medium-sized (SME) enterprises, employing between one and 249 people. While those SMEs had a total turnover of £11bn, the 3.6% of large companies' turnover was £153bn, fifteen times more.[387] At the EU level, 290,000 food-manufacturing SMEs account for 48% of turnover, while the 3% of firms which are large take 51.6% of total food-manufacturing sector turnover.[388]

Today UK manufacturers have 2.2% of the global food and drink export market, whereas French food companies have 4.7% and German 5.6%.[389] The EU is by far the UK's biggest food export market. In 2018, 61% of UK exports went to the

EU, worth €13.8bn, while the UK imported €32.3bn of food and drink products from the other twenty-seven members of the EU.[390] The UK's top food export market is its only land-based neighbour, Ireland, one of the twenty-seven, of course. The UK's top-ten export products are actually dominated by whisky; three more are alcoholic and the others mostly meaty (see Table 4.10).

With industrialization from the late eighteenth century, people rapidly moved away from the land, partly pulled by jobs and partly pushed by the awful conditions on the land. Today, there are vastly more jobs off the land than on it, and a quarter of all UK food industry employees were from the EU in 2018.[391] The UK has not mastered its urban–rural tensions well. A running theme in UK food policy concerns movement. As we saw in Part One, Britain has a chequered history of outsourcing its food supplies around the world. But movement has been troublesome in other respects, too. Supermarketization meant people travelled further and further to get their food; and now that trend is being partly reversed by food being home-delivered, direct to them.

To the British shopper, a main impact of the food retail revolution since the 1970s has been the emergence of super-market power – based on self-service, which persuades the consumer to replace shopworkers. Self-service began in the USA in 1916 with Clarence Saunders' store in Memphis, Tennessee, and arrived much later in the UK. The first US-style self-service supermarket in the UK was opened by the then powerful Co-operative in Southsea in March 1948. Thus began the Americanization of UK food shopping, and the process of restructuring (critics say 'eviscerating') towns and

Product	2018	Change 2017–18		
		Value, £	Value, %	Volume, %
Whisky	£4.8bn	£342.3m	7.7	3.0
Chocolate	£749.5m	£32.0m	4.5	3.9
Cheese	£675.4m	£60.1m	9.8	10.8
Salmon	£644.9m	−£84.6m	−11.6	−14.2
Wine	£630.4m	£56.1m	9.8	21.3
Gin	£614.4m	£80.1m	15.0	11.6
Beef	£536.6m	£35.1m	7.0	1.9
Beer	£489.2m	−£36.5m	−7.0	−6.3
Breakfast cereals	£481.6m	£52.7m	12.3	13.2
Pork	£465.5m	£6.7m	1.5	3.2

Table 4.10
Top ten UK food and drink exports, 2018
Source: FDF, 2019.[391]

cities – hence the boarded-up town centres today. Out-of-town shopping malls also came to the UK from the USA, the legacy of the Austrian-born US architect Victor Gruen, who first successfully designed a mall ten miles outside Minneapolis in 1952. The car-centred era of the food economy had begun.[392] This format paved the way for a revolution in logistics, which in turn accelerated concentration in market share by those who exploited it.

In 1979, Tesco had 7.2% of the UK grocery market, Sainsbury 6.1% and Asda a mere 1.5%. By 1990–91 Tesco had 12%, Sainsbury 12.4%, Asda 8.4%, Morrisons 1.7%. By 2018, Tesco had 28%, Sainsbury 16%, Asda 15.6% (see Table 4.11[393]). Today, the large British food retailers are being challenged by two German retailers, Aldi on 6.9% and Lidl on 5%, who operate on a different economic model of more restricted choice. They offer 3,000–6,000 items in a store rather than the 30,000–40,000 items of the superstores. The big UK retailers then began to ape the smaller-range 'local' stores. The Co-operative Group, which had started the British supermarket revolution back in 1948, was early to go this route, having already been diminished by the revolution it pioneered. By 2018, although its market share was again slowly growing, it was from a low base of 5.9%. This 'relocalization' of food shopping suggests the joys of sitting in a traffic jam to go shopping had begun to pall, but whether the British will build exercise into daily life by food shopping on foot or bicycle depends on whether town planning encourages this, as it should.

The changing dynamics of the retail market are the source of much fascination to economists and investors,[394] but at what point does this concentration become anti-competitive?

Company	Ownership structure	Country base	GB market share, %*
Tesco	FTSE 100	UK	27.7
Sainsbury	FTSE 100	UK	15.7
Asda	Walmart	USA	15.5
Morrisons	FTSE 100	UK	10.5
Aldi	Albrecht family	Germany	7.6
Co-op	Non-profit	UK	5.9
Lidl	Schwartz Gruppe (family)	Germany	5.2
Waitrose	Employee share partnership	UK	5.2
Iceland	Management buyout plus Brait SE	UK	2.2
Symbols and independents	Private	UK	1.6
Other outlets	n/a	UK	1.8
Ocado	FTSE 100	UK	1.2

* Percentages are rounded up.

Table 4.11
GB food retail market share, ownership structure and base, 2018
Source: Kantar Worldpanel[393] and author, 2019.

Most economists accept the rule of thumb that a company is on or near monopoly influence when it has 25% or more of market share, but Tesco has had that for years with impunity. If we look at market concentration by store throughput, not just company name, the concentration is even greater.

In 2016, 87,141 shops supplied groceries (food and other domestic products) worth £180.3bn to the UK's then 65 million consumers. Of this UK market, 368 hypermarkets (owned by the big retailers) took £16.4bn; 5,584 supermarkets (owned by the big retailers) took £86.3bn; 46,980 convenience stores took £38bn; 4,623 discounters took £18.2bn; online took £9.7bn; and 29,586 other kinds of shops took £11.8bn.[395] Thus 5,952 of large-format stores took 56.9% of all sales.

The battle for market share today is fought over store format and style as well as ownership. Experimentation is emerging, tapping into consumer frustration, but also pushing it beyond what is really needed. Start-ups in the large cities offer a box of ready-to-cook ingredients, as though it's hard to chop one's own vegetables and control portion size. This model of retailing-as-catering goes beyond the veg box schemes pioneered by the organic movement and now dominated by Riverford or Abel & Cole, who provide fruit and vegetables for the customer to decide what to cook. Many of these so-called 'third party specialists', which provide a recipe and contents for just one meal, might not survive. But who knows which it will be of Farmdrop, Quiqup, Home Run, Grocemania, Good Sixty, Easy food, or EasyFood (the latter the latest brand experiment by Sir Stelios Haji-Ioannou)?[396] The big retailers watch such developments acutely, and all have expanded their delivery systems since 2000.

A revolution in home delivery has created in a decade an entirely new logistics wedge within the food system. Just Eat was bought in January 2020 by the Dutch delivery firm Take-away.com, creating a £6.2bn company. Uber (founded as a cab company, US-owned), Deliveroo (founded in 2013, UK-owned but in which, in 2020, Amazon began to buy a stake), and the mid-player Ocado (UK-founded by former Goldman Sachs bankers, now in a 50–50 joint venture with Marks & Spencer) all vie for delivery dominance. Ocado is solely a delivery retailer and pioneered highly roboticized vast warehousing outside cities. It now licenses and sells its software development and logistics expertise to retailers abroad. Within retailing, technologists working for Moby, based in Shanghai, are pioneering a 'staffless store', while others are experimenting with robot delivery vehicles or drones. These investments are forays and experiments into just how little labour can be used and how software is the source of power. The buzz of drones could replace vans (and pollination naturally done by bees, but that is a different story); robot delivery could compete with humans walking; van deliveries might proliferate, reinforcing streets as unsafe for children to play in or take exercise.

These new dynamics and modes of competition have implications for the human-scale environment. Car use to shop was encouraged by locating stores away from town centres. The 1970s rise of mega out-of-town superstores is now being altered by new, smaller stores. The big difference is that these are not independent stores but small ones owned and run by giant companies. Shops of all kinds, not just food, close daily. Stoke-on-Trent lost 23% of its shops in 2013–19, Eastbourne 20.5%, Lincoln 14.7%. A vicious circle occurs of declining footfall, rising internet shopping, squeezed consumer spending and uncertain confidence, all of which shapes who captures consumer food spending, and ultimately even pension investment funds.[397] But it has helped board up town centres. Small independent food shops have declined – although the number of independent butchers grew, albeit from a very low base.

This retail revolution has altered property prices. Retailers' own property portfolios can be vast assets. By 2007, Tesco was Europe's biggest property company, with property assets then worth £28bn. Its property division yielded £139m annual profits from its 139 stores.[398] It and others began to sell and lease back their stores, taking the chance to profit from the asset boom. Then the commodity crisis came in 2007–8. A decade later, after the selling off and leasing back, and with the domestic property market still high, the retailers were sweating their property assets by successfully building flats on top of stores. The rise of the German discounters meant that their property management teams became the growth drivers of retail property value, entirely in towns and near high concentration of populations.[399] Rural populations are still car-dependent. By 2016, the shift to sell property – on sell-and-lease-back terms – had largely slowed down, yet still forty property transactions worth £1.18bn were traded.[400] In 2018, there were forty-four transactions worth £1.06bn. 44% of deals by value in 2018 were for institutions such as insurance or pensions, 19% by property companies, 13% by the retailers themselves and 8% by overseas investors.[401]

While big profits were made under these property deals, the tensions caused by the concentration of power still squeezed primary producers. Food manufacturers had come out of the Second World War relatively strong, and, as we saw earlier, farmers were enticed to modernize by state subsidies from 1947 onwards, but it was the retailers who gradually took control once the practice of Retail Price Maintenance (RPM) was ended in 1964. Under the Retail Prices Act 1964, fiercely contested within the Conservative Party at the time, food manufacturers could not set the price at which retailers had to sell their goods.[402] After the abolition of RPM, no longer did retailers peg their prices to what manufacturers wanted; they could 'stack it high, sell it cheap'.

Today, as Table 4.12 shows, the food retailer sector vies with manufacturers and caterers as to which of them adds the most value (GVA). The message, a theme throughout this book, is again that primary producers receive relatively little compared to others further down the chain. The EU was slow to respond to this unfairness, initially by banning 'unfair practices' and more recently in 2019 by developing a system of making transparent where value is taken in particular commodity supply chains – meat, fruit, vegetables, eggs, sugar, olive oil and some arable crops. The EU based its action on public support in an EU-wide 2018 opinion poll in which 88% supported strengthening farmers' role in the food supply chain. Whatever happens to UK–EU relations, UK moves in this direction need to be continued, and rapidly.[403]

Although retailers gate-keep between primary producers and manufacturers and consumers, the competition between them has lowered the rates of return on capital employed (ROCE) compared to manufacturing or even food service since 2013. And while ROCE tells us something about

Sector	£bn
Agriculture	10.3
Fishing and aquaculture	1.0
Agricultural wholesaling	2.3
Agricultural supply industry	1.0
Food and drink supply industry (e.g. machinery)	0.4
Food and drink manufacturing	31.1
Food and drink wholesaling	12.6
Food and drink retailing	30.3
Non-residential catering	36.4
Total	125.4

Table 4.12
GVA in the UK food chain, 2018, £bn
Source: Defra. Agriculture in the UK chart 14.2.[404]

potential for returns to investors (and possibly pensions), what is important for the present discussion is how retailers use their power to squeeze margins elsewhere in pursuit of their own sales. The Grocery Supply Code of Practice was created in 2009 to respond to years of claims of unfair practice by retailers in their dealings with farmers. In the decade since the Code was adopted, Christine Tacon, the Adjudicator, and her team had success in shining an independent light onto complex intra-chain negotiations and tackled some key unfairness such as deliberate late payments.[405] But in 2018, 43% of suppliers to the supermarkets still felt they were dealt with in a manner which infringed the Code by the retailers. While some argue that the GCA remit should be widened – myself included – the government rejected this in 2017. Table 4.13 provides the 2018 overview of how well the retailers fare in complying with the Code.[406] But the market squeeze continues.

Wage rates and differentials are also key factors in market power, not just profits or value-adding. The gap between highest and lowest paid within enterprises tells us about corporate values. Oxfam's international analysis in 2018 suggested that, in less than five days, the highest-paid chief executive at a UK supermarket earns the same as a woman picking grapes on a typical farm in South Africa will earn in her entire lifetime.[407] Just 10% of the cash returned to shareholders on average across the three biggest UK supermarkets in 2016 would be enough to lift more than 30,000 workers on South African grape farms to a living wage. Comparing a number of traded foods – orange juice, bananas, green beans, tea, prawns, canned tuna – across three periods (1996–8, 2000–2002, 2015), Oxfam found that inputs for the developing-world farmers had risen from 3%

Retailer	Consistently well	Mostly	Rarely	Never
Aldi	58	39	3	0
Tesco	39	58	3	0
Waitrose	41	54	5	0
Sainsbury	37	58	5	0
Morrisons	37	56	7	0
Lidl	43	50	7	0
Marks & Spencer	35	57	7	1
Asda	28	64	7	1
Co-op	27	61	11	0
Iceland	27	57	14	1

Table 4.13
How well retailers comply with the UK Grocery Code, %
Source: Groceries Code Adjudicator. Groceries sector survey 2018.[406]

of what the UK consumer paid in 1996–8 to 5% in 2015, while small-scale farmers and workers saw their share drop from 7.6% to 5.7% of the final price. Meanwhile, reported Oxfam, the UK supermarkets' share rose from 41.3% to 52.8%.[407] This injustice is what Fairtrade systems were created to prevent; and they have had some success.[408] But much more remains to be done, as a large three-year study for the Department for International Development by Prof. Chris Cramer and colleagues at SOAS, University of London, found in 2014. Even with Fairtraded products, the primary workers and women did not share in the Fairtrade premium as much as the local Fairtrade co-operative itself.[409,410] The SOAS report upset many in the Fairtrade movement, but also marked a time when some of the big retailers began to break away from Fairtrade and instead to institute their own systems. It remains to be seen whether this signals them actively wanting to break the small niche Fairtrade has in the entire food market.

It is also a shame that while development NGOs such as Oxfam highlight the unequal returns accrued by low-income farmers in developing countries who feed into global food supply chains, there is less discussion about UK inequalities and systematic unfair apportioning of returns from food. Yet, as the National Audit Office showed in its 2019 review of post-Brexit plans, 16% of UK farmers made a loss between 2014–15 and 2016–17, despite receiving direct payments from the EU's CAP, and 42% of farmers would have made a loss between 2014–15 and 2016–17 if they had not received direct payments and everything else stayed the same. As has been said earlier, if farm taxpayer welfare keeps farming afloat, this is hardly a ringing endorsement of the sector's economic

Sector	Number of outlets	Meals, millions	Food purchases, £m	Food and beverage sales, £m	Food and beverage sales, £m, by whether group or independent	
					Group	Independent
Restaurants	30,829	788	2,297	12,374	7,232	5,142
Quick-service restaurants	35,061	2,280	2,928	14,210	11,193	3,017
Pubs	39,849	746	1,145	5,490	3,265	2,225
Hotels	43,871	611	1,832	10,324	5,676	4,648
Leisure	20,302	519	829	4,168	1,672	2,496
Staff catering	16,415	702	867	2,372	2,123	249
Healthcare	32,423	904	647	862	790	72
Education	34,192	1,168	749	1,366	1,180	186
Services	3,068	258	224	285	285	0
Total	256,010	7,976	11,518	51,451	33,416	18,035

Table 4.14
The UK food service market, 2018
Source: Backman UK foodservice market 2018.[413]

health. It suggests a dependency culture for farmers and cheap inputs for off-farm sectors.

More attention is needed on the the UK hospitality (food service) industry, in which turnover and concentration have risen remarkably in recent years. The UK has Europeanized and now eats in a myriad of cafés and restaurants, snacking on takeaways, in short breaks, and while travelling.[411] Catering has many SMEs but increasingly, despite varied fascias, the public consumes from 'combines'. Four companies are the largest eating-out companies globally:[412] McDonald's, Yum! Brands (owner of Taco Bell, KFC and Pizza Hut), the coffee chain Starbucks, and Restaurant Brands (owner of Burger King). In contract catering, two conglomerates dominate: Compass, which is UK-headquartered, and Sodexho of France. There are thousands of small contract caterers, many highly profitable, but the big companies have come to dominate UK markets (see Table 4.14).[413] In 2018, there were over a quarter of a million food outlets in the UK, producing 7,977 million meals, made from food purchases costing £11.5bn and retailed together with drink at well over four times that money. The number of outlets are quite spread across the sub-sectors, but sales to the healthcare (hospitals) and education sub-sectors are dwarfed by the eating-out markets (restaurants, quick-service restaurants, pubs and hotels).

LAND CONCENTRATION

The concentration of food power reviewed thus far is relatively recent; today's giant firms were either entirely new or at most founded in the late nineteenth century, and the delivery sector is very new. The concentration of land ownership, however, began much earlier. The continuing concentration of UK farm size was discussed earlier (see 'Food problem 2', pp. 249–52). When Henry VIII annexed monastery lands and broke up the church's land ownership, he began a process of land concentration maintained to this day. Enclosures in the seventeenth and eighteenth centuries privatized common lands. In 2018, the Ministry of Defence instituted the first major enclosure of land since the nineteenth century when it took over land in Cumbria for military training. Technically, Cumbria Council deregistered the common land at (suitably named) Warcop to enable the MOD to keep it.[414]

Land ownership in both town and country raises questions of access and use as well as wealth. We need a new Doomsday Book to clarify who really owns what. The Land Registry does not give a complete picture because large estates are often not sold (but held in trusts or offshore) and therefore not registered. Kevin Cahill worked out in 2002 that 189,000 families owned two thirds of UK land. But Guy Shrubsole in 2019 estimated that about half of England is owned by just 25,000 people (see Table 4.15).[415]

Our problem today is that a massive concentration of ownership coincides with a time when the UK needs to be more flexible about land use than it has been at any time since the Second World War. The problem is not just ownership or use but value; it is a good investment. British land values rose by 169% in 2006–16. As Mark Twain is reputed to have said: 'Buy land, they don't make it any more.'* Savills 2017 Agricul-

---

* There is little evidence he said this, but he and this saying were witty enough for it to be true.

Group	English land owned, %
Aristocracy and gentry	30
Corporations	18
Oligarchs and city bankers	17
Unaccounted	17
Public sector	8.5
Home owners	5
Conservation charities	2
Crown and royal family	1.4
Church	0.5

Table 4.15

Estimate of land ownership in England

Source: Shrubsole. *Who Owns England?*[415]

tural Land Market Survey valued Great Britain's combined 39.8 million acres of farmland at £185.7bn (see Figure 4.25).[416] And Knight Frank calculates that in the last fifty years (1969–2019), those land values have risen 3,660%.[417]

This is a lot of money but pales into insignificance when compared to the housing market's value. In 2018, Great Britain's housing stock was worth £7.14trn. At January 2018 values, that housing stock (if converted to cash) was sufficient to buy Google, the International Space Station, the top twenty UK house-builders, all the oil left in the North Sea, all Bitcoin in circulation, Amazon, Apple, Coca-Cola, McDonald's, all companies in the FTSE100 and FTSE250, the top fifteen mortgage lenders and the English Premier League![418] Prime UK arable land sold in 2018 for an average of nearly £9,000 per acre, with average grade 3 farmland making £7,500 per acre. Grazing land sold for £4,400–£5,500 per acre, Savills reported.[419] Today's land values are twice those of 1900 in real terms and provide one of three peaks across the 120 years since 1900. Values dropped in and after the First World War, rose slowly across the Second World War, but rocketed when the UK integrated into the Common Market in 1970–75, dropping back slowly until 2003, when they again rose, peaking in 2014, after which they have dropped with uncertainties about European links.[420]

SUBSIDIES FOR WHAT?

The rise and fall of land values brings us to the question of subsidies again. Critics of the EU have long complained about the subsidies associated with the Common Agricultural Policy (CAP), but in truth the UK subsidized its farming long before its EU membership. The UK, USA and the six countries who founded the Common Market, now the EU, all began to subsidize farming in the 1930s and accelerated it after 1945. Mark Cocker, in his lyrical exploration of whether Britain can save its wildlife before it is it too late, argued that 'EC membership did not so much change overall policy as reinforce it.'[421] In some respects that is true; both before and after the UK joined the EEC in 1973, it was accepted that the state had a role in supporting farming and was committed to food security. But how this was delivered did change. Entering what became the EU, the UK moved from a subsidy system based on deficiency payments to a system where prices were fixed in advance. The UK deficiency payment system meant that, if market prices fell below officially set targets, the British government paid farmers the difference between the target price and the market price, but only for those supplies for which buyers could be found. But both the CAP and the UK's deficiency payment system of 1947–73 rejected notions of 'free markets' which had in practice been so ruinous before 1939.

The assumption that subsidies are needed and are a state responsibility is anathema in neo-liberal economics. Prof. Dieter Helm, the Oxford University economist who chairs Defra's Natural Capital Committee, has stated that UK farmers suffer 'subsidy addiction'.[422] Subsidies indeed rose to become 40% of farm incomes in 2000. They amounted to 120% of farm incomes in the mid-2000s, dropped back to 60% in 2014, rose again and then fell again.[423] A subsidy at 120% of income means that the subsidy is far greater than the income derived from selling the farm produce. What an indictment, indeed, but surely, if anyone is addicted, it is those *after* the farmgate who benefit from being sold otherwise unprofitable produce

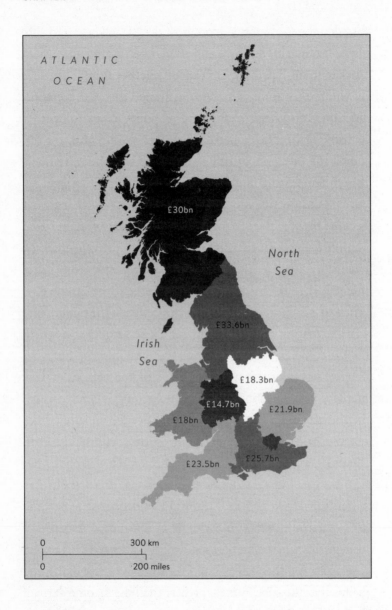

Figure 4.25
Total value of agricultural land and woodland in 2016
Source: Savills. GB agricultural land.[416]

	Great Britain	England
Total 2016 Value	£185.7bn	£137.7bn
Total Area (acres)	39.8m	21.9m
1-year % change	-2.9%	-3.1%
10-year % change	149%	171%

	North of England	South-East England
Total Area (acres)	6.4m	3.9m
1-year % change	-2.9%	-2.5%
10-year % change	134%	153%

	East Midlands	West Midlands
Total Area (acres)	2.8m	2.2m
1-year % change	-1.1%	-0.9%
10-year % change	188%	215%

	East of England	Wales
Total Area (acres)	3.2m	4.1m
1-year % change	-6.2%	-0.9%
10-year % change	177%	131%

	South-East England	Scotland
Total Area (acres)	3.5m	13.8m
1-year % change	-3.9%	-3.0%
10-year % change	210%	89%

at low prices. Subsidies are actually a transfer from the public purse to those who benefit from the production of 'cheap' food supplies.

A different and even more biting criticism of subsidies is that they have gone to those who need help the least. In 1995–2016, the top 10% of farms (by size) received 77% of all 'covered commodity' subsidies; and the top 1% received 26% of all subsidies, or $1.7m per recipient. A study by Greenpeace Unearthed found that one in five of the top 100 recipients of EU CAP subsidies were billionaires.[424] Two thirds of the £2.3bn single-payment budget – £1.6bn – went to the top 20% of claimants while the bottom 40% of claimants received only £95m combined – just 4% of the total subsidies. A National Audit Office review of 2017 data showed that the top 11% of subsidy recipients received 50% of total direct payments, and the bottom 20% received just 2% (Figure 4.26).[425]

Some of this was 'old' money – people who have been landowners for some time – such as the Queen, the Dukes of Westminster, Buccleuch and Northumberland, the Earls of Rosebery and Iveagh, and the Earls Bathurst. And some was 'new' money, such as Mohsin Al-Tajir, the son of a billionaire former UAE ambassador to the UK, whose farm specializes in Highland Wagyu beef, and Sir James Dyson, the vacuum cleaner billionaire. Sir James, a prominent backer of leaving the EU, owns 35,000 acres, farmed as Beeswax Dyson.[426] In 2017, it received £2.8m in EU subsidies. The company states that its subsidies were for environmental stewardship and infrastructure, and that it invested £92m into improving the farms, such as building anaerobic digester plants to provide power for 10,000 homes.

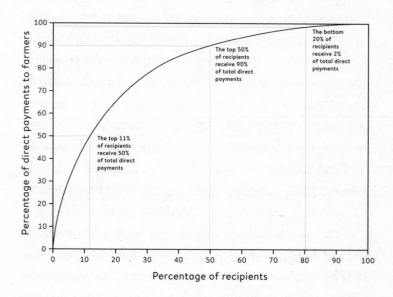

Figure 4.26
Distribution of direct payments (subsidies) to farmers in 2017
Source: NAO. Report: Early review of the new farming programme.[425]

While concentration of landownership has deep politics in Scotland and Wales,[427,428] and worldwide,[429] in England the issue has been more muted until recently. While Scotland has initiated means for buying back land under community control – tailored for crofters – the government in London has partly sidestepped the issue and partly created an entirely new avenue for policy. Defra's 2018 'Health and harmony' consultation paper introduced a new 'public pay for public goods' approach, specifically to link farm payments to ecosystems management.[430] The 2018 and 2020 Agriculture Bills and other announcements promised a maintenance of subsidies at EU CAP Levels for a few years, thereafter tapering down. HM Treasury (like Defra) has long wished to cut subsidies altogether, and it is likely that ecosystems payments would compensate for some loss of EU payments.[431] The connection with food production is set to be severed. A pilot Payment by Results scheme was trialled on some Suffolk and Norfolk farmers in East Anglia, paid to plant nectar plots for bees and other pollinators, and on nineteen farmers in Wensleydale, Yorkshire, to manage species-rich meadows. The latter were reported as approving of the greater flexibility over how to meet the goals.[432] Whether such subsidies tackle the fundamental problem that intensive agriculture has been subsidized to help wreck ecosystems is doubtful.

The economists' desire to cut subsidies does not wholly alter this problem of power within the food system. Really the UK ought to tackle the unfair spread of income across the food system. Whether there are zero subsidies or subsidies only for ecosystems support or only for other public goods takes us back to a central challenge for UK food security.

What is land for? Are we prepared to acknowledge and create a policy framework which will deliver all the functions we want from our food system? Switching subsidies from food to ecosystems misses the point. Both 'services' are needed. But why is there need for subsidies at all? At present, simply to abolish subsidies would create a cascade of consequences that would be undesirable for food security – farms going under, more concentration of landownership, more imports. But if Defra and HM Treasury decide to phase out subsidies, they need to be absolutely clear with both farmers and the consuming public what this will actually mean for food security and the countryside, and that a policy of full-cost pricing must be phased in. In the extreme, simply cutting subsidies could herald a policy framework in which UK land is used only for expensive unsubsidized food – 'local', high quality for the élite – while mass, cheap food is imported from where land and labour are cheaper. Somehow, as I argued in relation to the first 'Food problem', more of what consumers pay for food needs to be equitably distributed to SMEs rather than the big economic actors. We cannot expect good food if those whom we want to grow, process and transport high-quality healthy food to us are being unjustly treated.

Food problem 10: Food labour, education and skills

Labour productivity has been a policy sore spot for British governments since the nineteenth century. Priding itself as the first industrial nation from the late eighteenth century, the UK was actually being overtaken in efficiency and output terms by Germany and then others from the mid-nineteenth century.

Fear of being left behind forced a reluctant British state to approve and begin to invest in state education, conscious that Bismarck's *Gymnasium* school system in Germany was nurturing clever working-class young people. More class-ridden than continental Europe, the UK had resisted any social mobility 'ladder' until the 1870 Education Act. The running sore of food labour failings discussed in this section illustrates a theme of this book: the UK being a 'reluctant state', having to be dragged – sometimes by crisis – into action.

The UK is once more confused about food productivity and efficiency. 'Productivity' is often posited as the key measure for labour efficiency when it is itself in fact problematic. It needs to be recast and to combine rather than separate ecological, social, health and economic criteria. We need a less heavy-handed focus on output per unit of food labour, and more integration with wider societal goals. In recent years, academics, UN bodies and even UK governments have tentatively begun to do this. Indices for happiness have been designed and refined,[433,434] and ones for hunger and nutrition,[435] and indices for sustainable economic welfare have been piloted.[436] The thinking is interesting. If we do not know what we are aiming for and fail to set performance indicators accordingly, we should not be surprised if policy flails around. The issue is whether monetizing 'natural capital' helps us readjust the food system. I am not alone in being doubtful, although it has been well promoted inside government in recent years, or certainly in relation to land use.[437,438] This marks a policy change, definitely, but is unlikely to resolve the basic problem of what we want labour to do. The long-term policy question – what is land for? – is unlikely to be well resolved if we get rid of workers. Replacing them through automation – as we will see in the next section – might tick the box of productivity improvement but undermine capacity to enhance the 'multi-functionality' of food systems. If land workers are gone or bread is made in roboticized food factories, where are the skilled eyes and brains to ensure quality and ecosystems are aligned? And what will the displaced labour do?

Enhancing rather than deskilling food labour is, it seems to me, essential if we want to make the UK more food-secure. The labour process has to be viewed through a multi-criteria lens. Good work is not just necessary to enhance food as nutritional 'fuel', but also for culture, social life, land use, health, identity, pleasure and, yes, of course, the ecosystems to which the term 'natural capital' is now often applied. To reduce this web of functions to mere 'capital' filters the complexity of these impacts and values across the food system down to over-simplified and distorted financial value. 'Natural capital' confirms public policy as a process of arbitrated choices which weigh up costs against benefits, and calculate 'returns' on that capital. This cost-benefit approach to public policies is part of the simplistic economics we must critically assess if we really want to make the UK more food-secure for the long-term. It requires us to stand back and review whether food is a matter of so-called 'public goods', a notion associated with the US economist Paul Samuelson since 1954.[439] Actually, in those terms, food has quietly been privatized and financialized rather than celebrated as a public good for its own sake.

'Public goods' in theory are the free services from which we all can benefit – clean air, the sky, fine views, knowledge, national security. They may in fact be maintained and funded by the state or taxpayers or business but everyone benefits, and if someone has access to them this does not stop others also benefiting (they are 'non-rivalrous' in the jargon). The suggestion made in Defra's 2018 'Health and Harmony' consultation paper was that this thinking should now be applied to food, particularly farm subsidies.[440] UK agriculture (actually English because both Wales and Scotland were well down the route of linking their land use) was to be judged by environmental public goods. Subsidies would be maintained as at present but be phased down and replaced by environmental land management subsidies, almost certainly at lower subsidy levels. Food mysteriously almost disappeared from this document; also human health. As we saw in Part One, belatedly but welcomed, a separate National Food Strategy process was then set in train led by Henry Dimbleby at Defra; let us hope that does not wander into this blind alley.

What this notion of environmental public goods actually raises is how society chooses the criteria against which we judge what a good (not just efficient) food economy is. I propose that the extent, location and wages of food labour are one such area. Food work is a running sore within UK food policy. We do not take it seriously. We undervalue food skills. Having imported food using other people's land and labour in the slow transition after the 1846 repeal of the Corn Laws discussed in Part One, we now simply import food labour to fill gaps we have not been prepared to fund and train people for ourselves – be that vets to inspect meat quality in abattoirs, or waiters, baristas, chefs in food service, or farm workers prepared to pick fruit and vegetables in all weathers, or workers to make sandwiches in sandwich factories up the A1.[441] The UK will not be food-secure in the way that is needed for the twenty-first century unless it invests in food skills, and decides to enhance and nurture, not just specialist food labour skills in decent rather than low-waged jobs, but to produce a new generation of food citizenship across British society. The lesson to draw from the current state of food labour is that the UK still does not fully appreciate and value food as central to a decent society. We are still locked into an early-industrial mindset of food work as something to be stepped away from, left to a servant class. At the same time, there has been a welcome rise of interest in parts – think celebrity chefs – but less glamour goes with the mundane work; decidedly not with regard to hard farm labour.

Food work is arguably the oldest labour force in the world, and also still the largest. Whether hunter-gathering or beginning settled agriculture, humans have had to expend energy to be fed. With industrialization from the late eighteenth century, a transition began. Divisions of labour were extended. Machinery – canals, roads, rail, shipping – brought food on an unprecedented scale to burgeoning towns and cities which no longer fed themselves.[442] Over the last two or three centuries, the pattern of food work in the UK shifted. The UK led the global trend from being land-based towards an urbanized world. In 1400, an estimated 74% of the population was employed in agriculture (1.84 million people out of a population of 2.5 million). By 1800, it was about 36% (3.23 million out of 9.1 million).[443] In 2018, it was 0.7% (460,000 out of 66 million).[444] Today, there are age limits on child labour, but not so in the past. What food work there is, as we have seen earlier, is mostly by labour forces off the land. Only an eighth of UK food work today is on the land.

The UK food system includes some highly remunerated work alongside low pay. TV chefs can earn huge sums. Captains of food industries, too. Often characterized as a low-wage/low-skill sector, the food economy now needs to unlock this pay lock-in, which is partly a cultural block. Food offers ample opportunities for skills development,[445] yet there is a consistent flow of reports which point to exploitation and low pay and even, in extreme, to modern slavery. The 'healthy' salad bought in the UK may have been picked in south-east Spain in hot plastic greenhouses by migrant labour in poor conditions, with some earning less than half the legal minimum wage, according to one investigation by Felicity Lawrence in 2011. The Anti-Slavery Society commented at the time that this was the 'spectre of *de facto* state sanctioning of slavery in twenty-first-century Europe'.[446] The low price consumers are prepared to pay for what we eat – perhaps unknowingly – locks in such abuse. And we throw much of that salad away.

The complexity of modern food supply chains makes policing labour standards hard. Voluntary schemes such as the Ethical Trading Initiative (ETI) stepped into the gap.[447] Progressive companies, NGOs and trades unions worked hard to make this the norm. The application of legal minimum wages was supposed to create a baseline below which food labour cannot fall, but today in the UK there are in fact two official baselines. One is the National Living Wage (NLW), introduced by the Conservative government, which took effect in April 2016. This applied to workers over twenty-five years of age.[448] It was rather clumsily overlaid onto the other baseline, the National Minimum Wage (NMW) put in place two decades earlier under Labour's National Minimum Wage Act 1998. This gave the then new Low Pay Commission power to monitor and advise on adequacy and rates, which it has done ever since.

In 2018, the Resolution Foundation (whose focus is on the living standards of those on middle and low incomes) was clear that the NLW and NMW had improved the pay situation for the low-paid within three years. In 2015–18 there was a drop in the proportion of employees on low pay – paid less than two thirds of median hourly pay – the first drop in forty years.[449] But, a year earlier, the Foundation had concluded that the NLW had also *not* accelerated productivity in low-productivity sectors.[450] Specifically, it singled out food as low paid: 'The industries in which low pay was most common were accommodation and food services (58%), wholesale and retail (33%), and agriculture (31%).' Canteen workers' pay, for example, rose much more slowly than that of other low-paid workers in 2013–17. The Foundation also expected that 21% of agricultural workers, 21% of wholesale and retail workers, and 35% of hospitality sector workers would be paid at the wage floor, i.e. minimum rate, in 2020. The Resolution Foundation found that:

- 18% of employees earned less than two thirds of the median hourly wage, equivalent to 4.9 million people.
- 14% of men and 22% of women fell below this threshold.
- 36% of part-time employees were low paid compared to 11% of full-time employees.
- The share of employees on low pay was highest in Nottingham (24%) and Sheffield (23%).

In 2018, Her Majesty's Customs and Revenue (HMRC) released data showing that hospitality – food and hotels – was the worst-performing industry in the UK. 200,000 workers were paid less than the NMW.[451] In the same year, private-sector data – collected from agency wage payment data – suggested that the effect of reduced EU migrant labour in hospitality was pushing wage rates a little higher. The data indicated that the average hourly pay for UK catering workers over twenty-five years of age had risen to £8.60, 39p above the new NLW's rate of £8.21, which had begun in April 2019. Other age groups were above the NLW, too: for 21- to 24-year-olds it was £8.35, 65p above the NLW; for 18- to 20-year-olds it was £7.37, £1.22 higher; and people under eighteen years old were being paid £6.52, £2.32 higher than the NLW.[452] This might be good news compared to the HMRC data, but the sums are hardly princely.

As I keep stressing, the army of food labour across the entire UK food system is vast, 3.9 million employees in 2018. Many millions more people work on UK food in other countries from which the UK sources food. Oxfam, for example, reminds chocolate lovers: 'in the global cocoa value chain, only eight traders and grinders now control around 75% of the global trade in cocoa, and less than 6% of the value of a chocolate bar reaches cocoa farmers. This is a sharp decline from the 1980s, when farmers received 18% of the value created in the chain . . .'[453] There is even greater unwaged labour in the form of domestic cooking and service provision. Female de-ruralization is a global phenomenon, yet in the UK there is also an upsurge of interest in farming and other food sectors among women. The World Bank has called for better data on whether there is a 'feminization' of agriculture under way across the world.[454] Food can be a domestic commercial economic activity, and is a well-trodden route into industry and the waged economy for migrant women, as it enables them to break out of conventional unpaid roles in the economy as mothers, cooks and domestic labour.

The gender aspects of the food labour problem have been inadequately reviewed by formal parliamentary processes – and barely covered by academics with regard to the UK food labour force – although Brexit has brought general labour availability to the fore. The House of Commons Environment, Food and Rural Affairs (EFRA) Committee conducted an inquiry into agricultural labour and, despite uncertainties, considered that UK farming relied on an average of 20% EU migrant labour, mainly from Romania and Bulgaria. Some sectors were particularly reliant: '58% of members of the National Pig Association employ at least one migrant worker, and 63% of all staff employed by members of the British Meat Processors Association are from other EU countries (mainly those of Central and Eastern Europe).[455] The EFRA Committee took more evidence in 2018 which confirmed labour leaving the UK. The government dismissed such concerns as 'anecdotal'.

Using ONS Labour Force Survey data, Oxford University's Migration Observatory has suggested that the UK's foreign-born population rose from 3.8 million to 8.7 million in the period 1993–2015. In the same period, the number of foreign citizens increased from nearly 2 million to more than 5 million. In 2017, the UK population stood at 14.4% foreign-born (up from 7% in 1993) and 9.5% foreign citizens (up from 4% in 1993).[456] The location of migrants is uneven across the country (see Figure 4.27). ONS data show that Inner London had 42% and Outer London 36% people born outside the UK,

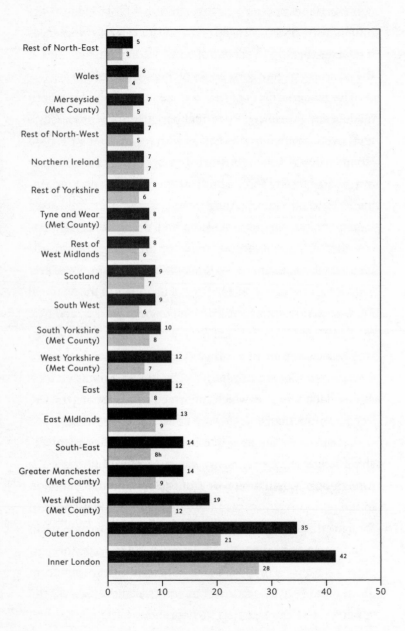

with the West Midlands at 19%. The region with the least foreign-born people was England's North-East (excluding Tyne and Wear).[457]

London – which voted heavily for staying in the EU – actually has the greatest number of migrants, 3,355,000 foreign-born people in 2017. A general rule appears to be that those regions with most 'foreigners' were actually most liberal and in favour of staying in the EU. The exceptions are small towns which have experienced a rush of immigrants brought in for economic reasons, such as Asians to work in the Lancashire textile industries as the white working class left or were undercut,[458,459] and the farm labour to cultivate and pick horticultural crops such as in much-cited Boston, Lincolnshire, or through gangster-run labour in East Anglia.[460,461]

The government's formal adviser on migration is the Migration Advisory Committee. In September 2018, it released its summary report.[462] Overall, it concluded that migrants 'have no or little impact on the overall employment and unemployment outcomes of the UK-born workforce', but it then noted that the effects were greater on 'lower-skilled' sectors. Noting the particular dependency of agriculture on migrant labour for picking, it recommended a new Seasonal Agricultural Worker Scheme (SAWS). This was a system whereby farms which needed a big influx of labour for harvesting or fieldwork could bring in a temporary workforce. SAWS had been in place since 1945 but was abolished in 2014 by the Conservative–LibDem coalition, in the belief that with access to

■ Foreign-born
░ Foreign-national

Figure 4.27
Share of migrants in the total population 2017, by region
Source: ONS/Oxford Migration Observatory.[456]

EU labour and membership meaning freedom of movement, there was little need for SAWS any more. The Brexit Referendum showed there was. Even when it closed on 12 September 2013, SAWS was still granting temporary visas for 21,150 workers from beyond the EU.[463] In 2018, under pressure from irate horticulturalists who already had unharvested crops, the government introduced a 'new' SAWS, but only as a 'pilot' allowing 2,500 non-EU workers and to run until December 2020.[464] This is no solution. In 2017 horticulture alone employed 60,000 seasonal workers. In evidence to government, G's Fresh Ltd, the largest horticulture firm in England, growing on 6,201 ha in the UK, stated that it uses 2,500 workers annually.[465] 65% of its full-time staff are EEA nationals. The UK horticulture industry has argued that, without migrant labour, there will be many fewer 'British' strawberries picked.[466,467] In autumn 2019, reports of unharvested crops proliferated.

In 2017, the British Hospitality Association (now called UK Hospitality) expected there would be a deficit of a million workers in its sector by 2029 due to unreplaced EU migrant labour if the UK left the EU, plus other factors.[468] KPMG, the consultancy which conducted this research for the BHA, advised that an extra 60,000 workers a year would be needed on top of the 200,000 new recruits required each year simply to replace the job 'churn'. The sector is famous for constant labour turnover, as people enter and leave. KPMG looked at the official statistics on migrant labour and compared them with a survey of BHA members. Although official statistics gave 12.5% of the UK hospitality sector as EU migrant labour, KPMG concluded that the real presence was nearer 25%. In 2016, for instance, 62,000 EU people joined the UK hospitality sector, with 43% of 'lower' categories of work filled by EU migrants.

At the same time, the hospitality and food service sector is experiencing considerable restructuring with the growth of eating out and takeaway food, noted earlier for their ancillary health impacts. Delivery companies such as Uber Eats, Deliveroo and Just Eat have created entirely new segments in the food chain. As we have seen earlier, they do not produce food, but merely control the software that allows them to hire 'gig' workers to deliver it. Some have now developed 'dark kitchens', realizing that, instead of being dependent on the quality of the café or restaurant whose food they deliver, they could create specialist kitchens run on more industrial principles, dedicated to delivery rather than sit-down guests eating out. Specialist dark-kitchen consortia emerged, such as FoodStars in London,[469] which was bought by Uber in 2018 for $150m. The battle for where food labour works is taking a new turn.

Investors from the software industry see this as natural expansion territory. Estimates of what the 'food-to-go' market might become worth vary wildly from £8.1bn to £21bn. It depends on what is considered food out of the home. But whatever it is, analysts agree it is witnessing rapid growth at a time of over-capacity in other food markets. The large 'gig' delivery companies are actually software companies which manage labour, and run it on gig economy lines, with all the associated problems summarized by the 2017 Taylor Review.[470] These include: casualization, low/no employment rights, zero-hours contracts, lack of pension, time pressures, low wages. The Taylor Review (chaired by Matthew Taylor, chief executive of the Royal Society of Arts) reported on its inquiry into the scandal of low-paid exploitative gig economy labour, and made many recommendations for how to civilize and humanize such work.[471] The government responded in February 2018 with a range of measures as part of its Industrial Strategy.[472] This was welcome and overdue. Exploitation can only be prevented by better pay, sick pay, full working conditions; all are needed to stop temporary workers becoming exploited workers. Workers had been made to register as self-employed, meaning employers did not pay their tax. Weakened trade union rights do not help. Government still reified 'flexibility' but it had been stung by the naked exploitation.

Mobile labour forces are not new to the food system. Economists often favour them on a supply-and-demand basis. At its most extreme, slavery served the sugar industry,[473] and the indentured-labour system was also used by the British to take workers from India to Guyana, for example, for plantation work.[474] The British food labour problem today is still a matter of poor investment in skills and education. British employers are free-riding on the back of countries who have paid and trained staff only to see them migrate and take their skills elsewhere, filling gaps in the labour force the indigenous population resists, rightly or wrongly. Why there is that resistance is complex – pay and conditions, naturally, but also reputation, status, identity. All these can combine. This criticism applies not just to food, of course; the NHS free-rides on other countries' training of skilled workers. Unless UK food work is more valued, this lock-in will be a source of vulnerability to food security.

So, besides revaluing food labour, where are workers to come from? The next section discusses promises that technology could in fact replace that labour, while some analysts wonder whether lessons could be learned from the past.[475] Prior to 1900, there were open borders; cross-European seasonal movement of labour was common. There was an enormous annual exodus of Iberian workers into southern France, for instance, and Londoners went out to Kent to pick hops and fruit seasonally. The Taylor Review was in some respects entering the policy space where it should be possible to consider how such seasonality requires something better to the benefit of land use and the people. In Part Three, I suggest why a more regionalized approach to food governance and skills might help.

Be that as it may, we should remember that today there is little labour planning akin to that conducted by War Agriculture Committees or which led to use of the Women's Land Army, created in 1917 to fill the gap of farm labour recruited and killed in Flanders; and little recognition that, in 1940, recruitment began again. Unless there is planning, exploitation can run rife. UK controls on use of gang labour were put in place in 1967, but had to be overhauled and renewed after the shocking drowning of twenty-three Chinese cockle pickers in Morecambe Bay in 2004 exposed the use of hidden labour.[476] These issues were rife in the nineteenth century, but why had such exploitation returned? Great credit must go to those who campaign on this matter. That such campaigning is needed shows how weakened trades unions have become – addressing these problems was central to the more civilized frameworks pursued by way of trade union rights.[477]

Unless primary production is completely industrialized and monocropped, some flexibility for the purposes of harvesting, by the use of temporary and casual work, is likely. There are moments when food simply has to be harvested or else it is wasted. The nature of land-based work is inevitably seasonal. FeedBack, the NGO which champions waste reduction, has even mooted a modern 'gleaning' movement. Running across this issue are nastier ethics – racism, anti-migrant hostility, exploitation. It has been easy for some politicians to play on anti-migrant sentiment – one thinks of the 2016 Referendum – only then for politicians to admit that migrant labour is actually needed. If not from the EU, where from? No wonder there are calls for a new fully fledged Seasonal Agricultural Workers Scheme.[478]

The food labour issue should not be fudged. It will not disappear.[479] The policy options range widely: fixed or rigid caps on migration; quotas with visas for particular sectors or skills sets; youth only, to allow young people in as part of travelling the world, then leaving (the Australian system); a points system, allowing people in only if they meet criteria set by the UK as needed; ad hoc labour deals as part of trade deals (as has been mooted by India: we buy your services if you allow more of our emigrants); a rapid investment in and encouragement of the UK labour force, taking labour from other markets; and, finally, trying to make more food tasks obsolete by technology such as robots. So which is it to be?

Food problem 11: Science, technology and engineering in the age of big data

The questions which have long troubled UK science and technology policy are: for whom is this being done? Who will benefit? Is it for private gain or the public good? The impact of science, technology, engineering and mathematics (STEM) on food has been a remarkable mixture of benefits and harms, but they need a fundamental reset again today. As was shown in Part One, food defence – the capacity to protect supply lines – is now a matter of cybersecurity, not just the navy or military; the air force role is perhaps less direct. The issue of biosecurity, too, is of great significance and was recognized in an updated framework in 2014.[480] Plants and entire ecosystems can be fundamentally altered by the release of predators, invasive species and diseases. Zoonoses – diseases from animals – can be devastating. Trade has to be carefully monitored, which in turn requires investment in having the right expertise and training of personnel who can ensure it is done. Growing food was never a simple matter; and today it has been made vastly more fragile by globalization's ceaseless movement of goods, foods and people.

The threats from globalization might be realized by scientists but have barely percolated into public policy, let alone into how the UK public eats. We assume we can 'eat the world'. I have argued that, although this is changing, and has been a benefit of Europeanization in part, the British have rarely placed a high value on their food.* Cars, houses and holidays can easily take priority over eating the optimum diet. Our

---

* If the reader needs to travel back, please read books such as Elspeth Huxley's 1965 *Brave New Victuals* or Derek Cooper's 1967 *The Bad Food Guide*, or Christopher Driver's 1981 *The British at Table 1940–80*, or John and Mary Postgate's 1994 *A Stomach for Dissent*, their biography of Raymond Postgate, founder of the *Good Food Guide* after the Second World War. The common complaint is brown food, badly cooked and drab. It is what we were known for and have begun the transition away from.

access to feast-day food every day is built on the just-in-time logistics system and on the assumption now hard-wired into UK culture that food will always flow into our local supermarket. Part of the purpose of this book is to question both those assumptions. So what can STEM add?

Conscious that food waste is a driver of global food insecurity, the UK Institute of Mechanical Engineers, for instance, proposed that engineering could help resolve waste.[481] Indeed, there are many practical issues within waste management to which engineering skills can be applied – using the waste as biomass for fuel, preventing waste by improved storage – but the resolution of the food waste problem is not just a material problem for engineers and others, but a social and cultural one. The circular economy needs *political* champions.

It was a positive move, therefore, when the nine UK research councils (grouped now under the UK Research and Innovation umbrella) combined to create the Global Food Security (GFS) Programme in 2010. It was a timely and important response to the global food security crisis which had surfaced in 2007–8.[482] The crisis gave the UK an impetus to create a better, more coherent position on UK food security and the role of science and innovation within that. The G8 rich nations were in shock about food supply, which they had assumed was a problem elsewhere, not for them; but they began to think aloud.[483,484,485] While initially framed as calling for more food to be produced globally in an age of climate change – as though there is an overall problem of scarcity when there is actually an overall opportunity to cut waste – more nuanced arguments and analyses emerged.[486,487,488,489] These linked production to ecosystems generally, and to the need for consumer change.[490] The GFS was undoubtedly an important initiative while focusing globally more than on the UK. There was, of course, a whiff of that age-old British reflex to address others rather than put our own house in order. To be fair, GFS gave examples of how the global situation would affect the UK, such as the spread of animal and plant diseases from abroad and the impact of climate change on pollinators, and its champion scientist, Tim Benton, was exemplary in bringing the UK into focus.[491,492,493] Britain's environmental impact is small in the overall global picture, but its historical legacy is immense, having exported models of land and animal use round the world when an imperial power. We too need to reflect on the role of the sciences in food.

UK science hosts some appropriate approaches, asking, 'What can *we* do?' The northern universities consortium's *IKnowFood* project[494] and the N8 Agri-Food collaboration give hope that a globally informed but UK-focused direction might at last be now emerging.[495] In February 2019, the GFS spelled out why UK food resilience itself was at stake.[496] A really positive avenue of work started in 2012 when GFS began a public engagement about food matters.[497] A 2017 survey of UK public attitudes showed a welcome and positive appetite for dietary change, among young people particularly, and that British adults generally saw the value of beginning to change diets now if it meant protecting future generations.[498] 66% of the public agreed that food contributes to climate change. By 2017, the GFS programme was being subsumed into a new technical focus instilled into the merger of the previously separate research councils, now asked to be merely 'drivers of innovation and exports'. What this ought to be doing, surely, is to champion significant national dietary change in the manner Sweden began in the 2000s,[499,500,501,502] and the Nordic Council does across the region.[503,504]

To argue against the possibility of major structural or dietary change as too hard ignores how change has been normal in the food system and incessant since settled agriculture began, and towns and cities started to develop.[505] In the last 250 years, the scale and pace of change have accelerated to a previously unimaginable degree, partly due to the unleashing of STEM-based innovation. Technology has replaced labour, yet it remains a problem. Engineering has reconfigured the UK landscape. Satellites guide tractors. Algorithms underpin the logistics revolution, and combine with industrial management to tell the East Anglian pea farmer when to harvest the crops, guaranteeing peas arrive in sequence to enable the pea-freezing factory to manage production. Yet, also, agrichemicals which replace the hoe by the liquid cosh have those deep consequences for biodiversity, and drive extinction rates.

The impact of what has been facilitated by science enters our mouths daily. It is remarkable. In the 1930s, UK farming could achieve average wheat yields of about 2 tonnes per hectare, and by the 2010s, it was 8 tonnes per hectare.[506] But as a recent review of the global situation noted, this has been 'more production, more calories, but less nutrition'.[507] It has also favoured technical solutions over social reorganization, instead of enabling social engagement to frame the direction that technological change will take, which might be better.

The problem here is that the UK, despite a proud history of science and innovation, has too little clarity about where the 'public interest' in food science lies today. In the Second

World War, desperate to increase UK food supply, state encouragement to invest in high-input, high-output agriculture held sway, and afterwards this productionist approach dominated food research and development (R&D). Initially, this was heavily government-funded, but investment was pulled away towards a private and 'near market' focus after the 1971 Rothschild Report.[508] And then the publicly owned research stations such as those for plant breeding were privatized under Margaret Thatcher.[509] The world-famous Plant Breeding Institute (PBI) at Cambridge, for example, was founded in 1912. This and a network of twenty-three Research Institutes and eighteen Units were destroyed in a few years and the skills were dispersed due to privatization. The remnants of PBI were sold off to Unilever in 1987 and the buildings bulldozed in 2009. UK plant-breeding capacity was seriously undermined by this intellectual and technological vandalism. The baton for protecting the public interest was increasingly picked up by the vibrant civil-society sector – the environmental, health, consumer and animal welfare NGOs, which gradually worked together, not least at EU level.

In budget terms, the EU has been an important source of public-interest science funding in the UK. The EU science budget was €70bn for 2014–20,[510] rising to €100bn for the 2020–27 9th Framework programme (Horizon Europe). Food was singled out to be a link between science, technology and society.[511] This is as it should be, but this societal focus is being weakened in the UK in favour of technical innovation for business. In 2015, the UK public sector spent 1.7% of national GDP on all research but aspired to raise this to 2.3% by 2027 by injecting more private funding to deliver a mix of public and private.[512] In 2016, the total government budget for Science, Engineering and Technology was £1.1bn, down in real terms since 2013 due to an HM Treasury-led 'austerity' squeeze.[513] These sums included university research funding. Severance from EU STEM networks and research generally would be a mistake. Since 2005, the UK contribution to EU science research budgets has grown, but the UK has been a major beneficiary, winning back far more than it has paid in.

Food companies had and continue to have significant R&D budgets of their own. In 2013, for instance, Associated British Foods spent 0.19% of its £12.3bn turnover on R&D. This is small compared to the 7.53% that Rolls-Royce spent from its £12.2bn turnover. Tate & Lyle, the sugar company, did not disclose its budget (but like all sweetness companies funds research). Food companies in the FTSE 100, the UK's largest manufacturers, averaged under 5%, with the food sector investment being lower than average.[514]

ARGUMENTS OVER AND IN SCIENCE

Genetic modification (GM) has been a particular focus for debate about the role of science in food. GM use was restricted by the EU while being favoured elsewhere in the world. Although a small part of the research picture, it became a symbol because it raised the question: who profits from that R&D and those industrial innovations? This question also applies beyond GM to emerging technologies such as nanotechnology.[515,516,517] Nanotechnology is the use of minute particles to create particular effects; they are invisible to the eye. Like GM, it passes power to the lab and the funder who seeks the effect the particle is designed to deliver. It is already being

applied on farms, in processing, in packaging and in food sup-
plements. They are used as carriers of 'smart' (always smart,
never not smart, note!) 'delivery of nutrients, anti-caking
agents, antimicrobial agents, fillers for improving mechanical strength and durability of the packaging material', to cite
one summary paper.[518] But where is the public consultation?
Next to nothing at the UK level, and left to the EU, which
has already been deservedly criticized for adopting a 'soft'
regulatory approach.[519] The European Food Safety Authority
began a consultation to update its 111-page guidance in 2018
just when UK attention was otherwise engaged on Brexit.[520]

While some scientists decry this as injecting unnecessary
politics into neutral science, others know that such ethical and social responsibilities are impossible to avoid. If not
addressed before application and if civil society is not engaged in how to frame the technology, the chance of hostile reaction later is increased. GM products such as Golden
Rice might have been declared safe by New Zealand, Australia and Canada but have been criticized for offering inappropriate technical fixes for poor people in the global South and
for taking undue environmental risks. People in the developing world were not consulted before its development; it
was sold to them. Proponents might argue that a GM wheat
developed and marketed for coeliac sufferers by the Institute of Sustainable Agriculture in Spain should be allowed or
that a high-oleic soybean oil developed by Calyxt and planted
by US farmers has the health profile of olive oil, but others
counter: why is this necessary and who owns the patents and
are they restricted? This is ultimately a battle about intellectual property rights as much as about science. Safety issues

are inevitably raised, and can be complex to resolve. On GM the EU is pilloried by some US critics as anti-science, but, following the food safety scandals of the 1980s and 1990s, the EU was right and popular with the public when it adopted a precautionary approach and committed to prioritize prevention over remediation.[521] It applied this, for example, when restricting the use of chlorine to 'wash' chicken after slaughter, which is permitted in the USA.[522] Hormone implants in beef rearing, widely used in the USA, are restricted in the EU on similar grounds.[523]

Perhaps the most pressing example of where science and food policy meet is the over-use and misuse of antibiotics. In his 1945 Nobel Prize for Medicine speech, Sir Alexander Fleming had warned of the danger of antimicrobial resistance.[524] The threat today is immense.[525] Even with considerable financial incentives, new drugs are unlikely to be able to replace those becoming ineffective.[526,527] European Medicines Agency data show the UK used 429.63 tonnes of pharmaceuticals for food-producing animals in 2014. This was low compared to some other European countries such as Spain, Cyprus, Italy, Portugal, Hungary and Belgium,[528] and the English Chief Medical Officer provided honourable leadership on the issue.[529,530,531] City of London financiers, led by Jeremy Coller, have also pioneered the development of a huge $1trn coalition of fifty-four investors committed to work towards stopping misuse and overuse.[532] But routine use continues.

UK science – both natural and social – needs a reboot, particularly now that food trade and security are again a concern.[533,534,535,536] A socially useful STEM system, guided by considerations of food security rather than solely by a search for profits, could be a powerhouse for rebuilding what a Manchester University research group calls the 'foundational economy'.[537] The group estimates that about 40% of the UK workforce underpins life for the rest with jobs 'engaged in providing households with basic goods and services' and providing the infrastructure for a decent life.[538] Food is part of this infrastructure but its foundational role has been mismanaged and is fragile. If resilience is the goal, then STEM and social sciences need to make that feature a core purpose for helping reorient the foundational economy. The funders and shapers of STEM work need to listen to the concerns of domestic life, transport users, care services, healthcare, energy networks, water users, if we are to innovate for enhanced food security. If consumers were co-creators of research, would nanotechnology really be presented as a key way forward?

Consider the huge investment in logistics and food handling made over the last half-century in the form of trucking, or creation of vast new docks such as Tilbury, or the computerized and software-dependent global-tracking systems on which the food flows summarized in previous pages depend. The UK's second Road Investment Strategy (RIS2) allocated £28.8bn for 2021–5, up from the £15bn in the 2015 RIS1.[539] The private-sector Forth Ports' £1bn investment in expanding Tilbury from 2017 may sound huge, and it is, but it is designed partly to help the car import–export trade.[540] Why fund more cars when they plague our towns, keep children indoors, stop exercise being built into daily life by bicycling rather than motoring? They have their place, of course, but the point is that social values and certainly unintended societal impacts follow from such investment in technology.

It might help the flow of imports, making them arrive cheaper and faster, but is that aiding the transition to a more sustainable society? The government, under a then new Prime Minister, Boris Johnson, set out to accelerate this import–export approach to infrastructure, by promising more freeports where flow of goods are exempt from tax.[541] Meanwhile next to no investment has been promised to fund sustainable UK horticulture or to resolve the UK's food labour problems.

INFRASTRUCTURE AND TECHNOLOGIES

The National Infrastructure Commission in theory has a role to shape what the UK needs in the future. While it does have a welcome long-term perspective, its assumption is to favour large-scale rather than devolved types of infrastructure. The initial £56bn funding for the HS2 train link might ultimately save, say, thirty minutes on the current intercity express London–Manchester route, but we can only imagine how much better those funds would be for millions of people in North-West and North-East England if they were spent upgrading local transport to meet local needs across a wider region, let alone be spread more equitably across the country.[542] What the UK food system really requires from the Commission is to map how to develop a low-carbon, more bio-regional food delivery system. Infrastructure research and planning are necessary not for the sake of more huge trucks on motorways but for bio-regionalized hubs and less traffic.

Meanwhile ever more automation, application of robotics and information technology are being designed for the food system. On the one hand, redundancy for workers is being planned through automation, while, on the other hand, consumers are being built into production as unpaid workers. As the US sociologist Alvin Toffler prophesized, we are all being turned into a fusion of producers and consumers – the prosumer.[543] The supermarket checkout teller is already being replaced by self-check-out technology. 900,000 UK jobs were expected to be lost from all retail (not just food) in 2014–25.[544] 40,000 shops of all kinds are expected to close, increasing the phenomenon of boarded-up town centres. Technologists became excited about the small six-wheel food delivery 'Starship' which can hold and deliver twenty food items and was trialled by Just Eat in Greenwich, London, and the Co-op in Milton Keynes. It had reported costs of £1–£3 per delivery compared with £4–£15 if the same food was delivered by a human in a van. But Starship came with the disadvantage of only being able to operate within a three-mile radius. Meanwhile, driverless vans are being designed using the geographical mapping already conducted by US software and big-data giants.

Agriculture, too, is being primed for a technical transition. A recent review listed imminent changes such as these: 'digital' farming which uses sensors and precision location to target particular plants; satellite mapping which refines where fertilizers are applied more effectively; drones which zoom over fields to see how animals are doing, thus sitting the 'farmer' behind a screen and removing the need to go round fields on a quad bike (perish the thought of 'walking'!); augmented reality to let the landowner 'see' what the land would look like with different cropping; gene editing, which removes undesirable genes from plants or animals (unlike genetic modification, which fuses); and vertical farming, which brings crop production indoors, all-year round, and into urban areas.[545]

In the horticulture sector, robotics are being developed for use on the land for seeding, pollination, harvesting, distribution and packaging. Autonomous tractors have been trialled at Harper Adams University, designed to remove the human altogether. In Spain, the Universidad Politécnica de Madrid's *Rosphere* ('hamster ball') rolls over land to gather information on soil, water and other features.[546] As though anticipating the demise of bees and natural pollinators from agrichemical misuse, Harvard University's Robobee has been developed to pollinate flowers; it is a tiny drone weighing 175 milligrams and the size of a 50p coin. Dogtooth Technologies, a UK robotics company, is developing strawberry picking by the stem, while other researchers are looking at vacuum apple pickers. Octinion, a Belgian firm, is working on a robotic 'hand' which picks the actual fruit. FTNON, a Netherlands group, has built 'sensory arms' which can de-core lettuces accurately. In massive so-called 'dark', automated warehouses, camera-using robots are being developed to shift products.

Such 'techie' innovations are fascinating, of course. While we can wonder at the inventiveness, their impact on humans and the foundational economy receives less attention. Mindful of the social consequences of unemployment, in 2016 the OECD published its review of the risks from automation to jobs in twenty-one of its member states. It concluded that only 9% of jobs were actually at risk.[547] (Surely 9% is a lot of jobs!) While South Korea and Estonia could anticipate 6% job losses, Germany and Austria were expected to lose 12%, and the UK 10%. The OECD concluded: 'It is mostly low skill and low-income individuals who face a high risk of being automatable.' The low-paid are hit once again. This echoed a much-cited 2013 study by Frey and Osborne for the Oxford Martin School.[548] They looked at the effects of computerized machine learning and robotics on jobs or tasks that are repetitive or have sequences of repetition. Here is a delicate tension. Automation can replace labour by speeding up remaining labour. It can also de-skill and turn craft into faster routinized actions. The power moves to the technologist, marginalizing the ousted worker. A dishwashing job can more easily be automated than an event planner's, a telemarketer's more easily than a surgeon's, a court clerk's more easily than a fashion designer's. But what then happens? And is this putting human and ecological benefit at the heart of progress?

Applying Frey and Osborne's methodology to the UK, Deloitte concluded there would be job losses in elementary occupations and factory-processing jobs, with a growth of jobs in the already affluent regions of London and South-East England, and a reduction elsewhere.[549] The food jobs they identified as likely to grow included chefs, who are expected to increase in number by 102,000, despite a 57% likelihood of elements of their jobs being automated. Jobs likely to see a fall in employment included retail sales and checkout workers, which Deloitte estimated as 97% likely to be automated; 72,000 job losses are anticipated. 35% of all UK jobs (not just food) were estimated to be at risk from aspects of automation. This is much more than the OECD's 9%. Meanwhile the investment is pouring in. The International Federation of Robotics reported a doubling of robots in the food sector worldwide in 2011–16,[550] and in 2017 the strongest growth sectors for robotics were the metal industry (+55%), the electrical/electronics industry (+33%) and the food industry (+19%).[551] In 2018, the UK had 71 robots per 10,000 workers; the world average is 74. South Korea has 631, Germany 309, Sweden 223 and Denmark 211.[552] The Royal Society of Arts has estimated that only 14% of UK businesses are investing in robots.

Analysts who wish to improve UK productivity are troubled by this but give less attention to those whose jobs will go.[553] Are we surprised that German food manufacturing uses robots more than the UK, when UK culture historically and currently is more reliant on cheap human labour? It was the German Domino's Pizza which trialled delivery of pizzas by robots and the German Metro retailing giant which took a part in developing the self-driving Starship delivery machine. But the German industrial tradition – encouraged by the British after 1945 – was for a collaborative workplace model. In this, robots are not simply to reduce labour but to enhance the labour process.[554] Decisions are negotiated by and in work councils, collaborations between workers and management. Or that is the theory.

A general verdict on robotics and food might be one of uneven development. The McKinsey Global Institute cautions that 'more jobs will change than be automated away',[555] yet its own study of the 'automation potential' for robotization suggested that accommodation and food service scored 73% (ripe for automation); manufacturing 60%; agriculture 58%; transport and warehousing 57%; and retail 53%. It saw automation's impact set to roll throughout the twenty-first century.[556] The British horticulture industry – heavily reliant on EU migrant labour for picking and fieldwork – was deeply troubled by anti-migrant sentiment in Brexit. If any industry would like to automate, it might be that; but it is cautious. Fruit and vegetables are soft, and although developments are underway, such as by Plymouth University for Hall Hunter (a big supplier of berries to large supermarkets), mass use of robotics is some way off. Nick Marston of British Summer Fruits estimates it will be ten years before such machinery could be as good as humans.[557] Ocado, meanwhile, already uses a 'fleet' of 1,100 robots in its giant automated warehouses. In food service, a Californian robot has been designed which can make 372 pizzas an hour, five times faster than a human.[558]

BIG DATA

The emergence of big data raises yet another set of important questions for STEM research on food. Data are often said to be neutral but in reality it matters very much who frames, collects, funds and uses that data. The revelations of how Cambridge Analytica had harvested Facebook information on people's behaviour, which was then sold and used to target them with sometimes false messages to warp US voting intentions might have worried political commentators,[559] but it barely ruffled food data harvesting. Your supermarket already knows what you do – behaviour is more important than what you think. Today, food should be featuring in a debate about who controls the data collected on us all as we buy. The massive increase in computer power, the explosion of search engines, the ubiquity of mobile phones as the means by which people relate with each other and the world – all this means power filters rapidly and remarkably into distant hands. Consumers in effect donate data about their behaviour which enables others to collate and allocate how their profile fits within wider demographics. 'Profiling' is now an industry within what Shoshana Zuboff calls 'surveillance capitalism'.[560]

The UK state began to collect data on food in the nineteenth century. It was useful when reviewing strategic issues in the 1905 Royal Commission on Food Supply in Time of War (see p. 120). Data gathering accelerated in the Second World War, with the application of techniques developed to ascertain what the public thought about issues. Mass Observation, for instance, began in 1937 with a study of the depressed mill town of Bolton, Lancashire, by a small body of remarkable researchers led by Charles Madge, Humphrey Jennings and Tom Harrisson.[561] They were determined to record and share how people actually lived and what people thought – an anthropology of everyday UK life.[562] Mass Observation's techniques started off in amateurish mode but its experience quickly grew, and it was picked up, dovetailed with polling – drawing on US experience[563] – and centralized by the state in the 1940s. Its data are a goldmine for historians today, as they reflect the sensitivities of so-called 'ordinary' people's lives – magnificently in diaries such as Nella Last's in the Lake District in the 1940s.[564] This type of people's history has returned with BBC Radio's Listening Project, for example, but the collection of knowledge about what people do and think is not always so benign. It is mostly about control. Critically, such data have now been financialized and combined – hence the term 'big data' – to give overviews of remarkable power.

The UK state had learned in the First World War how important public sentiment about food was for national morale. It rapidly amplified and applied those lessons in 1939–45.[565,566,567] Today, companies, as well as the state, are the harvesters and controllers of data about what people think, do and aspire to with regard to food; this is why analysts talk of the surveillance society and surveillance culture. In public health, the word 'surveillance' has a positive meaning, as it refers to the monitoring of disease patterns such as the incidence of food poisoning. Epidemiology is the science of interpreting and deriving predictions and control methods to protect the public health from outbreaks going out of control. Drugs, containment, isolation, quarantine systems all derive from that role of public-health medicine (or social medicine) as intervention.[568]

Today, food data have become a surveillance frontline in a different way, shifting the ethos from protection as a public good to harvesting and utilizing data for top-down rather than bottom-up benefit. A study by the consumer group Which? found a 'staggering' level of data collection occurring in and from UK homes, which it judged to be the downside of the trend towards smart homes. Which? tested seventeen electronic goods people have in their homes – smartphones, TVs, toothbrushes – and found, for example, fifteen minutes of use of a smart TV sent data to 700 external data gatherers.[569] This is not benign 'data sharing' but a combination of unwitting donation by the consumer plus unaccountable and hidden mining by machine makers. This was not declared on the label.

An army of consultancies – large and small – advise companies on business context, dynamics and opportunities, researching, collecting but not publishing data. Commercial confidentiality and non-disclosure agreements rule. Intellectual Property Rights (IPR) provide legal lock and key. STEM skills have refined the tracking and predicting of our every move. The arrival of blockchain cements this power, giving companies rather than the consumer information.[570] Credit and finance companies and social media now know (or will predict) what you think and what food you are likely to buy almost before you do. The company app young consumers downloaded onto their mobile phones, enticed by a witty ad, will harvest data on how they purchase and consume food. Cautiously and under duress, some industry analysts now talk of the 'democratization' of such data, but that seems unlikely unless there is a big redress in the form of rights of recall, access and sharing.[571]

Western democracies, which pride themselves on the value of liberty, have been very slow to recognize and debate this accrual of power. Legislation too has been slow. The EU, for example, belatedly passed the General Data Protection Regulation (GDPR) in 2016.[572] The UK translated this into a UK law in 2018, preparing for Brexit. This is supposed to reassert individual rights to privacy, and to enable consumers to withhold permission from others to keep data. The big-data horse had already bolted, however. The GDPR legislation begins well: 'The processing of personal data should be designed to serve mankind' but immediately softens it thus: 'The right to the protection of personal data is not an absolute right; it must be considered in relation to its function in society and be balanced against other fundamental rights, in accordance with the principle of proportionality.' The inevitable compromise between power and individual rights is confirmed. Where is this included in your food packaging?

Predictive software, consumer reliance, business-to-business networks, online purchasing, Google internet searching – all this had already transferred power to software and data harvesters who may be on the other side of the world. As was shown in Part One (see pp. 143–5), this has created vulnerabilities and opportunities for disruption of the food system. Software breakdowns, deliberate malware and ransomware interventions, and data 'hostage taking' are all part of modern criminality but also are the extension of how states and companies operate. It would be naïve, not just wrong, to suggest that the Age of the Internet is benign. It has been channelled. And food data are at the centre. If we really aspire to democratize food, then data and information, and the role of STEM within that, must be in the framework.

Food problem 12: Fraying food governance

In Part One, the problem of the UK's reluctance to engage with a modern regionalism was raised (see pp. 67–9), and again when setting out the scope of Part Two (see pp. 346–7). Now, after exploring the various lock-ins hindering how and whether the UK can address its food security, the theme is returned to again as our final 'food problem'. This is simply because governance is such an important cross-cutting issue for food. The UK is unlikely to address its food problems and begin the transition to a more sustainable food system unless we consider who must be engaged and what 'levers' they have to make a difference, either with us or on our behalf.

Some neo-liberal thinking – and not all is trite – dismisses
the issue with 'leave it to the market' or 'let the consumer
decide' or 'beware the nanny state'. These arguments, hopefully, have been addressed throughout Part Two, suggesting,
by contrast, that markets are in reality framed, carry assumptions, favour powerful over less powerful actors, filter and ex-
tract rather than share information. There is no one kind of
market economy. Markets can be shaped to favour interests,
to be more civilized or more brutal, to have funded safety
nets or have none, to favour finance capital over manufacturing or not, to keep wages low or raise the bar, to support
cheap food without internalizing the full costs or not. Markets are choices. And my point is that the UK is fudging these
critical food policy choices. We can civilize our food system
or let it undermine our future. Governance matters.

The market system – as it has been created – is not enabling the UK to institute the requisite reforms. The challenge
of food governance is itself a food problem, possibly even the
fundamental one. If we do not sort this out and improve how
we make decisions on food, the likelihood is that ecosystems,
public health, food security will all continue to drift or stum-
ble from crisis to crisis. Policy failures already fissure the food
system. Of course, there are and have been some inspiring actions, sound thinking and policy development which can be
and should be resoundingly welcomed. Some farmers build
their systems around ecosystems resilience. Some firms take
long-term health seriously. All take short-term health impacts seriously, unless fraudulent enterprises, not least for
brand- and reputational-risk avoidance. But the UK's political capacity to accelerate change, if we are to narrow the gap

between evidence and reality, requires governance reform. That is not happening. Local-authority structures, funding and powers are uneven and divided. No clear message even comes from the local authorities themselves, particularly in England. For good reason: they have been systematically and deliberately divided. But there are signs this is changing.[573] I write this knowing that, for many voters, the point of voting for Brexit was to do just that. The problem with isolating ourselves from our nearest neighbours, however, is that this might well be a mistaken belief that we can return the UK to its imperial past – letting others far away feed us, or to bring a halt to migration without thought to the food system. I have argued that, within the EU, we were already dependent but have been a signatory to this role. We ought to be growing more food here, and transforming our food systems, whether in or out of the EU. The problem is that our policymaking is providing little leadership. The National Food Strategy (Dimbleby) process might well provide just that. But this requires a cross-government transformation, a shift from ducking food security as a priority to making it very high indeed.

The UK food system operates within a weakened state. Political theorists call this the emergence of a 'hollowed-out' state.[574,575] Rod Rhodes, who first articulated this theory in 1994, then saw it as the state facing a choice as to whether just to shrink itself or to outsource itself. By 2017, he concluded it had done both. It has curtailed public functions and outsourced them to the private sector.[576] It has buildings, people on the payroll, laws and duties, but they have been reduced in numbers and power. It has sold public assets (water, county farms, buildings, land, agencies) and privatized them (school

meals, hospital catering, prisons, ports and military bases).
It may look like a functioning state from outside – and compared to the dire state of low-income countries, it is nirvana –
but it is not fit for a wealthy, mature democracy such as the
UK claims to be. And, certainly, it is not able or prepared to
unlock the lock-ins explored in this book or to get a grip on
food insecurity or food poverty. As we have seen, austerity
and funding cuts from 2010 to 2019 accentuated societal divides. That decade was particularly brutal in weakening the
regional state. Regional Development Agencies which could
have voiced the regional interest were axed when they should
have been strengthened and democratized. But the process
had begun from the late 1970s under UK governments of
Labour and Conservative leadership. The tone varied and the
mechanisms or safety nets changed considerably according
to political complexion, but the weakening of the state and
the ceding of power to corporate interests grew. Industries,
towns and whole regions of the UK were left adrift in the pursuit of what is often called globalization. (There are variants
of globalization, just as there are of the state.)

The local state, which was the pride of the late-Victorian
era, has been turned into what elsewhere in Europe would
be considered something laughable – bodies with little
power, less money, demoralized functionaries, and dwindled
or wounded local pride. The town halls, the theatres, the
schools, the swimming baths, the parks, the sewerage works,
the transport systems to get people about their everyday
lives of work and school and leisure, the roads, the housing –
all these are pot-holed; some are mothballed; buildings sold
off. Local authorities were turned into 'client states' by the

planning system. The march of giant one-stop, out-of-town hypermarkets, which locked Britain into a car culture while offering a cheaper vast range of too often fatty, sugary and ultra-processed foods, was oiled by deals known as 'planning gain'.[577,578] A supermarket would be approved and in return the local authority would get it to fund a roundabout or possibly a nursery, or a playground. This custom and practice had been growing for decades.[579] Today, once more, 'planning gain' is back with in-town sites.[580] In theory, framework plans are supposed to provide overview guidance.[581]

Amid the web of important but ill-serviced functions in which they still sit and often do a decent job, and despite conditions and despite central governments or political persuasions, local authorities had vital food responsibilities. In the past, markets were built and run, intended to provide good food for the people. Health inspections were conducted. Trading-standards systems were audited to stop cheats and frauds.[582] The local state was given, and welcomed, powers to ensure that – as the 1860 Food Act promised – British citizens' expectation that their food shall be 'of the nature, substance and quality demanded' would be met.[583] While Scotland and Wales were given new powers and governments in the 1990s, extended since, England's local authorities have been financially minced and their autonomy squeezed to the point where it is sometimes nominal. Food governance and power have centralized. As we saw in Part One, how can a local authority or Resilience Forum really protect the local population from food insecurity in time of crisis? They cannot.

No wonder there is political malaise in the country. This state of affairs locks in, rather than helping harness public engagement in resolving UK food problems. Any decent country would do as the UK engineered for Germany after 1945, and as other European and Western countries enjoy. We would have solidly tiered food governance: local powers, locally funded (with top-up where equitable), and regional and national powers where appropriate for better co-ordination. We would also not do as the UK has done to divide and rule even over whether an area can have a more powerful mayor. This area has no mayor, that area has one with restricted and different powers to others. Region is thus set against region.

Since the 1980s, as power generally concentrated with only partial devolution, there was in fact a remarkable civic flowering of food culture with food festivals, food movements, the Sustainable Food Cities network, a localist food renaissance, a rise of interest in food culture. There is much in this of which to be very proud, but there is a limit to what can be done on a shoestring. Localities lack food powers and funds. It will take time to turn round the UK food system but it is unlikely to happen unless there is a renaissance of bottom-up food governance to rebalance top-down control.

The movement which campaigned against food adulteration from the 1820s to the 1870s knew this would require tougher laws and institutions to protect and enhance local food supplies.[584,585] It took decades, but eventually by-laws allowed local authorities to finance water systems, pay for covered and wholesale markets, regulate shops, all to enable the citizen to gain access to an improved diet. In the twentieth century, civic campaigning moved on to actual food provision, demanding better food for everyone, and providing for the needy. As we saw, the 1906 Education (Provision of Meals)

Act was arguably one of the first acts of the welfare state. We need not be dewy-eyed about its success, as it actually was hardly used until the First World War required mothers to work in factories rather than at home feeding their children (and men).[586,587] But the powers were there and could kick in vigorously in 1939–45, funding a huge programme of school kitchens, for example.

Now consider today. What local authority can do much about food's impact on climate change or to build exercise into daily life? A growing network of cities – the Sustainable Food Cities network – set out to nurture this kind of change and do heroic work, but they are not yet turning cities into carbon sinks. They lack suitable powers. Or which cities are reversing biodiversity loss? Some, it is true, take their green spaces seriously, but many more have allowed planning agreements to site houses on floodplains, or build them without carbon in mind, or put roads on green fields, or sell off school playing fields for building, and continue to spray pavement 'weeds' with noxious herbicides (leaving the public to wonder what has happened to the bees and insects).[588] Their finances and central government encourage such dereliction. Yet it is at this 'local' level that climate change impacts are expected to strike, much as flooding becomes real if it is your house, your area. Cities are concentrations of vulnerable populations from a sustainable-food perspective. An EU-wide study concluded that all 571 cities looked at were likely to be affected by climate change, whether drought or floods.[589] Its high-impact scenario predicted Southern European cities would experience droughts fourteen times worse than today and that Wrexham, Carlisle, Glasgow, Aberdeen, Derry and Chester were likely to be the worst-hit UK towns and cities for river flooding, with Dublin, Cork and Waterford the worst in Ireland. How can these conurbations act unless given powers to protect themselves and to reconnect with their hinterland to regenerate ecosystems to be more resilient?

And which local authority can curtail rather than collude with car culture? Not many; it would be electoral suicide, they say, when our continued reliance on cars for mobility wastes fossil fuels and pollutes urban air! And which have really got citizenship food skills taught in schools? Actually, here there *has* been progress, with pioneering work by civil society helping and supporting teachers and catering staff to do this.[590] School heads, teachers and school cooks are restrained by centrally set curricula, and by food budget of a pound or so per child, but there are ways through the policy thicket. The curriculum can be refined.

Which local authority can really hold powerful marketing companies to account about warping food choices of young people? They could control planning permission for fast-food shops and try to reverse how these have emerged on routes around schools. But as we saw with Cambridge University's FEAT data (see p. 301), fast food clusters around people on low incomes. So is it any wonder that no UK body has set sustainable-diet criteria for their catering contracts? And that caterers in other countries are re-skilling cooks to favour the Planetary Diet while little happens in the UK, other than magnificent pioneering work in the private restaurant sector through bodies such as the Sustainable Restaurants Association?

While the UK has many inspiring projects and pioneers,

they remain the minority and fragmented, often competing for funds; noisy and growing, to be sure, but not yet tipping the mass. This is not because people cannot see it; it is because the frameworks do not normalise the right action or link projects to become a national food force. This energy needs support and to be, as business says, 'scaled up'. That requires laws, frameworks, infrastructure, encouragement, support and training. Towns need to reconnect with their hinterlands. Big cities need to rethink how and where they source their food. If the UK is to take its food security seriously, there must be a transformation of food governance at all three immediate levels: local, regional and national – not just in relation to Europe or the rest of the world.

We need to tap into the huge experience outside this country of how to help build local food resilience.[591] There is a thirst for such work here. Wales has its Food Manifesto group and the legal framework of the Well-Being of Future Generations (Wales) Act 2015.[592] In Scotland, Nourish Scotland,[593] and the Good Food Scotland legal framework is emerging.[594] At time of writing, this appears to have useful powers but lacks specific ecological public-health targets. In England, there is the Sustainable Food Cities network and civic interest – a precondition – in place, but no legal commitment, no budgets. There is no Sustainable Food System Act – or some such commitment. The UK *does* have a vibrant food debate, fuelled by well-organized civil-society networks, by active professions and scientists, and informed by robust debate with the various food industries. And there are many inside the food industries who read the writing on the wall, too, and who think and do much in recognition. What is missing is institutional reform, mechanisms which can provide policy coherence, and which engage with the consuming public without either patronizing or infantilizing it, on the one hand, or glorifying it as in control when patently it is not, on the other hand.

Social processes to reform food governance such as the above are what the UK ought to be engaging in. These processes could be shaped by a revitalized policy agenda. This is the genuine route to evidence-based policy. The UK is not alone in facing food challenges of such scale. Other rich societies have not dissimilar constellations of food problems; some more, some less. Nor can we tackle this on our own. Offshoring the problems is not an option. The UK does not have an Empire to feed it. Nor are we in a strong position to trade our way out of these difficulties. The strand of politics which argues that we should simply buy our food flies in the face of land use evidence. It is a soft neo-imperialism. To use others potentially or already worse affected by climate change would be immoral. To switch supplies of fresh fruit and vegetables from the Netherlands (which faces flooding) and Spain (which faces desertification) to Morocco or West Africa (which face the same) would be idiotic. We must sort out our own governance with and mindful of others, our neighbours and beyond. The route to long-term food security is to make our food system more resilient and to steer a sane course between autarky and neo-imperialism. Part Three outlines what, I believe, this involves.

Accelerating the 'Great Food Transformation'

The evidence points firmly to the need for the UK to create a food culture in which sustainable diets from a sustainable food system are the norm. This 'Great Food Transformation' is needed to realign food production with human and eco-systems health in a socially just and economically sustainable form. The 'raise production' food policy in post-1945 reconstruction was honourable in intent and successful in feeding more people, but has unleashed destructive forces which now threaten the underpinnings of our existence, not least through the loss of biodiversity which Darwin called the 'web of life'. It has also failed to resolve old social and political problems and played a part in new ones too – all reviewed in Part Two. In those pages, I argued that there are many lock-ins which maintain rather than prevent or resolve the UK's food problems.

Part Three now focuses on what the UK could do to address all this. It is an overview of what I think we should be doing and what the British public could now debate, amend and then demand from our policymakers. It is ambitious but framed within the evidence.

First, we must do a bit of political ground clearance; there are things we can do as a country, and some only with others.

The UK is by no means the major political force it was or sometimes thinks of itself as being. Some humility is in order but we can play – and in part already do play – a significant role in working out what we, with others, need to do. Many of Britain's food problems are shared with other rich over-consuming societies. We can learn from others, and they from us, about the vulnerabilities and how to address them.

I am optimistic that awareness of the need for change has grown. Some pessimists argue that, even if the UK became overnight a paragon of twenty-first-century food virtue, we are so small in population (67 million people out of 512 million in Europe and 7.4 billion in the world in 2018), and small as an economic power compared to the EU, the USA, China or India, that our improvements would barely alter the looming crises. This may be true objectively but it ignores the politics for three reasons. Firstly, we are among the richest economies in the world. Our political economy has impact. If we were to follow the evidence, we would now be on the path to a radical but reasonable global realignment of people, ecosystems, health and decent living through food. Food reform would be building a better society. Secondly, if the UK were to come clean that it needs to put its own house in order, this would provide useful leadership among other rich nations as well as valuable 'democratic experimentation' about which measures are most effective. Thirdly, we cannot expect the political powerhouses of China, India and Latin America to take the data seriously unless we act and are seen to act. The UK's much-vaunted leadership role is somewhat dented – not least by falling off our pragmatic pedestal over Brexit. How we as a rich post-imperial country address our twenty-first-century food security challenge offers a chance for some moral and political merit.

The problem of UK food security outlined in Part One will not be resolved unless we address the food problems and lock-ins outlined in Part Two. Piecemeal action is unlikely to be effective in the time and at the scale needed. A common vision for the UK food system is sorely required but also one which addresses local and regional interests. Our policymakers now face the task of answering big questions. Are our populations being well and sustainably fed? Are our food and land resources being cared for? Is what we are doing now integrating human and ecosystems health without dumping problems elsewhere or exploiting others? Is this economics just and sound? The answer is 'No, despite presure.' Current market frameworks are only tentatively and patchily engaged with these questions.

The British state was known for incremental policy development. The food problems we face, however, will not be surmounted by a 'reluctant' or 'hollowed-out' state, or a state which assumes rational consumers determine market dynamics, or which simply hands over power and responsibility to a new channel of lowest-common-denominator-marketized politics. Even powerful food companies now recognize they cannot do it alone, but they also remain committed to growing their companies, which means more unnecessary foods, more savvy marketing, too much hedging of bets. They know there are some things they can do: cut out some plastic from packaging, or GHGs from production lines, or reward some ethical producers rather than squeeze them. But they cannot resolve climate change or transform working lives or reverse obesogenic environments, in a piecemeal fashion. They are too bound by the need to assuage shareholders' demands for profitability or to fill the coffers of investment (and sometimes our pension) funds. Meeting all this means facing complexity systemically and transforming food decision-making.

No wonder, despite our food problems being urgent,[1,2] our food politics has drifted. The warning lights were on for food in the 1990s.[3,4,5,6,7,8,9,10,11] By 2018 the IPCC gave the world twelve years to act on reducing GHGs or a 2°C increase in global warming would be unstoppable.[12] And the extent of obesity and the number of overweight people had overtaken hunger, bringing a double whammy to health. Western diets had raised meat production when consumption needed to be reduced. The impact of diets high in fat, sugar and salt (HFSS) on health now warps not just our NHS but healthcare globally. The rise of ultra-processed foods brings profits to food processors and provides factory employment, of course, but it distorts eating patterns.* Processing is not all bad. It enables foods which otherwise are hard to eat to be palatable.[13,14] Baking bread does this for wheat. Cooking makes beans palatable, too. Processing has its place, but ultra-processing is like a runaway train which needs to be slowed down and shunted into a siding. These products and the companies which make them really ought to be seen by investors as stranded assets. No wonder a major 2018 report on how well the UK's top food companies were performing on access to decent nutrition found that 69% of products failed to meet health ratings, and 85% were unsuitable to market to children, according to WHO standards.[15]

---

* Many workers and unions in the big food companies know this only too well but are caught: jobs versus public health.

The vast spending power of marketers compounds such problems and dwarfs weakly funded health promotion. In 2015, it was estimated that £300m was spent advertising confectionery, snacks, fruit, veg and soft drinks, of which 5% went on fruit and vegetables.[16] Much more marketing is 'below the radar'; product placement in TV and films was made legal in 2010.[17] Surely it should be sustainability-audited or the decision reversed. A new national framework ought to rein back the runaway production and consumption of HFSS foods. It would help if national guidelines were the basis for food contracts in both the public *and* private sectors. Some changes which would have considerable impact within the food system actually need action from outside. Inequalities of income, access, power and life expectancy all require macro-economic intervention, if we are to narrow gross disparities. Tackling Britain's food problems to put us on a path to sustainability will not be easy. Industry insiders know this as well as civil-society campaigners outside the policy tent. You don't need to be wearing a suit or to have a university degree to read the writing on the wall. Happily, compared to even a decade ago, there is growing and widespread agreement, even within business circles, that big changes are in order; this will be more than incremental change at a normal pace.[18] No wonder some baulk at it.

In Part One, I explored UK food security, arguing that just because our country is relatively rich does not mean it is therefore food-secure – whatever meaning of 'security' one uses! Part Two then suggested that our structural insecurity is compounded by a range of deep food problems. The ground on which twentieth-century food progress was laid is now unstable. Yet this instability is held in place by lock-ins. How the food system has been run, the unwritten bargain with consumers – cheaper, more plentiful, easier – has undermined food capacity. It is literally unsustainable yet persists. This is our problem, our food system. UK food policy needs to change. Now, Part Three outlines what might be done.

CHAPTER 5

What We Ought to Do:
A 'Great Food Transformation'

Change of something as enormous and complex as a food system can happen by crisis or choice, can occur slowly and incrementally or fast and headlong, with planning and preparation or by *force majeure* or because of events. Wars devastate but they also remake food politics, breaking old ties, opening up opportunities, not always for the good. The Brexit promise seriously underestimated the scale of the UK's food supply ties to Europe, but the threat of no deal knocked more heads together, hence the shock – felt by a Brexiting government in possession of its secret Yellowhammer no-deal planning, we must remember – at realizing that our massive, 'efficient', just-in-time food supply system might grind to a halt in parts (e.g. Dover or Holyhead) within a couple of days. This showed how few lessons had been learned by politicians from the fuel protest blockade by farmers and lorry drivers from 7 to 14 September 2000.[1]

When we review the full picture of the UK's food system, it becomes clear we need to halt the drift of UK food policy; this requires a long-term approach too rare in politics. Governments edge into the territory, here or there, only to wander off. Ministers move, governments fall, lessons fade, minor modifications are said to suffice. These are signs that institutional learning is not in place to make them pay attention. They can always blame someone else – Brussels, predecessors, foreigners. As we saw in Parts One and Two, few laws stipulate effort to maintain or improve food security; even the Civil Contingency Act is vague on food; the Resilience Forums are noble but weak, faced with structural crises. Industry has been happy to be left alone; mild corporate responsibility is not up to tackling the range of what needs to be tackled. That is why we need a better long-term food policy to improve food security, strengthen food defences and feed the people better and more sustainably. That means addressing food problems coherently rather than singly – not easy but neccessary.

Our challenge is to reform the UK food system *away* from the following features:

- A food system whose plentiful food is based on a food-insecure model of production, processing, distribution and consumption.
- Weak food defence systems.
- Stretched and risky food supply chains, based on price, choice and quality rather than ecosystems or societal resilience.
- Inadequate food governance which neither provides full national-policy guidance nor gives powers and resources to the local and regional (or devolved) authorities.
- Patterns of consumption and production which prioritize some criteria such as cost, availability and range, but which distort health, the environment, society and the political economy in doing so.

- A culture of consumer choice which is rationalized as the rule of market forces, as though market forces cannot be altered, and given new terms and conditions, and as though consumers really are in control, yet which leaves them under-informed.
- The warping of public food messages by a huge adspend that outclasses health promotion, and too often ignores or 'greenwashes' sustainability, thus undermining support for a decent food culture.
- An economic system which concentrates power in relatively few commercial entities' hands yet shrouds itself in the mythology of tight market dynamics while under-rewarding those who produce the food.
- Rewarding those who process food, too often turning it into HFSS value-added ultra-processed food products but marginalizing primary producers.
- Social structures which have shaped food inequalities between rich and poor, cities and rural areas, the South-East of England and the rest of the UK.
- City and town planning which has restricted capacity for urban living to be people-centred, placing the car at the core of food-planning processes, thus altering how physical activity (which 'burns off' dietary intake) can be taken and how people access food.
- Land use which entrenches particular patterns of food production to the detriment of ecological public health, and restricts access to new entrants.
- Financial gain from food mostly being made by after-farmgate and fishing sectors, thus squeezing primary

production, and setting food as a low-waged industry, demeaning its skills and value.

- Divisions between rural and urban Britain with an infrastructure which fragments regional identities and concentrates control into central state power in London, maintaining these divisions with different powers (and too few over food) given to Wales, Scotland, Northern Ireland, cities and metropolitan areas.

Although this combination is sobering, I must stress again that, over the last four decades or so, the UK has also witnessed a remarkable flowering of democratic understanding and experimentation about these kinds of food problems. The bigger picture emerges here and there. Some ministers have come to realize this. They move on, but campaigners work hard to push some of the issues up the policy agenda. New, confident social movements have sprouted to address this or that fault, arguing for specific change. Change agents inside companies have listened to NGOs outside and begun some new ways of doing business and making food a more decent sector to work in. Consultancies (and apps) advise on how to cut waste in kitchens. Food festivals have popped up around the country, championing the local and building new food identities and commerce. Towns, villages and cities set up food councils and inquiries. Transition towns spawned food gatherings, building community cohesion through food. Campaigns expose complacencies and deficiencies. Scandals about food quality and adulteration forced legislators to toughen relaxed or underfunded regulations. Food labels were slowly won which gave more (but still not enough) information about contents, nutrients and allergens to consumers, but which encouraged processors to alter product recipes. Manufacturers and caterers were embarrassed into checking what previously they had assumed or denied. This country – infamous up to the 1950s for bad food and a cavalier attitude of disrespect for food and growers[2,3,4] – saw a partial flowering of a better food culture and a smattering of localism. Britain adopted a European café and restaurant culture. All these features have reignited interest in food and injected new skills and pleasure into the British food scene. It's not all bad!

And yet . . . the audit of where the UK food system is, presented in earlier pages, is not good overall. The features we need to dismantle remain. We could and should be doing much more and better. Food insecurity and declining home production ought to be permanently debated, reviewed and high on the national agenda. They barely feature until crises loom, as it began to over Brexit disruption. Why do we wait until we are in crisis mode to realize our food governance, like our food security and defence, is weak and out of date? It inadequately links pressures in one area, say, environmental, with others, say, trade. The UK food system is fissured by risks, however full the supermarket shelves are. The country's social and economic inequalities are entrenched. The massive social divisions in and over food have widened unnecessarily, sometimes due to forces outside the food system such as the casualization of work, austerity politics and cuts in local-authority support, summarized in Part Two.

If we want to do something about our food problems and to put UK food onto a sustainable, secure footing, we must create a new framework which delivers for the complex mix of demands that has been sketched in this book. Such a framework is needed to guide the process of change that must now unfold. This cannot and will not be done overnight. The country's food security must be central to the new overall vision for the food system.

Among many things this must do is to resolve, for instance, the botched priorities on what land is for. Here is an example of something politicians are timid about. UK land use has been warped by becoming a capital bargaining tool. Land is money. If food-growing land can be re-zoned as housing land, its value rockets. Too much prime land has been built on. Land strategy should be based on land's multi-functionality, of course; it must meet requirements for water, carbon, food, forests, views, biodiversity and more. But which takes priority? And how can these be addressed simultaneously? In practice, we act in contradictory ways; we spray pesticides – in effect a liquid hoe to reduce or replace labour and thus direct costs – and thereby we destroy the biodiversity we say we want. Gardeners pour chemicals over town gardens with barely a thought, and inadequate protection. In 2012, an estimated 701,148 kg of 'active substances' were applied to 299,419 hectares by farmers, public authorities and gardeners, mostly glyphosate.[5] And we cover land with tarmac and now with solar farms, instead of retrofitting houses and buildings with solar panels. It is more profitable to 'grow' houses than food on prime land with a view. And so on. Food growing is caught up in this welter of contradictory demands and treatments. Food production ought to be intrinsic to land use, not to the detriment of other features but nested, and mutually reinforcing for resilience. 65% of our land is 'farmed' but too often in a way that is inappropriate. Estate agents sell land for the view. To cut through this mess, we need human and ecosystems health to take a central role in food and land planning.

Too much UK land is given over to animal production, an argument understandably perceived by many but not all farmers as a threat. It is inescapable, however, that we have made cattle and sheep our competitors in land use; farmed animals generally consume around a third of grain production. In the next thirty years, however, a phased reduction of such animal output is needed. Ecological public-health criteria must reshape land use: more horticulture, less intensively farmed animal culture. If we want more diverse re-wooding and more varied tree cover – an issue on which there is at last some consensus – we need to do this properly, which probably means less grain production on prime land just to feed animals elsewhere. The uplands need to be regenerated; for too long they have been dominated by unprofitable sheep, with farmers kept just afloat by subsidies. If there is anywhere to rewild, it is the uplands, but they are sensitive in social terms, and there's little agreement as yet what 'rewilding' means in practice, let alone how or whether to fund it. The uplands are culturally iconic in the North, Wales and Scotland.* People may think the bare moors are natural; they are man-made, deforested, grazed and razed by sheep.[6] Attempts to begin significant rewilding in mid-Wales, for example, met

---

* I was a farmer on the Lancashire hills and know only too well the dogged resilience of hill farmers; the need to help and listen to them in the transition was well mapped in the 2019 Food, Farming and Countryside Commission. And even though I know we must re-tree vast tracts, my spirits lift when I see or walk on the moors and stretch my eyes.

opposition from some local interests.[7,8] Lives, ties and sentiments are at stake, which is why rural populations need to be directly engaged in the big changes required ahead. Some see this kind of thinking as driven by anti-meat or anti-animals bias. It is actually the result of applying multi-criteria thinking. Animals have their place; ruminants can sequester carbon, not just emit it, but they are also big water users, and can have either a beneficial or a harmful impact on biodiversity. Farm animals, as I have said earlier, need to be shepherded back into a better agri-ecological niche.

I have taken the question of land use and animal production as an illustration of the need to unravel many complexities across the food system. A series of deep-rooted tensions between state, companies, consumers and the public interest over food is now coming to a head. The naïve anti-planning thinking espoused by some neo-liberals has probably run its course. Politics may keep it alive, of course, but events are narrowing the options. The lack of planning for Brexit, for instance, became a worry even for anti-planning ministers, and Project Yellowhammer preparations (coded 'Official Sensitive') forced a reluctant government to see the value of preparing for the worst. Yellowhammer plans were published only in heavily truncated form and only after being leaked.[9] Yet still many people apparently favoured a 'no-deal' Brexit. This suggests perhaps that they either were used to being fed, or had a wholly inadequate appreciation of how food gets to the shops. It also exposed the limitations of national debate about food security. Even warnings from industry, who knew only too well the fragility of just-in-time food supply chains, barely dented government thinking until the reality of no-deal loomed large. We might think this bizarre – surely big business always gets its way, no? – until we remember that this is precisely the mix of denial and ignorance which characterized 1930s food policy.

Whatever one's views of Brexit, surely there is now a wider appreciation that security of food supply should feature in any political vision for the future. As was discussed in Part One, if the UK adopts an Atlanticist approach to food trade, the consequences are different to those that follow from going more globalist, let alone a version of continued Europeanization. The stakes on food standards have already been raised. In everyday terms it's a choice: fresh peaches and Mediterranean olive oil or tinned US peaches (and Spam?) and US olive oil; Latin American or US hormone-reared beef versus beef reared without growth hormones?[10,11,12]

Table 5.1 sketches seven distinct options for how the UK could frame its food security, with some of their implications, returning to themes introduced in Part One (see pp. 55–8). *Atlanticists* see the UK as turning its back on Europe, perhaps even becoming an honorary fifty-first US state. *Globalists* hedge their bets about particular trade deals, and suggest we simply trade food from anywhere. *Imperialists* want food from wherever (cheap) land and labour can be assured, and see the future as rekindling old food links and ties. *Outer Europeans* say we can get the kind of Mediterranean foods UK consumers have grown accustomed to from other parts of the Mediterranean. *Euro-reformers* propose that, if the UK severs EU food links, they will push to rebuild the links, urging a speed-up of EU internal reforms to allow the UK to return at a later date. UK food security requires close European links. *Nationalists*

Policy vision	Focus for food source	Some of what it means for UK farming and food	Some of what it means for consumers	Potential hotspots
Atlanticist	N. America/ USA	Competition from even more intensive production	Cheap beef and a possible welcome back to Spam and tinned peaches?	Food standards: chlorinated chicken, hormone-fed beef
Globalist	Anywhere, everywhere	Food deals subsumed within wider trade deals	Cheapest food	Traceability
Imperialist	Commonwealth countries	Competition more likely from Africa than the Antipodes	More food from Southern and West Africa	Far-off labour conditions can unravel
Outer European	South and east shores of Mediterranean	EU on the cheap	Less from EU, more from Turkey, Morocco, Israel	Geo-political uncertainties
Euro-reformer	Reformed EU or EFTA	Keeping to EU standards without the subsidies	More of the same	Divisiveness of return, reform and remain politics
Nationalist	UK first	Self-reliance	Higher prices	Loss of some favourite foods
Disinterested	Food is assumed, but sourcing is not a priority	Default values dominate	Assumption that supermarket shelves fill themselves	Volatility if difficulties or shortages emerge

Table 5.1

Some policy visions for the future of the UK food system

Source: Author.

counter that only more UK production will ensure food security. One strand argues for a bio-regionalism, growing more here sustainably. Another argues, whatever the format, British is best. There is also, perhaps sadly, a seventh vision we might term *Disinterested*. It is not really a vision, but at best a modern version of Nelson's statement at the sea battle of Copenhagen in 1801. Putting his telescope deliberately to his blind eye, he is reputed to have said, 'I see no ships', able to ignore what he did not want to see. This is the view not to take part and simply to cede policy to others. It ducks responsibility but is still detectable, shamefully, among policymakers. Each of these visions has different implications for supply and consumers. Each has adherents above and below the surface of national debate. They cross ostensible party lines. Yet on the choice hangs the overall framework for food security. It must be debated and clarified. The issues discussed throughout this book cut across each policy direction, implying different potential hotspots.

Deciding these huge long-term policy orientations will shape the food system. Whichever path, the UK will need to pursue a vision of a good (or better) food system with specific targets, political commitments, delivery mechanisms and funds to meet them. The positive news from the scientists is that we can, if we want, again overcome the Malthusian problem. In 1798, Malthus had painted a sober picture of population growth outstripping the capacity of farming to feed people.[13] His fearful analysis was in effect addressed in the nineteenth century by exploiting imperial power for food.[14] The UK used other people's land to feed itself, in a mix of colonialism, navy power and trade. This bought the UK time to begin to invent other ways of increasing food output for a rising population. But the imperialist approach twice nearly brought the UK to its knees in the First and Second World Wars. In the 1940s, thankfully, a rethink began which took food security more seriously. This centred on the productionist model, applying new science and technology to maximize output growth. Actually it improved food security by exploiting ecosystems. This worked but at a cost, even at the micro-farm level.[15,16,17,18,19] It also concentrated power and lengthened supply chains, making new sectors wealthy while breaking the link between primary producers and end consumers. Marketing reshaped food reality: eat, eat, eat. Result: diet-related ill-health.

Now a third phase for post-Malthusian UK food security is upon us. Simply producing more will not resolve our food problems. Although the UK population is growing, the rate is far slower here than globally. How the UK consumes is perhaps a more immediate driver of the food system's impact.[20] Global modelling studies seem reassuring; they suggest that it will be and is possible to feed all the world healthily and within environmental limits by 2050, but only with radical dietary change.[21,22,23,24] This is something the UK food politics cannot avoid. Our food system, our diets, our food policies must change, and on multiple levels and fronts if, that is, we want to make the UK more food-secure.

The creation of a resilient UK food system for food security

To address this task, we need to adopt a more complex approach – what is known in the policy world as a 'multi-criteria' framework. It sounds geeky, but is not. When we go shopping or consider buying a car, or think about children and friends, we do not apply a crude on–off, simplistic formula to the process. We can both love and be irritated, want and not want, think about price and aesthetics. We juggle different criteria: what we can afford, low interest rates, identity, aspirations, pleasure, utility, many values. In everyday life, we humans can and do apply really subtle multiple criteria to normal, everyday decisions. That is essentially what multi-criteria frameworks introduce into food policy: clarity about the co-existence of many criteria by which to judge progress.

If we apply the six-headings approach to sustainability outlined in Part One (see pp. 200–201), we can bring coherence to what we want from a 'Great Food Transformation' for the UK. Using this, the task is to achieve a better integration of:

1. public health in order to tackle over-, under- and malconsumption and to prevent diet-related health burdens;

2. environmental improvement, not just to reduce negative impacts on climate change, biodiversity, water, air, seas, but to reverse those and to make our food system truly resilient;

3. social and cultural aspects of food to enhance its role in how people live and to reverse its being a driver of social injustice, consigning millions of British people to worse or shortened lives;

4. a new political economy of food which provides decent waged and respected work via food at fully costed and fair prices.

All these aspirations must also be woven together to deliver:

5. high-quality food and diverse diets which people like to eat and meet sustainable dietary guidelines, while

6. being democratically accountable and subject to lively food governance at all levels – local, regional and national within the UK – as well as internationally (with neighbours and the rest of the world).

To apply these criteria would provide direction for what will in fact be a considerable change for UK food policy and governance. Dictators could simply push this through, but we live in a democracy. This makes the process both harder and better! The change will endure and grow, if there is public engagement and democratic processes which treat people (not just animals) as sentient beings, as citizens not just consumers. Citizens' juries and deliberative democracy show the way. The UK's vibrant civil society has already offered pointers for how to do it,[25,26,27,28] and the National Food Strategy review led by Henry Dimbleby (from June 2019) rightly recognized the need to extend this and throw the weight of government behind any countrywide (actually English) process.[29] It would be unprecedented to do this for food security. Whether motivated by food defence or food sustainability, this or any new strategy will not be done and dusted in a year. But since food is a matter of hearts and minds, not just keeping the shelves full or ordering people to change, it must happen.[30,31,32] At the same time we must face Britain's idiosyncrasies. Our diet has normalized ultra-processed foods more than others in Europe. Our cultural reflex is often said to be that food is good if it is cheap; the marketers tell us that is our number one concern, so there is no need for complicated democratic processes. Price is clearly important (and in all cultures), but polls and studies also show we bring many other values to the table.[33,34] We want our food to be British, but are less sure of what that is.[35] We want it safe but have to assume it, because food is a trust relationship.[36] We like it to taste nice, but our tastes change. In short, we apply many criteria already, and they are in flux, subject to competing demands and aspirations. And they need clarification, recalibration and realignment to achieve food security.

FOOD SUPPLY FOR RESILIENCE

The core theme of this book has been that national food security policy is adrift and too often our national policy is complacent or absent. If the UK is to deliver its commitment to zero carbon by 2050 – which is in national as well as international interests – we must speed up change while defending our food interests. At present, we are doing neither. Here and there, there are positive moves, but too little, too slowly, too messily. And too often by using other countries' resources, land and labour.

A *new Food Resilience and Sustainability Act with legally binding targets and delivery mechanisms* should map the new overall direction for the UK food system and set processes in train. The underpinning of food safety, for example, already exists in the Food Safety Act 1990 and Food Standards Act 1999 and legislation as a member of the EU (transferred to the UK in Brexit), but this says little about sufficiency of supply or addressing the lock-ins to unsustainability reviewed in Part Two. The UK has minimum obligations – enshrined for example in international law, and under legal agreements such as the UN International Covenant on Economic, Social and Cultural Rights (ICESCR) Article 11 (discussed in Part One, pp. 125–7) – but twenty-first-century British consumers and food industries deserve and need more than these.[37] Whether closely aligned to the EU or not , the UK needs to get a grip on its own targets. This new Food Resilience and Sustainability Act should go beyond the ICESCR's loose notion of 'adequate' food and nail down what we mean by sustainable diets, and take on board the evidence for how and where change is needed. If we don't set targets for diets and food which are low carbon and tasty, affordable but not displacing damage onto future generations, i.e. meet multi-criteria objectives, we simply rob peter to pay paul.

While the Climate Change Act 2008 creates targets for CO_2e by 2050, something of equal weight is needed to link production and consumption and apply the multi-criteria appropriate today.* Some early thinking has emerged around the idea of a 'Green New Deal',[38] and in Scotland's Good Food Nation.[39] Even before the December 2019 election, climate change rose up the national agenda, but the scope of change required has not yet been translated into action across the food system. That is why we need new food legislation – to deliver on the aspiration. We can note that a number of countries have placed the 'right to food' in national constitutions or law: Brazil in 2010, South Africa in 1996, and India with its National Food Security Act in 2013. The UK needs something

---

* In 2015/16 Kerry McCarthy MP introduced a Food Waste Reduction Bill recognizing systemic features; https://services.parliament.uk/bills/2015-16/foodwastereduction.html.

itself both to underpin the direction of the food system and to embed the rights of consumers within it, and to reconnect production and consumption.

The government should conduct *a special joint Food Defence Review*, a process which should be scrutinized by both the Parliamentary Defence and the Environment, Food and Rural Affairs Committees.* The terms of reference should cover not just 'old' threats such as to road, sea and air, but also the 'new' such as cyber, digital, artificial intelligence, and social disruption from unaccountable foreign powers. For a country with our geographical advantages – likely to grow if climate change modelling is correct – the UK is drifting into deeper over-reliance on external sources. Today, as I have argued, the UK lacks sufficient military or naval power to protect extended supply lines. The National Cyber Security Agency is a start on new threats, but Cabinet ministers (of many political persuasions) still naïvely believe the UK can simply switch supplies to other continents, as though there are no geopolitical tensions and the UK still 'rules the waves'! The Border Force's handful of small ships are hardly a sufficient fleet to protect supply lines in the case of difficulties.

For a country as blessed as is the UK with (mostly) benign weather, rich (but depleting) soil, (misused yet wonderful) land, and (massive amounts of) capital and skills, it is ludicrous that we produce so little food. The country is often

---

* The precedent for such a joint select committee for food was when the then Agriculture and Health Committees combined in 1998 to review Food Safety and Standards, pending the creation of the new Food Standards Agency. The joint committees' work could be a useful sounding board for intra-Whitehall policy development.

presented as overcrowded, but one can travel for many miles seeing no one in or working on the fields. Almost certainly we need more people from the UK committed to working in food, from farm to food service. They require training and support. We have to *set goals to increase production more appropriately and only on sustainable lines*. The UK food system must be encouraged by *a clear, legally binding framework with targets* which forge synergies across sectors and between supply and demand. We need more food direct for home consumption, from shorter supply lines. This should not be a slide into autarky (extreme nationalism as self-sufficiency) but stem from a desire to be a decent nation contributing to global targets for issues as varied as carbon emissions, water use, biodiversity loss, fair wages, skills enhancement and inequality reduction. And not to be parasitic on other, weaker economies' lands and labour. Africa, Latin America and Asia need to feed themselves on short rather than global supply lines.

We should not rely on UK economic power and financial wealth to buy our way out of problems. Some of the problems coming towards us could break the economy. The tentative moves to readjust UK food policy which began after the 2007–8 commodity price crisis, only to be stopped in 2010, need to be resuscitated. *The Cabinet Food Sub-committee needs to be restarted too*. Whatever happens to the Dimbleby National Food Strategy, the wasted years of the 2010's mean we are in a period of rapid catch-up. Brexit has sapped energy. NGOs and public pressure must ensure progress towards a redesign is not derailed. One essential task that is part of all this is *an Audit of what could be grown more in the UK*. Current supply may be 'sufficient', benchmarked to current patterns of demand, but is not if we apply sustainability criteria. Our home production has been in slow decline from the 1980s. Improved UK food security almost certainly means *raising UK food production* figures from 2018's 53% by value and from 61% 'self-sufficiency' to at least 80%, or a level to which the country could resort in crisis. A certain amount of importation is welcome, and will be demanded; and rates can obviously vary by product. Advice from agronomy, sustainability and food sector experts should inform the Audit, as should regional thinking.

The broad direction of rebuilding food primary production for sustainability is already clear: more diversity of planting, more grain for humans and less for livestock production, more regional horticulture, a switch in mode of livestock production, reskilling farmers to grow more fruit and vegetables in rotation. Land use must adjust more closely to ecological public-health and societal needs: fewer grain-fed animals, more horticulture, less agri-culture. The UK cannot grow rice or mangoes or bananas but it could grow 100% of apples, pears and soft fruit, and a more diverse range of vegetables. The barriers to appropriate sustainable home production need to be removed – better pay and conditions for workers, incentives to release land to young growers, better price structures, more regional targets and infrastructure. Although the argument is often made that the UK should maintain its meat and dairy focus because animal production suits our climate and land, this is really a side argument. Land use and ecological public health both point to the need to rebuild horticulture. Our farm animals need to be walked back into an appropriate ecological niche. Our farmers and growers need support in this transition. A sustainable food policy must be people-centred too.

ECOLOGICAL PUBLIC HEALTH

Sustainability is both the key to food defence and an end in itself. The link between human and environmental health is the base on which policy and planning must now be built. Good-quality food requires us to treat ecosystems carefully, not to mine them. Diet is a major cause of public ill-health, not just obesity but a range of non-communicable diseases too. Drug bills and hospital care that arise from failing to prevent food being a cause of poor health are a gross waste of time, money and effort. Too much diet-related unhealthiness is shaped by social and economic inequalities. The value of antibiotics for health emergencies has been undermined by profligate and normalized use in the food chain, as the O'Neill review recognized, although the writing had been on the wall for decades.[40,41] At the same time, UK food industries pour out too many ultra-processed foods high in fats, salt and sugar, and advertising and marketing practices continue to distort dietary choice. No wonder the UK has the highest rate of consumption of such foods in Europe.[42]

With good reason, in 2019 Dame Sally Davies set out in her final report as Chief Medical Officer for England the kind of radical but reasonable Preventive Actions which should be implemented to tackle the huge and costly burden that poor diet puts on people's lives, life expectancy and the NHS.[43] She was correct to urge the use of laws and regulations to institute change.* *A radical reorientation of budgets to increase the percentage of health budgets which go on preventive measures* is needed. In the 2010s, the share of NHS budgets allocated to

---

* Annex A of the CMO Dame Sally Davies's 2019 special report gives a long list of what should be done.

public health declined. In 2017–18, it was only £2.5bn out of a £130bn total budget; less than 2% is ludicrous. It should double within at least five years, sold to the public simply as 'prevention is better than cure'. We need to consider taxing the drivers of unhealthy, unsustainable diets. A *tax on food advertising and e-media* is suggested below.

Ideally, a body such as a Royal Commission should be charged with mapping a *new set of multi-criteria principles for the UK food system*. Defra's 2011–12 Green Food Project detailed some but not enough; it was ignored by Defra anyway.[44,45] And the 2010 Defra Food 2030 strategy had already been mistakenly axed by the Coalition government. The UK has excellent scientists who could be co-ordinated by suitable bodies such as the Royal Society and British Academy (both natural and social sciences), with professional bodies, to formulate and debate how such principles could be implemented, drawing on the previous efforts.[46,47,48] The country's food industry must not be left patchily to develop frameworks defining sustainability on its own. This should be a government-facilitated process. Historically, when confronted by huge challenges such as we face over food, UK governments have turned for advice and evidence either to 'standing', i.e. permanent, bodies or to one-off specially commissioned ones such as Royal Commissions. That the standing Royal Commission on Environmental Pollution was summarily closed in 2010 was an act of governmental vandalism. Ad hoc Royal Commissions can be lengthy processes but the magisterial 1905 Royal Commission on Food Supply and Raw Materials in Time of War was completed in two years. It can be done. They have become unfashionable for other reasons; governments do not like to be given strong advice. But food security requires just that.

A short-term *Food Resilience and Sustainability Task Force* should be set up, answering to a new Cabinet food security sub-committee, and drawing on existing bodies such as the Committee on Climate Change, the Standing Advisory Committee on Nutrition, the Environment Agency, and expert food-related committees such as the National Infrastructure Commission, National Cybersecurity Centre plus relevant professional bodies such as the Royal Society and British Academy. This Task Force should conduct an initial review within, say, twelve months, and make proposals for UK food resilience and sustainability.* It should include within its review a comprehensive look at good practice across the food system.† The temptation to lecture other countries while ignoring our own deep failings must be avoided. Meanwhile the terms of reference for a new *National Food Resilience and Sustainability Council* should be enshrined in the new law. This should begin the process of setting targets, and take note of international experience of using scientific

---

* We must resist the anti-expert nihilism sometimes expressed in anti-statist political circles. Until 2011, bodies such as the Royal Commission on Environmental Pollution and the Sustainable Development Commission could have provided some of the necessary expertise and advice suggested here. They were abolished in 2011. Select Committees in Parliament such as the EAC and EFRA Committees struggle to fill the gap. Their role is rightly and properly more immediately locked into assessment of government performance, rather than into providing evidence-based strategic advice.

† The Food, Farming and Countryside Commission hosted by the Royal Society of Arts did useful preliminary work mapping good practice for aspects of farming. We need this too for horticulture and fishing, but also for short-chain systems, for enlightened processing and retailing, and for the giant sector of food service.

advice to build sustainable food system policy thinking, such as in Scandinavia and The Netherlands.[49,50] The task ahead needs cool, clear, trustworthy data and policy recommendations which prioritize the public interest and address relevant food sector concerns.

Food policy will continue to drift unless we have *new UK-wide Sustainable Dietary Guidelines*. These need to be required by law (like the USA's dietary guidelines) and made available and translated or implemented by a body such as the British Standards Institute in the form of a Publicly Available Specification (PAS). HM Government in collaboration with the devolved governments in Scotland, Wales and Northern Ireland should institute this new UK-wide sustainable dietary guide and PAS to expand and build upon the Public Health England and the NHS Eatwell Plate. That currently includes only minimal elements of environmental guidance.* This is no longer acceptable. The new National Food Resilience and Sustainability Council should work with Public Health England (PHE) and others appropriately thereafter regularly to update them, and the PAS likewise. These will become the benchmark for food planning. Again, the UK should note and learn from the experience of other governments which have begun to develop sustainable-consumption advice.[51,52] We should not, for instance, continue to advise people to eat fish twice a week ('oily' fish once a week) without transforming our fishing policy. Nor should we continue weakly to advise consumers to

---

* One is to consume sustainable fish. The other is not explicit but evidence from the Carbon Trust for PHE in 2016 persuaded it to recommend lower meat consumption in the 2016 Eatwell Plate revision.

'eat less red and processed meat' (in tiny writing at the bottom-left edge of the 'plate') as the Eatwell Plate does, without translating that to sea and land use, fishing and farming.

Public advice on food matters crosses many ministerial boundaries – which is why sub-committee co-ordination is so necessary. The Food Standards Agency (FSA) has been weakened from when it led the (voluntary but effective) salt reduction programme. Today it contributes little on environmental and cultural aspects of diet. It has key responsibilities in relation to microbiological and toxicological safety, but not for nutrition or labelling policies, which were reallocated by the Coalition government in the 2010s. Public Health England, meanwhile, has become more important. It has a deeper public-health perspective, yet made little progress under the Public Health Responsibility Deal. It has regained its stride with the sugar levy and providing underpinning on child obesity, but its powers, too, are inadequate. If nothing else, the FSA should regain integrated responsibility for safety, nutrition and labelling, and include full sustainability criteria. Only this will deliver its legal duty to 'put consumers first'. Consumer trust also needs to be rebuilt by ensuring that representatives of the agricultural, chemical or food industries are no longer allowed to be members of the FSA Board, and members of FSA advisory committees should no longer include employees of, or consultants to, those industries.[53,54] All evidence used by scientific committees to make their decisions and offer advice should be in the public domain. Some argue that the FSA should be merged into Public Health England. This would certainly create a more powerful body, fit to stand up to industrial lobbies. *Whether separate or combined, both the FSA and PHE should incorporate a multi-criteria framework for defining high-standard food,* in line with advice from the proposed National Food Resilience and Sustainability Council.

CULTURE AND SOCIETY

British consumers need help. A more food-secure country would invest in *Food Citizenship* throughout the economy and society. Every person needs appropriate skills for the age of climate change and to be engaged in the Great Food Transformation. If we want to reduce plastic in food chains, as the public says it does,[55] this requires us to cook more – nutritious everyday foods – and to buy more discriminatingly, not just to replace polythene wrapping, for instance, with potato starch 'lookalike' plastic. A wholesale restructuring of how food is handled, sold and used is overdue, in which companies need to be held to account, but this also requires citizen reskilling. In the 2000s, campaigns to re-introduce cooking skills into schools helped win some change in the primary curriculum in England and Wales, but not in secondary schools or further and higher education. It barely touched private-sector catering, which today dominates the vast food service sector. The Great Food Transformation needs everyone to understand how our diets are a vehicle for national security. School curricula could build on pioneering work such as Food for Life, which now covers 10,000 schools.[56] If we can have a system of road skill classes and proficiency before people are allowed to drive cars on their own, we can surely have food equivalents to ensure sustainability. A new strand of National Vocational Qualifications and food sustainability certification would repurpose both private- and public-sector catering. This would incorporate lessons from food waste reduction in the kitchen programmes, for instance, and link waste reduction with skills being fostered by campaigns and pioneering projects such as the Royal Academy of Culinary Arts' Adopt-A-School, or the taste-focused Taste Education. These and many like them are all reframing and experimenting with ideas about future food citizenship. Their efforts ought to be brought under one umbrella, perhaps a *Food Citizenship Education Council*, rather than competing. In England, the Department for Education ought to facilitate this.

UK society is highly unequal. This inequality restricts our food progress. *Inequality reduction must be a principle at the heart of UK food security policy*. We should remember how rationing in the Second World War was a socially just programme which improved health for the poor and morale whatever a person's station. Inequality reduction requires Treasury action – taxation, infrastructural investment and other long-term fiscal measures – as well as commitment to less divisive wage structures, education and training. An immediate positive change could come from the introduction of high-quality, sustainable diets for young people into all educational establishments. Private and academy schools must not be exempted from such food standards. And the costs of sustainable diets, as defined by the new National Food Security Council, should be central to any welfare reform and payments. The goal is to invest in ill-health prevention and reduce NHS costs. We need to reinvigorate and fund the Beveridge and Boyd Orr public-health principle of prevention being the best approach.

Politicians can be easily seduced by the argument that

science and technology can and will solve food problems. New technologies, as we saw in Part Two, already proliferate in the world of food. All the sciences, not just STEM subjects, are needed to reframe food systems for sustainability. UK *research and development programmes should accelerate their contribution to UK food resilience and sustainability targets*. The work of the Government Office for Science and Chief Scientific Advisers aligns with existing UN Sustainable Development Goals, and should help the UK food system meet the Committee on Climate Change's zero carbon target set in 2019, and to update and advise the new National Food Security Council, the Sustainable Dietary Guidelines and other food-related targets. UK Research Councils have taken a lead in recent years on international food security but, until recently, little on UK food security – alas, a sign of the reflex to advise others while not leading ourselves. UK Research and Innovation's call in late 2019 for research to focus on the UK food system was thus very welcome, and should speed up collaboration by the Social Sciences, Natural Sciences and STEM subjects.[57] The nine Research Councils should adopt, for example, national-inequality reduction and sustainable food as two core goals for research strategies.*

A *new regional system of urban and rural food and farm colleges* is necessary. This could build on remaining institutions but with improved links between higher and further education at local and regional levels. In the nineteenth century, colleges of agriculture were founded, broadly one for each

---

* The UKRI research call used the multi-criteria approach pioneered by the Centre for Food Policy.

county, to be a beacon for the dissemination of good practice. A wider, whole-food-system approach is needed today. This new generation of joint urban–rural colleges of food will nurture skills and training for town and country. Shoreline areas, for example, could be linking the growth of offshore windfarms to seafood production, with mussel farms. Inland regions need to re-emphasize horticulture. We should note the USA's land grant system of nationally designated seats of learning and public advice. This began in 1862 and has changed and adapted over the years. The UK shamefully wrenched its agriculture colleges from local control – even closing and selling some off to universities, which too often saw little value in them or decided that they cost too much. This new cohort of agri-food colleges would reconnect town and country, be hubs for revitalized regional food economies, and become focus points for *regional food resilience*, places which understand their locality and respond to local needs and advise on the building of a better food infrastructure.

All *public and private food contracts should be required to apply the new Sustainable Dietary Guidelines*. The translation of best evidence into best practice should not be left to whim or vagaries of cost and whether a manager is interested. The lead that the Culinary Institute of America – the other CIA – took in collaborating with Harvard University's Chan School of Public Health shows what can be done.[58] The UK should develop such an approach on a national scale. Public-sector catering bodies and professional bodies such as the Sustainable Restaurants Association should be encouraged to merge advice and to disseminate expertise nationally; better co-ordination of the Skills Councils such as People 1st and

Lantra is needed, together with bodies such as UK Hospitality and the Food and Drink Sector Council. Some coherence in the plethora of schemes and projects is overdue. They may keep consultants in business but are not shifting the food system fast enough.

A persistent failure in UK food policy is that advertising budgets outspend health promotion by excessive amounts. Giant corporations obey the law but ride roughshod across health. A wasteful consumerism rules in food (and not just food). Food waste is a cultural act of planetary stupidity which must be reversed. That WRAP began within government but is now a contract-seeking charity is unacceptable. *WRAP should be re-awarded its centrality and funds*. Waste reduction throughout the food system, from farm to consumers, is one key to food security. *Taxation on food advertising* would help bring over-supply and over-purchasing as a source of waste more under control. The national debate about lax regulation of (mostly US-based) e-media is underway, but the food element needs careful scrutiny. Freedom of expression is used to justify misinformation. The notion of the 'watershed' for children's TV-watching habits is outdated and sidestepped by companies via social media. The sums raised should be hypothecated to health promotion.

POLITICAL ECONOMY

The role of public subsidies in the UK food system has been reviewed earlier (pp. 370–77). It is surely counter-productive that subsidies are used to keep farmers afloat. It would be more helpful if they received a decent return for their labours. The initial EU CAP system of subsidizing agriculture to produce food has gradually been altered to include environmental purposes. The English Agriculture Bill proposes to turn this further towards rewarding mainly environmental land management as a 'public good'. This public-good argument seems reasonable but must include food as a value in itself. Whatever happens politically, it seems essential for farming to receive far more than the current 5–6% of gross value added (GVA) in the food chain. Given the small sums that primary producers receive of the £225.7bn UK consumers spent on food and drink in 2018 (see p. 73), surely it would both make sense and be publicly acceptable for it to be legally binding that *primary producers receive at least double current GVA, i.e. 10-12% overall.* This would vary by product but be a sector guide.

Power is imperfectly distributed in the UK food system. The answer must be to *strengthen competition policy* and think it through properly for the food system. Concentration is higher in some sectors and some regions than in others. If the US could break up AT&T to create smaller telephone companies, is it unrealistic to break up Tesco, which hovers near 30% of the market, or to create new legal *regional concentration limits*? This may sound radical, but either UK capitalism must reassert the logic of being a 'market economy' or it must come clean and accept that it supports oligarchy. The UK food system is no longer – if it ever was – a simple mix of producers and consumers. The food system is labyrinthine. Supply chains witness bitter fights for profitability far from the farm. Long-established tensions between the urban and the rural, rich and poor, producers and consumers, home production and imports, now need to be reconfigured. The Competition and Markets Authority has overseen concentration rather than stopped it. Although EU Competition Commissioners flexed their muscles on occasion and brought US corporate giants into engagement, this has not been replicated in the UK; nor indeed enough in the EU. New competition thresholds need to be set and powers over intervention-willing institutions are required, with no retailer having more than, perhaps, 15% of a market at national, regional or local levels, and with *duties to source more of what is sold from the region* – an incentive to revitalize the local food economy.*

Distorted food prices are among the most tricky issues which must be faced in the Great Food Transformation. 'Cheap food' has been a default UK policy since the 1846 repeal of the Corn Laws. Consumers today may still seek lower prices but in fact they pay more over time; it may seem as though food prices have declined but this is because food has taken a declining share of household expenditure. False and short-term accounting is at the heart of the UK's current food policy mess. Over the next thirty years, *UK food culture must shift to a full cost-accounting approach.* Apparently cheap food does not include expensive externalized costs, let alone uncosted damage to health, the environment and society. People with low incomes cannot afford to spend more on better diets, because their incomes are squeezed. Yet the more affluent who can consume better (e.g. more fruit) still often eat a less than ideal sustainable diet, but nevertheless gain in life expectancy through their overall advantages. The

---

* Note should be taken of the 2018 French *Loi Agriculture et Alimentation*, whose three aims are to ensure fair prices, deliver health, and protect the environment.

entire population needs to shift to more sustainable diets. Politics must now decide how to unlock this lock-in.

Almost certainly, if current food supply chains remain long, food prices will have to rise to include the full costs of present production methods in terms of health and the environment. They would rise if primary producers were to be paid more, as proposed above. This has macro-economic implications which cannot be ducked. The NHS pays a huge bill for perfectly legal but inadequate and distorted diets. If we maintain the burden of costs across the economy as they currently are – cheap food, expensive housing, rising health bills, impediments to building exercise into everyday life – these costs will damage the economy. One option is to aim for shorter regional food supply chains, with fewer sectors each adding value and taking their cut, and with more of what consumers pay for food filtering down to better-rewarded primary producers. Another is to raise incomes and living standards to enable all people to eat well and sustainably. *Either we must pay higher food prices or we shorten food chains.* Outsourcing more abroad is neither acceptable nor 'taking back control'. As they stand, UK food costs have been at the low-to-middle end of the range across Europe.[59,60] Even that is arguably too low. An authoritative review of options on this issue – including the case for higher wages and/or welfare to include those costs – is a priority, and both the *National Minimum Wage and the National Living Wage should be recalibrated to include the cost of sustainable diets.*

The UK has no overt national food price policy. Politicians duck the issue. Policy is tacitly left to HM Treasury. Housing takes huge chunks out of people's wages, yet food is just assumed to be something to aim to get ever cheaper. Mediation in this conflict is by default left to supermarkets as the price setters and food chain gatekeepers. Another intervention to break this policy logjam would be to consider a *new legal duty to pay the full environmental and health costs at each stage of any food supply chain*. Powers to do this and the methods for estimation could be specified in new food legislation. A prerequisite is greater transparency about where the money is made down food supply chains. This probably requires an expansion of powers for the Competition and Markets Authority, certainly new duties to investigate and publish, and a strengthened and expanded Grocery Code Adjudicator. Food costs should also be included in the remit of the new National Food Security Council proposed below.

The food revolution from the mid-twentieth century has altered how we live. A vast infrastructure of property and roads, energy sources and water pipes is the invisible underpinning of how Britain eats. The *National Infrastructure Commission should include a focus on food resilience for future national investment*. If the UK food system is to scale up sustainability throughout, NIC's role in mapping national infrastructure becomes vital for food security. Huge sums of money are being spent on the HS2 high-speed link,* for instance, which might be better spent investing to enable people to walk or bike to food shops. In the Netherlands and Denmark, physical activity has been built into daily life – and here engineering *is* crucial – by normalizing bicycling and local hubs, almost whatever the weather. This could happen

---

* The official estimate has already risen from an initial £35bn to £56bn (2018), with estimates in the Cook Review sayings it's nearer £100bn.

throughout the UK. This would contribute a food element to any Green New Deal or variant of that strategy.[61] A *food resilience and sustainability infrastructure plan* should map this thirty-year transition and would simultaneously reinvigorate town centres and meet ecological public-health principles. The benefits from making streets walking- and bicycling-friendly for all age and income groups would be quick.

The movement for ethical and socially responsible investment has shown over the last two decades how investment can be reoriented to incentivize the good and withdraw from the bad. After years of pressure and recognition that price signals can support health in the case of tobacco and more recently sugar, HM Treasury should now apply *an escalator tax to discourage the production of HFSS foods and support the rebirth of a UK sustainable horticulture.* Too much of UK food manufacturing might be better viewed as stranded assets. *Pension funds should begin to disinvest from manufacturers of HFSS foods.* HM Treasury and the National Audit Office should also begin to provide better advice on *performance metrics* for the food industry to apply, ones which would help analyse whether overall food supply is decoupling from unhealthy and unsustainable food production. Useful opening ideas on such metrics have been developed by the Food Foundation and Food Climate Research Network.[62] The phasing out of our current 2.2 mt of plastic packaging waste and 7 mt of food waste should feature within new national metrics.

UK food security is at risk from unnecessary, exploitative and high food imports. It would be folly to try to grow rice here or oranges and mangoes (big in the juice market), but that the UK produces only 12% of the inadequate amounts of fruit we consume is a market failure. Distorted health outcomes have reinforced institutionalized land misuse by the UK, allowing farmers to be paid to rip up orchards (and hedges) in the 1990s. The new National Food Resilience and Sustainability policy would gradually put trade into its proper policy place, rejecting on the one hand any soft neo-colonial use of others' land, ecosystems and cheap labour, and on the other hand inappropriate, unsustainable UK first production (tasteless strawberries from polytunnels in midwinter?). For nearly forty years, UK governments have addressed the growing food trade gap by simply exporting more of our food. This has not worked; the gap has risen almost inexorably, not least since once the British began to realize the pleasures of Mediterranean produce, we did not want to reverse it; who would choose tinned US peaches over fresh ones, or lard over olive oil, or Spam over pork for that matter? Trade has its place but must not dominate or distort food supply. A more just trading system would ensure that *primary producers in far-off lands are properly paid*. International development should help them to feed more needy proximal people than us. This commitment would actually require us to get a grip on our land policy. Again, it is England which has been slow to engage with this problem; Scotland and Wales are further ahead.[63,64]

The advantage of imports is that they extend the range of foods and the seasons. We should see imports as 'icing on the (of course wholesome) cake', not the cake itself. Trade, moreover, can be a misnomer for the pursuit of cheap commodities then used in ultra-processed foods. A food economy which colludes with the ploughing up of distant virgin land,

and the deforestation of that land for animal feed, or which guzzles food from territories with scarce water – without declaring this on the label – cannot hold its head up high.

GOVERNANCE AND POLITICS

No rethink about food governance would be complete unless it grasped the abject failure of English local-authority structures – and this is mostly but not only an English problem. The UK is a highly centralized state, with too much power and wealth concentrated nationally and in London. In the 1990s, Scotland and Wales were given differing powers and England little power. A divisive bidding system for city mayors maintained this mixture of begging bowl and divisive politics. Meanwhile local authorities have been starved of funds and powers, breeding resentments not of their making. If this is to be a United Kingdom, similar and equal rights need to be given to all regions.[65] There are different approaches, ranging from those who argue we should simply give existing authorities more money to others who say it is time to create new regional bodies.[66] We need both.

We must reinvigorate local democracy and reverse creeping centralization. Food can be a vehicle for this. *A new set of regional structures with food-planning responsibilities* would be welcome across the entire UK. Italy, France and Germany all have them but the UK does not. The Regional Development Agencies set up under Labour were abolished in 2010 when they should have been strengthened. There were nine English regions: the North-East, North-West, Yorkshire and the Humber, West Midlands, East Midlands, Eastern, South-East, London and South-West. There is an argument that new regional bodies with food powers should not be elected but have powers delegated from others which are elected, such as unitary authorities, cities or local authorities.* Scotland, Wales and London, however, have elected bodies; six new ones started in 2017 and a few more are to follow. There is little coherence to their food powers. Whether new bodies are delegated from directly elected local authorities or not, they do need *clear local accountability* and to be a vehicle for *rebuilding more resilient bio-regional food economies*.

Critics argue that the UK presently suffers from excess HFSS 'food from anywhere'. Genuinely local foods are a rare offer, despite the public desire being reportedly high. The blockage is weak links between local populations, growers and processors. The market system is not working. The new agri-food colleges proposed above could help the renaissance, as would the new food regional bodies just suggest. The goals should be to *shorten food chains*, and return added value from the consumer to sustainable appropriately local food production. They could accelerate the reversal partly underway from US-style out-of-town malls and hypermarkets.[67]

Finally, there is the matter of parliamentary scrutiny. Either the Environment, Food and Rural Affairs (EFRA) Committee should receive an enlarged remit with less focus on farming or *a new Food Security Committee should be created*, working jointly with other select committees, as appropriate. I prefer the latter. The EFRA Committee is dominated by agricultural

---

* Interesting discussions are being held under the All-Party Parliamentary Group (APPG) on Reform, Decentralisation and Devolution.

concerns but, to be fair, has broadened its focus at times. The Health Committee rarely or never considers the environment. The Environmental Audit Committee often provides the best multi-criteria approach to food matters,[68] even though food is not its main focus. Longer-term strategic food issues have tended to be conducted by the House of Lords Environment Committee. This is bizarre, and was recognized by their Lordships when setting up a short-term overview committee for 2019–20.[69] *The Lords should create a Food Policy Committee; ideally so should the Commons.*

Too much or too little: a case for food optimism

The previous pages set out a radical but reasonable set of proposals. Is this all too much to tackle? Anyone who discusses, works in or simply analyses the UK food system – or if outside the UK looks at their own country – knows that the task I have outlined is considerable but feasible. The UK is not alone in needing to begin this kind of radical food transformation. On a positive note, the intellectual and public mood has changed compared to twenty years ago; this Great Food Transformation is no longer pie-in-the-sky, it is inevitable. Many more people across the food system now accept that things cannot go on as they have. Some say that this must be done through incremental rather than systemic change, and that a slow pragmatic approach would minimize the danger of unintended consequences – destroying what is good in pursuit of constraining the bad. Those are risks, it is true, but food security already faces a multiple emergency.

The scale of what is going wrong with our food system

is sometimes hard to appreciate. It is understandable to think 'It will be all right on the night'. Alas, the data suggest otherwise. Things are not 'all right'. The trends are sobering. This is why we need institutional reform. We cannot expect change unless the policymakers have structures which enable this to be done democratically but well – at local, regional and national levels.

It is surely better to begin managed change than to wait for crisis. The UK, as we saw in Part One – not least in the history of Beveridge being ignored in 1936 (see pp. 38–9) – has form here. Powerful voices in politics and Whitehall have a default arrogance that other countries will feed us or that we will muddle through. That would be a fundamental mis-reading of twenty-first-century geo-politics. The UK is not as powerful as it was. Its food system is fragile. Its food defence is weak. The challenges looming over food are real yet have been largely ignored. The Chief Medical Officers across the UK have warned about obesity.[70,71,72,73] The Chief Scientist's Foresight reports set out cases for food reform on different issues across the 2000s.[74,75,76,77] One incumbent of that post even talked of a 'perfect storm' brewing – to little avail thus far.[78,79,80] The hard truth is that the UK food system has not been restructured adequately or systemically enough. There have also been enough early warnings, often at the global or European level, it is true, but enough close at hand to be taken seriously. Urging the country to address this evidence–policy–action gap was my motivation for writing this book.

I have argued that the British food system is *highly exposed*. The sheer banality of that exposure is part of the problem. We think that as long as there is food on the supermarket shelves, all is well in the world. It is not. Or we think that change can be left to individuals. It cannot. The Great Food Transformation requires change to happen collectively, across the population, allowing for diversity. If you and your friends/colleagues/family were to eat a low-carbon, healthy, low-impact diet, while the town you live in does the reverse, the net effect is negative. The point is that *together* we need to alter our consumption, and *together* the food supply chains need radical reform. This collective strategy is what the UK ought to begin in the 'radical but reasonable' terms I have sketched. Consumption change has to be population-wide to affect and guide production.

This process will require enormous effort and goodwill. That Brexit walked the country into this realization is perhaps a good thing. No-deal assessments certainly exposed a lot to a wider audience. But many, myself included, had concluded as much already. The British people need help to realize change is coming, and must engage with what must now begin. Our need for good, clear, inclusive leadership on food is clear. Whatever happens to the National Food Strategy, the concern must not be allowed to dissipate. That can happen. A moment of change began in 2007–10 and was squashed. Another is upon us ten years later. Even politicians who are disdainful of expert input need help and advice. The alternative is worse. Amid national and international debate about the direction and 'soul' of capitalism, food can offer some direction. As has been discussed, the UK food system could be taken in multiple different directions in the name of food security: Atlanticist, globalist, neo-colonialist, outer European, reformed EU, nationalist or bio-regionalist (see p. 438). The latter means each region trying to produce appropriately and sustainably, thus delivering decentralized food resilience across the country. The range of food problems explored in Part Two suggests that they require us to get our act together to sort out our food insecurity. This is why we need the kind of new legislation, targets, structures and policies outlined here. The alternative is to bury our heads in the sand.

This book has explored where the tensions and fault-lines lie in the UK food system. Others might sketch the food problems slightly differently, but they encounter the same data, the same or similar lock-ins. I am confident that, when food security is discussed, the search for solutions requires us to address the kind of data, ideas and options explored in these pages. Food security seems a simple and mundane matter until we look into it, and then we find it is deeply sensitive and complicated. It is more fragile than most British people might have expected. How a nation feeds its people, whether it feeds them all to decent standards, whether it applies sound criteria for doing so, and who gains or loses from reform, these are all tests for whether a country is civilized. How we feed Britain matters. Whether we address our food problems is now a test not just for the food system but for democracy and British capitalism itself. We must not duck the historic responsibilities, or the trends look set to haunt us and their realities to bite us. We can and must do better than that.

List of Abbreviations

AHDB: Agriculture and Horticulture Development Board

AI: Artificial Intelligence

AQEG: Air Quality Expert Group (of Defra & Governments of Scotland, Wales & N. Ireland)

BAPEN: British Association for Parenteral and Enteral Nutrition

BEIS: Department for Business, Enterprise, Industry and Science

bn: billion

BD: bulk density (of soil)

BMI: body mass index

CAFO: concentrated animal-feeding operation

CAP: Common Agricultural Policy

CCA: Civil Contingencies Act (2004)

CCC: Committee on Climate Change

CGI: computer generated imagery

cm: centimetre

C:N: carbon to nitrogen ratio (of soil)

CNI: Critical National Infrastructure

CO_2: carbon dioxide

CO_2e: carbon dioxide equivalent

COP: Conference of the Parties (of the 1992 UN
    Convention on Biological Diversity)

Defra: Department for Environment, Food and Rural Affairs

DPE: Designated Point of Entry (ports)

DPH: Director of Public Health

DPI: Designated Point of Import (ports)

EAC: Environmental Audit Committee of the House of
    Commons

EFRA: Environment, Food and Rural Affairs Committee of
    the House of Commons

ETI: Ethical Trade Initiative

EU: European Union

EUIPO: European Union Intellectual Property Office

Europol: agency for European law enforcement co-operation

FAO: Food and Agriculture Organization of the United
    Nations

FCR: Feed Conversion Ratio

FCRN: Food Climate Research Network

fmcg: fast-moving consumer goods

FLWS: Food Loss and Waste Accounting and Reporting
    Standard

FPI: First Point of Introduction (ports)

GB: Great Britain

GDP: Gross Domestic Product

GDPR: General Data Protection Regulation 2016 of the EU
    (also turned into UK law in 2018)

GFS: Global Food Security (programme of the joint UK
    Research Councils)

GHG: greenhouse gas

GM: genetic modification (of plants and animals)

GPS: global positioning system

H_2O: water

ha: hectares

HACCP: Hazards Analysis Critical Control Point

HFSS: high in fat, sugar and salt

HMRC: Her Majesty's Revenue and Customs

HS2: High-speed train programme no. 2

IARC: International Agency for Research on Cancer

ICESCR: International Covenant on Economic, Social and
Cultural Rights 1966

IPBES: Intergovernmental Science-Policy Platform on
Biodiversity and Ecosystem Services

IPCC: Intergovernmental Panel on Climate Change

IPR: Intellectual Property Rights

IT: information technology

JCNSS: Joint Committee on the National Security Strategy
of the Houses of Lords and Commons

JIT: just-in-time (delivery systems)

JRF: Joseph Rowntree Foundation

km: kilometre

LB: London Borough

LEP: Local Enterprise Partnership

Lo-Lo: lift-on, lift-off

m: million

m^3: cubic metres

MOD: Ministry of Defence

Mha: million hectares

MIS: Minimum Income Standard

mt: million tonnes

$MtCO_2e$: million tonnes of CO_2 equivalents

NAO: National Audit Office

NDNS: National Diet and Nutrition Survey

NHS: National Health Service

NIC: National Infrastructure Commission

N: Nitrogen

NLW: National Living Wage (introduced in 2016)

NMW: National Minimum Wage (under the NMW 1998 Act)

NO: nitrogen oxide

ODI: Overseas Development Institute

OECD: Organisation for Economic Co-operation and Development

OHCHR: Office of the High Commissioner on Human Rights (UN)

ONS: Office for National Statistics

PAC: Public Accounts Committee

PAN-UK: Pesticides Action Network UK

PAS: Publicly Available Specification

PBI: Plant Breeding Institute (at Trumpington, Cambridge, 1912–87)

PFMA: Pet Food Manufacturers Association

PHE: Public Health England

POST: Parliamentary Office for Science and Technology

PV: photovoltaic

R&D: Research and Development

RDA: Regional Development Agencies

RF: Resilience Forum

RN: Royal Navy

ROCE: return on capital employed

RoRo: roll-on, roll-off (lorry-ship systems)

RPM: Retail Price Maintenance (a price-fixing scheme
    ended in 1964)

RSPB: Royal Society for the Protection of Birds

SAWS: Seasonal Agricultural Worker Scheme

SMC: Social Mobility Commission

SME: Small and medium-sized enterprise

SOC: soil organic carbon

STEM: science, technology, engineering and mathematics

TACCP: Threat Assessments Critical Control Points

TEU: 20-foot equivalent unit shipping container

TIFF: Total Income from Farming (a figure calculated
    annually by Defra)

TN: total nitrogen

trn: trillion (a million million – 1,000,000,000,000)

TRR: Transport Resilience Review

UCL: University College London

UDHR: Universal Declaration of Human Rights 1948

UK: United Kingdom

UN: United Nations

UNEP: United Nations Environment Programme

USA: United States of America

WCRF: World Cancer Research Fund (AICR in the USA)

WHO: World Health Organization (of the UN)

WRAP: Waste and Resources Action Programme (formerly
    government, now private)

WTO: World Trade Organization

WWF: World Wildlife Fund

WWT: Wildfowl and Wetlands Trust

Acknowledgements

Many people fed me with ideas for this book, which has emerged in many drafts over three extraordinary years in British politics before I sat down to write this final version in 2019. I have also drawn on many discussions, mostly unattributable or held under the Chatham House rule to protect people. As I went round the country, I would ask people what they thought was needed and what they saw as the successes, challenges and potential directions. This book draws on those discussions, sometimes long, sometimes in intense snippets, held with colleagues and peers concerned about what a rich but divided country such as the UK might or can do, and how and why its food system is as it is.

In particular, I am grateful to Jean Adams, Tony (A. J.) Allan, David Baldock, David Barling, Jason Beedell, Tim Benton, Mike Berners-Lee, Simon Billing, Rosie Boycott, Thomas Burgoine, Tom Burke, Simon Capewell, Martin Caraher, Mike Clarke, Charlie Clutterbuck, Dan Crossley, Kath Dalmeny, Sue Davies, Olivier De Schutter, Henry Dimbleby, Bob Doherty, Liz Dowler, James Elliott, Andrew Fearne, Yiannis Gabriel, Tara Garnett, Dave Goulson, Mike Hamm, Corinna Hawkes, Michael Heasman, Mario Herrero, Tim Hess, Colin Hines, Vicki Hird, Donald Hislop,

Patrick Holden, Tom Hunt, John Ingram, Lisa Jack, Philip James, Jonathan Jones, Felicity Lawrence, Tony Lewis, Tim Lobstein, Philip Lymbery, Jennie Macdiarmid, Graham MacGregor and the Action on Sugar and CASH teams, Tom Macmillan, Claire Marris, Terry Marsden, Pamela Mason, Alan Mathews, Gary McFarlane, Martin McKee, Peter Melchett (RIP), John Middleton, Erik Millstone, Kevin Morgan, Donal Murphy-Bokern, Michael O'Connor, Alison Parente, Will Parente, Kate Pickett, Jonathan Porritt, Jules Pretty, Claire Pritchard, Sue Pritchard, Geof Rayner, Mike Rayner, Ben Reynolds, Aileen Robertson, Laura Rodrigues, Johan Rockström, Patti Rundall, Laura Sandys, Lindy Sharpe, Guy Shrubsole, Geetie Singh, Fiona Smith, Pete Smith, Shaun Spiers, Marco Springmann, Carolyn Steel, Peter Stevenson, Gunhild Stordalen, Chloe Sutcliffe, Boyd Swinburn, Geoff Tansey, Anna Taylor, Bill Vorley, Pam Warhurst, Guy Singh Watson, Rebecca Wells, Martin White, Richard Wilkinson, Walter Willett, Duncan Williamson, Graeme Willis, Michael Winter and Amanda Wood. They have all put up with my musings, and provided data and critical policy thought.

I also thank many people in daily food research and policy worlds for discussions and data while I mulled analyses presented here. They include my endlessly patient family and friends, above all Liz Castledine and Alfie Stephenson-Boyles, who kept me going, and fed me ideas and options when I was writing. I salute, as ever, my colleagues at the Centre for Food Policy at City, University of London, and our MSc and PhD programme students, visiting fellows, and speakers at Food Thinkers seminars; also the team for the EAT–*Lancet* Food in the Anthropocene Commission (which reported in January 2019 on the global challenge) and its panoramic thinking; the various Chatham House food projects and conferences on food security since 2006, most recently the diet and net zero UK work; the London Food Board and the Mayor's Food Brexit group with London Resilience; the Food Climate Research Network at Oxford University; the Zero Carbon Britain team and Graduate School of Environment at CAT, Machynlleth; the Fine Whiners endlessly and rigorously but reasonably; the Trustees and tenants of Borough Market, London, where I was Trustee (2007–17), who reminded me of daily SME realities; Peter Schmidt and Monica Guarinoni at the European Economic and Social Committee, who showed me the value of EU policy development (and its risks); Sustain, the Food Foundation, Eating Better, and Compassion in World Farming, the UK civil-society coalitions, provided constant energy and interventions; as have Tristram Stuart of Feedback and Lindsay Boswell of FareShare and colleagues about food waste; the team at the Food Research Collaboration which worked patiently to build understanding of Food Brexit realities; the IFSTAL teams at eight universities (Oxford, Reading, Warwick, SOAS, Birkbeck, the Royal Veterinary College, the London School of Hygiene and Tropical Medicine, and City, University of London), where we discussed how to understand food system dynamics; the students at the Royal College of Defence Studies who always ask big strategic questions; the Sustainable Restaurants Association and Chefs Manifesto group who see the potential for Britain's food service sector to shape change; Colin and Ruth Tudge and the now hundreds of participants at the Oxford Real Farming Conference, which they set up and where such good fundamental questions are asked alongside questions over the road at the older conference; the Cooks Livery Company of the City of London, which has supported Centre for Food Policy meetings and whose armed forces links remind me how the UK state once had to be taught but did learn the value of feeding people well; Jill Rutter and Joe Owen at the Institute for Government; and the various research projects which have asked me to contribute and from which I learn so much, most recently the IKnowFood project led by Bob Doherty at York, FIT4FOOD2030 led by Amsterdam University, and the many organizations which have hosted me in recent years. I also pay tribute to the BSSRS discussion groups which set me on this road.

Many people spoke with me or wrote to me from their daily roles working in food trades and food analysis, such as Matt Boyns, David Frost, Sean Leather, John Pelham, Freya Robinson, Tim Smith and Dave Wilkinson. I'm grateful to the people who educated me about cybersecurity risks, some anonymous, and also my colleague Muttukrishnan Rajarajan at City and Lisa Jack at Portsmouth. Various erudite lawyers, some anonymous, improved my understanding of the legal duties on food: Fiona Smith, Michael Cardwell, Chris Newdick and Ross Cranston. From the food industries, I have learned much by listening to and discussing with key people including Andrew Opie (British Retail Consortium), James Walton (IGD), Christine Tacon (Groceries Code Adjudicator), Ian Wright (Food and Drink Federation), Minette Batters, Guy Smith and Terry Jones (National Farmers Union), Laurence Olins and Nick Marston (British Summer Fruits), Andrew Kuyk (Provision Trades Federation), Sara Jayne

Stanes (Royal Academy of Culinary Arts), Kate Nichols and Ufi Ibrahim (UK Hospitality), Raymond Blanc (Sustainable Restaurants Association). Many civil servants in Defra, the Department of Health and Social Care, the Food Standards Agency, the National Audit Office, Public Health England, the Department of Health, the Welsh and Scottish governments, and the Houses of Commons and Lords have invited me to meetings or summoned me to hearings, and inevitably answered me patiently in turn. The same is true of the various MPs and Lords in the UK Parliament who prodded and held government to account amid Brexit perturbations and deliberations. As ever, I am in debt to the statisticians at the Office for National Statistics, Her Majesty's Revenue & Customs, and the Department for Environment, Food and Rural Affairs, the Department for Transport and the Department for Health and Social Care, plus various Port Authorities and the Civil Aviation Authority.

My editor, Simon Winder, and the team at Penguin – Richard Duguid, Eva Hodgkin, Mark Handsley, Matt Hutchinson, Pen Vogler, Ilaria Rovera, Francisca Monteiro – have been endlessly patient and supportive. Simon and I began to discuss such a book in 2012, just when a hard period of work fell on me, due to a colleague's serious and distressing illness, necessitating a doubling of my workload. The issue of UK food security, however, did not go away; indeed, to some extent it has come ever to the fore, not least with the Brexit processes. I am particularly grateful to Simon for sticking with me and the topic. As the song has it, I hope we can see more clearly now.

For permission to cite data or figures, my thanks go to:

the Green Alliance; the Imperial War Museum; StepChange, the UK debt charity, for interview data on debt-related food poverty; Peter Backman of Peterbackmanfs for data on the food service sector; the FEAT team at the University of Cambridge for their data tracking food outlets; Sir Michael Marmot for use of UCL's Institute of Health Equity analyses; John Pelham and Richard King of the Andersons Centre for information on subsidies; Joseph Poore of Oxford University; and Sarah Phillips and colleagues at the Local Data Company, who generated data they hold on food shopping figures across Britain especially for me. I am most grateful to them.

Finally, although many people contributed to my thinking for this book, its content remains my responsibility, not that of any of those named above.

London, January 2020

References

PART ONE: OUR FOOD SECURITY PROBLEM

Chapter 1: Food and the National Interest

1.   Hannington, W. *Unemployed Struggles 1919–1936*. London: Lawrence & Wishart, 1977 [1936].

2.   Boyd Orr, J. *Food, Health and Income: Report on Adequacy of Diet in Relation to Income*. London: Macmillan and Co., 1936.

3.   Ostry, A. S. *Nutrition Policy in Canada, 1870–1939*. Vancouver: University of British Columbia Press, 2006.

4.   M'Gonigle, G. C. M. and Kirby, J. *Poverty and Public Health*. London: Gollancz, 1936.

5.   BMA. *Nutrition and the Public Health: Proceedings of a National Conference on the Wider Aspects of Nutrition, April 27–28–29, 1939*. London: British Medical Association, 1939.

6.   Alston, P. Statement on visit to the United Kingdom, by Professor Philip Alston, United Nations Special Rapporteur on extreme poverty and human rights. Geneva: Office of the UN Commissioner for Human Rights, 2018.

7.   Alston, P. Visit to the United Kingdom of Great Britain and Northern Ireland – report of the Special Rapporteur on extreme poverty and human rights. UN General Assembly. Human Rights Council Forty-First Session, 24 June–12 July 2019, Agenda Item 3. A/HRC/41/39/Add. 1. Geneva: UN Human Rights Council, 2019.

8.   Social Metrics Commission. Measuring poverty 2019. London: Social Metrics Commission, 2019.

9.   Astor, W. A. and Rowntree, B. S. *British Agriculture: The Principles of Future Policy*. London and New York: Longmans, Green, 1938.

10.   Astor, W. A. and Rowntree, B. S. *British Agriculture: A Report of an Inquiry Organized by Viscount Astor and B. Seebohm Rowntree* (abridged edn). Harmondsworth: Penguin Books, 1939.

11. Williamson, H. *Story of a Norfolk Farm*. London: Faber & Faber, 1941.

12. Vernon, J. *Hunger: A Modern History*. Cambridge, Mass.: Harvard University Press, 2007.

13. Women's Group on Public Welfare. *Our Towns: A Close-Up – a Study Made during 1939–42*. London: Oxford University Press, 1943.

14. Boyd Orr, J. *Food and the People: Target for Tomorrow No. 3*. London: Pilot Press, 1943.

15. Collingham, L. *The Taste of War: World War Two and the Battle for Food*. London: Allen Lane, 2011.

16. Mukerjee, M. *Churchill's Secret War: The British Empire and the Ravaging of India during World War II*. New York: Basic Books, 2010.

17. Driver, C. *The British at Table 1940–1980*. London: Chatto & Windus, 1983.

18. Titmuss, R. M. 'War and Social Policy', in Titmuss R. M., ed. *Essays on the Welfare State*. London: Allen and Unwin, 1958.

19. Lang, T., Millstone, E. P., Lewis, T., et al. Feeding Britain: food security after Brexit. London: Food Research Collaboration, 2018.

20. Burch, D. and Lawrence, G. eds. *Supermarkets and Agri-Food Supply Chains*. Cheltenham: Edward Elgar, 2007.

21. Cox, A., Ireland, P., Lonsdale, C., et al. *Supply Chains, Markets and Power: Mapping Buyer and Supplier Power Regimes*. London: Routledge, 2002.

22. Gereffi, G. and Lee, J. 'Why the world suddenly cares about global supply chains'. *Journal of Supply Chain Management* 48(3), July 2012, 24–32.

23. Monbiot, G., Grey, R., Kenny, T., et al. Land for the many: Changing the way our fundamental asset is used, owned and governed – report to the Labour Party. London: Labour Party, 2019.

24. Willett, W., Rockström, J., Loken, B., et al. 'Food in the Anthropocene: The EAT–*Lancet* Commission on healthy diets from sustainable food systems'. *The Lancet* 393(10170), 2 February 2019, 447–92. https://doi. org/10.1016/S0140-6736(18)31788-4 (published online 16 August 2019).

25. Owen, J. and Lloyd, L. Costing Brexit: What is Whitehall spending on exiting the EU? London: Institute for Government, 2018.

26. IfG. Civil service staff numbers. London: Institute for Government, 2018.

27. 'A new furrow: How Brexit could change the face of rural Britain'. *The Economist*, 30 August 2018. https://www.economist.com/ britain/2018/08/30/how-brexit-could-change-the-face-of-rural-britain.

28. 'No-deal Brexit preparations: the leaked Operation Yellowhammer document'. *Sunday Times*, 18 August 2019.

29. Lang, T. 'No-deal food planning in UK Brexit'. *The Lancet* 394(102019), 7 September 2019: 814–15. http://dx.doi.org/10.1016/S0140-6736(19)31769-6.

Chapter 2: Why UK Food Security Matters

1. Defra. Agriculture in the UK 2017. London: Department for Environment, Food and Rural Affairs, 2018.

2. Foreman, S. and MAFF. *Loaves and Fishes: An Illustrated History of the Ministry of Agriculture, Fisheries and Food, 1889–1989.* London: HMSO, 1989.

3. Hammond, R. J. *Food: The Growth of Policy.* London: HMSO/Longmans, Green, 1951.

4. Defra. Food statistics pocketbook 2017. London: Department for Environment, Food and Rural Affairs, 2017.

5. Foreign and Commonwealth Office. UK Overseas Territories. London: HM Government, 2018. https://www.gov.uk/government/policies/uk-overseas-territories.

6. Hayter, T. *Aid as Imperialism.* Harmondsworth: Penguin Books, 1971.

7. Barrett, C. B. and Maxwell, D. G. *Food Aid after Fifty Years: Recasting Its Role.* London: Routledge, 2005.

8. Shaw, D. J. *The UN World Food Programme and the Development of Food Aid.* Basingstoke: Palgrave Macmillan, 2001.

9. Graves A. R., Morris, J., Deeks, L. K., et al. 'The total costs of soil degradation in England and Wales'. *Ecological Economics* 119, November 2015: 399–413. https://doi.org/10.1016/j.ecolecon.2015.07.026.

10. Haygarth, P. and Ritz, K. 'The future of soils and land use in the UK: soil systems for the provision of land-based ecosystem services'. *Land Use Policy* 26, Supplement 1, December 2009: S187–97.

11. GAD. Mortality insights from GAD. Government Actuary's Department. London: December 2018.

12. Raleigh, V. What is happening to life expectancy? London: The King's Fund, 2018. https://www.kingsfund.org.uk/publications/whats-happening-life-expectancy-uk (accessed 18 December 2018).

13. Hiam, L., Harrison, D., McKee, M., et al. 'Why is life expectancy in England and Wales "stalling"?' *Journal of Epidemiology and Community Health,* 72(5), 2018, 404–8

14. LSP. Mortality trends of people in different socio-economic circumstances in England. London: Longevity Science Panel, 2018. https://www.longevitypanel.co.uk.

15. Lang, T. 'The Agriculture Bill has no vision for food', in Spiers, S., ed. *Inside Track.* London: Green Alliance, 2018.

16. Gove, M. Letter to Neil Parish MP, chair of the EFRA Commission, House of Commons, 30 October 2018. London: Department for

Environment, Food and Rural Affairs, 2018. https://www.parliament.
uk/documents/commons-committees/environment-food-rural-affairs/
correspondence/181030-Secretary-of-State-to-Chair-Food-strategy.pdf
(accessed 6 June 2019).

17. Sustain. A national food strategy? Brexit Forum News, January 2019.

18. Beveridge, S. W. *Food Control*. Oxford: Oxford University Press, 1928.

19. Manton, K. 'Sir William Beveridge, the British government and plans
for food control in time of war, *c*. 1916–1941'. *Contemporary British
History*, 23(3), 2009: 363–85. https://doi.org/10.1080/13619460903080192
(published online 4 September 2009).

20. Wilt, A. F. *Food for War: Agriculture and Rearmament in Britain before the
Second World War*. Oxford: Oxford University Press, 2001.

21. Manton, 'Sir William Beveridge'.

22. Astor, W. A. and Rowntree, B. S. *British Agriculture: The Principles of
Future Policy*. London and New York: Longmans, Green, 1938.

23. Astor, W. A. and Rowntree, B. S. *British Agriculture: A Report of an Inquiry
Organized by Viscount Astor and B. Seebohm Rowntree* (abridged edn).
Harmondsworth: Penguin Books, 1939.

24. Astor, W. A. and Rowntree, B. S. *The Agricultural Dilemma: A Report of
an Enquiry Organised by Viscount Astor and Mr. B. Seebohm Rowntree*.
London: P. S. King, 1935.

25. Astor, W. A. and Rowntree, B. S. *Smallholdings Studies: Reports of Surveys
Undertaken by Some Agricultural Economists*. London: Longmans, 1938.

26. Astor, W. A. and Rowntree, B. S. *Mixed Farming and Muddled Thinking: An
Analysis of Current Agricultural Policy*. London: Macdonald, 1946.

27. Pember Reeves, M. *Round about a Pound a Week*. London: Virago, 1979 [1913].

28. BMA. *Nutrition and the Public Health. Proceedings of a National Conference
on the Wider Aspects of Nutrition, April 27-28-29, 1939*. London: British
Medical Association, 1939. Boyd Orr, J. *Food, Health and Income: Report on
Adequacy of Diet in Relation to Income*. London: Macmillan, 1936.

29. Boyd Orr, J. *Food and the People*. London: Pilot Press, 1943.

30. Boyd Orr, J. 'Nutritional Science and State Planning', in Boyd Orr, J., ed.
What Science Stands For. London: Allen and Unwin, 1937.

31. Beveridge, S. W. *Social Insurance and Allied Services*, Cmd 6404. London:
HMSO, 1942.

32. G8 leaders' statement on global food security. http://www.whitehouse.
gov/news/releases/2008/07/20080708-6.html, 2008.

33. US President response to G8 leaders' statement on global food security.
Washington DC: President of the United States, 2008. http://www.
whitehouse.gov/news/releases/2008/07/20080708-6.html.

34. 'L'Aquila' joint statement on global food security. L'Aquila Food Security Initiative (AFSI)'. Rome: G8 Leaders, 10 July 2009. http://www. g8italia2009.it/static/G8_Allegato/LAquila_Joint_Statement_on_Global_Food_Security%5B1%5D,0.pdf.

35. Ambler-Edwards, S., Bailey, K., Kiff, A., et al. Food futures: Rethinking UK strategy. A Chatham House report. London: Royal Institute of International Affairs (Chatham House), 2009.

36. Food matters: towards a strategy for the 21st century. London: Cabinet Office Strategy Unit, 2008.

37. Defra. Ensuring the UK's food security in a changing world: a Defra discussion paper. London: Department for Environment, Food and Rural Affairs, July 2008.

38. Defra. UK food security assessment: detailed analysis. London: Department for Environment, Food and Rural Affairs, 2010.

39. Defra. Food 2030. London: Department for Food, Rural Affairs and Environment, 2010.

40. Lang, T., Millstone, E. P., Lewis, T., et al. Feeding Britain: food security after Brexit. London: Food Research Collaboration, 2018.

41. Lang, T., Millstone, E. P. and Marsden, T. A food Brexit: time to get real – a Brexit briefing. Falmer: Science Policy Research Unit, University of Sussex; Cardiff University Sustainable Places Institute; and City University of London, 2017.

42. Benton, T. G. British food: What role should UK producers have in feeding the UK? Independent report to Morrisons supermarket. Bradford: Morrisons and University of Leeds, 2017. www.leeds.ac.uk/download/481/british_food_makers_report (accessed 17 August 2018).

43. Foresight. The future of food and farming: challenges and choices for global sustainability. Final report. London: Government Office for Science, 2011.

44. Willett, W., Rockström, J., Loken, B., et al. 'Food in the Anthropocene: the EAT-*Lancet* Commission on healthy diets from sustainable food systems'. *The Lancet* 393(10170), 2 February 2019: 447–92. https://doi.org/10.1016/S0140-6736(18)31788-4.

45. Sage. 'Meltdown in the UK supply chain: What went wrong and why? And what lessons can be learned in the aftermath?' Newcastle upon Tyne: Sage, 2018.

46. Pennycook, R. and Dickinson, H. Letter to Prime Minister May and Mr Barnier from the chair and chief executive of the British Retail Consortium, 4 July 2018. London: British Retail Consortium, 2018.

https://brc.org.uk/news/2018/there-will-be-food-supply-issues-in-the-event-of-a-cliff-edge-brexit.

47. Ibid.

48. Peck, H. 'Resilience in the food chain: a study of business continuity management in the food and drink industry. Final report to the Department for Environment, Food and Rural Affairs. July 2006'. Shrivenham/London: Defra/The Resilience Centre, Department of Defence Management & Security Analysis, Cranfield University, 2006.

49. Defra. Agriculture in the UK 2018. London: Department for Environment, Food and Rural Affairs, 2019.

50. Ward, M. UK trade, 1948–2017: statistics CBP 8261. London: House of Commons Library, 2018.

51. Defra. Food security and the UK: an evidence and analysis paper. London: Department for Environment, Food and Rural Affairs – Food Chain Analysis Group, 2006. http://webarchive.nationalarchives.gov.uk/20130402151656/http://archive.defra.gov.uk/evidence/economics/foodfarm/reports/documents/foodsecurity.pdf (accessed 23 February 2016).

52. FAO, IFAD, IMF, et al. Price volatility in food and agricultural markets: policy responses. Rome: Food and Agriculture Organization, IFAD, IMF, OECD, UNCTAD,WFP, the World Bank, the WTO, IFPRI and the UN High Level Task Force (HLTF), 2011.

53. Mason, P. and Lang, T. *Sustainable Diets: How Ecological Nutrition Can Transform Consumption and the Food System*. Abingdon: Routledge Earthscan, 2017.

54. Pirog, R. and Benjamin, A. Calculating food miles for a multiple ingredient food product. Ames, Iowa: Leopold Center for Sustainable Agriculture, Iowa State University Ames, 2005.

55. Pretty, J. N., Ball, A. S., Lang, T., et al. 'Farm costs and food miles: an assessment of the full cost of the UK weekly food basket'. *Food Policy* 30(1), February 2005: 1–19.

56. Smith, A., Watkiss, P., Tweddle, G., et al. The validity of food miles as an indicator of sustainable development. Report to DEFRA by AEA Technology. London: Department for the Environment, Food and Rural Affairs, 2005.

57. Fleskens, L., Nainggolan D., Termansen, M., et al. 'Regional consequences of the way land users respond to future water availability in Murcia, Spain'. *Regional Environmental Change* 13(3), 2013: 615–32.

58. Medland, L. A harvest of bare living conditions: a Moroccan enclave within the global food system. PhD thesis. Bristol: University of Bristol, School of Sociology, Politics and International Studies, 2019.

59. Aznar, C., MacGregor, A., Rosenberg, G., et al. Ad brake: primary school children's perceptions of unhealthy food advertising on TV. London: Centre for Social Research and Cancer Research UK, 2016.

60. Action on Sugar. Nutrition, health and cartoon animation on food and drink packaging. London: Action on Sugar, Action on Salt, Children's Food Campaign, 2019.

61. OHA. Health costs of obesity soaring as junk food companies pour millions into advertising. London: Obesity Health Alliance, 2017. http://obesityhealthalliance.org.uk/2017/10/11/press-release-health-costs-obesity-soaring-junk-food-companies-pour-millions-advertising/.

62. Hughes, L. 'More spent on treating obesity-related conditions than on the police or fire service, says NHS chief'. *Telegraph*, 7 June 2016.

63. Monteiro, C. A., Moubarac, J.-C., Levy, R. B., et al. Household availability of ultra-processed foods and obesity in nineteen European countries. *Public Health Nutrition* 21(1), 2018: 18–26. https://www.doi.org/10.1017/S1368980017001379.

64. Rauber, F., Louzada, M. L. da Costa, Steele, E. M., et al. Ultra-processed food consumption and chronic non-communicable diseases-related dietary nutrient profile in the UK (2008–2014). *Nutrients* 10(5), 2018: 587. https://www.doi.org/10.3390/nu10050587.

65. Fiolet, T., Srour, B., Sellem, L., et al. 'Consumption of ultra-processed foods and cancer risk: results from NutriNet-Santé prospective cohort'. *BMJ Open Access* 360(k322), 2018: http://dx.doi.org/10.1136/bmj.k322.

66. Srour, B., Fezeu, L. K., Kesse-Guyot, E., et al. Ultra-processed food intake and risk of cardiovascular disease: prospective cohort study (NutriNet-Santé). *British Medical Journal* 365: l1451, 2019. http://dx.doi.org/10.136/bmj.l51. doi: 10.1136/bmj.l1451.

67. Davies, S. C. Annual report of the Chief Medical Officer, 2018: Health 2040 – Better health within reach. London Department of Health and Social Care, 2018.

68. Bennett, J. E., Pearson-Stuttard, J., Kontis, V., et al. 'Contributions of diseases and injuries to widening life expectancy inequalities in England from 2001 to 2016: a population-based analysis of vital registration data'. *Lancet Public Health* 3(12), 2018: Pe586–e97. https://doi.org/10.1016/S2468-2667(18)30214-7 (published online 1 December 2018).

69. Black, S. D., Morris, J. and Townsend, P. Inequalities in health: report of research working group. London: Department of Health and Social Services, 1980.

70. Acheson, D. Independent inquiry into inequalities in health (the Acheson Report). London: The Stationery Office, 1998.

71. Marmot M, ed. Marmot Review: Fair society, healthy lives. Strategic review of health inequalities in England post-2010. London: Marmot Review (University College London), 2012.

72. FSA. Biannual public attitudes tracker: Wave 13. Food Standards Agency Social Science team. London: Food Standards Agency, 2017.

73. Maguire, E. R. and Monsivais, P. 'Socio-economic dietary inequalities in UK adults: an updated picture of key food groups and nutrients from national surveillance data'. *British Journal of Nutrition* 113(1), 2015: 181–9.

74. Caraher, M. and Coveney, J. Food Poverty and Insecurity: The Poor in a World of Global Austerity, in Caraher, M. and Coveney, J., eds. *Food Poverty and Insecurity: International Food Inequalities*, pp. 1–9. Switzerland: Springer International Publishing, 2016.

75. Caraher, M. and Furey, S. *The Economics of Emergency Food Aid Provision: A Financial, Social and Cultural Perspective*. Basingstoke: Palgrave Macmillan, 2018.

76. FRC. Food Brexit briefings. London: Food Research Collaboration hosted at the Centre for Food Policy, City University of London, 2016–19. https://foodresearch.org.uk/food-brexit-briefings/.

77. Millstone, E. P., Lang, T. and Marsden, T. 'Food Brexit and chlorinated chicken: a microcosm not a single issue'. *Political Quarterly*, 90(4), 2019: 645–53.

78. Food, Farming and Countryside Commission. About us. London: Royal Society of Arts, 2019. https://www.thersa.org/action-and-research/rsa-projects/public-services-and-communities-folder/food-farming-and-countryside-commission.

79. Lightfoot, W., Burke, J., Craig-Harvey, N., et al. Farming tomorrow: British agriculture after Brexit. London: Policy Exchange, 2017.

80. Parker, G., Pickard, J., Donnan, S., et al. 'Liam Fox seeks to narrow focus for post-Brexit US trade deal: Trade minister seeks accord on services as problems loom on goods and agriculture'. *Financial Times*, 23 October 2017. https://www.ft.com/content/2f8c8a8a-b711-11e7-8c12-5661783e5589.

81. Wasley, A. Dirty US meat could flood into UK after a Brexit trade deal. London: Bureau of Investigative Journalism and the *Guardian*, 21 February 2018.

82. Millstone, Lang and Marsden. Food Brexit and chlorinated chicken.

83. Gove, M. Interview on BBC Radio 4 about the case for leaving the EU, 19 April 2016. http://www.bbc.co.uk/news/uk-politics-eu-referendum-36080568.

84. Gove, M. Interview on BBC Radio 4, *Today* programme, 3 July 2016.

85. Mason and Lang, *Sustainable Diets*.

86. Garnett, T. and Strong, M. The principles of healthy and sustainable eating patterns. Swindon: Global Food Security programme (BBSRC et al.), 2015.

87. Welsh Government. The Well-Being of Future Generations (Wales) Act 2015. Cardiff: Welsh Government, 2015. http://gov.wales/topics/people-and-communities/people/future-generations-act/?lang=en (accessed 11 November 2016).

88. Scottish Government. Good food nation. Edinburgh: Scottish Government, 2016.

89. Spence, P. Chlorinated chicken: Why you shouldn't give a cluck. London: Adam Smith Institute, 2017.

90. Stone, J. 'Britain could slash environmental and safety standards "a very long way" after Brexit, Tory MP Jacob Rees-Mogg says. The MP said standards that were "good enough for India" could be good enough for the UK'. *Independent*, 6 December 2016. http://www.independent.co.uk/news/uk/politics/brexit-safety-standards-workers-rights-jacob-rees-mogg-a7459336.html; http://www.independent.co.uk/news/uk/politics/brexit-safety-standards-workers-rights-jacob-rees-mogg-a7459336.html.

91. Codex Alimentarius Commission. Membership. Rome: Food and Agriculture Organization and World Health Organization, 2018. http://www.fao.org/fao-who-codexalimentarius/about-codex/members/en/ (accessed 26 August 2018).

92. Foresight. Tackling obesities: future choices. London: Government Office of Science, 2007.

93. Wanless, D. Securing our future health: Taking a long-term view. London: HM Treasury, 2002.

94. Wanless, D. Securing good health for the whole population. London: HM Treasury, 2004.

95. Barling, D. and Lang, T. 'A reluctant food policy? The first five years of food policy under Labour'. *Political Quarterly* 74(1), 2003: 8–18.

96. Policy Commission on the Future of Farming and Food (Curry Commission). Report of the Policy Commission on the Future of Farming

and Food. London: Cabinet Office, 2002. http://archive.cabinetoffice.gov.uk/farming/.

97. Lang, T. and Rayner, G. Why health is the key to farming and food. Report to the Commission on the Future of Farming and Food chaired by Sir Don Curry. London: UK Public Health Association, Chartered Institute of Environmental Health, Faculty of Public Health Medicine, National Heart Forum and Health Development Agency, 2002.

98. Competition and Markets Authority. J Sainsbury PLC/Asda Group Ltd merger inquiry: 18 May 2018–23 May 2019. London: Competition and Markets Authority of HM Government, 2019. https://www.gov.uk/cma-cases/j-sainsbury-plc-asda-group-ltd-merger-inquiry (accessed 6 June 2019).

99. Woolton, T. E. *The Memoirs of the Rt Hon. The Earl of Woolton*. London: Cassell, 1959.

100. Sitwell, W. *Eggs or Anarchy. The Remarkable Story of the Man Tasked with the Impossible: to Feed a Nation at War*. London: Simon & Schuster, 2016.

101. Britnell, G. E. 'The war and Canadian wheat'. *The Canadian Journal of Economics and Political Science/Revue canadienne d'économique et de science politique* 7(3), 1941: 397–413.

102. Heywood, S. J. How the Civil Service is preparing for Brexit. London: HM Government, 2017. https://civilservice.blog.gov.uk/2017/07/11/how-the-civil-service-is-preparing-for-brexit/Govuk.

103. Healey, D. *The Time of My Life*, p. 121. London: Michael Joseph, 1989.

104. Lang, T. and Heasman, M. *Food Wars: The Global Battle for Mouths, Minds and Markets*, 2nd edn. Abingdon: Routledge Earthscan, 2015.

105. UK2070 Commission. Fairer and stronger – rebalancing the UK economy. The first report of the UK2070 Commission. Sheffield: University of Sheffield, University of Manchester, University College London and the Lincoln Institute (USA), 2019.

106. Goulson, D. *The Garden Jungle*. London: Jonathan Cape, 2019.

107. Smit, J., Ratta, A. and Nasr, J. *Urban Agriculture: Food, Jobs and Sustainable Cities*. New York: UN Development Programme Habitat II Series, 1996.

108. Steel, C. *Hungry City: How Food Shapes Our Lives*. London: Chatto and Windus, 2008.

109. Butler, S. 'Ocado invests in "vertical farms" to grow produce near distributors'. *Guardian*, 10 June 2019.

110. 100 Resilient Cities. https://www.100resilientcities.org/ (2019).

Chapter 3: The State of UK Food (In)Security

1. Wilde, O. *An Ideal Husband*. London: Methuen, 1912 [1895].
2. ONS. UK trade: November 2018. London: Office for National Statistics, 2018.
3. Defra: UK Trade & Investment. UK food and drink – international action plan: an export action plan for the UK food and drink sector. London: Department for Environment, Food and Rural Affairs, 2013.
4. Defra. Agriculture in the UK 2018.
5. Ibid.
6. NAO. Report: early review of the new farming programme (Department for Environment, Food and Rural Affairs). HC 2221, Session 2017–2019, 5 June 2019. London: National Audit Office, 2019.
7. Strutt and Parker. Farm support, the new Environmental Land Management system and the funding gap – effect on net profits by farm type and productivity. London: Strutt and Parker, September 2019.
8. HM Treasury and Defra. A vision for the Common Agricultural Policy. London: HM Treasury and Department for Environment, Food and Rural Affairs, 2005.
9. ONS. UK trade in goods estimates and the 'Rotterdam effect'. London: Office for National Statistics, 2015.
10. BBC News. Dominic Raab under fire over Dover–Calais comments. London: BBC News, 8 November 2018. https://www.bbc.co.uk/news/uk-politics-46142188 (accessed 7 June 2019).
11. Hotten, R. Brexit: can firms stop stocks running low? London: BBC News, 13 November 2018. https://www.bbc.co.uk/news/business-46195749 (accessed 13 November 2018).
12. Benton, T. G. British food: what role should UK producers have in feeding the UK? – Independent report to Morrisons supermarket. Bradford: Morrisons and University of Leeds, 2017. www.leeds.ac.uk/download/481/british_food_makers_report (accessed 17 August 2018).
13. Defra. Agriculture in the UK 2017.
14. Matthews, A. Possible transitional arrangements related to agriculture in the light of the future EU–UK relationship: institutional issues. Research Study for the European Parliament AGRI Committee. Brussels: European Parliament DG Internal Policies: Agriculture and Rural Development/ Policy Department Structural and Cohesion Policies, 2017.
15. FSDF. FSDF leads delegation to see Michael Gove on no deal planning for food logistics. Reading: Food Storage and Distribution Federation, 2018.

16. De Ruiter, H., Macdiarmid, J. I., Matthews, R. B., et al. 'Total global agricultural land footprint associated with UK food supply 1986–2011'. *Global Environmental Change* 43, March 2017: 72–81. https://doi.org/10.1016/j.gloenvcha.2017.01.007.

17. De Ruiter, H., Macdiarmid, J. I., Matthews, R. B., et al. 'Global cropland and greenhouse gas impacts of UK food supply are increasingly located overseas'. *Journal of the Royal Society Interface* 13(114), 2016. http://dx.doi.org/10.1098/rsif.2015.1001.

18. De Ruiter, H., Macdiarmid, J. I., Matthews, R. B., et al. 'Exploring a "Healthy Foodshed": Land Use Associated with UK Fruit and Vegetables Supply', in Niewöhner, J., Bruns, A., Hostert, P., et al., eds. *Human–Environment Interactions 6: Land Use Competition: Ecological, Economic and Social Perspectives*, pp. 247–61. Switzerland: Springer International Publishing, 2016.

19. European Commission. Generalised Scheme of Preferences. Brussels: European Commission DG Trade, 2018. http://ec.europa.eu/trade/policy/countries-and-regions/development/generalised-scheme-of-preferences/index_en.htm (accessed 24 May 2019).

20. Hestermeyer, H. What is the most-favoured-nation clause? UK Trade Forum, 2017. https://uktradeforum.net/2017/11/30/what-is-the-most-favoured-nation-clause/ (accessed May 2018).

21. Ibid.

22. BRC. A fair Brexit for consumers: the customs roadmap. London: British Retail Consortium, 2017.

23. ONS: Woodland Research. Provisional woodland statistics (2019 edn). London: Office for National Statistics, 2019.

24. HSBC UK: Agriculture. Forward planning 2019. Coventry: HSBC, 2019.

25. Defra. Horticulture statistics 2017. London: Department for Environment, Food and Rural Affairs, 2018.

26. Andersons (Midland) and Pelham, J. The impact of Brexit on the UK soft fruit industry. London: British Summer Fruits, 2017. http://www.seasonalberries.co.uk/2017/06/latest-news/summer-fruit-prices-set-to-soar-as-a-result-of-brexit-urgent-action-needed-to-ensure-essential-workforce.html.

27. Willett, W., Rockström, J., Loken, B., et al. 'Food in the Anthropocene: The EAT–*Lancet* Commission on healthy diets from sustainable food systems'. *The Lancet* 393(10170), 2 February 2019: 447–92. https://doi.org/10.1016/S0140-6736(18)31788-4.

28. Robertson, H., Marshall, D., Slingsby, E., et al. Economic, biodiversity, resource protection and social values of orchards: a study of six orchards by the Herefordshire Orchards Community Evaluation Project. Report commissioned by Natural England from the Bulmer Foundation. London: Natural England, 2012.

29. Brown, P. *The Apple Orchard: The Story of Our Most English Fruit.* London: Penguin Books/Particular Books, 2016.

30. MAFF. The Apple Orchard Grubbing Up Regulations. Statutory Instrument (coming into force on 5 February 1991). London: Ministry of Agriculture, Fisheries and Food, 1991.

31. G's. G's: The G's story. Ely: G's Group, 2018. https://www.gs-fresh.com/gs-group/the-gs-story/.

32. Mellard Reade, T. 'On a section through Glazebrook Moss, Lancashire'. *Quarterly Journal of the Geological Society* 1878(34): 808–10.

33. Riverford Organic. About Riverford. Buckfastleigh: Riverford Organics, 2018. https://www.riverford.co.uk/aboutus.

34. Growing Communities. Transforming food and farming through community-led trade. London: Hackney Growing Communities, 2018. http://www.growingcommunities.org/.

35. Barcombe Nurseries, near Lewes, Sussex. https://www.barcombenurseries.co.uk/.

36. De Ruiter, Macdiarmid, Matthews, et al. 'Total global agricultural land footprint'.

37. De Ruiter, Macdiarmid, Matthews, et al. 'Exploring a "Healthy Foodshed"'.

38. Willett, Rockström, Loken, et al. 'Food in the Anthropocene'.

39. Springmann, M. 'Modelling report on alternative production and consumption scenarios for the UK. Report to the Food, Farming and Countryside Commission'. Oxford: Oxford Martin School, 2019.

40. Springmann, M., Godfray, H. C. J., Rayner, M., et al. 'Analysis and valuation of the health and climate change cobenefits of dietary change'. *Proceedings of the National Academies of Science* 113(15), 2016: 4146–51. https://doi.org/10.1073/pnas.1523119113.

41. Maxwell, S. 'The Evolution of Thinking about Food Security', in Devereux, S. and Maxwell, S., eds. *Food Security in Sub-Saharan Africa*, pp. 13–31. London: ITDG Publishing, 2001.

42. Maxwell, S. and Smith, M. 'Household Food Security: A Conceptual Review', in Maxwell, S. and Frankenberger, T., eds. *Household Food Security: Concepts, Indicators, Measurements: A Technical Review*, pp. 1–72. New York/Rome: UNICEF and IFAD, 1995.

43. Lang, T. and Barling, D. 'Food security and food sustainability: Reformulating the debate'. *The Geographical Journal* 178(4), 2012: 313–26. https://doi.org/10.1111/j.1475-4959.2012.00480.x (published online 23 August 2012).

44. Sen, A. K. *Poverty and Famines: An Essay on Entitlement and Deprivation.* Oxford: Clarendon Press, 1981.

45. Gross, R., Schoeneberger, H., Pfeifer, H., et al. The four dimensions of food and nutrition security: definitions and concepts. Rome: Food and Agriculture Organization, 2000. http://www.fao.org/elearning/course/fa/en/pdf/p-01_rg_concept.pdf (accessed 28 January 2018).

46. Alston, P. Statement on visit to the United Kingdom, by Professor Philip Alston, United Nations Special Rapporteur on extreme poverty and human rights. Geneva: Office of the UN Commissioner for Human Rights, 2018.

47. Alston, P. Visit to the United Kingdom of Great Britain and Northern Ireland – Report of the Special Rapporteur on extreme poverty and human rights. UN General Assembly, Human Rights Council Forty-First Session, 24 June–12 July 2019, Agenda Item 3. A/HRC/41/39/Add. 1. Geneva: UN Human Rights Council, 2019.

48. Collingham, L. *The Taste of War: World War Two and the Battle for Food.* London: Allen Lane, 2011.

49. Pickett, H. Farm assurance schemes and animal welfare: How the standards compare. Godalming and Edinburgh: Compassion in World Farming and OneKind, 2012.

50. Hammond, R. J. *Food: The Growth of Policy.* London: HMSO/Longmans, Green, 1951.

51. Beveridge, S. W. *Food Control.* Oxford: Oxford University Press, 1928.

52. Hammond, R. J. *Food and Agriculture in Britain 1939–45: Aspects of Wartime Control.* Stanford, Calif.: Stanford University Press, 1954.

53. Zweiniger-Bargielowska, I. *Austerity in Britain: Rationing, Controls, and Consumption, 1939–1955.* Oxford: Oxford University Press, 2000.

54. HM Government. Agriculture Act 1947 (Chapter 48 10 and 11 Geo 6).

55. Le Gros Clark, F. and Titmuss, R. M. *Our Food Problem and Its Relation to Our National Defences.* Harmondsworth: Penguin Books, 1939.

56. Hammond. *Food: The Growth of Policy.*

57. Hammond. *Food and Agriculture in Britain 1939–45.*

58. Hewitt, N. The convoys that helped save Britain during the Second World War. London: Imperial War Museum, 2018.

59. Beveridge. *Food Control.*

60. Manton, K. 'Sir William Beveridge, the British government and plans for food control in time of war, *c.*1916–1941'. *Contemporary British History* 23(3), 2009: 363–85. https://doi.org/10.1080/13619460903080192 (published online 4 September 2009).

61. Woolton, T. E. *The Memoirs of the Rt Hon. The Earl of Woolton*. London: Cassell, 1959.

62. Sitwell, W. *Eggs or Anarchy. The Remarkable Story of the Man Tasked with the Impossible: to Feed a Nation at War*. London: Simon & Schuster, 2016.

63. Smith, D. F. 'Nutrition Science and the Two World Wars', in Smith, D. F., ed. *Nutrition in Britain: Science, Scientists and Politics in the Twentieth Century*, pp. 142–65. London: Routledge, 1997.

64. Edgerton, D. *Britain's War Machine*. London: Penguin Books, 2012.

65. Holling, C. S. 'Resilience and stability of ecological systems'. *Annual Review of Ecology and Systematics* 4, November 1973: 1–23.

66. Benton, T. G. and Thompson, C. 'Food system resilience'. *Food Science and Technology* 30(3), 2016: 20–24.

67. Himanen, S. J., Rikkonen, P. and Kahiluoto, H. 'Codesigning a resilient food system'. *Ecology and Society* 21(4), 2016: 41. https://doi.org/10.5751/ES-08878-210441.

68. Selye, H. *The Stress of Life*. New York: McGrawHill, 1956.

69. Millstone, E., van Zwanenberg, P., Levidow, L., et al. Risk-assessment policies: differences across jurisdictions. Seville: European Commission Joint Research Centre: Institute for Prospective Technological Studies, 2008.

70. Millstone, E. P. and van Zwanenberg, P. 'The politics of scientific advice'. *Science and Public Policy* 28(2), 2001: 99–112.

71. Courtenay, P. P. *Plantation Agriculture*. London: G. Bell & Sons, 1965.

72. Mintz, S. W. *Sweetness and Power: The Place of Sugar in Modern History*. Harmondsworth: Penguin Books, 1985.

73. FAO. FAO capacity development. Rome: Food and Agriculture Organization of the UN, 2019.

74. Nyéléni Declaration. Declaration of Nyéléni: World Forum on Food Sovereignty. http://www.landaction.org/spip/spip.php?article37, 2007.

75. Windfuhr, M. and Jonsén, J. Food sovereignty: towards democracy in localized food systems. Bourton-on-Dunsmore (UK): ITDG Publishing, 2005.

76. Herrera, R. and Kin, C. L., eds. *The Struggle for Food Sovereignty: Alternative Development and the Renewal of Peasant Societies Today*. London: Pluto Press, 2015.

77. Pimbert, M. Towards food sovereignty: Reclaiming autonomous food systems. London and Munich: International Institute for Environment and Development, Rachel Carson Centre and the Centre for Agro-Ecology and Food Security, Coventry University, 2009.

78. Rosset, P. 'Food sovereignty and alternative paradigms to confront land-grabbing and the food and climate crisis'. *Development* 54(1), 2011: 21–30.

79. Ibid.

80. Brem-Wilson, J. 'Towards food sovereignty: interrogating peasant voice in the United Nations Committee on World Food Security'. *Journal of Peasant Studies* 42(1), 2015: 73–95. http://dx.doi.org/10.1080/03066150.2014.968143.

81. Fairlie, S., Hamer, E., Fernandes, J., et al. Making food sovereignty a reality: recommendations for post-Brexit agricultural policy. Landworkers Alliance, 2017.

82. UN. Universal Declaration of Human Rights. Adopted and proclaimed by General Assembly resolution 217 A (III) of 10 December 1948. Geneva: United Nations, 1948.

83. Bailey, R. Growing a better future: food justice in a resource-constrained world. Oxford: Oxfam International, 2011.

84. Gottlieb, R. and Joshi, A. *Food Justice*. Cambridge, Mass., and London: MIT Press, 2013.

85. FEC. Food justice: the report of the Food and Fairness Inquiry. Brighton: Food Ethics Council, 2010.

86. De Schutter, O. 'The specter of productivism and food democracy'. *Wisconsin Law Review* 2014(2): 199–233.

87. Lang, T. 'Towards a Food Democracy', in Griffiths, S. and Wallace, J., eds. *Consuming Passions: Food in the Age of Anxiety*. Manchester: Manchester University Press, 1998.

88. Lang, T., Barling, D. and Caraher, M. *Food Policy: Integrating Health, Environment and Society*. Oxford: Oxford University Press, 2009.

89. Johnson, B. 'Face it: it's all your own fat fault'. *Daily Telegraph*, 27 May 2004.

90. Friedman, M. *Capitalism and Freedom*. Chicago: University of Chicago Press, 1962.

91. ONS. National population projections: 2016-based statistical bulletin. London: Office for National Statistics, 2017.

92. MAC. EEA migration in the UK: Final report. London: Migration Advisory Committee, 2018.

93. Rienzo, C. and Vargas-Silva, C. Migration in the UK: an overview 2018. Oxford: COMPAS/The Migration Observatory, University of Oxford, 2018.

94. UN DESA. World population prospects: the 2017 revision. New York: United Nations Department of Economic and Social Affairs: Population Division, 2017.

95. Dyson, T. *Population and Development: The Demographic Transition*. London: Zed Books, 2010.

96. Pearce, F. *Peoplequake: Mass Migration, Ageing Population and the Coming Population Crash*. London: Eden Project Books (Random House), 2010.

97. Sen, A. Hunger in the contemporary world. London: London School of Economics, Suntory and Toyota International Centres for Economics and Related Disciplines, 1997.

98. Sen. *Poverty and Famines*.

99. Drèze, J., Sen, A. K. and Hussain, A. *The Political Economy of Hunger: Selected Essays*. New Delhi and Oxford: Oxford University Press, 1999.

100. Lang, T. and Heasman, M. *Food Wars: The Global Battle for Mouths, Minds and Markets*, 2nd edn. Abingdon: Routledge Earthscan, 2015.

101. Willett, Rockström, Loken, et al. 'Food in the Anthropocene'.

102. Ranganathan, J., Waite, R., Searchinger, T., et al. How to sustainably feed 10 billion people by 2050. Washington DC: World Resources Institute, 2018.

103. Fears, R., Canales, C., ter Meulen, V., et al. 'Transforming food systems to deliver healthy, sustainable diets – the view from the world's science academies'. *The Lancet Planetary Health* 3(4), April 2019: e163–5. http://dx.doi.org/10.1016/S2542-5196(19)30038-5.

104. Springmann, M., Clark, M., Mason-D'Croz, D., et al. 'Options for keeping the food system within environmental limits'. *Nature* 562(7728), 2018: 519–25. https://doi.org/10.1038/s41586-018-0594-0.

105. Springmann, M., Mason-D'Croz, D., Robinson, S., et al. 'Global and regional health effects of future food production under climate change: a modelling study'. *The Lancet* 387(10031), 7 May 2016: 1937–46. https://doi.org/10.1016/S0140-6736(15)01156-3 (published online 2 March 2016).

106. CWF. Why we need a UN Framework Convention on Food Agriculture. Godalming: Compassion in World Farming, 2018.

107. JiJi. 'Nation's food self-sufficiency rate hits 23-year low as rice consumption decline continues'. *Japan Times*, 10 August 2017.

108. Ricardo, D. *On the Principles of Political Economy and Taxation*. Cambridge: Cambridge University Press, 2015 [1817].

109. Mazzucato, M. *The Entrepreneurial State: Debunking Public vs Private Sector Myths*. London: Penguin Books, 2018.

110. Ministry of Agriculture and Food. Food security. Oslo: Government of Norway, 2015. https://www.regjeringen.no/en/topics/food-fisheries-and-agriculture/mat/innsikt/matsikkerhet/id2357158/ (accessed 8 June 2019).

111. Defra. Ensuring the UK's Food Security in a Changing World: A Defra Discussion Paper. London: Department for Environment, Food and Rural Affairs, July 2008.

112. Defra. Agriculture in the United Kingdom 2017. London: Department for Environment, Food and Rural Affairs, 2018.

113. Ricardo. *On the Principles of Political Economy and Taxation*.

114. Malthus, T. R. *The Grounds of an Opinion on the Policy of Restricting the Importation of Foreign Corn: Intended as an Appendix to 'Observations on the Corn Laws'*. London: John Murray and J. Johnson and Co., 1815.

115. Burnett, J. *A History of the Cost of Living*. Harmondsworth: Penguin Books, 1969.

116. Inter-Departmental Committee on Physical Deterioration (chaired by Sir Almeric W. Fitzroy). *Report of the Inter-Departmental Committee on Physical Deterioration*: vol. 1. Cd. 2175. London: HMSO, 1904.

117. Inter-Departmental Committee on Physical Deterioration (chaired by Sir Almeric W. Fitzroy). *Minutes of Evidence for the Report of the Inter-Departmental Committee on Physical Deterioration*: vol. 2. Cd. 2186. London: HMSO, 1904.

118. Royal Commission on Supply of Food and Raw Material in Time of War. *The Report of the Royal Commission on Supply of Food and Raw Material in Time of War*. 3 vols. Cd. 2643, 2644, 2645. London: HMSO, 1905.

119. BSSRS. Bread: Who makes the dough? London: British Society for Social Responsibility in Science Agricapital Group, 1977.

120. Sharpe, R. P., Barling, D. and Lang, T. Final report on the investigation into ethical traceability in the UK wheat–flour–bread supply chain. Report to DG Research. Framework 6: Science & Society. London: Centre for Food Policy, City University, 2006.

121. Whitley, A. *Bread Matters*. London: Fourth Estate, 2006.

122. Paulus, I. *The Search for Pure Food*. Oxford: Martin Robertson, 1974.

123. Berger, N. *The School Meals Service: From Its Beginnings to the Present Day*. Plymouth: Northcote House, 1990.

124. Beveridge, *Food Control*.

125. Vernon, J. *Hunger: A Modern History*. Cambridge, Mass.: Harvard University Press, 2007.

126. Atwater, W. O. Foods, nutritive value and cost. US Department of Agriculture, Farmers Bulletin 23. Washington DC: US Department of Agriculture, 1894.

127. Atwater, W. O. Methods and results of investigations on the chemistry and economy of food. US Department of Agriculture, Bulletin 21. Washington DC: Department of Agriculture, 1895.

128. Atwater, W. O. and Woods, C. D. Investigations upon the chemistry and economy of foods. Connecticut (Storrs): Agricultural Experimental Station, 1891.

129. BMA. *Nutrition and the Public Health: Proceedings of a National Conference on the Wider Aspects of Nutrition, April 27–28–29, 1939.* London: British Medical Association, 1939.

130. Rowntree, B. S. *How the Labourer Lives.* London: Thomas Nelson & Sons, 1913.

131. Rowntree, B. S. *The Human Needs of Labour.* London: Longmans, 1921.

132. Rathbone, E. *The Disinherited Family: A Plea for the Endowment of the Family.* London: Edward Arnold, 1924.

133. Hannington, W. *Unemployed Struggles 1919–1936.* London: Lawrence & Wishart, 1977 [1936].

134. Stapledon, S. G. *The Land: Now and Tomorrow.* London: Faber & Faber, 1935.

135. Le Gros Clark, F. and Titmuss, R. M. *Our Food Problem and Its Relation to Our National Defences.* Harmondsworth: Penguin Books, 1939.

136. Astor, W. A. and Rowntree, B. S. *British Agriculture: A Report of an Inquiry Organized by Viscount Astor and B. Seebohm Rowntree,* abridged edn. Harmondsworth: Penguin Books, 1939.

137. Astor, W. A. and Rowntree, B. S. *The Agricultural Dilemma: A Report of an Enquiry Organised by Viscount Astor and Mr. B. Seebohm Rowntree.* London: P. S. King, 1935.

138. UN. Universal Declaration of Human Rights.

139. De Schutter, O. The transformative potential of the right to food. Final report of the Special Rapporteur on the right to food to the twenty-fifth session of the Human Rights Council. UN doc. A/HRC/25/57. Geneva: Human Rights Council, 2014.

140. Eide, W. B. and Kracht, U., eds. *Food and Human Rights in Development:* vol. I: *Legal and Institutional Dimensions and Selected Topics.* Antwerp: Intersentia, 2005.

141. Eide, A. Right to adequate food as a human right. UN Human Rights Study, Series No. 1. Geneva: United Nations, 1989.

142. UN OHCHR. International Covenant on Economic, Social and Cultural Rights. Adopted and opened for signature, ratification and accession by General Assembly resolution 2200A (XXI) of 16 December 1966, entry into force 3 January 1976, in accordance with article 27. Geneva: United Nations Office of the High Commissioner on Human Rights, 1966.

143. EHRC. International Covenant on Economic, Social and Cultural Rights. Manchester: Equality and Human Rights Commission, 2018.

144. UN OHCHR. Table of pending cases on Human Rights before the Office of the UN Commissioner on Human Rights. Geneva: United Nations Office of the High Commissioner on Human Rights, 2019. https://www.ohchr.org/en/hrbodies/cescr/pages/pendingcases.aspx (accessed 21 March 2019).

145. HM Government. Civil Contingencies Act 2004. London: HMSO, 2004. http://www.opsi.gov.uk/acts/acts2004/ukpga_20040036_en_1.

146. Lang, T., Millstone, E. P., Lewis, T., et al. *Feeding Britain: food security after Brexit*. London: Food Research Collaboration, 2018.

147. Benton. British food.

148. McFarlane, G., Lewis, T. and Lang, T. Food, Brexit and Northern Ireland: critical issues. London: Food Research Collaboration and Chartered Institute of Environmental Health, 2018.

149. DOH. Directors of Public Health in local government: roles, responsibilities and context. London: Department of Health, 2013.

150. Library HoC. Local authorities' public health responsibilities (England). London: House of Commons, 2014.

151. Middleton, J. 'Life and death in Sandwell: Where public health and economic health meet'. *Journal of Local Government Policy Making* 16(4), 1990: 3–9.

152. Middleton, J. and Reynolds, L. Lansley's wonderful plan, by Clostridium difficile. Blog piece, 1 February 2012. http://abetternhs.wordpress.com/2012/02/01/cdiff/ (accessed 12 March 2013).

153. Middleton, J. and Saunders, P. '20 years of local ecological public health: the experience of Sandwell in the English West Midlands'. *Public Health* 129(10), 2015: 1344–52. https://www.sciencedirect.com/science/article/abs/pii/S0033350615003303.

154. Lang, T. 'No-deal food planning in UK Brexit'. *The Lancet* 394(102019), 7 September 2019: 814–15. http://dx.doi.org/10.1016/S0140-6736(19)31769-6 (published online 4 August 2019).

155. Kirkby, D. 'Leeds company helping the "Brexit preppers" stockpile over no deal fears'. *Yorkshire Post*, 4 February 2019. Moshakis, A. 'Worst case

scenario: the "preppers" gearing up for disaster'. *Observer*, 28 January 2018.

156. Elgot, J. 'Grayling defends giving Brexit ferry contract to company with no ships'. *Guardian*, 2 January 2019.

157. Bold, B. 'Engine to lead government's £100m no-deal Brexit campaign'. *Campaign*, 31 July 2019. https://www.campaignlive.co.uk/article/ engine-lead-governments-100m-no-deal-brexit-campaign/1592659.

158. Parker, G. 'Sajid Javid to unveil £2bn extra Brexit cash for no-deal planning: Pot includes £434m to stop UK running out of vital medicines and £138m information campaign'. *Financial Times*, 31 July 2019.

159. Groves, J., Sculthorpe, T., Wilcock, D., et al. 'Top mandarin's bombshell No Deal warning: Food up 10%, police unable to protect public, direct rule in Ulster, worse recession than 2008 says leaked letter'. *Daily Mail*, 2 April 2019.

160. 'No-deal Brexit preparations: the leaked Operation Yellowhammer document'. *Sunday Times*, 18 August 2019.

161. HM Government. Don't Panic – Prepare, e.g. via: https://www.bradford. gov.uk/media/1951/dontpanicbooklet.pdf. London: HM Government, 2019.

162. Cabinet Office. Civil Contingencies Act (2004) – Duty to communicate with the public. The Ten Step Cycle – an informal guidance note. London: HM Government, 2011.

163. Lang. 'No-deal food planning in UK Brexit'.

164. Cabinet Office. Public Summary of Sector Security and Resilience Plans 2018. London: Cabinet Office, 2018.

165. Cabinet Office. Government Security Classifications. 21 May 2018. London: Cabinet Office, 2018.

166. Defra, FSA and BSI. PAS 96 (4th edn): Guide to protecting and defending food and drink from deliberate attack. London: British Standards Institute, Department of Environment, Food and Rural Affairs, and Food Standards Agency, 2017.

167. Peck, H. Resilience in the food chain: a study of business continuity management in the food and drink industry. Final report to the Department for Environment, Food and Rural Affairs, July 2006. Shrivenham/London: Defra/The Resilience Centre, Department of Defence Management & Security Analysis, Cranfield University, 2006.

168. Collingham. *Taste of War*.

169. Hammond. *Food: Growth of Policy*.

170. Sitwell. *Eggs or Anarchy*.

171. Zweiniger-Bargielowska. *Austerity in Britain.*

172. HM Government. National security strategy and strategic defence and security review 2015. London: HM Government, 2016.

173. Home Select Committee. Home Office delivery of Brexit: customs operations. London: House of Commons Home Select Committee, 2017.

174. Dunlop, T. 'UK Border Force fleet size "worryingly low"'. *UK Defence Journal*, 2017.

175. Home Office. Press release: Home Secretary bolsters Border Force fleet in the Channel. 31 December 2018. London: Home Office, 2018.

176. Dunlop, 'UK Border Force fleet size "worryingly low"'.

177. Getlink. Paris: Getlink, 2019. https://www.getlinkgroup.com/uk/group/operations/security/ (accessed 30 March 2019).

178. Committee D. 'Sunset for the Royal Marines?' London: House of Commons, 2018.

179. Oral Statement by the Rt Hon. Theresa May to Parliament: Home Secretary's statement on border security. 20 February. London: The Home Office, 2012. https://www.gov.uk/government/speeches/home-secretarys-statement-on-border-security (accessed 9 June 2019).

180. Defence Committee. Restoring the Fleet. Third report. London: House of Commons Defence Committee, 2016. https://www.globalsecurity.org/military/library/report/2016/restoring-the-fleet_uk-house-of-commons_20161121.pdf.

181. Ibid.

182. Defra, FSA and BSI. PAS 96 (4th edn): Guide to protecting and defending food and drink from deliberate attack.

183. JCNSS. Cyber security of the UK's critical national infrastructure. Third report of Session 2017–19. HL Paper 222/HC 1708. London: House of Lords and House of Commons Joint Committee on the National Security Strategy, 2018.

184. NCSC. London, 2019. https://www.gov.uk/government/organisations/national-cyber-security-centre (accessed 9 June 2019).

185. Cabinet Office. Interim cyber security science & technology strategy: Future-proofing cyber security. London: HM Government Cabinet Office, 2017.

186. James, N. C. K. 'Cyberterrorism: How food companies are planning for threat of cybersecurity risks'. *Food Quality and Safety*, 18 May 2018. https://www.foodqualityandsafety.com/article/cyberterrorism-food-industry-cybersecurity-risks/ (published online 18 May 2018).

187. Atherton, M. 'Food firms advised to boost cyber security after attack'. *Food Manufacture.* https://www.foodmanufacture.co.uk/

Article/2017/06/12/Food-firms-told-to-improve-their-computer-system-security (published online 12 June 2017).

188. Hellard, B. Grocers to use blockchain to track food by 2020. ITPRO newsletter, 30 April 2019. https://www.itpro.co.uk/blockchain/33546/grocers-to-use-blockchain-to-track-food-by-2020.

189. Ismail, N. 'What sectors are investing the most and least in cyber security?' *Information Age*. https://www.information-age.com/sectors-investing-most-least-cyber-security-123473207/ (published online 4 July 2018).

190. EUIPO, Europol. Intellectual property crime theft assessment 2019. European Union Intellectual Property office and Europol, 2019.

191. NAO. Progress of the 2016–2021 National Cyber Security Programme. HC1988, 2017–19. London: National Audit Office, 2019.

192. PAC. Defence Equipment Plan 2018–28. Seventy-Seventh Report of Session 2017–19. HC1519. London: House of Commons Public Accounts Committee, 2019.

193. PAC. Ministry of Defence Nuclear Programme. Sixty-First Report of Session 2017–19. HC1028. London: House of Commons Public Accounts Committee, 2018.

194. Allison, G. 'How much will it cost to fix the Type 45 Destroyer fleet?' *UK Defence Journal*, 13 July 2018. 'Type 45 Daring Class Destroyer'. *Naval Technology*, 2019. https://www.naval-technology.com/projects/horizon/.

195. HM Government. National security strategy and strategic defence and security review 2015.

196. DfT. Transport statistics Great Britain 2017. London: Department for Transport, 2017.

197. DfT. Domestic road freight statistics United Kingdom 2017. London: Department for Transport, 2018.

198. NIC. Future of freight: interim report. London: National Infrastructure Commission, 2018.

199. Steer/Airlines UK. Assessment of the value of air freight services to the UK economy. London: Steer plc and Airlines UK, 2018.

200. AirportWatch. Heathrow never mentions imports, only exports – but imports larger by tonnage and by value than exports. London: AirportWatch, 25 November 2015.

201. NIC. Future of freight.

202. Porritt, J. *The World We Made*. London: Phaidon, 2013.

203. IMO. Initial IMO strategy on reduction of GHG emissions from ships. Resolution MEPC.304(72), 13 April 2018. London: International Maritime Organization, 2018.

204. DfT. Port freight statistics 2017: notes and definitions. London: Department for Transport, 2017.

205. Owen, J., Shepheard, M. and Stojanovic, A. Implementing Brexit: customs. London: Institute for Government, 2017.

206. DfT. DfT statistics: road freight statistics: Table RFS 0104 Goods lifted by commodity: annual 2004–2017. London: Department for Transport, 2018.

207. Lang, T. 'Food miles'. *Slow Food*, 19 May 2006: 94–7.

208. Paxton, A. The food miles report. London: Sustainable Agriculture, Food and Environment (SAFE) Alliance, 1994.

209. Smith, A., Watkiss, P., Tweddle, G., et al. The validity of food miles as an indicator of sustainable development. Report to DEFRA by AEA Technology. London: Department for the Environment, Food and Rural Affairs, 2005.

210. MacGregor, J. and Vorley, B. 'Fair miles'? The concept of 'food miles' through a sustainable development lens. London: International Institute for Environment and Development, 2006.

211. Rai Chi, K., MacGregor, J. and King, R. Fair miles: recharting the food miles map. Oxford: International Institute for Environment and Development and Oxfam GB, 2009.

212. Desrochers, P. and Shimizu, H. Yes, we have no bananas: a critique of the 'food miles' perspective. Washington DC: George Mason University Mercatus Centre, 2008.

213. RAC Foundation. Mobility facts. London: RAC Foundation, 2019.

214. Bates, J. and Leibling, D. Spaced out: perspectives on parking policy. London: RAC Foundation, 2012. https://wwwracfoundationorg/assets/rac_foundation/content/downloadables/spaced_out-bates_leibling-jul12pdf.

215. DfT. National travel statistics England 2017. London: Department for Transport, 2018.

216. Adeh, E. H., Selker, J. S. and Higgins, C. W. 'Remarkable agrivoltaic influence on soil moisture, micrometeorology and water-use efficiency'. *PLoS ONE* 13(11), 2018. https://doi.org/10.1371/journal.pone.0203256.

217. Osborne, M. Fraunhofer ISE proves Agrophotovoltaics pilot project feasibility. PV-Tech, 24 November 2017. https://www.pv-tech.org/news/fraunhofer-ise-proves-agrophotovoltaics-pilot-project-feasibility.

218. Ban Ki-moon. 'UK must stop investing in fossil fuels in developing countries'. *Guardian*, 24 February 2019.

219. CCC. Biomass in a low-carbon economy. London: Committee on Climate Change, 2018.

220. Ajanovic, A. 'Biofuels versus food production: Does biofuels production increase food prices?' *Energy* 36(4), 2011: 2070–76. https://doi.org/10.1016/j.energy.2010.05.019.

221. Daugbjerg, C. and Swinbank, A. 'Globalization and new policy concerns: the WTO and the EU's sustainability criteria for biofuel'. *Journal of European Public Policy* 22(3), 2015: 429–46.

222. OECD. Agricultural market impacts of future growth in the production of biofuels. Report of Working Party on Agricultural Policies and Markets to the Committee for Agriculture of the Directorate for Food, Agriculture and Fisheries. AGR/CA/APM(2005)24/FINAL. Paris: Organisation for Economic Cooperation and Development, 2006.

223. OECD/IEA. *Biofuel Support Policies: An Economic Assessment.* Paris: Organisation for Economic Co-operation and Development/International Energy Agency, 2008.

224. DfT. Transport statistics Great Britain 2017.

225. European Commission. Energy prices and costs in Europe. Brussels, COM(2019) 1 final. Report from the Commission to the European Parliament, the Council, the European Economic and Social Committee and the Committee of the Regions {SWD(2019) 1 final}. Brussels: European Commission, 2019.

226. ETC. Mission statement. London: Energy Transitions Commission, 2018. http://www.energy-transitions.org/ (accessed 30 January 2019).

227. BEIS. Energy trends: March 2018. London: Department for Business, Energy and Industrial Strategy, 2018.

228. DfT. Port freight statistics (2016 revised). London: Department for Transport, 2017.

229. Morgan, A. Sustainable supply chains – more than a concept? Paper to Food CIM Annual Conference, 24 March 2016. Sutton Bonington: ESPRC Centre for Innovative Manufacturing in Food (Universities of Loughborough, Nottingham and Birmingham), 2016.

230. Getlink. Getlink company data. Paris: Getlink, 2019. https://www.getlinkgroup.com/uk/group/our-business/ (accessed 29 January 2019).

231. FSA. Ports designations. London: Food Standards Agency, 2012. https://www.food.gov.uk/business-guidance/port-designations (accessed 26 August 2018).

232. Bridger, R. Airport freight: the facts. London: AirportWatch, 2009.

233. BRC. A fair Brexit for consumers: the customs roadmap. London: British Retail Consortium, 2017.

234. Lewis, T. Post-Brexit food trade across the UK's borders: some inconvenient truths. Food Voices blog. London: Food Research Collaboration, 2018.

235. HMRC. Port health authorities: monitoring of food imports. London: HM Revenue and Customs. Guidance, 2012. https://www.gov.uk/guidance/port-health-authorities-monitoring-of-food-imports#choosing-a-port (accessed 26 August 2018).

236. O'Carroll, L. 'Post-Brexit port checks could disrupt fresh food supplies, say freight bosses'. *Guardian*, 3 May 2018. https://www.theguardian.com/politics/2018/may/03/post-brexit-port-checks-could-disrupt-fresh-food-supplies-say-freight-bosses?utm_source=esp&utm_medium=Email&utm_campaign=Brexit+briefing+16&utm_term=274147&subid=25525508&CMP=ema-3239.

237. HMRC. Port health authorities: monitoring of food imports.

238. DfT. Modern ports: a UK Policy. London: Department for Transport, 2000.

239. DfT. *National Policy Statement for Ports*. London: The Stationery Office, 2012.

240. Maritime UK. Ports. London: Maritime UK, 2018.

241. Cohen, D. Who owns Britain? Open Democracy, 2018. https://www.opendemocracy.net/neweconomics/who-owns-britain/.

242. Nightingale, L. Forth Ports' new owner sells minority stakes. London: Lloyd's List, 2018.

243. DP World. Shipping Alliance chooses DP World's UK ports for ten trade routes to US and Asia. Dubai: DP World, 2017. http://web.dpworld.com/wp-content/uploads/2017/03/2017_03_08_UK-Shipping-Alliance_-Eng.pdf (accessed 26 August 2018).

244. Cave, A. London Gateway will reopen capital to the world's largest ships. *Daily Telegraph*, 2 November 2013.

245. Brogan, C. How Imperial's findings on post-Brexit borders caught the eyes of politicians (a study conducted for the BBC on M20/M2). London: Department of Civil and Environmental Engineering, Imperial College London, 2018. https://www.imperial.ac.uk/news/186530/how-imperials-findings-post-brexit-borders-caught/ (accessed 20 July 2018).

246. Tendall, D. M., Joerin, J., Kopainsky, B., et al. 'Food system resilience: Defining the concept'. *Global Food Security* 6, October 2015: 17–23.

247. DfT. Maritime 2050: navigating the future. London: Department for Transport, 2019.

248. DfT. Transport resilience review: a review of the resilience of the transport network to extreme weather events. Cm 8874. London: Department for Transport, 2014.

249. Ibid.

250. EA. National Flood and Coastal Risk Management Strategy consultation. Rotherham: Environment Agency, 2019.

251. CILT. Importance of ports within the food supply chain. Chartered Institute of Logistics and Transport's Ports, Maritime & Waterways Forum Event, Thursday, 29 October 2015, Port of Tilbury. London: Chartered Institute of Logistics and Transport, 2015.

252. CCC. Net zero – the UK's contribution to stopping global warming. London: Committee on Climate Change, 2019.

253. Issa, 'N. Eurotunnel unveils security upgrade in France'. ITV News, 18 January 2017.

254. Peck. Resilience in the food chain.

255. Morgan, A. and Baker, P. Resilience of the food supply to port disruption. Defra Project FO0108. Final report. London: Department of Environment, Food and Rural Affairs, 2012.

PART TWO: TACKLING FOOD PROBLEMS IS THE KEY TO SECURITY

1. HM Government. Government gives details on setting a UK net zero emissions target. London: House of Commons, 2019. https://www.parliament.uk/business/news/2019/june/government-gives-details-on-setting-a-uk-net-zero-emissions-target/.

2. United Nations. Sustainable Development Goals, agreed at the UN Summit, 27–29 September 2015. New York: United Nations Department of Economic and Social Affairs: Division for Sustainable Development, 2015. https://sustainabledevelopment.un.org/post2015/summit.

3. Willett, W., Rockström, J., Loken, B., et al. 'Food in the Anthropocene: The EAT–*Lancet* Commission on healthy diets from sustainable food systems'. *The Lancet* 393(10170), 2 February 2019: 447–92.

Chapter 4: Our Food Problems: Recognizing the Lock-in

1. Laureys, S., Pellas, F., Van Eeckhout, P., et al. 'The locked-in syndrome: What is it like to be conscious but paralyzed and voiceless?' *Progress in Brain Research* 150, 2005: 495–511. https://doi.org/10.1016/S0079-6123(05)50034-7.

2. Smith, E. and Delargy, M. 'Locked-in syndrome'. *British Medical Journal* 330, 2005: 406. https://doi.org/10.1136/bmj.330.7488.406 (published online 17 February 2005).

3. Hill, A. 'Locked-in syndrome: Rare survivor Richard Marsh recounts his ordeal'. *Guardian*, 7 August 2012.

4. Lang, T. 'Sustainable Development', in Gabriel, Y., ed. *Organizing Words: A Critical Thesaurus for Social and Organizational Studies*, pp. 292–4. Oxford: Oxford University Press, 2008.

5. Willett, W., Rockström, J., Loken, B., et al. 'Food in the Anthropocene: the EAT–*Lancet* Commission on healthy diets from sustainable food systems.' *The Lancet* 393(10170), 2 February 2019: 447–92. https://doi.org/10.1016/S0140-6736(18)31788-4.

6. Macdiarmid, J. 'Is a healthy diet an environmentally sustainable diet?' *Proceedings of the Nutrition Society* 72(1), 2012: 13–20. https://doi.org/10.1017/S0029665112002893.

7. Brundtland, G. H. *Our Common Future: Report of the World Commission on Environment and Development (WCED) Chaired by Gro Harlem Brundtland.* Oxford: Oxford University Press, 1987.

8. Lang, T. and Mason, P. 'Sustainable Diets: A Bundle of Policy Problems in Search of Answers', in Burlingame, B. and Dernini, S., eds. *Sustainable Diets: Transdisciplinary Imperative.* Wallingford: CABI, 2018.

9. Elkington, J. *Cannibals With Forks: The Triple Bottom Line of 21st Century Business.* Oxford: Capstone, 1997.

10. Mason, P. and Lang, T. *Sustainable Diets: How Ecological Nutrition Can Transform Consumption and the Food System.* Abingdon: Routledge Earthscan, 2017.

11. Bruce-Lockhart, C. and Terazono, E. 'From bean to cup, what goes into the cost of your coffee? Farmers get just 1p from a £2.50 brew, so why is your morning brew so expensive?' *Financial Times*, 4 June 2019.

12. Englberger, L., Aalbersberg, W., Ravi, P., et al. 'Further analysis on Micronesian banana, taro, breadfruit and other foods for provitamin carotenoids and minerals'. *Journal of Food Composition and Analysis* 16, 2003: 219–36.

13. Englberger, L. 'Revisiting the Vitamin A fiasco: going local in Micronesia', in Burlingame, B. and Dernini, S., eds. Sustainable Diets and Biodiversity: Directions and Solutions for Policy, Research and Action, pp. 126–33. Rome: Food and Agriculture Organisation of the United Nations, and Bioversity International, 2010.

14.   Banana Link. Who earns what from field to supermarket? Norwich:
      Banana Link, 2018. http://www.bananalink.org.uk/who-earns-what-from-
      field-to-supermarket (accessed 24 July 2019).

15.   Mendick, R. 'Sour truth behind Morrisons' "For Farmers" milk'. *Daily
      Telegraph*, 14 November 2018.

16.   Sharpe, R. P., Barling, D. and Lang, T. 'Ethical Traceability in the UK
      Wheat–Flour–Bread Chain', in Coff, C., Barling, D., Korthals, M., et al.,
      eds. *Ethical Traceability and Communicating Food*, pp. 125–65. New York:
      Springer, 2008.

17.   Howard, P. H. *Concentration and Power in the Food System: Who Controls
      What We Eat?* London: Bloomsbury, 2016.

18.   Brexit: Future UK agriculture policy. Briefing number 8218, 31 January
      2018. London: House of Commons Library, 2018.

19.   Defra. Health and harmony: the future for food, farming and the
      environment in a Green Brexit. Cm 9577. London: Department for
      Environment, Food and Rural Affairs, 2018.

20.   Strutt and Parker. Farm support, the new Environmental Land
      Management system and the funding gap – reports 1 & 2. London: Strutt
      and Parker, June and September, 2019.

21.   Food, Farming and Countryside Commission. *Fork in the Road*. London:
      Royal Society of Arts, 2019.

22.   Food, Farming and Countryside Commission. Field guide for the future.
      London: Royal Society of Arts, 2019.

23.   Murray, C. J. 'Health effects of dietary risks in 195 countries, 1990–2017:
      a systematic analysis for the Global Burden of Disease Study 2017. *The
      Lancet* 393(10184), 11 May 2019: 1958–72 (published online 3 April 2019).
      https://doi.org/10.1016/S0140-6736(19)30041-8.

24.   NHS. Health – food and diet: Poor diet now killing more than smoking.
      London: National Health Service, 2019. https://www.nhs.uk/news/food-
      and-diet/poor-diet-now-killing-more-than-smoking/.

25.   Scarborough, P., Bhatnagar, P., Wickramasinghe, K. K., et al. 'The
      economic burden of ill health due to diet, physical inactivity, smoking,
      alcohol and obesity in the UK: an update to 2006–07 NHS costs'. *Journal
      of Public Health* 33(4), December 2011: 527–35. https://doi.org/10.1093/
      pubmed/fdr033.

26.   NHS. Health matters: obesity and the food environment – The costs
      of obesity. London: National Health Service, 2017. https://www.gov.
      uk/government/publications/health-matters-obesity-and-the-food-
      environment/health-matters-obesity-and-the-food-environment--2
      (accessed 29 July 2019).

27. Kanavos, P., van den Aardweg, S. and Schurer, W. Diabetes expenditure, burden of disease and management in 5 EU countries. London: LSE Health, London School of Economics, 2012.

28. Murphy-Bokern, Donal. *Environmental impacts of the UK food economy with particular reference to WWF Priority Places and the North-East Atlantic*. Godalming: WWF, 2008.

29. Lamb, H. *Fighting the Banana Wars and Other Fairtrade Battles*. London: Rider/Ebury, 2008.

30. Barratt Brown, M. *Fair Trade: Reform and Realities in the International Trading System*. London: Zed Press, 1993.

31. Groceries Code Adjudicator. What Groceries Code Adjudicator does. London: HM Government, 2019. https://www.gov.uk/government/organisations/groceries-code-adjudicator (accessed 29 July 2019).

32. Lee, M. M., Falbe, J., Schillinger, D., et al. 'Sugar-sweetened beverage consumption 3 years after the Berkeley, California, sugar-sweetened beverage tax'. *American Journal of Public Health* 109(4), 2019: 637–9.

33. Crist, E., Mora, C. and Engelman, R. 'The interaction of human population, food production, and biodiversity protection'. *Science* 356, 2017: 260–64.

34. Ripple, W. J., Wolf, C., Newsome, T. M., et al. 'World scientists' warning to humanity: a second notice'. *BioScience* 67(12), December 2017: 1026–8. https://doi.org/10.1093/biosci/bix125.

35. Dowler, C. Revealed: the millionaires hoarding UK fishing rights. London: Unearthed/Greenpeace, 2018.

36. Bonham-Carter, V. *The Survival of the English Countryside*. London: Hodder and Stoughton, 1971.

37. Willett, Rockström, Loken, et al. 'Food in the Anthropocene'.

38. Clark, M., Tilman, D. 'Comparative analysis of environmental impacts of agricultural production systems, agricultural input efficiency, and food choice'. *Environmental Research Letters* 12(6), 2017; https://doi.org/10.1088/1748-9326/aa6cd5/meta.

39. Defra. Agriculture in the UK 2017. London: Department for Environment, Food and Rural Affairs, 2018.

40. EA. The state of the environment: water resources. London: Environment Agency, 2018.

41. Phelps, L. N. and Kaplan, J. O. 'Land use for animal production in global change studies: Defining and characterizing a framework'. *Global Change Biology* 23(11), 2017: 4457–71. https://doi.org/10.1111/gcb.13732.

42. Margulis, L. and Sagan, D. *Microcosmos*. New York: Touchstone, 1986.

43. Fraser, E. D. G. and Rimas, A. *Empires of Food: Feast, Famine and the Rise and Fall of Civilizations*. London: Random House, 2010.

44. Rae, A. Land cover atlas of the United Kingdom. Sheffield: Sheffield University Department of Urban Studies and Planning, 2017.

45. CCC. Land use: reducing emissions and preparing for climate change. London: Committee on Climate Change, 2018.

46. EA. Environment Agency Chair calls for new approach to flood and coastal resilience. Press release, 9 May 2019. Rotherham: Environment Agency, 2019.

47. BEIS. Digest of UK energy statistics (DUKES). London: Department for Business, Energy and Industrial Strategy, 2018.

48. BEIS, Office for National Statistics. 2017 UK greenhouse gas emissions, provisional figures. London: Department for Business, Energy and Industrial Strategy, 2018.

49. CCC. UK climate change risk assessment 2017: synthesis report – priorities for the next five years. London: Committee on Climate Change, 2016. Challinor, A., Adger, W. N., Di Mauro, M., et al. UK climate change risk assessment evidence report; chapter 7, 'International dimensions'. Report prepared for the Adaptation Sub-Committee of the CCC, London. London: Committee on Climate Change, 2016.

50. ONS. Final UK greenhouse gas emissions national statistics: 1990–2016. London: HM Government/Office for National Statistics, 2018.

51. Poore, J. and Nemecek, T. 'Reducing food's environmental impacts through producers and consumers'. *Science* 360(6392), 1 June 2018: 987–92. https://doi.org/10.1126/science.aaq0216.

52. Scarborough, P., Appleby, P. N., Mizdrak, A., et al. 'Dietary greenhouse gas emissions of meat-eaters, fish-eaters, vegetarians and vegans in the UK'. *Climatic Change* 125(2), July 2014: 179–92. https://doi.org/10.1007/s10584-014-1169-1.

53. Behrens, P., Kiefte-de Jong, J. C., Bosker, T., et al. 'Evaluating the environmental impacts of dietary recommendations'. *Proceedings of the National Academies of Science* 114(51), 4 December 2017: 13412–17. https://doi.org/10.1073/pnas.1711889114.

54. Warwick HRI and Biffa. Nitrogen UK, 2005.

55. Bauer, S. E., Tsigaridis, K., Miller, R. 'Significant atmospheric aerosol pollution caused by world food cultivation'. *Geophysical Research Letters* 43(10), 28 May 2016: 5394–5400.

56. Air Quality Expert Group. Air pollution from agriculture. London: Department for Environment, Food and Rural Affairs; Scottish

Government; Welsh Government; and Department of the Environment in Northern Ireland, 2018.

57. Misselbrook, T. H., Gilhespy, S. L., Cardenas, L. M., et al. Inventory of ammonia emissions from UK agriculture 2014 (Submission report November 2015). DEFRA Contract SCF0102. London: Department for Environment, Food and Rural Affairs, 2015.

58. Rockström, J., Steffen, W., Noone, K., et al. 'A safe operating space for humanity'. *Nature* 461(7263), 2009: 472–5.

59. Steffen, W., Richardson, K., Rockström, J., et al. 'Planetary boundaries: Guiding human development on a changing planet'. *Science* 347(6223), 2015: 1259855. https://doi.org/10.1126/science.1259855.

60. Ibid.

61. Reay, D. *Nitrogen and Climate Change: An Explosive Story*. Basingstoke: Palgrave Macmillan, 2015.

62. Stern, N. *The Stern Review of the economics of climate change. Final report.* London: HM Treasury, 2006.

63. Environmental Audit Committee. UK progress on reducing nitrate pollution. Eleventh report of session 2017–19. HC656. London: House of Commons, 2018.

64. Withers, P. J. A., Forber, K. G., Lyon, C., et al. 'Towards resolving the phosphorus chaos created by food systems'. *Ambio* (published online 21 September 2019). https://doi.org/10.1007/s13280-019-01255-1.

65. Ibid.

66. WWAP, UN-Water. United Nations world water development report 2018: nature-based solutions for water. Paris: UNESCO and United Nations World Water Assessment Programme, 2018.

67. NIC. Announcement of National Resilience Study (due to report 2020): New resilience study to examine how infrastructure can withstand future challenges. London: National Infrastructure Commission, 2018.

68. NIC. Preparing for a drier future: England's water infrastructure needs. London: National Infrastructure Commission, 2018.

69. EFRA Committee. Regulation of the water industry. Eighth report of session 2017–19. HC 1041. London: House of Commons Environment, Food and Rural Affairs Committee, 2018.

70. EA. State of the environment.

71. Ibid.

72. Moncrieff, C. and Draisey, Z. Saving the Earth: a sustainable future for soils and water. Woking: WWF-UK, Angling Trust and Rivers Trust, 2018.

73. Allan, J. A. 'Virtual water – the water, food and trade nexus: useful concept or misleading metaphor?' *Water International* 28(1), March 2003: 4–11.

74. Allan, J. A. *Virtual Water: Tackling the Threat to Our Planet's Most Precious Resource.* 1st edn. London: I. B. Tauris, 2011.

75. Hess, T. and Sutcliffe C. 'The exposure of a fresh fruit and vegetable supply chain to global water-related risks'. *Water International* 43(6), 2018: 746–61. https://doi.org/10.1080/02508060.2018.1515569 (published online 15 October 2018).

76. Sutcliffe, C. and Hess, T. The global avocado crisis and resilience in the UK's fresh fruit and vegetable supply system. Swindon: Global Food Security Programme, 2017.

77. Allan. 'Virtual water – the water, food and trade nexus'.

78. Allan. *Virtual Water.*

79. Elliott, J. and Tipper, W. A. Protecting standards in UK food and farming through Brexit. London: Green Alliance, 2018.

80. Keane, B. 'Meat-free diets could cut our "water footprint" in half, say scientists'. *The Conversation*, 10 September 2018. http://theconversation.com/meat-free-diets-could-cut-our-water-footprint-in-half-say-scientists-102926.

81. Vanham, D., Comero, S., Gawlik, B. M., et al. 'The water footprint of different diets within European sub-national geographical entities'. *Nature Sustainability* 1(9), 10 September 2018: 518–25.

82. Damkjaer, S. and Taylor, R. 'The measurement of water scarcity: Defining a meaningful indicator' *Ambio* 46(5), September 2017: 513–31.

83. Rice Association. Rice in the UK. London: Rice Association/Nabim, 2019. http://www.riceassociation.org.uk/content/1/3/rice-in-the-uk.html.

84. Chapagain, A. K. and Hoekstra, A. Y. The green, blue and grey water footprint of rice from both a production and consumption perspective. Value of Water Research Report Series No. 40. Delft and Twente, NL: UNESCO–IHE Institute for Water Education, 2010.

85. Ercin, A. E., Aldaya, M. M. and Hoekstra, A. Y. The water footprint of soy milk and soy burger and equivalent animal products. Delft, NL: UNESCO–IHE Institute for Water Education, 2011.

86. Worldpanel K. Sparkling growth: bottled water value sales. *The Grocer* 241(8397), 2019.

87. Arthur, R. 'UK bottled water sales reach 4bn litres, with "robust growth" to continue'. *Beveragedaily.com*, 14 March 2019.

88. Haygarth, P. and Ritz, K. 'The future of soils and land use in the UK: soil systems for the provision of land-based ecosystem services'. *Land Use Policy* 26(Supp 1), 2009: S187–97.

89. Willis, G. Back to the land: Rethinking our approach to soil. London: Campaign for the Protection of Rural England, 2018.

90. Withers, P., Edwards, A. C. and Foy, B. 'Phosphorus cycling in UK agriculture and implications for phosphorus loss from soil'. *Soil Use and Management* 17(3), 2006: 139–49. https://doi.org/10.1111/j.1475-2743.2001. tb00020.x.

91. Juniper, T. *What Nature Does for Britain*. London: Profile Books, 2015.

92. Mihelcic, J. R., Fry, L. M. and Shaw, R. 'Global potential of phosphorus recovery from human urine and feces'. *Chemosphere* 84(6), August 2011: 832–9.

93. Kasprak, A. 'The desert rock that feeds the world: A dispute over Western Sahara's phosphate reserves could disrupt food production around the globe'. *The Atlantic*, 29 November 2016.

94. Graves, A. R., Morris, J., Deeks, L. K., et al. 'The total costs of soil degradation in England and Wales'. *Ecological Economics* 119, November 2015: 399–413.

95. Moncrieff and Draisey. Saving the Earth.

96. EAC. Soil health. London: House of Commons Environmental Audit Committee, 2016.

97. POST. Securing UK soil health. London: Parliamentary Office on Science and Technology, 2015.

98. SSA. Facts & figures. https://sustainablesoils.org/facts-figures-1/. Sustainable Soils Alliance, 2017.

99. Edmondson, J. L., Davies, Z. G., Gaston, K. J., et al. 'Urban cultivation in allotments maintains soil qualities adversely affected by conventional agriculture'. *Journal of Applied Ecology* 51(4), August 2014: 880–89. https://doi.org/10.1111/1365-2664.12254.

100. Defra. Science and research projects: the total costs of soil degradation in England and Wales. SP1606. London: Department for Environment, Food and Rural Affairs, 2011.

101. Food, Farming and Countryside Commission. Field guide for the future.

102. IPBES. Summary for Policymakers (SPM) of the IPBES Assessment Report on land degradation and Restoration, Bonn: Intergovernmental Science-Policy Platform on Biodiversity and Ecosystem Services, 2018.

103. Silva, V., Mol, H. G. J. and Zomer, P., et al. 'Pesticide residues in European agricultural soils – a hidden reality unfolded'. *Science of the Total Environment* 653, 25 February 2019: 1532–45.

104. PAN-UK. The hidden rise of UK pesticide use: Fact-checking an industry claim. Brighton: Pesticides Action Network UK, 2018.

105. Taskforce on Systemic Pesticides. 'Worldwide Integrated Assessment of the impact of systemic pesticides on biodiversity and ecosystems'. *Environmental Science and Pollution Research*, 22(1), 2015: 1–154.

106. Bozzini, E. *Pesticide Policy and Politics in the European Union: Regulatory Assessment, Implementation and Enforcement.* London: Palgrave Macmillan, 2017.

107. Cohen, J., Mole, N. and Tyrrell, K. Brexit and pesticides: UK agriculture at a crossroads. London: Food Research Collaboration, 2018.

108. Ramandutty, N., Mehrabi, Z., Waha, K., et al. 'Trends in global agricultural land use: implications for environmental health and food security'. *Annual Review of Plant Biology* 69, 2018: 789–815. https://doi.org/10.1146/annurev-arplant-042817-040256

109. Landrigan, P. J., Fuller, R., Acosta, N. J. R., et al. '*Lancet* Commission on Pollution and Health'. *The Lancet* 391(10119), 2017: 462–512. http://dx.doi.org/10.1016/S0140-6736(17)32345-0.

110. CBD. Text of the Convention on Biological Diversity. Rio de Janeiro: Convention on Biological Diversity, 1992.

111. CBD. Strategic Plan 2011–2020: Aichi Biological Diversity Targets. Rome: Convention on Biological Diversity, 2010.

112. JNCC. Biodiversity Indicators 2018: C1 Protected Areas. Peterborough: Joint Nature Conservation Committee, 2018.

113. JNCC. UK Post-2010 Biodiversity Framework: Implementation Plan. 1st Annual Report. Peterborough: Joint Nature Conservation Committee, 2013.

114. Defra. UK Biodiversity Indicators 2018. London Department for Environment, Food and Rural Affairs; Scottish Government; Welsh Assembly Government; Department of Agriculture, Environment and Rural Affairs of Northern Ireland; and Office of National Statistics, 2018.

115. JNCC. 6th National Report to the Convention on Biological Diversity – United Kingdom of Great Britain and Northern Ireland. Peterborough: Joint Nature Conservation Committee, 2019.

116. Hayhow, D. B., Burns, F., Eaton, M. A., et al. State of nature. Sandy: State of Nature Partnership [fifty conservation organizations], 2016.

117. Ibid.

118. Defra. Wild bird populations in England, 1970 to 2017. London: Department for Environment, Food and Rural Affairs, 2018.

119. NFFN. What is the Nature Friendly Farming Network? St Neots, Cambs.: Nature Friendly Farming Network, 2019. https://www.nffn.org.uk/.

120. JNCC. Biodiversity Indicators 2018: C1 Protected Areas.

121. Marine Management Organisation, Centre for Environment, Fisheries and Aquaculture Science. Blue Belt Programme annual update: financial year 2017/18. London: HM Government, 2018.

122. Tree, I. *Wilding: The Return of Nature to a British Farm*. London: Picador, 2018.

123. Monbiot, G. *Feral: Searching for Enchantment on the Frontiers of Rewilding*. London: Allen Lane, 2013.

124. Lachat, C., Raneri, J. E., Smith, K. W., et al. 'Dietary species richness as a measure of food biodiversity and nutritional quality of diets'. *Proceedings of the National Academies of Science* 115(1), 2 January 2018: 127–32 (published online 9 November 2017). http://dx.doi.org/10.1073/pnas.1709194115.

125. Tutwiler, A. Mainstreaming agrobiodiversity in sustainable food systems: the value of an agrobiodiversity index. Rome: International Institute for Sustainable Development – SDG Knowledge Hub, 2016.

126. Khoury, C. K., Achicanoy, H. A., Bjorkman, A. D., et al. 'Origins of food crops connect countries worldwide'. *Proceedings of the Royal Society B*. 283(1832), 15 June 2016. http://dx.doi.org/10.1098/rspb.2016.0792.

127. EEA. Public awareness: biodiversity (data from special Eurobarometer 436). Copenhagen: European Environment Agency and Directorate-General Environment of the European Commission, 2017.

128. Defra, ONS. Attitudes and knowledge relating to biodiversity and the natural environment, 2007–2011: from the Survey of Public Attitudes and Behaviour towards the Environment. London: Department for the Environment, Food and Rural Affairs, 2011.

129. Eurobarometer. Attitudes towards biodiversity. Flash Eurobarometer 379. Brussels: Eurobarometer of the EU, 2013.

130. Laville, S. and Taylor, M. 'Nearly 1m tonnes every year: supermarkets shamed for plastic packaging'. *Guardian*, 17 January 2018.

131. 'Power list: packaging'. *The Grocer*, 16 May 2018, pp. 26–33.

132. Laville, S. 'Chinese ban on plastic waste imports could see UK pollution rise'. *Guardian*, 7 December 2017.

133. Quinn, I. 'Wrap's UK pact on plastic is "world first initiative"'. *The Grocer*, 2018(4).

134. Lebreton, L., Slat, B., Ferrari, F., et al. 'Evidence that the Great Pacific Garbage Patch is rapidly accumulating plastic'. *Scientific Reports* 8(1), 22 March 2018: article no. 4666. http://dx.doi.org/10.1038/s41598-018-22939-w.

135. Geyer, R., Jambeck, J. R. and Lavender Law, K. 'Production, use, and fate of all plastics ever made'. *Science Advances* 3(7), 19 July 2017: e1700782. http://dx.doi.org/10.1126/sciadv.1700782.

136. Secretariat of the Convention on Biological Diversity. Impacts of marine debris on biodiversity: current status and potential solutions. Montreal: Convention on Biological Diversity, Scientific and Technical Advisory Panel of the Global Environment Facility (GEF) and UN Environment Programme, 2012.

137. Li, J., Green, C., Reynolds, A., et al. 'Microplastics in mussels sampled from coastal waters and supermarkets in the United Kingdom'. *Environmental Pollution* 241, October 2018: 35–44. http://dx.doi.org/10.1016/j.envpol.2018.05.038.

138. ITV. 'All wild and shop-bought mussels tested in UK ingested plastics, study shows'. London: ITV Reports, 2018.

139. Environmental Investigation Agency, Greenpeace UK. Checking out on plastics: a survey of UK supermarkets' plastic habits. London: Greenpeace UK, November 2018.

140. Alliance to End Plastic Waste. Addressing an issue of global proportions. London: Alliance to End Plastic Waste, 2018.

141. Hetu. The Refill-Larder Shop, 201 St John's Hill, London SW11 1TH. www.hetu.co.uk. 2018.

142. Hines, C. Food co-ops: How to save money by getting together and buying in bulk. London: Friends of the Earth, 1976.

143. WEN. Low packaging aisles. London: Women's Environmental Network, 2004.

144. BBC News. 'Bring your own containers, says Waitrose'. London: BBC, 4 June 2019. https://www.bbc.co.uk/news/business-48498346 (accessed 5 June 2019).

145. European Commission. Closing the loop: Commission adopts ambitious new Circular Economy Package to boost competitiveness, create jobs and generate sustainable growth. Brussels: European Commission, 2015.

146. European Commission. The Circular Economy: Communication 'Towards a circular economy: a zero waste programme for Europe'. Brussels: European Commission, 2014. http://ec.europa.eu/environment/circular-economy/index_en.htm.

147.   Ellen MacArthur Foundation. The new plastics economy: Rethinking the
       future of plastic. Cowes: Ellen MacArthur Foundation, World Economic
       Forum and McKinsey & Company, 2016.

148.   Nestlé UK. Press release: Nestlé accelerates action to tackle plastic waste.
       Croydon: Nestlé UK, 15 January 2019.

149.   Kropotkin, P. A. *Fields, Factories and Workshops: or Industry Combined
       with Agriculture and Brain Work with Manual Work*, new edn. London:
       S. Sonnenschein, 1901.

150.   Herrero, M., Thornton, P. K., Power, B., et al. 'Farming and the geography
       of nutrient production for human use: a transdisciplinary analysis'.
       The Lancet Planetary Health 1(1), 1 April 2017: e33–42. http://dx.doi.
       org/10.1016/S2542-5196(17)30007-4.

151.   Ricciardi, V., Ramankutty, N., Mehrabi, Z., et al. 'How much of the world's
       food do smallholders produce?' *Global Food Security* 17, June 2018: 64–72.

152.   Willis, G. Uncertain harvest: does the loss of farms matter? London:
       Campaign for Protection of Rural England, 2017.

153.   HSE. Fatal injuries in agriculture, forestry and fishing in Great Britain
       2018/19. London: Health and Safety Executive, 2019.

154.   FSA. Biannual public attitudes tracker: Wave 13. Food Standards Agency
       Social Science Team. London: Food Standards Agency, 2017.

155.   SERIO. Understanding of consumer attitudes and actual purchasing
       behaviour, with reference to local and regional foods – report to DEFRA.
       Plymouth: University of Plymouth Socio-Economic Research and
       Intelligence Observatory, 2008.

156.   Mintel. Attitudes to healthy eating – UK – February 2015. London:
       Mintel, 2015.

157.   Mintel. The ethical food consumer UK 2015 report. London: Mintel,
       2015.

158.   WRAP. Consumer attitudes to food waste and food packaging. Banbury:
       Waste Resources Action Programme, 2013.

159.   Kemp, K., Insch, A., Holdsworth, D. K., et al. Food miles: Do UK
       consumers actually care? *Food Policy*. 35(6), 2010: 504–13.

160.   Poore and Nemecek. 'Reducing food's environmental impacts'.

161.   Committee on Climate Change. Land use.

162.   Strutt and Parker. Farm support, the new Environmental Land
       Management system and the funding gap – reports 1 and 2. London: Strutt
       and Parker, June and September, 2019.

163.   Gerber, P. J., Steinfeld, H., Henderson, B., et al. Tackling climate change
       through livestock – a global assessment of emissions and mitigation

opportunities. Rome: Food and Agriculture Organization of the United Nations, 2013.

164. Steinfeld, H., Gerber, P., Wassenaar, T., et al. Livestock's long shadow: environmental issues and options. Rome: Food and Agriculture Organization of the United Nations, 2006.

165. Buckwell, A., Nadeu, E., Mathijs, E., et al. What is the safe operating space for EU livestock? Brussels: The Rural Investment Support for Europe (RISE) Foundation, 2018.

166. Tree. *Wilding*.

167. Gerbens-Leenes, P. W., Nonhebel, S. and Ivens, W. P. M. F. 'A method to determine land requirements relating to food consumption patterns'. *Agriculture Ecosystems and Environment* 90, 2002: 47–58.

168. FCRN. Feed conversion. Oxford: Food Climate Research Network, 2018. https://www.fcrn.org.uk/research-library/feed-conversion-efficiency-aquaculture-do-we-measure-it-correctly (accessed 10 March 2019).

169. Tolkamp, B., Wall, E., Roehe, R., et al. Review of nutrient efficiency in different breeds of farm livestock. Project IF0183 for the Department of Environment, Food and Rural Affairs. Penicuik: Scottish Agricultural College, 2010.

170. Cassidy, E. S., West, P. C., Gerber, J. S., et al. 'Redefining agricultural yields: from tonnes to people nourished per hectare'. *Environmental Research Letters* 8, 2013: 034015. http://dx.doi.org/10.1088/1748-9326/8/3/034015.

171. Berners-Lee, M., Kennelly, C., Watson, R., et al. 'Current global food production is sufficient to meet human nutritional needs in 2050 provided there is radical societal adaptation'. *Elementa: Science of the Anthropocene* 6(1), 2018: 52: http://doi.org/10.1525/elementa.310.

172. Mottet, A., de Haan, C., Falcucci, A., et al. 'Livestock: On our plates or eating at our table? A new analysis of the feed/food debate'. *Global Food Security* 14, September 2017: 1–8.

173. Tolkamp, Wall, Roehe, et al. Review of nutrient efficiency in different breeds of farm livestock.

174. Cassidy, West, Gerber, et al. 'Redefining agricultural yields'.

175. Ranganathan, J., Waite, R., Searchinger, T., et al. How to sustainably feed 10 billion people by 2050. Washington DC: World Resources Institute, 2018.

176. Tanner, T. and Rana, A. Foodprint: The Event. 25 July. London: Sustainable Restaurant Association, 2019.

177. PFLA. Pasture for life. Cirencester: Pasture-fed Livestock Association, 2018. https://www.pastureforlife.org/.

178. Food, Farming and Countryside Commission. Our future in the land – final report.

179. Searchinger, T. D., Wirsenius, S., Beringer, T., et al. 'Assessing the efficiency of changes in land use for mitigating climate change'. *Nature* 564(7735), 2018: 249–53.

180. Tilman, D. and Clark, M. 'Global diets link environmental sustainability and human health'. *Nature* 515(7528), 2014: 518–22. http://dx.doi.org/10.1038/nature13959.

181. Evans, S. 'Analysis: UK's CO2 emissions fell for record sixth consecutive year in 2018'. *Carbon Brief* 2019. https://www.carbonbrief.org/analysis-uks-co2-emissions-fell-for-record-sixth-consecutive-year-in-2018.

182. Cassidy, West, Gerber, et al. 'Redefining agricultural yields'.

183. Foley, J. A., Ramankutty, N., Brauman, K. A., et al. 'Solutions for a cultivated planet'. *Nature* 478(7369), 2011: 337–42.

184. Tree. *Wilding*.

185. Battle, L. 'Rewilding revives a country estate: The Knepp Estate ceased farming to become a natural habitat that attracts wildlife, environmentalists and campers'. *Financial Times*, 28 September 2018.

186. IPCC. Climate change and land – IPCC special report on climate change, desertification, land degradation, sustainable land management, food security, and greenhouse gas fluxes in terrestrial ecosystems. Geneva: Intergovernmental Panel on Climate Change, 2019.

187. Scottish Government. Statistics. Health and Community Care: Health of Scotland's population – Diet. https://www2.gov.scot/Topics/Statistics/Browse/Health/TrendDiet (accessed 20 March 2019). Edinburgh: Scottish Government, 2017.

188. Defra. Horticulture statistics 2017. London: Department for Environment, Food and Rural Affairs, 2018.

189. Kentish Cobnuts Association. About us: https://kentishcobnutsassociation.org.uk/. West Malling, Kent, 2019.

190. CALU. CALU technical note 050402: Hazel and walnut production. Bangor: Bangor University Centre for Alternative Land Use, 2006.

191. O'Neil, C. E., Keast, D. R., Nicklas, T. A., et al. 'Nut consumption is associated with decreased health risk factors for cardiovascular disease and metabolic syndrome in U.S. adults: NHANES 1999–2004'. *Journal of the American College of Nutrition* 30(6), 2011: 502–10.

192. AHDB. UK cattle yearbook 2018. Stoneleigh Park, Warwickshire: Agriculture and Horticulture Development Board, 2019.

193. AHDB. Monthly slaughter statistics, February 2019. Stoneleigh Park, Warwickshire: Agriculture and Horticulture Development Board, 2019. http://beefandlamb.ahdb.org.uk/markets/industry-reports/uk-statistics/.

194. Stevenson, P. J. Industrial livestock production: the twin myths of efficiency and necessity. Godalming: Compassion in World Farming, 2015.

195. Pickett, H. Nutritional benefits of higher welfare animals. Godalming: Compassion in World Farming, 2012.

196. Steinfeld, H., Gerber, P., Wassenaar, T., et al. Livestock's long shadow: environmental issues and options. Rome: Food and Agricultural Organization, 2006.

197. Gerber, P., Steinfeld, H., Henderson, B., et al. Tackling climate change through livestock: a global assessment of emissions and mitigation opportunities. http://www.fao.org/3/i3437e.pdf (accessed 3 March 2014). Rome: Food and Agricultural Organization, 2013.

198. Delgado, C. L., Rosegrant, M. W., Steinfeld, H., et al. 'Livestock to 2020: the next food revolution'. *Outlook on Agriculture* 30(1), 2001: 27–9.

199. WCRF. Diet, nutrition, physical activity and cancer: a global perspective. Third expert report. London: World Cancer Research Fund, 2018.

200. WCRF/AICR. Food, nutrition and the prevention of cancer: a global perspective. London and Washington DC: World Cancer Research Fund/American Institute for Cancer Research, 1997.

201. WCRF/AICR. Food, Nutrition, Physical Activity and the Prevention of Cancer: a Global Perspective. Washington DC / London: World Cancer Research Fund/American Institute for Cancer Research, 2007.

202. WCRF. Meat, fish and dairy products. London: World Cancer Research Fund/American Institute for Cancer Research, 2018.

203. Bouvard, V., Loomis, D., Guyton, K. Z., et al. 'Carcinogenicity of consumption of red and processed meat'. *The Lancet Oncology* 16(16), 1 December 2015: 1599–1600.

204. Ibid.

205. Scarborough, Appleby, Mizdrak, et al. 'Dietary greenhouse gas emissions of meat-eaters, fish-eaters, vegetarians and vegans in the UK'.

206. Glotz, J. 'Rising to the plant-based challenge – the future of meat'. *The Grocer*, 2018: 12–13.

207. Dietary Guidelines Advisory Committee. Scientific report of the 2015 Dietary Guidelines Advisory Committee. Washington (DC): USDA and US Department of Health and Human Services, 2015.

208. Nelson, M. E., Hamm, M. W., Hu, F. B., et al. 'Alignment of healthy dietary patterns and environmental sustainability: a systematic review'. *Advances in Nutrition* 7(6), 1 January 2016: 1005–25. doi:10.3945/an.116.012567.

209. Lang, T, and Mason, P. 'Sustainable diet policy development: implications of multi-criteria and other approaches, 2008–2017'. *Proceedings of the Nutrition Society* 77(3), December 2017: 1–16. doi:10.1017/S0029665117004074.

210. Hollywood, J. and Piri, M. Don't have a cow man: the prospects for lab grown meat. London: Adam Smith Institute, 2018.

211. Yu, D. 'Dairy and meat alternatives stay on top of U.S. food investors' mind'. *Forbes* (first published online 8 June 2019).

212. Cornish, C. 'Could we save the world if we all went vegan?' *Financial Times*, FT Magazine, 22 September 2018. https://www.ft.com/content/3b210ddc-bba0-11e8-8274-55b72926558f.

213. Willett, W., Rockström, J., Loken, B., et al. Supplementary Appendix to Willet, Rockström, Loken, et al. 'Food in the Anthropocene'. *The Lancet* 393(10170), 2019: 1–37. http://dx.doi.org/10.1016/S0140-6736(18)31788-4.

214. O'Sullivan, C. UK pig farmers support lifting the ban on feeding pigs with leftovers, while experts say safety concerns can be overcome. London: Feedback, 2018.

215. Macdiarmid, J. I., Clark, H., Whybrow, S., et al. 'Assessing national nutrition security: the UK reliance on imports to meet population energy and nutrient recommendations'. *PLoS ONE* 13(2), 2018: e0192649. http://dx.doi.org/10.1371/journal.pone.0192649.

216. PHE. Health matters: obesity and the food environment. London: Public Health England, 2017.

217. WCRF. Diet, nutrition, physical activity and cancer.

218. Eurostat. EU proportion of overweight and of obese women, 2014. Brussels: European Commission, 2017.

219. Diabetes UK. Number of people living with diabetes doubles in twenty years. London: Diabetes UK, 2018.

220. FSA, PHE. National diet and nutrition survey: results from years 7 and 8 (combined) of the Rolling Programme (2014/2015 to 2015/2016). London: NatCen, Food Standards Agency and Public Health England, 2018.

221. Roberts, C., Steer, T., Maplethorpe, N., et al. National diet and nutrition survey: results from years 7 and 8 (combined) of the Rolling Programme (2014/2015 to 2015/2016). London: Food Standards Agency and Public Health England, 2018.

222. Green, R., Milner, J., Dangour, A. D., et al. 'The potential to reduce greenhouse gas emissions in the UK through healthy and realistic dietary change'. *Climatic Change* 129(1–2), 2015: 253–65.

223. Milner, J., Green, R., Dangour, A. D., et al. 'Health effects of adopting low greenhouse gas emission diets in the UK'. *BMJ Open* 5(4), 2015. http://dx.doi.org/10.1136/bmjopen-2014-007364. doi: 10.1136/bmjopen-2014-007364.

224. OECD. Obesity update 2017. Paris: Organisation for Economic Cooperation and Development, 2017.

225. Ibid.

226. CEDAR, MRC Unit. Food Environment Assessment Tool (FEAT). Cambridge: University of Cambridge Centre for Diet and Activity Research and MRC Epidemiology Research Unit, 2017. http://www.feat-tool.org.uk/.

227. Duncan, P. and Butler, P. 'Children in poor areas exposed to five times as many fast food takeaways'. *Guardian*, 1 December 2017. https://www.theguardian.com/inequality/2017/dec/01/schoolchildren-poor-areas-exposed-fast-food-takeaways.

228. Ejlerskov, K. T., Stead, M., Adamson, A., et al. 'The nature of UK supermarkets' policies on checkout food and associations with healthfulness and type of food displayed: cross-sectional study'. *International Journal of Behavioral Nutrition and Physical Activity* 15(52), 2018. http://dx.doi.org/10.1186/s12966-018-0684-2.

229. Keaver, L. and Webber, L. Morbid obesity in England, Wales, and Scotland. Paper to European Congress on Obesity (ECO), Vienna, 23–26 May 2018. https://www.sciencedaily.com/releases/2018/05/180527105811.htm.

230. OECD. Obesity update 2017.

231. FSA, PHE. National diet and nutrition survey: results from years 7 and 8.

232. Food Foundation. Veg facts no. 44. London: Food Foundation, 2016.

233. PHE. Children consume more than a year's worth of sugar in 6 months. London: Public Health England, 2018.

234. PHE. Sugar reduction: the evidence for action. London: Public Health England, 2015.

235. Ejlerskov, Stead, Adamson, et al. 'The nature of UK supermarkets' policies on checkout food'.

236. Coker, T., Rumgay, H., Whiteside, E., et al. Paying the price: new evidence on the link between price promotions, purchasing of less healthy food and drink, and overweight and obesity in Great Britain. London: Cancer Research UK, 2019.

237. Richardson, B. and Winkler, J. Sugar reduction in post-Brexit UK: a supply-side policy agenda. London: Food Research Collaboration, 2019.

238. Monteiro, C. A., Moubarac, J.-C., Levy, R. B., et al. 'Household availability of ultra-processed foods and obesity in nineteen European countries'. *Public Health Nutrition* 21(1), 2018: 18–26.

239. Pickett, K. E., Kelly, S., Brunner, E., et al. 'Wider income gaps, wider waistbands? An ecological study of obesity and income inequality'. *Journal of Epidemiology and Community Health* 59(8), 2005: 670–74.

240. ONS. Statistical bulletin: Effects of taxes and benefits on UK household income, financial year ending 2017. London: Office for National Statistics, 2018.

241. Cominetti, N., Henehan, K. and Clarke, S. Low pay Britain 2019. London: Resolution Foundation, 2019.

242. Cheung, R. International comparisons of health and wellbeing in early childhood. London: Nuffield Trust and Royal College of Paediatrics and Child Health, 2018.

243. Soil Association. State of the nation: children's food in England 2018. Bristol: Soil Association, 2018.

244. Food Foundation. Children's future food inquiry. London: Food Foundation, 2019.

245. Food Foundation. The broken plate: the state of the nation's food health report. London: Food Foundation, 2019.

246. Foresight. Tackling obesities: future choices. London: Government Office of Science, 2007.

247. Hawkes, C., Russell, S., Isaacs, A., et al. What can be learned from the Amsterdam Healthy Weight programme to inform the policy response to obesity in England? Rapid response briefing paper. London: University College London Obesity Policy Research Unit (OPRU), 2017.

248. Rudolf, M., Perera, R., Swanston, D., et al. 'Observational analysis of disparities in obesity in children in the UK: Has Leeds bucked the trend?' *Pediatric Obesity* 14(9), 2019: e12529. http://dx.doi.org/10.1111/ijpo.12529.

249. Eating Better. Are ready meals ready for the future? Brighton: Eating Better coalition, 2018.

250. Pearce, S. 'UK pet food market hits new high'. *Pet Business World*, 4 April 2018. https://www.petbusinessworld.co.uk/news/feed/uk-pet-food-market-hits-new-high.

251. German, A. J., Woods, G. R. T., Holden, S. L., et al. 'Dangerous trends in pet obesity'. *Veterinary Record* 182(1), 2018: http://dx.doi.org/10.1136/vr.k2.

252. Scarborough, P., Allender, S., Clarke, D., et al. 'Modelling the health impact of environmentally sustainable dietary scenarios in the UK'. *European Journal of Clinical Nutrition* 66(6), 2012: 710–15.

253. Springmann, M., Mason-D'Croz, D., Robinson, S., et al. 'Health-motivated taxes on red and processed meat: a modelling study on optimal tax levels and associated health impacts'. *PLoS One* 13(11), 2018: e0204139. doi:10.1371/journal.pone.0204139.

254. Caro, D., Frederiksen, P., Thomsen, M., et al. Toward a more consistent combined approach of reduction targets and climate policy regulations: the illustrative case of a meat tax in Denmark. *Environmental Science & Policy* 76, October 2017: 78–81. http://dx.doi.org/10.1016/j.envsci. 2017.06.013.

255. Springmann, Mason-D'Croz, Robinson, et al. 'Health-motivated taxes on red and processed meat'.

256. Burnett, J. *A History of the Cost of Living*. Harmondsworth: Penguin Books, 1969.

257. ThoughtWorks. Conscious consumption replaces decadent waste society as Britain is on the brink of a food revolution. London: ThoughtWorks, 2018. https://www.thoughtworks.com/news/groceryretail2030 (accessed 4 August 2019).

258. Ibid.

259. Lang, T., Barling, D. and Caraher, M. *Food Policy: Integrating Health, Environment and Society*. Oxford: Oxford University Press, 2009.

260. Scarborough, P., Matthews, A., Eyles, H., et al. 'Reds are more important than greens: How UK supermarket shoppers use the different information on a traffic light nutrition label in a choice experiment'. *International Journal of Behavioral Nutrition and Physical Activity* 12, 2015: 151–60.

261. National Consumer Council and Sustainable Development Commission. I will if you will. Report of the Sustainable Consumption Roundtable. London: Sustainable Development Commission, 2006.

262. Lang, T. 'The school meals business'. *Critical Social Policy* 3(8), 1983: 117–28. http://dx.doi.org/10.1177/026101838300300809.

263. Swinburn, B. A., Kraak, V., Allender, S., et al. 'The global syndemic of obesity, undernutrition, and climate change: The *Lancet* Commission report'. *The Lancet* 393(10173), 2019: 791–846.

264. Swinburn, B., Sacks, G., Vandevijvere, S., et al. INFORMAS (International Network for Food and Obesity/Non-Communicable Diseases Research, Monitoring and Action Support): Overview and key principles. *Obesity Reviews* 14, 2013: 1–12.

265. OHA. A 'watershed' moment: Why it's prime time to protect children from junk food adverts. London: Obesity Health Alliance, 2017.

266. Statista. Advertising in the United Kingdom – statistics & facts, 2017. https://www.statista.com/topics/1747/advertising-in-the-united-kingdom/.

267. O'Dowd, A. 'Spending on junk food advertising is nearly 30 times what government spends on promoting healthy eating'. *British Medical Journal* 359, 2017: j4677. doi:10.1136/bmj.j4677.

268. Action on Sugar, Action on Salt, Children's Food Campaign. Nutrition, health and cartoon animation on food and drink packaging. London, 2019.

269. Food Foundation. UK's restrictions on junk food advertising to children. International Learning Series 3. London: Food Foundation, 2017.

270. WHO Europe. Evaluating implementation of the WHO set of recommendations on the marketing of foods and non-alcoholic beverages to children. Progress, challenges and guidance for next steps in the WHO European Region. Copenhagen: World Health Organization Regional Office for Europe, 2018.

271. Tatum, M. 'The dark side of digital'. *The Grocer*, 2018: 26–33.

272. Tatum, M. 'The rise of the CGI Instagram celebrity'. *The Grocer*, 2019: 31–3.

273. Murphy, H. 'Influencers captivate the advertising sector'. *Financial Times*, 13 July 2019.

274. Cairns, G., Angus, K., Hastings, G., et al. 'Systematic reviews of the evidence on the nature, extent and effects of food marketing to children. A retrospective summary'. *Appetite* 62(7), 2013: 209–15.

275. Hastings, G., Stead, M., Macdermott, L., et al. Review of research on the effects of food promotion to children. Final report to the Food Standards Agency by the Centre for Social Marketing, University of Strathclyde. London: Food Standards Agency, 2004.

276. ASA, CAP. Non-Broadcast Code. CAP Code: History of Self-Regulation. London: Advertising Standards Authority and Code of Advertising Practice, 2019. https://www.asa.org.uk/type/non_broadcast/code_section/history-of-self-regulation.html.

277. Mason, P. and Lang, T. *Sustainable Diets: How Ecological Nutrition Can Transform Consumption and the Food System.* Abingdon: Routledge Earthscan, 2017.

278. RCPCH. Position statement: breastfeeding in the UK. London: Royal College of Paediatrics and Child Health, 2018.

279. Mayor of London. The London Food Strategy: healthy and sustainable food for London. London: Greater London Authority, 2018.

280. Dadhich, J. P., Smith, J., Iellamo, A., et al. Report on carbon footprints due to milk formula. Delhi: International Baby Food Action Network Asia and Promotion Network of India, 2015.

281. WRAP. Estimates of food surplus and waste arisings in the UK. Banbury: Waste and Resources Action Programme, 2017. http://www.wrap.org.uk/ sites/files/wrap/Estimates_%20in_the_UK_Jan17.pdf.

282. EFRA Committee. Food waste in England: Eighth Report of Session 2016–17. HC 429. London: Environment, Food and Rural Affairs Committee, 2017.

283. WRAP. WRAP restates UK food waste figures to support united global action. Swindon: Waste and Resources Action Programme, 2018.

284. Evans, D. Blaming the consumer – once again: the social and material contexts of everyday food waste practices in some English households. *Critical Public Health* 21(4), 2011: 429–40.

285. Schneider, F. 'Wasting food: an insistent behaviour'. Waste – The Social Context. Edmonton, Canada: Conference, 2008. http://wwwifracuk/ waste/Reports/Wasting%20Food%20-%20An%20Insistentpdf.

286. Defra. Our waste, our resources: a strategy for England. London: Department for Environment, Food and Rural Affairs, 2018.

287. Stephenson, W. Why plastic recycling is so confusing. London: BBC News Science and Environment, 2018.

288. Laville. 'Chinese ban on plastic waste imports could see UK pollution rise'.

289. WRAP. Estimates of food surplus and waste arisings in the UK.

290. Defra. Reducing and managing waste: anaerobic digestion and energy recovery from waste. Policy statement. London: Department for Environment, Food and Rural Affairs, 2013.

291. OIES. Biogas: a significant contribution to decarbonizing gas markets? Oxford: University of Oxford, Oxford Institute for Energy Studies, 2017.

292. WRAP. WRAP: our history. Banbury: Waste and Resources Action Programme, 2019. http://www.wrap.org.uk/about-us/our-history (accessed 20 March 2019).

293. WRAP. Courtauld 2025: cutting the cost of food and drink. Banbury: Waste and Resources Action Programme, 2017. http://www.wrap.org.uk/ food-drink/business-food-waste/courtauld-2025.

294. Ellen MacArthur Foundation. Towards a circular economy: business rationale for an accelerated transition. Cowes: Ellen MacArthur Foundation, 2015.

295. World Economic Forum/Ellen MacArthur Foundation/McKinsey & Company. Towards the circular economy: Accelerating the scale-up across global supply chains. Geneva: World Economic Forum, 2014.

296. Feedback. The food waste scorecard: an assessment of supermarket action to address food waste. London: Feedback, 2018.

297. Champions 12.3. Washington DC: World Resources Institute, 2016. https://champions123.org/.

298. SRA. One Planet Plate 'Rules': London Sustainable Restaurant Association, 2018. https://www.oneplanetplate.org.

299. Winnow. London: Winnow, 2017. www.winnowsolutions.com.

300. Stuart, T. Waste: Uncovering the global food scandal. London: Penguin Books, 2009.

301. Defra/ONS. Statistics on waste managed by local authorities in England in 2017/18. London: Department for Environment, Food and Rural Affairs/Office for National Statistics, 2018.

302. FAO. Food wastage footprint & climate change. Rome: Food and Agricultural Organization of the United Nations, 2015.

303. INHERIT. An INHERIT policy road map. Brussels: EuroHealthNet, 2018.

304. EC Platform on food losses and food waste. Brussels: European Commission: Directorate-General for the Environment, 2017. https://webgate.ec.europa.eu/flwp/.

305. EC. Mandate of sub-group on date marking and food waste prevention. Brussels: European Commission: Directorate-General for Health and Food Safety, 2018. https://ec.europa.eu/food/safety/food_waste/eu_actions/date_marking_en (accessed 20 March 2019).

306. World Economic Forum/Ellen MacArthur Foundation/McKinsey & Company. Towards the circular economy.

307. Ellen MacArthur Foundation. Towards a circular economy. Cowes: Ellen MacArthur Foundation, 2013.

308. World Economic Forum/Ellen MacArthur Foundation/McKinsey & Company. Towards the Circular Economy.

309. Van Zanten, H. H. E. Feed sources for livestock: Recycling towards a green planet. PhD thesis. Wageningen: Wageningen University, 2016.

310. Van Zanten, H. H. E., Mollenhorst, H., van Middelaar, C. E., et al. 'Global food security: land use efficiency of livestock systems'. *International Journal of Life Cycle Assessment* 5, 2016: 747–58.

311. OECD. Income inequality (2017 figures: https://data.oecd.org/inequality/income-inequality.htm). Paris: Organisation for Economic Co-operation and Development, 2019.

312. Thompson, E. P. 'The Moral Economy of the English Crowd in the Eighteenth Century', in Thompson, E. P., ed. *Customs in Common,* pp. 185–258. Harmondsworth: Penguin Books, 1993 [1971]: 185–258.

313. Polanyi, K. *The Great Transformation.* Boston: Beacon Press, 1957 [1944].

314. Riches, G. *Food Bank Nations: Poverty, Corporate Charity and the Right to Food.* Abingdon: Routledge, 2018.

315. Riches, G. and Silvasti, T. First World Hunger Revisited: Food Charity or the Right to Food? 2nd edn. Basingstoke: Palgrave Macmillan, 2014.

316. Canadian Association of Food Banks. 'Something has to give': Food banks filling the policy gap in Canada. HungerCount 2003. Toronto: Canadian Association of Food Banks, 2003.

317. Caraher, M., Cavicchi, A., Griffith, C. J. Old crises on new plates or old plates for a new crisis? Food banks and food insecurity. *British Food Journal* 116(9), 2014. doi:10.1108/BFJ-08-2014-0285.

318. Hansard. Food Banks. Debate in the (UK) House of Commons, 18 December 2013. columns 806–55. London: Hansard, 2013. http://www.publications.parliament.uk/pa/cm201314/cmhansrd/cm131218/debtext/131218-0003.htm.

319. Loopstra, R., Reeves, A., Taylor-Robinson, D., et al. 'Austerity, sanctions, and the rise of food banks in the UK'. *British Medical Journal* 350(1775), 2015. doi:10.1136/bmj.h1775.

320. Webb, S.and Webb, B. *English Poor Law Policy.* London: Longmans, Green, 1910.

321. Beveridge, W. H. B. *Voluntary Action: A Report on Methods of Social Advance.* London: G. Allen & Unwin, 1948.

322. Beveridge, W. H. B. and Wells, A. F. *The Evidence for Voluntary Action: Being Memoranda by Organisations and Individuals, and Other Material Relevant to Voluntary Action.* London: George Allen and Unwin, 1949.

323. Cooper, N., Purcell, S. and Jackson, R. Below the breadline: the relentless rise of food poverty in Britain. Manchester: Church Action on Poverty/Oxfam/Trussell Trust, 2014.

324. Douglas, F., Ejebu, O.-Z., Garcia, A., et al. The nature and extent of food poverty. Glasgow: NHS Scotland, 2015.

325. Trussell Trust. End of year stats 2018–19. Salisbury: Trussell Trust, 2019.

326. Independent Food Aid Network/Goodwin, S. Mapping the UK's independent food banks. Glasgow: Independent Food Aid Network, 2018. http://www.foodaidnetwork.org.uk/mapping (accessed 21 March 2019).

327. Hird, S. 'Are retailers getting food banks right?' *The Grocer*, 241(8420), 2019: 26–31.

328. De Schutter, O., Riches, G., Tarasuk, V., et al. 'Food banks are no solution to poverty'. Letter to the *Guardian*. London: *Guardian*, 25 March 2019.

329. APPG Inquiry into Hunger UK. Feeding Britain: a strategy for zero hunger in England, Wales, Scotland and Northern Ireland. The report of the All-Party Parliamentary Inquiry into Hunger in the United Kingdom. London: All-Party Parliamentary Group on Hunger, 2014.

330. Ashton, J. R., Middleton, J., Lang, T., et al. 'Open letter to Prime Minister David Cameron on food poverty in the UK'. *The Lancet* 383(9929), 10 May 2014: 1631 doi:10.1016/S0140-6736(14)60536-5 (first published online 30 April 2014).

331. London Food Link. Beyond the food bank 2017: London food poverty profile. London: Sustain/London Food Link/Trust for London, 2017.

332. Caraher, M. and Furey, S. Is it appropriate to use surplus food to feed people in hunger? Short-term Band-Aid to more deep rooted problems of poverty. London: Food Research Collaboration, 2017.

333. Defra. Food statistics pocketbook 2018. London: Department for Environment, Food and Rural Affairs, 2019.

334. Citizens UK. The living wage campaign. London: Citizens UK, 2012. http://www.citizensuk.org/campaigns/living-wage-campaign/.

335. D'Arcy, C. and Corlett, A. Taking up the floor: Exploring the impact of the National Living Wage on employers. London: Resolution Foundation, 2015.

336. Living Wage Foundation. Life on low pay. London: Living Wage Foundation, 2018.

337. Scott, C., Sutherland, J. and Taylor, A. Affordability of the UK's Eatwell Guide. London: Food Foundation, 2018.

338. FSA. Food and you survey, Wave 4 (conducted 2016). London: Food Standards Agency, 2017.

339. Pereira, A. L., Handa, S. and Holmqvist, G. P. Prevalence and correlates of food insecurity among children across the globe. Florence: UNICEF Office of Research, 2017.

340. JRF Analysis Unit. UK poverty 2018. York: Joseph Rowntree Foundation, 2018.

341. SMC. Measuring poverty 2019. London: Social Metrics Commission, 2019.

342. Russell, C. A., Elia, M. and BAPEN. Nutrition screening surveys in hospitals in the UK, 2007–2011. Redditch: British Association for Parenteral and Enteral Nutrition, British Dietetic Association, Royal

College of Nursing, NHS England, Scottish Government and Welsh Government, 2014.

343. Alston P. Statement on visit to the United Kingdom, by Professor Philip Alston, United Nations Special Rapporteur on extreme poverty and human rights. Geneva: Office of the UN Commissioner for Human Rights, 2018.

344. Alston, P. Visit to the United Kingdom of Great Britain and Northern Ireland – Report of the Special Rapporteur on extreme poverty and human rights. UN General Assembly. Human Rights Council Forty-First Session 24 June–12 July 2019. Agenda item 3. A/HRC/41/39/Add.1. Geneva: UN Human Rights Council, 2019.

345. Lambie-Mumford, H., Crossley, D., Jensen, E., et al. Household food security in the UK: a review of food aid. London: Department for Environment, Food and Rural Affairs, 2014.

346. Sustain. Written submission – Visit by the UN Special Rapporteur on extreme poverty and human rights, Philip Alston, to the UK from 5 to 16 November 2018. London: Sustain, 2018.

347. Alston, P. Visit to the United Kingdom of Great Britain and Northern Ireland – Report of the Special Rapporteur on extreme poverty and human rights.

348. Worstall, T. Why we shouldn't believe a word of Philip Alston's UN report on poverty in the UK. London: Adam Smith Institute, 2019.

349. Booth, R. UN report compares Tory welfare policies to creation of workhouses. London: *Guardian*, 22 May 2019.

350. Helliwell, J. F., Layard, R. and Sachs, J. D., eds. World happiness report 2019. New York: Sustainable Development Solutions Network/Earth Institute, Columbia University, 2019.

351. Mann, E., Long, M. A., Stretesky, P. B., et al. 'A question of justice: Are holiday clubs serving the most deprived communities in England?' *Local Environment* 23(10), 2018: 1008–22. doi:10.1080/13549839.2018.1518415.

352. StepChange. The high cost of credit – a discussion paper on affordable credit alternatives. London: StephChange, 2017.

353. Cooper, Purcell and Jackson. Below the breadline.

354. Douglas, Ejebu, Garcia, et al. The nature and extent of food poverty.

355. Lambie-Mumford, Crossley, Jensen, et al. Household food security in the UK.

356. Leather, S. The making of modern malnutrition: an overview of food poverty in the UK. London: Caroline Walker Trust, 1996.

357. Walker, C. and Church, M. 'Poverty by administration: a review of supplementary benefits, nutrition and scale rates'. *Journal of Human Nutrition* 32, 1978: 5–18.

358. Nelson, M. and Naismith, D. 'The nutritional status of poor children'. *Journal of Human Nutrition* 33, 1979: 33–45.

359. Cole-Hamilton, I., Lang, T. Tightening belts: a report on the impact of poverty on food. 2nd edn. London: London Food Commission, 1986.

360. Lang, T. and Caraher, M. 'Food poverty and shopping deserts: what are the implications for health promotion policy and practice?' *Health Education Journal* 58(3), 1998: 202–11.

361. ONS. Wealth in Great Britain, Wave 5: 2014 to 2016. Main results from the fifth wave of the Wealth and Assets Survey covering the period July 2014 to June 2016. London: Office for National Statistics, 2018.

362. Oxfam International. Public good or private wealth: Oxfam inequality report 2019. Oxford: Oxfam International, 2019.

363. Joyce, R., Pope, T. and Roantree, B. Briefing note: the characteristics and incomes of the top 1%. London: Institute for Fiscal Studies, 2019.

364. SMC. Social mobility in Great Britain: fifth state of the nation report. London: Social Mobility Commission, 2017.

365. Padley, M. A minimum income standard for London 2018. London: Trust for London/Centre for Research in Social Policy, Loughborough University, 2019.

366. FSA. Food and your Survey, Wave 4 (conducted 2016).

367. Taylor, A. and Loopstra, R. Too poor to eat – food insecurity in the UK. London: Food Foundation, 2016.

368. End Hunger UK. Shocking figures show hidden hunger. London: End Hunger UK Coalition, 2018. http://endhungeruk.org/shocking-figures-showing-hidden-hunger-show-need-find/ (accessed 21 March 2019).

369. UK2070 Commission. Fairer and stronger: Rebalancing the UK economy – the First Report of the UK2070 Commission: Sheffield: University of Sheffield/University of Manchester/University College London/Lincoln Institute (USA), 2019.

370. LGA. The future of non-metropolitan England: the freedom to lead local places. The post-Brexit England Commission final report. London: Local Government Association, 2019.

371. UK2070 Commission. Fairer and stronger: Rebalancing the UK economy.

372. Darmon, N. and Drewnowski, A. 'Contribution of food prices and diet cost to socioeconomic disparities in diet quality and health: a systematic

review and analysis'. *Nutrition Reviews* 73(10), 2015: 643–60. doi:10.1093/nutrit/nuv027 (first published online 27 August 2015).

373. Boyd Orr, J. *Food, Health and Income: Report on Adequacy of Diet in Relation to Income*. London: Macmillan and Co., 1936.

374. Ostry, A. S. *Nutrition Policy in Canada, 1870–1939*. Vancouver: University of British Columbia Press, 2006.

375. IHE. Marmot indicators briefing, 18 July 2017. London: University College London Institute of Health Equity, 2017.

376. Booth, W. *In Darkest England, and the Way Out*. London: International Headquarters of The Salvation Army, 1890.

377. Engels, F. *The Condition of the Working Class in England in 1844*. Harmondsworth: Penguin Books, 1987 (1845/1892).

378. Rowntree, B. S. *Poverty: A Study of Town Life*. London: Macmillan & Co., 1901.

379. Rowntree, B. S.. *Poverty and Progress*. London: Longmans, 1941.

380. IHE. Marmot indicators briefing, 18 July 2017.

381. Marmot, M., ed. Marmot Review: Fair society, healthy lives. Final report of the Strategic Review of Health Inequalities in England post-2010. London: Marmot Review (University College London), 2010.

382. Ibid.

383. RSA. People, public services, place and power: a new prospectus for research and action. London: Royal Society of Arts, 2018.

384. Bell, T. and Tomlinson, D. Is everybody concentrating? Recent trends in product and labour market concentration in the UK. London: Resolution Foundation, 2018.

385. Stones, M. 'Food manufacturing industry set for 3–4% growth'. Food Manufacture. Crawley: William Reed Business Media, 18 August 2018. https://www.foodmanufacture.co.uk/Article/2015/08/19/Food-and-drink-manufacturing-industry-set-for-3-4-growth.

386. Smith, A. *An Inquiry into the Nature and Causes of the Wealth of Nations*. London: Printed for W. Strahan; and T. Cadell in the Strand, 1776.

387. Grant Thornton. The food and drink industry: economic contribution and growth opportunities. London: Food and Drink Federation/Grant Thornton, 2017.

388. FDE. Data & trends of the European food and drink industry 2018. Brussels: FoodDrinkEurope, 2019.

389. Thornton. Food and drink industry.

390. FDE. Data & trends of the European food and drink industry 2018.

391. FDF. Industry statistics 2018. London: Food and Drink Federation, 2019. https://www.fdf.org.uk/statsataglance.aspx (accessed 26 March 2019).

392. Marshall, C. 'Southdale Center: America's first shopping mall – a history of cities in 50 buildings'. *Guardian*, 6 May 2015.

393. Kantar Worldpanel. Grocery marketshare Great Britain. London Kantar Worldpanel, 2019.

394. Winter, M. Changing food cultures: challenges and opportunities for UK agriculture. Nuffield Farming Lecture report. Exeter: University of Exeter/ Nuffield Farming Scholarships Trust, 2018.

395. USDA FAS. United Kingdom retail foods 2017. Washington DC: US Department of Agriculture Foreign Agricultural Service, 2018.

396. Farrell, S. 'The race to the last mile'. *The Grocer*, 2018: 26–30.

397. West, K. 'This supermarket in Wales is owned by a small council in Surrey. Why?' *Observer*, 27 January 2019, pp. 52–3.

398. Hall, J. and Russell, J. 'Tesco: Europe's biggest property company'. *Daily Telegraph*, 22 April 2017.

399. Quinn, I. 'Power list 2018: Who is pulling the property strings?' *The Grocer*, 9 February 2018. https://www.thegrocer.co.uk/people/power-list/ power-list-2018-who-is-pulling-the-property-strings/562893.article.

400. Colliers International, MSCI. UK supermarket investment report 2016. London: Colliers International, 2017.

401. Colliers International. UK grocery real estate review. London: Colliers International, 2019.

402. Mercer, H. The abolition of resale price maintenance in Britain in 1964: A turning point for British manufacturers? London: London School of Economics and Political Science, 1998.

403. European Commission. Fairness in the food supply chain: Commission proposes to increase price transparency. Brussels: Directorate-General for Agriculture and Rural Development, 22 May 2019. http://europa.eu/rapid/ press-release_IP-19-2629_en.htm (accessed 4 June 2019).

404. Defra. Agriculture in the UK. London: Department for Environment, Food and Rural Affairs, 2019.

405. Groceries Code Adjudicator. Groceries Code Adjudicator annual report and accounts 1 April 2017–31 March 2018. HC 1088. London: Groceries Code Adjudicator, 2018.

406. Groceries Code Adjudicator. Groceries sector survey 2018. London Office of the Groceries Code Adjudicator, 2018.

407. Wishaw, R. UK supermarket supply chains: Ending the human suffering behind our food. Oxford: Oxfam, 2018.

408. Fairtrade International. About Fairtrade Standards. Bonn: Fairtrade International, 2016. http://www.fairtrade.net/standards.html (accessed 13 July 2016).

409. Cramer, C., Johnston, D., Oya, C., et al. Fairtrade, employment and poverty reduction in Ethiopia and Uganda: final report to DFID. London: School of Oriental and African Studies, University of London, 2014.

410. Fairtrade International. Statement on SOAS report – Fairtrade, employment and poverty reduction in Ethiopia and Uganda, 16 May. Bonn: Fairtrade International, 2014. http://www.fairtrade.net/single-view+M5a2383b864f.html.

411. UK Hospitality. UK Hospitality management report 2018. London: UK Hospitality, 2018.

412. Forbes. Global 2000: The world's largest public companies 2018. Jersey City, NJ: Forbes Media, 2018.

413. Backman, P. UK food service market 2018. London: Peter Backman, 2019.

414. Bounds, A. 'Army takes control of common land in first UK enclosure in century: Cumbria council votes to deregister military training area despite fierce opposition'. *Financial Times*, 6 December 2018; https://www.ft.com/content/4abec6a4-f96b-11e8-af46-2022a0b02a6c.

415. Shrubsole, G. *Who Owns England?* London: William Collins, 2019.

416. Savills. GB agricultural land: market survey 2017. London: Savills World Research, 2017.

417. Knight Frank. The rural report 2019. London: Knight Frank LLP, 2019.

418. Savills. Valuing Britain. London: Savills, 2018.

419. Savills. GB agricultural land 2018: market survey. London: Savills Europe, 2018.

420. Cocker, M. *Our Place: Can We Save Britain's Wildlife before It is Too Late?* London: Jonathan Cape, 2018.

421. Ibid.

422. Greenfield, P. 'UK farmers are addicted to subsidy, says government adviser'. *Guardian*, 29 July 2017.

423. Ibid.

424. Dowler, C. and Carter, L. Common Agricultural Policy: Rich List receive millions in EU subsidies. London: Unearthed/Greenpeace, 2016. https://energydesk.greenpeace.org/2016/09/29/common-agricultural-policy-millions-eu-subsidies-go-richest-landowners/ (accessed 26 March 2019).

425. NAO. Report: Early review of the new farming programme (Department for Environment, Food and Rural Affairs). HC 2221 Session 2017–2019. London: National Audit Office, 5 June 2019.

426. Pooler, M. Brexiter James Dyson turns first farming profit as EU subsidies grow: Magnate who backed Leave turns round agricultural business as Brussels support nears £3m. *Financial Times*, 27 September 2018.

427. Cahill, K. *Who Owns the World? The Hidden Facts behind Landownership*. London: Mainstream, 2006.

428. Cohen, D. Who owns Britain? Open Democracy, 2018. https://www.opendemocracy.net/neweconomics/who-owns-britain/.

429. Pearce, F. *The Land Grabbers: The New Fight over Who Owns the Earth*. London: Transworld Publishers, 2012.

430. Defra. Health and harmony.

431. Strutt and Parker. Farm support, the new Environmental Land Management System.

432. Defra. Environmental farming scheme given green light. London: Department for Environment, Food and Rural Affairs/Natural England/Yorkshire Dales National Park Authority, 2018.

433. Helliwell, Layard and Sachs, eds. World happiness report 2019.

434. Blanchflower, D. G. and Oswald, A. J. 'International happiness: a new view on the measure of performance'. *Academy of Management Perspectives* 25(1), 2011: 6–22.

435. HANCI. The Hunger and Nutrition Committment Index (HANCI): Ranking governments on their political commitment to tackling hunger and undernutrition. Brighton: Institute of Development Studies, University of Sussex, 2016.

436. Jackson, T. and Marks, N. Measuring sustainable economic welfare – a pilot index 1950–1990. Stockholm: Stockholm Environment Institute/New Economics Foundation, 1994.

437. Natural Capital Committee. The state of natural capital: Protecting and improving natural capital for prosperity and wellbeing. Third report to the Economic Affairs Committee. London: Department of the Environment, Food and Rural Affairs, 2015.

438. FAO. Natural capital impacts in agriculture: Supporting better business decision-making. Rome: Food and Agriculture Organization, 2015.

439. Samuelson, P. A. 'The pure theory of public expenditure'. *Review of Economics and Statistics* 36(4), 1954: 387–9.

440. Defra. Health and harmony.

441. Sharpe, R. An inconvenient sandwich: the throwaway economics of takeaway food. London: New Economics Foundation, 2010.

442. Steel, C. *Hungry City: How Food Shapes Our Lives*. London: Chatto and Windus, 2008.

443. Allen, R. C. 'Economic structure and agricultural productivity in Europe, 1300–1800'. *European Review of Economic History* 3, 2000: 1–25.

444. Defra. Agriculture in the UK 2017.

445. Improve/Lantra/People 1st, et al. Feed your ambition: Skills Action Plan for the food supply chain. Heslington, York: Improve Ltd, 2011.

446. Lawrence, F. 'Spain's salad growers are modern-day slaves, say charities'. *Guardian*, 7 February 2011.

447. ETI. Ethical Trading Initiative. London: Ethical Trading Initiative, 2009. http://www.ethicaltrade.org/Z/home/index.shtml (accessed 8 February 2009).

448. BEIS. National Living Wage. London: Department for Business, Energy and Industrial Strategy, 2016.

449. Cominetti, Henehan and Clarke. Low pay Britain 2019.

450. D'Arcy, C. Low pay Britain 2018. London: Resolution Foundation, 2018.

451. Price, K. 'Hospitality shamed as HMRC releases minimum wage underpayments data'. *The Caterer*, 22 September 2018.

452. Price, K. 'Hospitality industry wages outstripping new NLW'. *The Caterer*, 31 October 2018.

453. Vázquez Pimentel, A., Macías Aymar, D. and Iñigo Lawson, M. Reward work, not wealth. Oxford: Oxfam International, 2018.

454. World Bank. Feminization of agriculture in the context of rural transformations: what is the evidence? Washington DC: World Bank, 2017.

455. EFRA Committee. Feeding the nation: labour constraints – Seventh Report of Session 2016–17 – HC 1009. London: Environment, Food and Rural Affairs Committee of the House of Commons, 2017.

456. Rienzo, C. and Vargas-Silva, C. Migration in the UK: an overview 2018. Oxford: COMPAS/The Migration Observatory, University of Oxford, 2018.

457. Ibid.

458. Seabrook, J. 'Blackburn: The town that stopped working'. *New Statesman*, 27 July 2018.

459. Seabrook, J. *City Close-Up*. London: Allen Lane, 1971.

460. Lawrence, F. 'The gangsters on England's doorstep'. *Guardian*, 11 May 2016.

461. Lawrence, F. *Not on the Label: What Really Goes into the Food on Your Plate*. 2nd edn. London: Penguin Books, 2013.

462. MAC. EEA migration in the UK: final report. London: Migration Advisory Committee, 2018.

463. Home Office. Ministerial statement by Rt Hon. Mark Harper MP: Seasonal Agricultural Workers Scheme and the Food Processing Sectors Based Scheme. London: HM Government, 2013.

464. Defra/Home Office. UK farmers given support for seasonal labour with new pilot scheme. London: Home Office and Department for Environment, Food and Rural Affairs, 2018. https://deframedia.blog.gov.uk/2018/09/06/new-pilot-scheme-to-bring-2500-seasonal-workers-to-uk-farms/.

465. GsF Ltd. Migration & EEA Labour at G's. 2017.

466. British Summer Fruits. How Brexit could crush our soft fruit industry, & the implications for food prices, the nation's health, the economy & food security. London: British Summer Fruits, 2017.

467. British Summer Fruits/Andersons. The impact of Brexit on the UK soft fruit industry. Louth: British Summer Fruits, 2017.

468. KPMG. Labour migration in the hospitality sector: a KPMG report for the British Hospitality Association. London: British Hospitality Association, 2017.

469. Bradshaw, T. 'Travis Kalanick's new venture buys UK "dark kitchens" business'. *Financial Times*, 26 March 2019. https://on.ft.com/2YqXd6n.

470. Taylor, M. Good work: the Taylor Review of modern working practices. London: Department for Business, Energy and Industrial Strategy, 2017.

471. Ibid.

472. HM Government. Good work – a response to the Taylor Review of modern working practices. London: HM Government, 2018.

473. Mintz, S. W. *Sweetness and Power: The Place of Sugar in Modern History*. Harmondsworth: Penguin Books, 1985.

474. Bahadur, G. *Coolie Woman: The Odyssey of Indenture*. London: Hurst & Co., 2013.

475. Nye, C. Who picked British fruit and veg before migrant workers? The Conversation. London, 2016.

476. The Gangmasters Licensing Authority was renamed the Gangmasters and Labour Abuse Authority in 2016. GLAA. The Gangmasters and Labour Abuse Authority. London: HM Government, 2016. http://www.gla.gov.uk/.

477. Clutterbuck, C. *Bittersweet Brexit: The Future of Food, Farming, Land and Labour*. London: Pluto, 2018.

478. Hughes, L and Daneshkhu, S. 'Michael Gove says UK farms need workers from around the world'. *Financial Times*, 20 February 2018.

479. McGuinness, T. and Garton Grimwood, G. Migrant workers in agriculture. Commons Briefing papers CBP-7987. London: House of Commons Library, 2017.

480. Defra. Protecting plant health: a plant biosecurity strategy for Great Britain. London: Department for Environment, Food and Rural Affairs/ Welsh Government/Scottish Government/Forestry Commission, 2014.

481. IME. Global food: Waste not want not. London: Institute of Mechanical Engineers, 2013.

482. Global Food Security Programme. The challenge. Swindon: Biotechnology and Biological Sciences Research Council/Global Food Security, 2019. https://www.foodsecurity.ac.uk/challenge/uk-threat/.

483. G8. G8 leaders statement on global food security, Toyako, 8 July 2008. http://www.whitehouse.gov/news/releases/2008/07/20080708-6.html.

484. G8. 'L'Aquila' joint statement on global food security. L'Aquila Food Security Initiative (AFSI), Rome, 10 July 2009. http://www.g8italia2009.it/static/G8_Allegato/LAquila_Joint_Statement_on_Global_Food_Security%5B1%5D,0.pdf.

485. G8. Final communiqué of G8 Lough Erne. London: HM Government, 2013.The G8 communiqué is at www.gov.uk/government/uploads/system/uploads/attachment_data/file/207583/Lough_Erne_2013_G8_Leaders_Communique__2_.pdf.

486. Beddington, J. Chief Scientific Advisor's speech to UK Sustainable Development 2009 conference, 18 March 2009. BBC: http://newsbbccouk/1/hi/uk/7951838stm. *Guardian*: http://www.guardiancouk/science/2009/mar/18/perfect-storm-john-beddington-energy-food-climate.

487. Godfray, H. C. J., Beddington, J. R., Crute, I. R., et al. 'Food security: The challenge of feeding 9 billion people'. *Science* 327(5967), 2010: 812–18. doi:10.1126/science.1185383.

488. Paillard, S., Treyer, S. and Dorin, B., eds. *Agrimonde: Scenarios and Challenges for Feeding the World in 2050*. Paris: Éditions Quæ, 2011.

489. PMSEIC (Australia). Australia and food security in a changing world. Canberra: Prime Minister's Science, Engineering and Innovation Council of Australia, 2010.

490. Global Food Security Programme. Environmental tipping points and food system dynamics. Swindon: UK Research and Innovation/Biotechnology and Biological Sciences Research Council (BBSRC), 2017.

491. Benton, T. G. British food: What role should UK producers have in feeding the UK? Independent report to Morrisons supermarket. Bradford: Morrisons and University of Leeds, 2017. www.leeds.ac.uk/download/481/british_food_makers_report (accessed 17 August 2018).

492. Benton, T. G. What might the UK food system look like in 5 (to 10) years' time? A scenarios exercise. Leeds: University of Leeds, 2017.

493. Benton, T. G. and Thompson, C. 'Food system resilience'. *Food Science and Technology* 30(3), 2016: 20–24.

494. IKnowFood. *IKnowFood* programme of the Universities of York, Manchester and Liverpool. York: York Management School, 2017–20.

495. N8 AgriFood consortium of Northern Universities. www.n8agrifood.ac.uk.

496. Global Food Security Programme. Exploring the resilience of the UK food system in a global context. Swindon: UK Research Councils, 2019.

497. Global Food Security/TNS-BRMB. Global Food Security Programme – Exploring public views. Swindon: Global Food Security Programme of the Joint Research Councils, 2012.

498. ComRes/Global Food Security Programme. Public attitudes to climatic shocks and their interaction with the food system. Swindon: Global Food Security Programme of the UK Joint Research Councils, 2017.

499. IFS (Sweden). A Taste of Food21: FOOD 21 – sustainable food production. Uppsala: Institute of Food Sciences and MISTRA (Foundation for Strategic Environmental Research), 2005. http://www-mat21.slu.se/eng/.

500. Livsmedelsverket (NFA (Sweden)). Find your way to eat greener, not too much and be active. Stockholm: Livsmedelsverket (National Food Administration), 2015.

501. Ministry of the Environment (Sweden)/UNEP. Task Force on Sustainable Lifestyles. Stockholm and Nairobi: Ministry of the Environment (Sweden)/UN Environment Programme, 2011.

502. National Food Administration/Swedish EPA. Environmentally effective food choices: Proposal notified to the EU, 15 May 2009. Stockholm: National Food Administration and Swedish Environmental Protection Agency, 2009.

503. Nordic Food Policy Lab. Solutions menu: a Nordic guide to sustainable food policy. Copenhagen: Nordic Food Policy Lab of the Nordic Council of Ministers, 2018.

504. NCM. Nordic nutrition recommendations 2012: Integrating nutrition and physical activity. Copenhagen: Nordic Council of Ministers, 2014.

505. Steel, C. *Hungry City*.

506. Piesse, J. and Thirtle, C. 'Agricultural Productivity in the United Kingdom', in Alston, J. M., Babcock, B. A. and Pardey, P. G., eds. *The Shifting Patterns of Agricultural Production and Productivity Worldwide*, pp. 149–91. Ames, Iowa: CARD Books (Center for Agricultural and Rural Development), 2010.

507. Ramankutty, N., Mehrabi, Z., Waha, K., et al. 'Trends in global agricultural land use: implications for environmental health and food security'. *Annual Review of Plant Biology* 69(1), 2018. doi:10.1146/annurev-arplant-042817-040256.

508. Rothschild, L. 'Report of the Organisation and Management of Government R&D (The "Rothschild Report")', in Office, C., ed. *A Framework for Government Research and Development*. London: HMSO, 1971.

509. Piesse and Thirtle. 'Agricultural Productivity in the United Kingdom'.

510. Schiermeier, Q. 'Horizon 2020 deal reached in Brussels'. *Nature*, 26 June 2013.

511. Vesper, I. '€100-billion budget proposed for Europe's next big research programme'. *Nature* 557(150), 3 May 2018. doi:10.1038/d41586-018-05105-0.

512. Royal Society. Royal Society responds to Budget 2018. London: Royal Society, 2018. https://royalsociety.org/news/2018/10/royal-society-budget-response/.

513. ONS. Government expenditure on science, engineering and technology, UK: 2016. London: Office for National Statistics, 2018.

514. Anon. 'R&D spending of FTSE-100 manufacturers averages below 5%'. *The Manufacturer*, 29 July 2013.

515. Berger, M. 'Nanotechnology in agriculture'. *Nanowerk*, 25 August 2014. http://www.nanowerk.com/spotlight/spotid=37064.php.

516. ETC. Nanotechnology: a tiny primer on nanotechnologies. Ottawa: ETC Group, 2005. http://www.etcgroup.org/content/tiny-primer-nano-scale-technologies-and-little-bang-theory.

517. FSA. Report on FSA regulatory review of the use of nanotechnology in relation to food. London: Food Standards Agency, 2008.

518. Singh, T., Shukla, S., Kumar, P., et al. 'Application of nanotechnology in food science: perception and overview'. *Frontiers in Microbiology* 8, 2017: 1501. doi:10.3389/fmicb.2017.01501 (first published online 7 August 2017).

519. Salvi, L. 'The EU's "soft reaction" to nanotechnology regulation in the food sector'. *European Food and Feed Law Review* 10(3), 2015: 186–93.

520. EFSA. Public consultation on the draft EFSA guidance on the risk assessment of the application of nanoscience and nanotechnologies in the food and feed chain. Part 1: Human and animal health. Parma: European Food Safety Authority, 2011.

521. Millstone, E. P. 'Science, risk and governance: radical rhetorics and the realities of reform'. *Research Policy* 38(4), 2009: 624–36.

522. Millstone, E. P., Lang, T. and Marsden, T. K. Should chicken and turkey meat washed in disinfectant be accepted in the UK after Brexit? Food Brexit Policy Briefing. London: Food Research Collaboration, 2017.

523. Millstone, E. P. and Lang, T. Hormone-treated beef: Should Britain accept it after Brexit? London: Food Research Collaboration, 2018.

524. Fleming, A. Penicillin. Nobel Prize Lecture. Stockholm: Nobel Laureates, 1945.

525. Jørgensen, P. S., Aktipis, A., Brown, Z., et al. 'Antibiotic and pesticide susceptibility and the Anthropocene operating space'. *Nature Sustainability* 1(11), 2018: 632–41. doi:10.1038/s41893-018-0164-3.

526. Review on Antimicrobial Resistance (Chair: Jim O'Neill). Securing new drugs for future generations: the pipeline of antibiotics. London: Wellcome Trust/HM Government, 2015.

527. Review on Antimicrobial Resistance (Chair: Jim O'Neill). Tackling drug-resistant infections globally: final report and recommendations. London: Wellcome Trust/HM Government, 2015.

528. EMA. European Surveillance of Veterinary Antimicrobial Consumption (ESVAC). London: European Medicines Agency, 2017.

529. Review on Antimicrobial Resistance. Securing new drugs for future generations.

530. Review on Antimicrobial Resistance. Tackling drug-resistant infections globally.

531. Davies, S. C. Annual report of the Chief Medical Officer, vol. 2: 2011: Infections and the rise of antimicrobial resistance. London: Department of Health, 2013.

532. FAIRR. $1 trillion investor coalition demands corporate action on 'systemic overuse' of antibiotics. London: Farm Animal Investment Risk & Return, 2017.

533. Millstone. 'Science, risk and governance'.

534. Millstone, E. P., van Zwanenberg, P., Marris, C., et al. Science in trade disputes related to potential risk: comparative case studies. ESTO Technical Report Series. Brussels: European Science and Technology Observatory, 2004.

535. Lang, T., Millstone, E. P., Lewis, T., et al. Feeding Britain: food security after Brexit. London: Food Research Collaboration, 2018.

536. Lang, T., Millstone, E. P. and Marsden, T. A food Brexit: time to get real – a Brexit briefing. Falmer: Science Policy Research Unit, University of Sussex/Cardiff University Sustainable Places Institute/City, University of London, 2017.

537. Bowman, A., Williams, K., Moran, M., et al. *The End of the Experiment? From Competition to the Foundational Economy.* Manchester: Manchester University Press, 2014.

538. Bentham, J., Bowman, A., de la Cuesta, M., et al. Manifesto for the foundational economy. Manchester: CRESC, University of Manchester, 2013.

539. KPMG. Assessment of the Chancellor's October 2018 budget – roads sector welcomes a surge in investment. London: KPMG, 2018.

540. Plimmer, G. 'Tilbury's £1bn drive to build a global trading port on Thames'. *Financial Times*, 5 February 2017.

541. Osler, D. New UK prime minister pledges to prioritise free ports. Lloyd's List. 25 July 2019.

542. Pendleton, A., Salveson, P., Kiberd, E. A rail network for everyone. London: New Economics Foundation/Friends of the Earth England, Wales and N. Ireland, 2019.

543. Gabriel, Y. and Lang, T. *The Unmanageable Consumer*. 3rd edn. London: Sage, 2015.

544. BRC. Retail 2020: fewer but better jobs. London: British Retail Consortium, 2016.

545. Knight Frank. Rural Report 2019.

546. Leahy, E. 'More human than human?' *Fresh Produce Journal* 2018: 30–32.

547. Arntz, M., Gregory, T. and Zierahn, U. The risk of automation for jobs in OECD countries: a comparative analysis. OECD Social, Employment and Migration Working Papers, no. 189. Paris: OECD Publishing, 2016.

548. Frey, C. B. and Osborne, M. A. The future of employment: how susceptible are jobs to computerisation? Oxford: Oxford Martin School, 2013.

549. Deloitte. From brawn to brains: the impact of technology on jobs in the UK. London: Deloitte, 2015.

550. Pooler, M. 'Robot army is transforming the global workplace'. *Financial Times*, 20 November 2017.

551. IFR. Industrial robot sales increase worldwide by 31 per cent. Results presented to CEO Roundtable, 20 June 2018. Frankfurt am Main: International Federation of Robotics, 2018.

552. IFR. Robots and the workplace of the future. Frankfurt am Main: International Federation of Robotics, 2018.

553. Mason, A. 'Could the UK miss out on the robotics revolution?' *The Grocer*, 2018: 26–31.

554. IFR. The impact of robots on productivity, employment and jobs. Frankfurt am Main: International Federation of Robotics, 2017.

555. Manyika, J., Chui, M., Miremadi, M., et al. A future that works: automation, employment and productivity. San Francisco: McKinsey Global Institute, 2017.

556. Ibid.

557. Kollewe, J. and Davies, R. 'Robocrop: world's first raspberry-picking robot set to work – autonomous machine expected to pick more than 25,000 raspberries a day, outpacing human workers'. *Guardian*, 27 May 2019.

558. Mason. Could the UK miss out on the robotics revolution?

559. Tett, G. 'Why we should open the Cambridge Analytica data vault'. *Financial Times*, FT Magazine, 24 April 2019.

560. Zuboff, S. *The Age of Surveillance Capitalism: The Fight for the Future at the New Frontier of Power*. London: Profile Books, 2019.

561. Heimann, J. M. *The Most Offending Soul Alive: Tom Harrisson and His Remarkable Life*. London: Aurum, 2002.

562. Mass Observation Archives. Archives of Mass Observation 1937–1950s, held at the University of Sussex. http://www.massobs.org.uk. Brighton: University of Sussex, 2015.

563. Worcester, R. *British Public Opinion: A Guide to the History and Methodology of Political Opinion Polling*. Oxford: Blackwell, 1991.

564. Last, N., Broad, R. and Fleming, S. *Nella Last's War: The Second World War Diaries of 'Housewife, 49'*. 2nd edn. London: Profile Books, 2006.

565. Zweiniger-Bargielowska, I. *Austerity in Britain: Rationing, Controls, and Consumption, 1939–1955*. Oxford: Oxford University Press, 2000.

566. Edgerton, D. *Britain's War Machine*. London: Penguin Books, 2012.

567. Collingham, L. *Taste of War: World War Two and the Battle for Food*. London: Allen Lane, 2011.

568. Rayner, G. and Lang, T. *Ecological Public Health: Reshaping the Conditions for Good Health*. Abingdon: Routledge Earthscan, 2012.

569. Laughlin, A. '*Which?* investigation reveals "staggering" level of smart home surveillance'. *Which?*, 1 June 2018.

570. Halliwell, J. 'How blockchain will change fmcg'. *The Grocer*, 26 April 2017: 30–32.

571. Southey, F. 'Food (and data) to go? Machine learning drives innovation in "digitally-led" retailers'. *FoodNavigator.com*. 20 March 2019. https://www.foodnavigator.com/Article/2019/03/20/Big-data-drives-innovation-in-food-to-go-sector.

572. European Union. General Data Protection Regulation 2016/679. Brussels: Council of the European Union, 2016. https://eur-lex.europa.eu/eli/reg/2016/679/oj/eng.

573. LGA. The future of non-metropolitan England.

574. Holliday, I. 'Is the British state hollowing out?' *Political Quarterly* 71(2), 2002: 167–76.

575. Rhodes, R. A. W. 'The hollowing out of the state', in Rhodes, R. A. W., ed. *Network Governance and the Differentiated Polity: Selected Essays*. Oxford: Oxford University Press, 2017.

576. Osler. New UK prime minister pledges to prioritise free ports.

577. FOE. How to . . . oppose a supermarket planning application: a short guide. London: Friends of the Earth, 2005.

578. House of Commons: Communities and Local Government Committee. Planning gain supplement. Fifth Report of Session 2005–06, HC 1024-1. London: The Stationery Office, 2006.

579. Loughlin, M. 'Planning gain: law, policy and practice'. *Oxford Journal of Legal Studies* 1(1), 1981: 61–97.

580. Planning Direct. Trends in supermarket planning applications. Ipswich: Planning Direct, 2013.

581. Wong, C., Ravetz, J. and Turner, J. The United Kingdom Spatial Planning Framework: a discussion. Manchester: Royal Town Planning Institute/ University of Manchester, 2000.

582. Wilson, B. *Swindled: From Poison Sweets to Counterfeit Coffee – the Dark History of the Food Cheats*. London: John Murray, 2008.

583. Lang, T. 'Food, the law and public health: three models of the relationship'. *Public Health* 120, October 2006: 30–41. doi:10.1016/j.puhe.2006.07.013 (first published online).

584. Accum, F. C. *A Treatise on Adulterations of Food and Culinary Poisons*. London: Longman, 1820.

585. Paulus, I. L. E. *The Search for Pure Food: A Sociology of Legislation in Britain*. Oxford: Martin Robertson, 1974.

586. Lang. School meals business.

587. Berger, N. *The School Meals Service: From Its Beginnings to the Present Day*. Plymouth: Northcote House, 1990.

588. Goulson, D. *The Garden Jungle*. London: Jonathan Cape, 2019.

589. Guerreiro, S. B., Dawson, R. J., Kilsby, C., et al. 'Future heat-waves, droughts and floods in 571 European cities'. *Environmental Research Letters* 13(3), 2018.

590. Food for Life Partnership. Food for Life Catering Mark. Bristol: Soil Association/Garden Organic, 2008. www.foodforlife.org.uk/resources/ catering/catering-mark.

591. FAO. FAO framework for the Urban Food Agenda. Rome: Food and Agriculture Organization, 2019.

592. Welsh Government. The Well-Being of Future Generations (Wales) Act 2015. Cardiff: Welsh Government, 2015. http://gov.wales/topics/

people-and-communities/people/future-generations-act/?lang=en
(accessed 11 November 2016).

593. Nourish Scotland. Nourish Scotland, the Scottish Food Coalition. Edinburgh: Nourish Scotland, 2019. http://www.nourishscotland.org.

594. Scottish Government. Good Food Nation Bill (consultation). Edinburgh: Scottish Government, 2018.

PART THREE: ACCELERATING THE 'GREAT FOOD TRANSFORMATION'

1. IPCC. Climate change and land – IPCC special report on climate change, desertification, land degradation, sustainable land management, food security, and greenhouse gas fluxes in terrestrial ecosystems. Geneva: Intergovernmental Panel on Climate Change, 2019.

2. Food, Farming and Countryside Commission. Our future in the land – final report. London: Royal Society of Arts, 2019.

3. FAO. *The State of Food and Agriculture 2000*. Rome: Food and Agriculture Organization, 2000.

4. FAO. *State of Food Insecurity 2000*. Rome: Food and Agriculture Organization, 2000.

5. FAO. *World Agriculture: Towards 2015/2030: An FAO Perspective*. Rome: Food and Agriculture Organization/Earthscan, 2003.

6. WHO. *Diet, Nutrition and the Prevention of Chronic Diseases*. Geneva: World Health Organization, 1990.

7. WHO. *Public Health Impact of Pesticides Used in Agriculture*. Geneva: World Health Organization, 1990.

8. WHO. *Medical Impact of the Use of Antimicrobials in Food Animals: Report of a WHO Meeting, Berlin, Germany, 13–17 October 1997*. Geneva: World Health Organization, Division of Emerging and Other Communicable Diseases Surveillance and Control, 1997.

9. WHO. *Obesity: Preventing and Managing the Global Epidemic. Report of a Global Consultation on Obesity*. WHO/NUT/NCD/98.1. Geneva: World Health Organization, 1998.

10. UNEP, Nellemann, C., MacDevette, M., et al. *The Environmental Food Crisis: The Environment's Role in Averting Future Food Crises. A UNEP Rapid Response Assessment*. Arendal, Norway: United Nations Environment Programme/GRID–Arendal, 2009.

11. WCRF/AICR. *Food, Nutrition and the Prevention of Cancer: A Global Perspective*. London and Washington DC: World Cancer Research Fund/ American Institute for Cancer Research, 1997.

12. IPCC. Global warming of 1.5°C, an IPCC special report. Summary for Policymakers of IPCC Special Report on Global Warming of 1.5°C approved by governments. Geneva: Intergovernmental Panel on Climate Change, 2018.

13. Martínez Steele, E., Popkin, B. M., Swinburn, B., et al. 'Processed foods and the overall nutritional quality of diets in the US: evidence from a nationally representative cross-sectional study'. *Population Health Metrics* 15(6), 2017.

14. Monteiro, C. A., Cannon, G., Levy, R., et al. 'NOVA: the star shines bright'. *World Nutrition* 7(1–3), 2016: 28–38.

15. ATNI. UK product profile 2019. Utrecht: Access to Nutrition Initiative, 22 May 2019.

16. Food Foundation. UK's annual fruit and veg advertising budget used up just 19 days into the new year. London: Food Foundation Peas Please Campaign, 2018. https://foodfoundation.org.uk/uks-annual-fruit-and-veg-advertising-budget-used-up-just-19-days-into-the-new-year/ (accessed 2 November 2019).

17. Tatum, M. 'Can product placement evolve in 2019?' *The Grocer* 241(8427), 2019: 26–30.

18. World Economic Forum/Deloitte. Shaping the future of global food systems: a scenarios analysis. Geneva/Cologne: World Economic Forum, 2017.

Chapter 5: What We Ought to Do: A 'Great Food Transformation'

1. BBC News. Countdown to crisis: Eight days that shook Britain. London: BBC World Service Education, 2000.

2. Cooper, D. *The Bad Food Guide*. London: Routledge & Kegan Paul, 1967.

3. Huxley, E. J. G. *Brave New Victuals: An Inquiry into Modern Food Production*. London: Chatto & Windus, 1965.

4. Driver, C. *The British at Table 1940–1980*. London: Chatto & Windus, 1983.

5. Goulds, A. J. Pesticide usage survey report 254 – Amenity pesticides in the United Kingdom 2012 – Section 1: Quantitative report. London: Department for Environment, Food and Rural Affairs, 2012.

6. Monbiot, G. *Feral: Searching for Enchantment on the Frontiers of Rewilding*. London: Allen Lane, 2013.

7. Wrigley, R. Welcoming Summit to Sea: https://www.rewildingbritain.org.uk/blog/welcoming-summit-to-sea. Steyning: Rewilding Britain, 2018.

8. Dean, L. 'Farmers fight rewilding plans'. Farmers Guardian. Preston: FGInsight, 2019.

9. HM Government. Yellowhammer Planning Assumptions, 2 August 2019. 'Official Sensitive'. London: HM Government, 2019.

10. Millstone, E. P. and Lang, T. Hormone-treated beef: Should Britain accept it after Brexit? London: Food Research Collaboration, 2018.

11. Lang, T. and Millstone, E. P. 'Post-Brexit food standards'. *The Lancet* 393(10177), 23 March 2019; doi:10.1016/S0140-6736(19)30540-9.

12. Millstone, E. P., Lang, T. and Marsden, T. 'Food Brexit and chlorinated chicken: a microcosm of wider food problems'. *Political Quarterly* 90(4), 2019: 645–53. doi:10.1111/1467-923X.12780.

13. Malthus, T. R. *An Essay on the Principle of Population, As It Affects the Future Improvement of Society with Remarks on the Speculations of Mr. Godwin, M. Condorcet and Other Writers*. London: Printed for J. Johnson, 1798.

14. Collingham, L. *The Hungry Empire: How Britain's Quest for Food Shaped the Modern World*. London: Bodley Head, 2017.

15. Conway, G. *The Doubly Green Revolution: Food for All in the 21st Century*. London: Penguin Books, 1997.

16. Shiva, V. *The Violence of Green Revolution: Third World Agriculture, Ecology and Politics*. London: Zed Books, 1991.

17. De Schutter, O. and Vanloqueren, G. 'The new green revolution: How twenty-first-century science can feed the world'. *Solutions Journal* 2(4), 2011: 33–44.

18. Glaeser B, ed. *The Green Revolution Revisited: Critique and Alternatives*. London: Routledge, 1987.

19. Holt-Giménez, E. and Altieri, M. 'Agroecology, food sovereignty and the new green revolution'. *Agroecology and Sustainable Food Systems* 37(1), 2012: 90–102.

20. Rayner, G. and Lang, T. *Ecological Public Health: Reshaping the Conditions for Good Health*. Abingdon: Routledge Earthscan, 2012.

21. Willett, W., Rockström, J., Loken, B., et al. 'Food in the Anthropocene: the EAT–*Lancet* Commission on healthy diets from sustainable food systems'. *The Lancet* 393(10170), 2019: 447–92.

22. IAP. Opportunities for future research and innovation on food and nutrition security and agriculture: the InterAcademy Partnership's global perspective. Washington DC and Trieste: The InterAcademy Partnership, 2018.

23. Ranganathan, J., Waite, R., Searchinger, T., et al. This is how to sustainably feed 10 billion people by 2050. Washington DC: World Resources Institute, 2018.

24. Springmann, M. 'Modelling report on alternative production and consumption scenarios for the UK. Report to the Food, Farming and Countryside Commission'. Oxford: Oxford Martin School, 2019.

25. Food, Farming and Countryside Commission. Our Future in the Land. Final report. London: Royal Society of Arts, 2019.

26. Food, Farming and Countryside Commission. Field Guide for the future. London: Royal Society of Arts, 2019.

27. *Which?* The future of food: Giving consumers a say. London: *Which?*, 2013.

28. Butterly, D. and Fitzpatrick, I. A people's food policy: Transforming the food system. Land Workers' Alliance/Global Justice Now/Ecological Land Co-op/The Centre for Agroecology and the Permaculture Association, 2018.

29. Defra. Developing a national food strategy: independent review 2019 (Dimbleby Review). London: Department for Environment, Food and Rural Affairs, 2019.

30. Ibid.

31. FSC. Resetting the table: a people's food policy for Canada. Montreal: Food Secure Canada, 2011.

32. Nordic Food Policy Lab. Solutions menu: a Nordic guide to sustainable food policy. Copenhagen: Nordic Food Policy Lab of the Nordic Council of Ministers, 2018.

33. FSA. Public attitudes tracker, Wave 18 (May 2019). London: Food Standards Agency, 2018.

34. Warde, A. *The Practice of Eating.* Cambridge: Polity Press, 2016.

35. ComRes. AgriBriefing Farming Survey – September 2019. London: ComRes and the Guild of Agricultural Journalists, 2019.

36. Kjaernes, U., Harvey, M. and Warde, A. Trust in food: an institutional and comparative analysis. Basingstoke: Palgrave Macmillan, 2007.

37. UN High Commissioner for Human Rights. International Covenant on Economic, Social and Cultural Rights. Adopted and opened for signature, ratification and accession by General Assembly resolution 2200A (XXI). U.N. Doc. A/6316 (1966), 993 U.N.T.S. New York: United Nations, 1966.

38. Green New Deal Group. The Green New Deal: a Bill to make it happen. Fifth full report. London: Green New Deal Group, 2019.

39. Scottish Government. Good Food Nation Bill (consultation). Edinburgh: Scottish Government, 2018.

40. Wallinga, D., Rayner, G. and Lang, T. 'Antimicrobial resistance and biological governance: explanations for policy failure'. *Public Health* 129(10), 2015: 1314–25.

41. Review on Antimicrobial Resistance (Chair: Jim O'Neill). Tackling drug-resistant infections globally: final report and recommendations. London: Review on Antimicrobial Resistance, 2016.

42. Monteiro, C. A., Moubarac, J.-C., Levy, R. B., et al. 'Household availability of ultra-processed foods and obesity in nineteen European countries'. *Public Health Nutrition* 21(1), 2018: 18–26. doi:10.1017/S1368980017 001379.

43. Davies, S. C. Time to solve childhood obesity: an independent report by the Chief Medical Officer. London: Department of Health and Social Care, 2019.

44. Defra. Green Food Project. London: Department for Environment, Food and Rural Affairs, 2012. http://engage.defra.gov.uk/green-food/.

45. Defra. Sustainable consumption report: Follow-up to the Green Food Project. London: Department for Environment, Food and Rural Affairs, 2013.

46. Scottish Government. Good Food Nation Bill (consultation).

47. Garnett, T. and Strong, M. The principles of healthy and sustainable eating patterns. Swindon: Global Food Security Programme (Biotechnology and Biological Sciences Research Council et al.), 2015.

48. Defra. Food 2030 strategy. London: Department for Food, Rural Affairs and Environment, 2010.

49. Lang, T. and Mason, P. Sustainable diet policy development: implications of multi-criteria and other approaches, 2008–2017. *Proceedings of the Nutrition Society* 77(3), 2018: 331–46.

50. Utviklingsfondet. A viable food future. Oslo: Utviklingsfondet (The Development Fund (Norway)), 2011.

51. Lang and Mason. Sustainable diet policy development.

52. Springmann, M., Wiebe, K., Mason-D'Croz, D., et al. Health and nutritional aspects of sustainable diet strategies and their association with environmental impacts: a global modelling analysis with country-level detail. *Lancet Planetary Health* 2(10), 2018: Pe451-e61. doi:10.1016/S2542-5196(18)30206-7.

53. Millstone, E. P. and Lang, T. Risking regulatory capture at the UK's Food Standards Agency? *The Lancet* 372(9633), 2008: 94–5.

54. Millstone, E. P. and Lang, T. Weakening UK food law enforcement: a risky tactic in Brexit. London: Food Research Collaboration, 2018.

55. WRAP/INCPEN. UK survey 2019 on citizens' attitudes & behaviours relating to food waste, packaging and plastic packaging. Banbury: Waste and Resources Action Programme, 2019.

56. Food for Life Partnership. Food for Life Catering Mark. Bristol: Soil Association/Garden Organic, 2008. www.foodforlife.org.uk/resources/ catering/catering-mark.

57. UKRI. Transforming the UK food system for healthy people and a healthy environment. Swindon: Biotechnology and Biological Sciences Research Council/UK Research and Innovation, 2019.

58. CIA/HSPH. Menus of Change Initiative. Hyde Park, NY: Culinary Institute of America/Harvard School of Public Health, Department of Nutrition, 2013. http://www.menusofchange.org/.

59. Schoen, V. and Lang, T. UK food prices – cooling or bubbling? London: Food Research Collaboration, 2014.

60. Eurostat. Comparative price levels for food, beverages and tobacco. Brussels: Eurostat, June 2019.

61. Pettifor, A. *The Case for the Green New Deal*. London: Verso, 2019.

62. FCRN/Food Foundation. Plating Up Progress (Part 1 and Part 2). Oxford and London: Food Climate Research Network/Food Foundation, 2019.

63. Peacock, P. Land: for the many, not the few? Limitations on the scale of land ownership – a discussion paper. Edinburgh: Land Lines, 2018.

64. Shrubsole, G. Who Owns England? London: William Collins, 2019.

65. UK2070 Commission. Fairer and stronger – Rebalancing the UK Economy. The first report of the UK2070 Commission. Sheffield: University of Sheffield/University of Manchester/University College London/Lincoln Institute (USA), 2019.

66. LGA. The future of non-metropolitan England: the freedom to lead local places. The post-Brexit England Commission final report. London: Local Government Association, 2019.

67. Steel, C. *Hungry City: How Food Shapes Our Lives*. London: Chatto & Windus, 2008.

68. Environmental Audit Committee. Our planet, our health. Twenty-First Report of Session 2017–19. London: House of Commons, 2019.

69. House of Lords. Inquiry to consider the links between inequality, public health and food sustainability – to report by March 31

2020. London: House of Lords Committee on Food, Poverty, Health and the Environment 2019. https://www.parliament.uk/food-pov-health-enviro-comm.

70. Davies. Time to solve childhood obesity.

71. Davies, S. C. Annual report of the Chief Medical Officer, 2011, vol. 1: On the state of the public's health. London: Department of Health, 2012.

72. Scottish Government Chief Medical Officer. A summary of the health of the nation 2017–18: Chief Medical Officer for Scotland's annual report. Edinburgh: Scottish Government, 2018.

73. Wales Chief Medical Officer. Chief Medical Officer for Wales annual report 2016–2017: Gambling with our health. Cardiff: Welsh Government, 2018.

74. Foresight. Tackling obesities: future choices. London: Government Office of Science, 2007.

75. Foresight. Foresight Land Use Futures Project. London: Foresight Programme of the Chief Scientist, 2008. http://www.foresight.gov.uk/OurWork/ActiveProjects/LandUse/LandUse.asp.

76. Foresight. The future of food and farming: challenges and choices for global sustainability. Final report. London: Government Office for Science, 2011.

77. Foresight. Foresight Land Use Futures Project. Land use futures: Making the most of land in the 21st century. Final project report. London: Government Office for Science, 2010.

78. Beddington, J. 'Food, energy, water and the climate: a perfect storm of global events?' Paper to 'Sustainable Development UK 09' Conference, QEII Conference Centre, London, 19 March 2009. London: Office of the Chief Scientific Adviser, 2009.

79. Poppy, G. M., Chiotha, S., Eigenbrod, F., et al. 'Food security in a perfect storm: using the ecosystem services framework to increase understanding'. *Philosophical Transactions of the Royal Society of London B: Biological Sciences* 369(1639), 2014; doi:10.1098/rstb.2012.0288.

80. RGS/WWF-UK. 'Navigating the "Perfect Storm": the international challenge of food, water and energy security'. RGS (and Institute of British Geographers) and WWF-UK Seminar, held at the RGS, Kensington, London, 9 February 2012. London: Royal Geographical Society, 2012.

Index

C

PELICAN BOOKS

Economics:
The User's Guide
Ha-Joon Chang

Human Evolution
Robin Dunbar

Revolutionary Russia:
1891–1991
Orlando Figes

The Domesticated Brain
Bruce Hood

Greek and Roman Political Ideas
Melissa Lane

Classical Literature
Richard Jenkyns

Who Governs Britain?
Anthony King

How to See the World
Nicholas Mirzoeff

The Meaning of Science
Tim Lewens

Social Class in the 21st Century
Mike Savage

The European Union:
A Citizen's Guide
Chris Bickerton

The Caliphate
Hugh Kennedy

PELICAN BOOKS

Islam:
The Essentials
Tariq Ramadan

Basic Income:
And How We Can Make It Happen
Guy Standing

Think Like an Anthropologist
Matthew Engelke

Hermeneutics:
Facts and Interpretation in the Age of Information
John D. Caputo

Being Ecological
Timothy Morton

Object-Oriented Ontology:
A New Theory of Everything
Graham Harman

Marx and Marxism
Gregory Claeys

The Human Planet:
How We Created the Anthropocene
Simon L. Lewis and Mark A. Maslin

Think Again:
How to Reason and Argue
Walter Sinnott-Armstrong

Parenting the First Twelve Years:
What the Evidence Tells Us
Victoria L. Cooper, Heather Montgomery, Kieron Sheehy

PELICAN BOOKS

Social Mobility:
And Its Enemies
Lee Elliot Major and Stephen Machin

National Populism:
The Revolt Against Liberal Democracy
Roger Eatwell and Matthew Goodwin

A Political History of the World
Jonathan Holslag

A Short History of Brexit
From Brentry to Backstop
Kevin O'Rourke

Our Universe:
An Astronomer's Guide
Jo Dunkley

The Art of Statistics:
Learning from Data
David Spiegelhalter

Chinese Thought:
From Confucius to Cook Ding
Roel Sterckx

This is Shakespeare
Emma Smith

What We Really Do All Day
Jonathan Gershuny and Oriel Sullivan

The Government of No One
Ruth Kinna

Plunder of the Commons
Guy Standing